Interdisziplinäre Studien zu Recht und Staat

In Verbindung mit
Dieter Grimm, Eric Hilgendorf, Joachim Hruschka,
Hermann Klenner, Ernst-Joachim Lampe, Stefan Oeter,
Britta Padberg, Manfred Rehbinder, Hubert Rottleuthner,
Rüdiger Schott

herausgegeben von
Gertrude Lübbe-Wolff, Werner Maihofer †,
Gerhard Sprenger und Winfried Brugger

Band 49

Michael Baurmann/Geoffrey Brennan/
Robert E. Goodin/Nicholas Southwood (eds.)

Norms and Values

The Role of Social Norms as Instruments of
Value Realisation

Nomos

Die Deutsche Nationalbibliothek lists this publication in the
Deutsche Nationalbibliografie; detailed bibliographic data
is available in the Internet at http://dnb.d-nb.de.

ISBN 978-3-8329-4063-8

1. Edition 2010
© Nomos Verlagsgesellschaft, Baden-Baden 2010. Printed in Germany.

This work is subject to copyright. All rights are reserved, whether the whole or part of the material is concerned, specifically those of translation, reprinting, re-use of illustrations, broadcasting, reproduction by photocopying machine or similar means, and storage in data banks. Under § 54 of the German Copyright Law where copies are made for other than private use a fee is payable to »Verwertungsgesellschaft Wort«, Munich.

Contents

Michael Baurmann, Geoffrey Brennan,
Robert E. Goodin and Nicholas Southwood
Introduction..7

I. Concepts and Justification

Philip Pettit
Norms, Commitment and Censure..19
Thomas Spitzley
The Importance of Being Honest..40

Robert Sugden
Is There a Distinction between Morality and Convention?....................47
Geoffrey Brennan
Hume's/Sugden's Psychopathy?..66

Nicholas Southwood
Norms, Laws and Social Authority...75
Stefan Huster
Social and Legal Norms..92

Bernd Lahno
Norms of Evaluation vs. Norms of Conduct...95
Michael Baurmann
Categorical Commitment and the Emergence of Norms.....................113

Edna Ullmann-Margalit
Surveillance, Privacy, Sanctions, Cleanliness:
Norms and Values in the Kitchen-Camera Case..................................123
Michael Biggs
Storm in a Teacup?..143

II. Empiricism and Efficacy

Cristina Bicchieri and Alex Chavez
Behaving as Expected: Public Information and Fairness Norms..........151
Werner Güth and Hartmut Kliemt
Normative Expectations...173

Lina Eriksson
Rational Choice Explanations of Norms: What They Can and Cannot Tell Us 179
Alan Hamlin
The Rationality and Functionality of Norms 198

Rainer Hegselmann and Oliver Will
Modelling Hume's Moral and Political Theory—The Design of HUME$_{1.0}$ 205
Giulia Andrighetto
The Micro-Macro Link as a Recursive Loop 233

Gerhard Schurz
Global Value Distribution and Value Clashes 239
Annette Schmitt
Why Still Criticize Huntington? 257

III. Social Values and Collective Choice

Werner Güth and Hartmut Kliemt
The Impossibility of Social Choice and the Possibilities of
Individual Values: Political and Philosophical Liberalism Reconsidered 267
A. Michael Kirmes
Political and Philosophical Liberalism Re-Reconsidered 282

Robert E. Goodin
Norms Honoured in the Breach 289
Holly Lawford-Smith
The Importance of Being Earnest, and the Difficulty of Faking It 299

Russell Hardin
The Story of Qiu Ju 309
Kieran Healy
Social Structure, Gifts and Norms in *The Story of Qiu Ju* 326

IV. Epilogue

Ernesto Garzón Valdés
Radical Evil, Absolute Evil, and Norms.
Responding to Extraordinary Violence 335

Authors 365

Michael Baurmann, Geoffrey Brennan, Robert E. Goodin and
Nicholas Southwood

Introduction

1. The Bridging-Function of Norms

1.1 Norms and Values

Values are constitutive of the self-conception of individuals and groups. The identification with fundamental values generates significant aims and commitments for social communities and their members. By accepting binding values and striving to realize them individually and collectively, personal aspirations and social integration become focused and meaningful.

Some values are practically universally valid: life, health, love, well-being, security, social recognition. Other values are embedded in a certain political order or culture: freedom, autonomy, self-realization, democracy, authority, duty, self-control, material welfare, sexual equality. In addition, many values are subject to a more or less dynamic development and alteration. In the contemporary climate, it is common to discern a change in values from 'materialism' to 'post-materialism' or from 'collectivism' to 'individualism'.

However, whatever the special content and characteristics of their particular values, individuals and communities must find ways and means to transform their basic value-orientations into individual and collective actions so that the values are actually realised. This includes a demand for efficient adaptation processes in the face of changes in values—and changes too in external circumstances that make specific actions realise relevant values less effectively. In this context *social norms* play a central role: they are artificially created or evolutionarily developed prescriptions that aim at aligning people's behaviour with the values it is socially supposed to serve. Seen from this view, social norms are instruments to realize certain values. And hence, the relation between norms and values is a topic of special interest. Understanding how norms succeed or fail to realize desired individual and collective values, and how norms should and could change in the light of changing circumstances seem to be issues not only of theoretical significance but also of crucial practical importance—especially in the face of new challenges to democratic societies such as globalization, terrorism, fundamentalism and cultural diversity.

To see social norms as instruments to realize values and to seek the conditions under which they can serve this purpose is not new. But it is a topic which deserves to be taken up again and to be studied with modern methods and insights. Moreover, present-day research in this area is fragmented and isolated. On the one hand, there are several empirical studies which deal extensively with values and the change in values; on the other, there are theoretical models focused directly on the emergence and maintenance of social norms. But seldom do we find the relation and the transfer-mechanisms between values and norms studied from an interdisciplinary perspective. And that is, we think, regrettable. An interdisciplinary approach could explain the potential of social norms to realise desired values in practice and explore the empirical mechanisms that work in favour of or against this function. The issues here revolve around the so-called 'bridging problem': how to bridge the gap between values, on the one hand, and conduct, on the other—how, in short, to put desired values into social practice.

1.2 The Bridging Problem: Values and Conduct

The bridging problem can be viewed in a number of different lights. It can be viewed as a *conceptual* problem. One version of this view is related to the principle 'Ought implies can'. Suppose values are making infeasible demands: then it would arguably make no conceptual sense to say that we ought or have reason to conduct ourselves in ways that are unavailable to us. A second version relates to whether it is a conceptual pre-requisite for something to be a value that it bears some appropriate relation to conduct: for example, that it be the kind of thing that we can translate into our everyday behaviour. If so, the bridging problem must be solvable in principle for a value even to count *as* a value. The conceptual aspects of the bridging problem refer also to the fundamental philosophical question of how moral and non-moral values can be justified and in what way justifications of values can be directly or indirectly transformed into reasons for actions.

The bridging problem can also be viewed as a *practical* problem concerning conduct: by which mechanisms are values empirically transformed into actual behaviour? Fallible human agents can fail to act in ways they have most reason to act because of cognitive and/or motivational failures. In the first case, agents fail to perceive what they have most reason to do. In the second, they fail to be appropriately motivated by values and reasons. They might fail to be motivated by these values and reasons at all; or values/reasons might simply not supply enough motivating force, compared with the clamour of other motivating considerations, to induce the required conduct. This practical aspect of the bridging problem is reflected in the long-standing concern of economics with invisible hand mechanisms and more generally with questions of institutional design, (a concern shared with political science) and of sociology with socialisation and social integration.

1.3 Formal Institutions as Instruments of Value Realisation

Practical aspects of the bridging problem are often seen to be solvable by *formal collective institutions* of various kinds. The processes of collective decision-making might, for example, enhance our appreciation of values through respect for procedural fairness, information pooling and deliberative refinement. Formal mechanisms of command and control can also tell us what to do; and formal institutions of sanctions and incentives can help motivate us to comply with those collective prescriptions.

But though sometimes necessary, formal institutional sanctioning is often costly and sometimes totally ineffective. Moreover, such institutions typically presuppose that some agents in the system already act in accordance with the desired values; and democratic systems further presuppose that the appropriate values and reasons are shared by a majority of the general population, who will in turn elect as their political representatives agents who will reliably promote those values. In short, the solutions assume that the bridging problem has already largely been solved. It may well be that institutions that are designed to enforce the values of a community can only emerge when those values already exhibit sufficient efficacy by themselves to operate as the basis for these institutions. We should be wary of 'solutions' to problems that ultimately involve simply assuming the problem away.

Moreover, formal institutional sanctions might fail in the deeper task of properly incorporating reasons and values into our everyday conduct. H. L. A. Hart famously distinguished between 'being obliged' in ways that are externally imposed and 'being under an obligation' in ways that are internally felt. Internalising reasons and values in our everyday conduct requires the latter; institutional sanctions on their own provide only the former. Institutional sanctions only produce external incentives to comply with norms and therefore support only an 'external point of view' towards the underlying values. However, there are good reasons to assume that a social order is not viable in the long run if people do not adopt an 'internal point of view' in regard to the basic values of their community. This is—as Hart argues—especially true in regard to the institutions of law. At first sight these institutions appear as paradigmatic evidence for the relevance and efficacy of external incentives and formal sanctions. But further insight reveals that a system of law itself can only exist if at least a relevant subgroup of the members of the law system accepts and voluntarily co-operates in maintaining the basic principles of the system and its underlying values.

1.4 Social Norms as Instruments for Value Realisation

The systematic limits on the capacity of formal institutions to bridge the gap between values and behaviour support the view that *social norms* play a crucial role in solving the bridging problem. Social norms implement an *informal social order* that is not imposed externally, but is created and enforced endogenously by the decentralised forces within the community itself. Unlike purely formal institutional sanctions, norms necessarily have an internal as well as an external aspect. Not only do we externalise norms by holding others accountable to them; we also internalise norms, taking a critical and reflective attitude towards people's conduct in light of them—including or excluding our own conduct. In this way social norms can transform an internal point of view towards individual and collective values to an internal point of view towards concrete behavioural demands. The distinction between attitudes to others' conduct and attitudes to our own allows logical room for two kinds of internalisation—one the weaker form in which the values govern our attitudes towards others; and the other, the strong form under which the internalisation is determinate over a wider range of our own actions. The level of 'internalisation' relevant for a critical and reflective attitude towards other people's conduct is considerably weaker than the level of internalisation necessary to motivate action.

For the bridging of values and behaviour the *aggregation, co-ordination* and *co-operation functions* of social norms are essential. Norms fulfil a general *aggregation function* insofar as they regulate individual and collective behaviour in such a way that an aggregated outcome is produced which incorporates the desired values. Norms can furthermore perform a special *co-ordination function* if a mutual adjustment of interpersonal behaviour is necessary to realize common aims and values. Norms enable co-ordination by helping us to know what to expect of one another, allowing us to anticipate others' behaviour and adapt our own conduct accordingly. Norms can also accomplish a *co-operation function* in situations in which actors risk producing a sub-optimal result because of conflicting incentives that generate dilemmatic outcomes. Social norms offer in these situations a set of incentives that stand against the incentives for opportunistic behaviour and make it more likely that the outcome will be one in which individual and collective values are achieved to a higher degree than in the case of unregulated behaviour.

In the fulfilment of their various bridging-functions, norms themselves often embody values such as fairness, reliability or trustworthiness. And by virtue of creating widely acknowledged expectations, even mere behavioural regularities may take on a certain normative force. People can become morally outraged when others act in ways that are inconsistent with the regular pattern—when others 'violate the norm'. This fact reminds us that bridges carry traffic in both directions. Behavioural regularities may develop value rationalisations, as well as values giving rise to norms. In an evolving environment, the behavioural regularities can also persist after the original value rationale has evaporated. Norms can come apart from the values and reasons that originally justified them. Not only can norms cease to represent faithfully the underlying values of which they are putative expressions—but the behavioural rigidities to which they give rise may well stand in the way of developing new modes of conduct better fitted to those values.

2. The Volume

Although many theorists across philosophy and the social sciences have noted that norms seem to play a bridging function, the question of *how* and to *what extent* norms are actually *capable* of doing this has received only very partial and incomplete response. Such discussions as there are have tended to occur in isolated and increasingly divergent places across disparate disciplines. Within philosophy, work at the general level proceeds in splendid isolation from work at the specific or applied level, and often vice versa. Focusing exclusively on the general runs the risk of missing important nuances, with insufficient attention to the different kinds of norms and values in place and the different ways in which norms function to promote and pursue values. Focusing exclusively on the specific and applied, on the other hand, leads to a kind of tunnel vision: rich appreciation of the particular often fails to give rise to any general lessons.

A second kind of polarisation is along more overtly disciplinary lines: between those whose aim and method is squarely philosophical and those whose aim and method is derived from economics, political science, sociology or perhaps sociobiology. Disciplinary divides are of course a well-known issue, but they seem especially problematic in relations to the study of norms. Philosophical inquiry uninformed by social scientific understanding of how norms function is prone to simplify and mislead. Empirical social scientific inquiry lacking adequate philosophical underpinning risks conceptual confusion.

The ambition of this volume—and of the conference that it reports—revolves an attempt to make a start on a unified account of the bridging function of norms, employing a perspective that is both philosophical and social scientific at one and the same time. The editors share the conviction that norms are best considered simultaneously through a variety of disciplinary lenses, and with the relation between practical examples and more abstract analysis always in view. A coherent, unified understanding of norms is essential in order to 'make norms work', and especially to change them so they 'work better' in the service of the values that supposedly justify and explain them.

Recent work in 'normativity' in various corners of philosophy, ethics and law and on the evolution of norms in economics and (in a very different way) in political science and sociology, makes this a timely topic. Different disciplines all have a stake in the analysis of norms. But work on norms from diverse disciplines is rarely brought into joint focus. The different arenas in which norms apply are interesting and important in their own right; but they are especially interesting as a sample of the wide range of instances of the more general and more abstract phenomenon of normative solutions to the problem of 'bridging' between values and conduct. The distinctive feature of this project lies, therefore, in its multi-level and multi-disciplinary approach. The participants of the volume are selected according to the criteria that they have a strong record of operating across disciplinary boundaries and that each brings a somewhat different mix of skills and disciplinary orientations to the task.

A comprehensive research enterprise in this area should refer at least to three subjects. First, to *conceptual and normative questions*: philosophy and ethics have to clarify the conceptual relation between norms and values and to analyse the problems of normative and evaluative justification. Second, to *empirical and explanative dimensions*: social theory, game theory, behavioural and institutional economics and psychology can contribute to revealing the dynamics of the evolution, maintenance and alteration of norms and to deepening our understanding of how social norms guide co-ordination and co-operation processes to enhance value realisation. Third, to the political field of *collective decisions*: political science, social and public choice theories can be deployed to explain the consequences of different forms of collective choice set-ups for the implementation of norms and values and can there throw some light on the values incorporated in collective choice rules themselves.

Accordingly we have structured the volume in three sections: *1. Concepts and Justifications. 2. Empiricism and Efficacy. 3. Social Values and Collective Choice.* In each section participants from different disciplines present their views on their topic, in an interplay of papers and comments. The first section starts with a paper by *Philip Pettit* in which he argues that values can derive from norms. He suggests that a basic norm of dialogue plays a crucial role in a naturalistic genealogy of the values that serve in turn to support various norms. *Bob Sugden* discusses the distinction between morality and conventions. He defends David Hume's view that 'moral principles' are ultimately to be understood as conventions about social practices of approval and disapproval: according to this view, the idea that any particular set of moral principles is unconditionally true dissolves under philosophical scrutiny. *Nic Southwood* analyzes the crucial differences between norms and laws focussing in particular on their objects, their sanctions and their internalisation conditions. He argues that the appreciation of these differences allows us to gain a better understanding of the different values norms and laws help to realize and to make some headway in explaining both their origin and evolution over time. In his paper *Bernd Lahno* confronts consequentialism with deontological ethics and rejects both views: no pure system of norms of evaluation combined with instrumental rationality can suffice as a proper guide in social interaction; no pure system of norms of conduct can adequately reflect all our basic moral intuitions. Lahno explains some conceptual difficulties in moral theory by the general tendency to reduce all norms to one of the two forms. The subject of *Edna Ullmann-Margalit*'s paper is the 'case of the kitchen-camera'. The case revolved around the installation of a closed-circuit TV camera, as a somewhat private initiative, in a university kitchen in an effort to ensure cleanliness. The installation evoked a passionate debate both directly—for and against the camera—and indirectly, about the proper procedures that might govern a decision as to whether the camera was installed or not. Taking off from this debate, the article explores some of the diverse general normative issues that the incident raises.

Cristina Bicchieri and *Alex Chavez* lead into the second section *Empiricism and Efficacy*. Using a modified version of the Ultimatum Game, they demonstrate that both fair behaviour and perceptions of fairness depend upon beliefs about what one *ought* to do in a situation—that is, upon *normative expectations*. Proposers and responders show a remarkable degree of agreement in their beliefs about which choices are considered fair. *Lina Eriksson* looks at the kind of questions about social norms that rational choice accounts can answer. By being more precise about what rational choice theories can tell us, the paper also raises important questions about social norms that such accounts do not answer, thereby identifying the gaps and suggesting possible extensions of the theory that might cover some of these shortcomings. The paper by *Rainer Hegselmann* and *Oliver Will* presents the first outlines of a computational model reconstructing Hume's moral and political theory, in particular his assumptions about the origin of virtue and government. The computational model has precisely defined assumptions, and the values of the parameters that are involved are made explicit. This makes it possible to study the interplay and robustness of a bunch of mechanisms and to analyze systematically under what assumptions virtues, specialization, and wealth prosper. The section ends with the paper by *Gerhard Schurz* in which he criticizes Huntington's view of world-cultures as historically enduring characteristics from an evolution-theoretic and empirical viewpoint. It seems that cultural evolution does not follow a uniform trend, but is subject to opposing evolutionary forces whose strength is dependent on the level of economic well-being and education. The location of cultural equilibria on the cultural world-map and the regions in which societies stay stable for a long time are largely dependent on the constellation of these forces.

The third section *Social Values and Collective Choice* is comprised of three articles. *Werner Güth* and *Hartmut Kliemt* claim the impossibility of social choice and argue for the possibilities of social values. The very notion of 'collective choice (making)' seems problematic for the methodological individualist, while the concept of forming an ordering of social states does not raise comparable problems. Several possibilities of construing the relationship between emergent outcomes and values are discussed. *Bob Goodin* offers an analysis of how norms can be honoured in the breach. Starting with the question how old norms are revised or new norms are adopted in the absence of any secondary rule of recognition, the paper discusses the question as to the strategies by which people might hope to persuade others to persist in adherence to a rule that the agent herself violates. In his article *Russell Hardin* takes Zhang Yimou's film, *The Story of Qiu Ju*, as an exemplary tale of the transition of traditional norms that are *local, informal, and personal*, to norms that are *abstract, formal, and impersonal*, with variation in degrees on all these dimensions, and then to institutionalized legal rules that trump many of the local norms.

Each of the main papers is followed by a commentary by one of the conference participants—in the spirit of engagement that guided the conference organisation and intellectual ambition.

The volume closes with *Ernesto Garzón Valdés'* paper on radical evil and norms. In the 20th century we have witnessed great calamities resulting from hatred and fanaticism which were perceived as expressions of 'radical evil' and thus impossible to comprehend, to prevent or to punish. However, Garzón Valdés argues that oblivion and impunity are morally unacceptable, and that the only means to oppose atrocities involve a persistent memory and the strict application of national and international penal law.

3. Prospects

What are the possible long-term prospects of such an interdisciplinary endeavour? In the ideal case, the various insights of the different disciplines would accumulate to an integrated theory of norms and values. Such a theory would, inter alia, clarify the conceptual relationship between norms and values, deal with the moral justification of norms through values, analyze and evaluate different processes of collective decision-making and of mechanisms by which norms are implemented, and would make well-grounded assertions about the empirical conditions for the stability and adaptability of norms as instruments of value realization. Such hopes for an integrated theory of norms and values are not overambitious and unrealistic. In recent years the relevant disciplines for such a project have worked on research agendas and produced insights which make a systematic integration under a common thematic framework promising.

Moral philosophy and *normative ethics*, at least since John Rawls's influential work, have been characterized by a return to the problem of the moral justification of the institutional structure of a society. In this context, conceivable justifications for common norms and values acceptable to people from different cultural backgrounds and different life circumstances are of special significance. The integration of these normative endeavours into a comprehensive perspective including empirical and explanatory social theory is promising because it rejects metaphysical or religious foundations and aims for a rational justification of norms and values on the basis of social practice and the empirical facts of life.

In *descriptive social theory* we can observe an ever-growing awareness of the crucial relevance of social norms for the stability and efficiency of any societal order and its formal and informal institutions: examples are the seminal studies on social capital by Robert Putnam, Elinor Ostrom's discovery of the potential for self-governing the 'commons', or the insights of evolutionary game theory into the emergence of spontaneous order. Psychology and experimental economics have contributed important findings about the role of values and normative commitments in many interactive settings. Recent revisionism within the tradition of 'classical' public choice theory have emphasized the importance of expressive and moral motives for democratic elections, and the role of trust and non-instrumental preferences on the part of political agents. These insights contribute substantially to our knowledge of rational procedures to achieve commonly accepted values and norms as a basis for social stability and integration. Against this background, it has become clear that the behavioural models in the tradition of rational choice need to be replenished to account for intrinsic motivation, moral principles of behaviour and 'soft' incentives like social recognition and esteem in the explanation of rule-following behaviour and conformity with social norms. From here a direct connection to ethics opens up.

Taken together, these research programmes and theories converge in a central point: they share the basic insight that formal institutions and extrinsic incentives alone are not capable of guaranteeing the realization of basic societal values but rather that informal and spontaneously evolved social norms play a decisive role. Furthermore, they agree in the assumption that the emergence and maintenance of social norms essentially depend on intrinsic motivation and commitment on the part of the individuals. Therefore, the ethical justification of norms through values as well as the legitimacy and rationality of collective choice procedures becomes directly relevant from the perspective of descriptive social theory. Equally, the insights derived from empirical study of the stability of social norms cannot be ignored by normative ethics if moral convictions and motives are empirically relevant factors in this context. The focus on the role of social norms as instruments of value realization and on the mechanisms and dynamics of their emergence, maintenance and alteration provides a common reference point for different disciplines that makes prospects for a unified theory of norms and values today more encouraging than it seemed even a few years ago. As editors, we see the papers assembled here as both evidence of, and instruments in, that convergence. And we are for that reason delighted to offer the collection to a wider audience.

This volume comprises papers and comments that were presented and discussed at a conference of the same title at the *Centre for Interdisciplinary Research (ZiF), Bielefeld University*, from 8 to 10 May 2008. We gratefully acknowledge the generous funding of the conference by the *Centre for Interdisciplinary Research*, the *Deutsche Forschungsgemeinschaft*, and the *Gesellschaft von Freunden und Förderern der Heinrich-Heine-Universität Düsseldorf*. We are especially grateful to the staff of the ZiF for their professional and friendly support in preparing and organizing the conference. We would also like to thank Lars Heilsberger for his excellent technical assistance in the preparation of this book.

I. Concepts and Justification

Philip Pettit

Norms, Commitment and Censure[*]

1. The Norm-normative Gap

There are many different stories about how norms emerge but under most of them, norms come about as a result of rationally intelligible adjustments between the parties. They are regularities that people are naturally motivated to comply with and naturally motivated to enforce, say by retaliation against offenders or by some other form of punishment. Under these stories, however, neither compliance nor enforcement need have any element of the normative. People will comply with a regularity because prudence dictates, not because they ought in an independent sense to do so. And people will enforce the regularity on the same basis—if enforcement is intentional—not because offenders ought in an independent sense to be punished.

These naturalistic theories of norms apply to a wide spectrum of social regularities, ranging from norms of etiquette to norms of decent behavior. With norms at the etiquette end it is understandable that they might be sustained from merely rational motives but with norms at the decency end it seems that something more strongly normative is relevant. In order to count as decent, after all, people will have to conform to norms of decency because they ought to conform, not just because it is rational for them to do so. A pressing problem for any naturalistic theory of norms, then, is to explain how some norms come to assume such a normative status in the minds of those who uphold them.

The problem might also be described, in a way that Herbert Hart (1961) made famous, as an issue about how people assume an internal perspective on norms that they instantiate and enforce. He recognized that the norms on the realization of which a legal system depends—the norms followed and applied by those who administer the system—are ones which insiders treat normatively and that any theory of law ought to make sense of this. Yet he saw that the more or less naturalistic account that he himself sketched of how such norms might emerge and gain a hold did not fully account for this internal perspective. The problem he faced is exactly the problem as to how norms—naturalistically explicable norms—gain a normative status in the minds of those who implement them.

If norms have a normative status then they do not obtain just in virtue of rationally intelligible compliance and enforcement. They must also engage the normative

---

[*] This paper emerged from discussion of a sketch of related ideas at a conference in the University of Bielefeld in May 2008. I am most grateful for the searching feedback I received there, especially from my commentator, Thomas Spitzley. I am also grateful for some well-directed comments received from Michael Baurmann.

counterparts of those two elements. The counterpart to compliance is commitment, the counterpart to enforcement is censure. When people comply with the norm on a normative basis, they must in some sense commit themselves to it. And when they enforce the norm, they must in some sense censure those who have offended: they must hold them to have reneged on the commitment. The problem raised by such a norm is that there is a gap between what it requires, on pain of penalty, and what is normatively required, on pain of censure. We might call this the norm-normative gap.

In this paper I shall address the problem by showing that there is at least one plausible, naturalistically explicable norm in the implementation of which commitment and censure inevitably make an appearance and play an important role. This is the norm of honesty in communication, which rules out any form of deception between interlocutors. It requires people not only to use their words honestly, matching them to the world, but also to perform in fidelity to their words, providing a match in the reverse direction.

The paper has four more sections. In the next I outline the conditions that must be satisfied for something to be a norm, indicating the sorts of naturalistic explanations that norms in that sense invite and the normative gap that those explanations leave in place. In the third section I analyze what honesty requires and show how we might expect a norm of non-deception to arise on a naturalistic basis. In the fourth section I explain why such a norm is bound to mobilize attitudes of commitment and censure, assuming a properly normative profile. And then in the fifth section I expand on the significance of this fact, looking at two forms of commitment, avowals and promises, that a flourishing norm of honesty may be expected to activate.

2. Naturalistic Norms

2.1 The Definition of Norms

As it is used in social theory, and perhaps more generally, the word 'norm' has two more or less obvious connotations. First, anything that deserves to be described as a norm of a group—an actual, not a would-be, norm—has to be a regularity that actually prevails amongst members. But, second, the regularity cannot be a matter of indifference amongst the people who sustain it. In order to have the status of a norm, a social regularity has to have a relatively high approval rating in the society; compliance must be expected to attract approval or non-compliance disapproval. This is not to say that it has to be approved in a strong normative sense. The norm may present as a regularity that is to everyone's liking, or that has a good chance of being to everyone's liking—it may have a high approval rating in that naturalistic sense—without displaying anything in the way of a moral or strongly normative claim on people's allegiance.

But these two connotations do not exhaust the associations of the word 'norm', as that is used in social contexts. Suppose that a regularity was behaviorally and attitudinally supported among the members of a certain society but that there was no connection between the approval rating and the behavioral compliance. Suppose, in other words, that people were not exposed to any extra incentive for complying by the existence of the approval rating: not by the formation of attitudes of approval or disapproval on the part of others, and not by exposure to associated rewards or penalties. In that case the regularity would scarcely count as a norm. This suggests that we ought to build a third connotation into our use of the term. We ought to stipulate that in order for a regularity to count as a social norm, it should not only be instantiated as a general rule, and not only have a high approval rating; in addition, that rating should help to explain why it is generally instantiated: it should play a policing role in sustaining the regularity.

This characterization of social norms leaves open a range of questions. Does a regularity count as generally instantiated if it is a regularity that applies only to those holding a certain office or meeting a certain qualification? How extensive is the pattern of approval or disapproval envisaged when it is said that the regularity has a high approval rating? Moreover, must the approval or disapproval be associated with the relevant type of behavior, considered in general, or will it suffice if it reliably appears, instance by instance? And what, finally, is required for the approval rating to help to explain the pattern of behavior? Must it contribute in some measure to the production of the behavior, at least among a number of those complying? Or will it do if it is there to reinforce the behavior, should the motives that normally produce it fail for one or another reason? Will it do, in other words, if it is a virtual or standby force that is triggered to support the behavior only on a need-to-act basis, when the 'red lights' are illuminated (Pettit 1995)?

I am happy to leave aside these questions, taking an inclusive view of norms. But there is one further question we cannot avoid. Is it essential for a social norm that the fulfillment of the three core conditions be a matter accessible to common awareness? It will be a matter of common awareness that the conditions are fulfilled if each is aware that the conditions are fulfilled; each is aware that each is aware of this; and each is disposed to answer positively for any question that may arise at a higher level in the potential hierarchy of awareness. I am happy to add this condition too, though some may prefer to take it as a condition that is almost inevitably fulfilled with norms rather than a condition that must be fulfilled if they are to count as norms.

The upshot is a generous, perhaps deflationary sense of norm. On this account, a behavioral regularity among the members of a group will constitute a norm just in case:

- nearly everyone conforms;
- the behavior has a high approval rating;
- this rating helps to police and promote the general conformity;
- and those conditions are fulfilled as a matter of common awareness.

2.2 The Variety of Norms

This account of norms is broadly in line with the approach of recent authors on the subject and ought not to generate any deep controversy (Hart 1961; Winch 1963; Ullmann-Margalit 1977; Coleman 1990; McAdams 1997; Sober/Wilson 1998; Elster 1999; Brennan/Pettit 2004). Where those accounts vary from that provided here, that is often because they are focused on particular sets of norms, not norms in general. Herbert Hart (1961, 84–85) concentrates, for example, on rules that generally prevail in a society, are supported by serious social pressure, are thought useful in some way for the life of the group, and are individually burdensome, however beneficial in group terms.

My account allows for a much larger range of norms. Thus, norms may obtain only in particular sub-groups, rather than prevailing generally in a society, and they may have a counterproductive impact on that group or on society as a whole. It may even be the case that norms obtain in virtue of each person thinking that compliance attracts approval, or noncompliance disapproval, when as a matter of fact few if any hold that attitude; the approval rating may be assigned in ignorance about people's actual attitudes (Miller/Prentice 1996; Pettit 2006). Still, the focus here will mainly be on norms of the kind that Hart has in mind, for it is those norms that assume a normative status amongst adherents and that raise the problem of the norm-normative gap.

Norms in the broad sense defined, including norms with normative status, have long been targets of explanation in social science. Sometimes the explanations focus on explaining the behavior, then in the second place the approval rating and its impact (Hardin 1982; Sugden 1986). Sometimes they focus on explaining the approval rating in the first place and the behavioral compliance in the second (Pettit 1990; McAdams 1997; Brennan/Pettit 2004). Sometimes they mobilize rational choice resources of explanation and sometimes they rely more heavily on evolutionary narratives, natural or cultural or mixed (Sober/Wilson 1998; Richerson/Boyd 2005).

I abstract here from those variations in explanatory strategy, remarking only that there is no need in any of these accounts to introduce a strongly normative element. The explanatory work is entirely done by naturalistic factors that may operate without people's going in for commitment rather than mere compliance, censure rather than mere punishment. It is for that reason that the accounts leave in place the problem of closing the norm-normative gap.

3. The Naturalistic Norm of Honesty

Most accounts of norms concentrate on regularities in non-linguistic behavior but there is no reason why they should not be extended to regularities of a communicative character as well. There might be a norm—a naturalistically explicable norm—against the use of coercive threats, for example. Or there might be a norm against the manipulative use of speech. In manipulation everything appears to be above board, unlike the case of coercion, but speakers rely on an underhanded power—say, their skill at spin or their intimidating presence—in order to secure a desired uptake. In this paper I concentrate on perhaps the most basic norm that is likely to arise in the space of words: a norm against deception—a norm of honesty.

3.1 The Meaning of Honesty

In order to understand what a norm of honesty would entail, we need to be clear about what counts as deception or dishonesty. The most obvious way in which speech is likely to deceive, or so it may appear, is through conveying an inaccurate or inadequate account of that which it purports to represent. Let us concentrate for the moment on the assertion that reports a public state of affairs: that it is raining, to take an occurrent state of affairs, or that Princeton lies just south of New York, to take one of a standing character. An assertion will be inaccurate if things are not as they are reported to be, and inadequate if the way they are reported to be does not provide all the information that is contextually required for the guidance of the hearer.

If I report things inaccurately or inadequately in making an assertion, does that mean that I am being deceptive and dishonest? And if I report things accurately and adequately does that mean I am being non-deceptive and honest? In each case the answer is, no. I may misreport things because of being misinformed or underinformed myself, not out of a deceptive wish to mislead the hearer. And if I report things accurately and adequately I may do so due to the lack of proper information, and may actually have meant to deceive. It is in virtue of the intent of a communication, not its content, that a report counts as non-deceptive or deceptive.

This observation suggests that what is required for non-deception or honesty is not accuracy or adequacy—if you like, truth—but rather sincerity. An assertion will be sincere just in case the belief it purports to express really is the belief of the speaker. My assertion reports that it is raining and expresses, or at least purports to express, my belief that it is raining. Whether or not the report is true, the assertion will be sincere just in case I believe that it is true: just in case it is a true expression of my belief.

What is it for an utterance to express or purport to express a belief as distinct from reporting on a state of affairs? Expressing and reporting are both forms of representation, in a broad sense of that term. When I express a belief that it is raining by reporting that it is raining, then I represent the environment as rainy and I represent myself as holding the belief that it is rainy. And I support both representations with full knowledge and with full consent, in the overt manner that is characteristic of speech; the representation does not occur behind my back. At a single stroke I describe the world and express the belief, where both the description and the expression are forms of linguistic representation.

Why does the self-representation count as expression, and the world-representation count as a report or description? The crucial contrast, as I see it, is the following. I may explain a descriptive misrepresentation of the world on the grounds that I misread the evidence—I thought the water on the glass was rain. But I cannot explain the expressive misrepresentation of my belief—say, the belief that it was raining—on similar evidential grounds. Suppose I spoke insincerely in reporting that it was raining and that I am challenged about this. I cannot explain the expressive misrepresentation of my state of belief—I cannot explain my insincerity—by claiming that I got that belief wrong: I misread the evidence on what I actually believed. Descriptive misrepresentation is explicable on grounds that the evidence that prompted it was misleading, expressive misrepresentation is not explicable in that way. For the moment I take that point of contrast as a given; it will assume a good deal of importance in the later argument.

What honest, non-deceptive assertion requires, then, is that it be sincere. The expressive self-representation that it involves must be accurate and adequate to the facts; the speaker must actually have the belief expressed, whether or not that belief is correct. But what of other speech acts? What of the question that communicates a desire for a certain information, the request that indicates the presence of a wish, or the command that conveys an order: an order, as it happens, that the issuance of the command will itself constitute?

Such speech acts represent attitudes of the speaker on a par with the belief that the assertion represents the speaker as having. And they represent those attitudes in an expressive manner, by the criterion just introduced, not in the manner of a report or description. In normal contexts a speaker cannot plausibly explain a misrepresentation of attitude on evidential grounds: on the grounds that he or she thought wrongly that they had the attitude expressed. As with assertions, these speech acts will be sincere and honest to the extent that the speaker really has the attitudes expressed, insincere and deceptive to the extent that the speaker lacks them.

We can sum up this discussion in three claims. When I represent myself as having a certain attitude, and it is understood on all sides that I cannot give an evidential explanation for having misrepresented myself, the representation at issue counts as an expression. When my expressive self-representation fails to be accurate or adequate to the type of attitude expressed, it counts as insincere. And when it is insincere, it is dishonest or deceptive.

3.2 Making Honesty a Norm

Honesty is something that each of us is bound to welcome from others. If I communicate with you honestly then I can extend and improve the epistemic representation of your environment and facilitate the achievement of your goals. I can make you aware of opportunities and obstacles of which you may not have been conscious, providing you with a new set of eyes and ears. And I can make you aware of failures in your own practical and theoretical reasoning, providing you with a new set of checks on how you think and plan. Assuming that I do not offend in other ways, say through resort to coercion or manipulation, I will be a friend in the forum of your informational gathering and informational processing: an amicus curiae, a friend of the court.

The welcome character of honest communication appears most vividly in the fact that the service I provide for you in such communication may be exactly like the service you provide for yourself when you stop and reason about the best thing to do or think, or when you seek out extra information (Pettit/Smith 2004; Pettit 2007). I collaborate with you epistemically, as we might say, when I communicate with you in this mode. I provide you in all sincerity with considerations that bear on how you conduct your thought and action. And assuming that I avoid coercion and manipulation, I offer these on a take-it-or-leave it basis, enabling you to make up your own mind, using your own reason. There is everything to celebrate about this service—at least if I am reasonably competent—and nothing to regret.

Given the benefits that each of us stands to gain from a norm of honesty, the appearance or stability of such a norm ought not to be surprising. Assume that each of us is aware of the benefits of someone's honesty to others. Assume that instances of dishonesty stand a good chance of being detected. Assume that for intrinsic or instrumental reasons each of us cares about being well thought of by others—that is, accepted, liked, regarded as a friend, not well thought of in any more normative terms. And assume that those assumptions are matters of common recognition and acceptance.

Under those plausible assumptions, it should be no surprise that the desire for the good opinion of others should lead each of us to be honest in our general dealings.[1] And so in those circumstances we may expect a norm of honesty to emerge and remain in place. People will generally be non-deceptive in their dealings with one another and this will be due, at least in part, to the fact they will be policed by the attitudes of approval and disapproval on the part of others (Brennan/Pettit 2004). To rehearse the clauses in our definition of norms, then, there will be compliance with the regularity of honesty; honesty will have a high approval rating; this approval rating will play a role in policing and promoting the regularity; and all of that will be a matter accessible to common awareness.

This account of how a naturalistic norm might emerge says nothing on the response that instances of dishonesty will merit, apart from the disapproval they will attract. Plausibly, they will prompt those who have been let down not to care about being honest in future dealings with the offender, at least not until the offender shows signs of reform. Such a response might actually attract esteem and would certainly not attract disesteem. Thus the pattern of behavior that appears under the norm is almost bound to have a conditional, tit-for-tat character.

---

[1] In those circumstances, indeed, it should be no surprise if each of us is disposed to pronounce on how all of us in the society welcome honesty and to expose and thereby penalize offenders; the disposition to pronounce in that manner would itself earn the good opinion of others, marking out the speaker as a congenial presence. I have spoken elsewhere of this development as one in which the norm is 'moralized' (Pettit 1990). But that may not have been the best word to use, if the argument of this paper goes through.

This being so, there is obvious room for a different, complementary explanation according to which conditional cooperation in honest communication has an appeal, quite independently of how far it connects with attitudes of approval or disapproval on the part of people generally. The idea is that in self-interested terms that are independent of the returns in esteem, it will be rational in familiar circumstances for each to follow something like a tit-for-tat maxim: be honest in an initial encounter with another and after that be honest with anyone who has been honest with you in the preceding encounter. If there are independent motives for adopting such a strategy, then they will provide a naturalistic push to complement the naturalistic pull of the desire for esteem. The appearance of a norm of honesty will be overdetermined.

The circumstances in which the independent case for conditional honesty is most plausible are those in which people experience recurrent prisoner's-dilemma interactions with random others. I can tell you about my source of food, you can tell me about yours, but we would each like to know about the other's source without letting the other know about ours. In a dilemma of this kind joint honesty scores over joint dishonesty but dishonesty is the dominant choice for each; it beats honesty both when the other is honest and when the other is dishonest. Robert Axelrod (1984) ran a famous computer simulation that displayed the merits of tit-for-tat in a society where such exchanges recur in an open-ended way. The strategy is going to be a viable one to adopt for the first time, even if no one else has done so. It promises to be robustly successful in competition with a wide range of rival strategies, such as permanent honesty, permanent dishonesty, or tit-for-double-tat. And it is going to be resistant—at least in general (Nowak/Sigmund 1993)—to the invasion of the population by numbers of individuals with rival strategies.

The benefits of this strategy make it likely that people will find it attractive and even that they are primed by their evolutionary history to find it attractive, as a great deal of evidence suggests that other species are primed.[2] But if people all display tit-for-tat in the sphere of communication then honesty will become a regular pattern—and no doubt be backed up by the forces of esteem; each party will be honest in initial encounters with others and each, therefore, will be honest in later encounters too. Indeed general honesty will emerge even if the parties vary the strategy a little, say through being willing to be honest with another, and only with another, who looks likely to be honest with them. This variant would not ensure initial honesty, nor would it ensure immediate retaliation for anyone who was dishonest in the preceding session. But under plausible circumstances it would predict the appearance of honesty in most communicative encounters.

I refer to these explanations of why a norm of honesty might emerge in a group in order to show that the appearance of such a norm is likely to be naturalistically explicable. Other accounts that would bear out the same lesson might appeal to the

---

2 For an example among vampire bats, see Wilkinson (1984; 1990); among stickleback fish, see Milinski/Pfluger et al. (1990); and among vervet monkeys, see Seyfarth/Cheney (1984, 541), who report that these monkeys "appear to be more willing to aid unrelated individuals if those individuals have behaved affinitively toward them in the recent past".

effects of cultural evolution in addition to the factors invoked in these accounts, or instead of them (Sober/Wilson 1998; Richerson/Boyd 2005). But we need not go into further detail. The point to emphasize is that there is no dearth of naturalistic accounts of why we should expect a norm of honesty to emerge and survive in human society.

This is the important point, because it highlights the problem of the norm-normative gap. The norm of honesty is taken by adherents to have a strong normative status, requiring commitment on the part of those who conform, not just compliance, and engaging censure on the part of those who enforce the norms, not just punishment. If the norm of honesty is naturalistically explicable, however, why does it display this normative status? Where does that normative status come from? And does its appearance mean that the naturalistic story does not identify all the factors relevant in explaining its appearance and stability?

One way of explaining the gap would be to postulate that the approval rating with the norm of honesty is normative in character, where the approval rating with certain other norms is not. In this case there is approval of conformity as right or desirable and of non-conformity as wrong or undesirable, where in those other cases, there is merely prudential approval and disapproval. But this explanation would be ad hoc. And besides, it would introduce an unexplained notion—perhaps even a naturalistically inexplicable notion—of normative approval and disapproval.

The challenge is to see if we can do better. And I think we can. There are grounds for holding that as a regularity of honest behavior gets established by a naturalistically explicable norm, it will inevitably give rise to the concept and practice of commitment and to the related concept and practice of censure.

4. The Normative Status of the Norm of Honesty

4.1 The Counsel-and-Consult Model

Suppose that we are confronted, with a human society in which the norm of honesty has been established on a naturalistic basis. To be concrete, suppose that the norm appears and stabilizes on a conditionally cooperative basis, reinforced by a prudential pattern of approval for honesty, disapproval for dishonesty. What sort of behavior would this sort of explanation lead us to expect?

When the norm is not overridden by other factors—for example, by a salient conflict of interests—we must certainly expect that human beings will counsel and consult one another, confident in their mutual honesty, about the lie of the land in which they operate. Rather than just relying on their personal sources of information, and personal styles of reasoning, they will seek and offer one another a wealth of epistemic advice. They will pool their information and put their minds together in exploring its implications. Those implications will bear on what to think and do, whether individually or together.

When I consult with you, under this pattern, I will presumably provide you with information about the opportunities in your natural environment for fulfilling certain desires, and about the opportunities that may arise because of a convergence of interests with third parties. I may tell you, for example, that a third party would be willing to provide you with a reward for choosing A rather than B and that, on the basis of my knowledge of your desires, you ought to approach that person and seek an offer of a reward. And in the same information-providing spirit I may make the same report about myself. I may say that I myself would be willing to provide you with a reward for choosing A rather than B and that you ought to consider approaching me with a view to securing an offer.

But the behavior that we can expect under a naturalistically explicable norm of honesty is not restricted to the sort of counseling and consulting described here. What we now have to see is that the sort of explanation sketched predicts that when I provide information about my disposition to reward your choice, I go beyond what I do when I provide information about someone else's disposition. I make an offer in a sense in which this involves a commitment and, should I not provide the reward offered, I expose myself to punishment in a sense in which it involves censure.

4.2 Expression and Excuse

In order to see why this is going to be so, we have to go back to a feature of regular assertion that was mentioned earlier. When I make an assertion that turns out to be false—inaccurate or at least inadequate—it is always an open possibility that I can explain why it is false in a way that establishes my sincerity and my honesty. I can show that the evidence at my disposal was misleading and that my assertion expressed the belief that I formed in response to the evidence. I asserted that it was raining and did so perfectly sincerely, taking the water on the windows to be evidence of rain.

Suppose now that I had communicated my belief that it was raining to you and that you took certain steps on the basis of that information. When you discover that I misinformed you, will the naturalistic, prudential norm of honesty lead you to see my communication as dishonest and a fit target of retaliation? Surely not. Or not at any rate if I get the opportunity of explaining to you that though my descriptive report was false, my representation of myself as someone who believed in the rain was not; I made the report sincerely. If I get the chance to explain this to you—or if you just see that I am in a position to provide such an explanation—then you will surely resist retaliation. You will take it that notwithstanding the disservice that I unwittingly performed, still your conditionally cooperative strategy does not require that I be penalized; in fact it requires that I not be penalized. The explanation of my disservice plays the role of canceling the retaliation that might seem to have been required under a strategy of conditional honesty. It counts in this context as an excuse.

The concept of an excuse may not be strictly definable on the basis of the naturalistic concepts introduced in this story. But a somewhat weaker claim certainly seems plausible. This is that we can explain the appearance of such a concept, invoking only naturalistic elements in the explanation (Pettit 2000). If we simulate the position of someone who is about to be penalized for dishonesty, within a relationship of manifest, conditional cooperation, we can readily imagine why that person might protest their sincerity; why the other party might accept the explanation provided for their mistake; and why in that context the word 'excuse', as we use it, would become accessible to both. With the sort of meaning that we give the term, the parties are in a position to recognize that what the first person has done is to provide an effective excuse for having told an untruth and on that account that the naturalistic norm of honesty does not support retaliation.

4.3 Commitment and Censure

The concept of an excuse, and the practice of invoking excuses, is bound to have a place under any norm of honesty, given that honesty requires sincere communication. It will be required in order to mark the crucial difference between speaking falsely but sincerely and speaking falsely and insincerely; it plays the role of showing how the first is not in breach of the norm but the second is. And now the big news. With the appearance of such a notion of an excuse, the concepts and the practices of both commitment and censure will also become available.

Suppose that you make a report to me, as in our earlier examples, about the current rain or the position of Princeton in relation to New York. You are bound to be aware of the excuse that you can make for the failure of such a descriptive report; this will be a matter of shared linguistic understanding, as I emphasized earlier. And so you can give yourself some comfort in making that report: you can expect to count as sincere and cooperative even if, as it turns out, the report is false. But the salience of this possibility means that you now have a way of playing safe—a way of hedging your bets—in any representation of yourself that looks risky. You can represent your beliefs or any other attitudes in a descriptive way, leaving room for invoking an evidential excuse in the event of the representation proving to be false.

Imagine now that I seek information on what you believe in some domain where you are not so clear about your beliefs. I ask whether you believe that Jones is trustworthy, for example, or whether you believe that the stock market is going to recover soon. You may simply express your belief on the matter, saying that Jones is indeed trustworthy or that the market will recover.[3] In this case you will have no excuse to offer, if it becomes clear from your behavior—as, plausibly, your caution

---

[3] Consistently with such expression, I may take the content of the belief to be probabilistic, as in saying that the chances are high that Jones is trustworthy or that the market will recover. In the terms that I go on to introduce, there will still be a commitment in that case but the commitment will not be as hazardous as in the case where the content is not probabilistically qualified.

in dealing with Jones or the market might later make it clear—that you do not really believe this. That emerges from our account of what it is to express such a belief. But anticipating this possibility, you may decline to represent your belief expressively and do so just descriptively. You may say that you believe, so far as you can tell, that Jones is trustworthy or that the market will recover: that that is what you find yourself inclined to say. And if you do opt for the descriptive representation of your belief then you will have an excuse available, as a matter of common awareness, should your later behavior belie the report. Your self-representation will allow excuses, not exclude them.

We can now introduce the notions of commitment and censure, at least in the domain of belief representation. Assume that the difference in significance between expressive and descriptive representation of a belief is a matter of common awareness. If it were not then anyone guilty of expressive misrepresentation could claim ignorance of what they were doing, explain that they meant to offer just a descriptive report, and thereby excuse the misrepresentation. And now suppose that, when asked whether Jones is trustworthy, or the market reliable, you express your belief in a way that, as a matter of common awareness, puts evidential excuses for misrepresenting it out of reach (McGeer 1996; 2008; Moran 2001). In that case it is natural to say that you commit to the belief. You manifestly forego resort to an evidential excuse for misrepresenting the belief to an addressee; you speak in a way that forecloses the possibility of invoking such an excuse. You put yourself in the hands of the other, denying yourself grounds on which to protest at punishment, should you prove not to hold the belief expressed.

The best way of explaining what occurs in this transaction is to start from the observation that when speakers report that they have such and such a belief, there are no rules in play that outlaw their evading or resisting a tit-for-tat penalty for misrepresenting the belief: say, resisting it, sincerely or insincerely, by seeking to explain and excuse the misrepresentation on evidential grounds. In the weakest sense of the term 'right', then, those who give a false report have a right to evade or resist punishment in that manner. They have a so-called 'liberty-right' to resistance: a right that consists in there being no rules or requirements in play, manifest to the parties, that would make resistance inappropriate (Hohfeld 1919).

When speakers foreclose an evidential excuse for self-misrepresentation in a manifestly intentional way, then they deny themselves unqualified access to this liberty-right of evading or resisting punishment. Consistency is a requirement of self-representation to which no one can be openly indifferent; it is a requirement, like attitudinal consistency, that does not depend for its appeal on contingently desiring this or that result. Speakers who deny themselves an evidential excuse for misrepresenting a belief are bound in consistency not to resist punishment by claiming to have misread the evidence. Having said that Jones is trustworthy, for example, consistency requires that, in the event of your not acting on that belief, you acknowledge the loss of your right to resist punishment in that manner. It is no longer the case that there is nothing manifest to the parties that rules out such resistance on your part; the requirement of consistency rules it out.

But now we can go one step further. By manifestly forgoing an evidential excuse for misrepresentation, speakers give their audience a 'claim-right' to punish them for misrepresentation, at least when there are no other excuses available. The right to punish that the audience enjoys counts as a claim-right insofar as it correlates with the loss of the liberty-right that the speakers have incurred. Otherwise put, it correlates with an obligation that the speakers have assumed not to resist punishment.

I said that it is natural to describe what you do in choosing to represent a belief expressively, forgoing an evidential excuse for any self-misrepresentation, as an act of committing to that belief. This is natural because, as we now see, the act of forgoing such an excuse has important, normative implications. It amounts to conferring a certain claim-right of punishment on your interlocutors. Alternatively, it means incurring an obligation not to evade or resist punishment by appealing to misleading evidence.

Once the notion of commitment is in place, the notion of censure also gets established. Censure always involves punishment, in my usage, if only the symbolic variety associated with casting a cold eye, wagging a finger or using sharp words. What distinguishes it from other forms of punishment, however, is that it is imposed on the assumption that it is appropriate or earned; it involves a penalty that the punisher has a right to apply. The commissive character of forgoing an excuse for self-misrepresentation explains why we should cast the punishment imposed on any misrepresentation as a case of censure. When the audience chastises you for not acting on a belief to which you committed, they don't just try to make you smart under their barbs; they assume a right to make you smart.

The upshot is clear. If a norm of honesty is in place in a communicative context—and this, by courtesy of naturalistic factors alone—it is inevitable that the notions of excuse, commitment and censure will make an appearance too. And with those notions in place, the very character of the norm will change. It will assume a status under which we can find room for saying that if you represented yourself in such and such a manner, then you ought not to do so and so; you are committed to not doing it. And if you do so and so, then you ought to accept that you are subject to censure. Although springing out of purely naturalistic sources, the norm will assume a normative profile in the understanding of participants.

4.4 The Inescapability of Commitment and Censure

Why would people ever commit to beliefs? Why would they ever put excuses beyond reach? There are two points to notice in response. The first is that committing yourself to a certain belief will have positive attractions in facilitating relations with others. By manifestly exposing yourself to a penalty for misrepresentation, denying yourself access to an excuse, you can make that representation all the more credible to others. Thus you can induce others to rely on you, guiding their behavior on the assumption that your representation is correct. And by proving to be reliable, you can build up mutually beneficial relationships of trust. Commitment is the high road to community.

But not only are there attractions of this kind attaching to commitment. It turns out that even if you wanted to, you could not indefinitely postpone commitment. At some level of linguistic communication, you will have to represent yourself on the excuse-excluding pattern; you cannot keep excuses available at every level of self-representation.

Suppose you want to hedge your bets on what you believe about Jones. In that case you will say that your impression is that you believe that Jones is trustworthy: that you find yourself inclined to say that he is, or something of that kind.[4] By taking this line you can get yourself off the hook, if you are proved to have misrepresented your belief; you will be able to appeal to a misreading of the evidence that you had about your beliefs at that first level. But is this ploy available at every possible level? Is the second-level belief that you would thereby represent yourself as having had open, for example, to the same possibility? Might you be able to explain having got it wrong by appeal to a misreading of the evidence at that level? And if so, what then of the third-level belief that you would represent yourself as having mistakenly held about the second-level belief? Might it be open to the same possibility as well?

On pain of infinite regress, these progressively higher-level beliefs cannot all be represented in the descriptive manner way that would keep the possibility of evidential excuse open. At some level you must express the belief held, foreclosing any excuse for getting it wrong (Bar-on 2004; McGeer 2005). The option for expression over description, then, is not a heroic choice in favor of commitment. When you represent what you believe to others you have to commit yourself at some level and have to expose yourself to the possibility of censure at that level. The only choice is whether to commit in the lower reaches of self-representation or in the higher.

5. Avowals and Promises

The conclusion of the argument so far is that even when people come to uphold a norm of honesty on a purely naturalistic basis, they are going to get themselves into a position where they are bound to conceive of their compliance with the norm as a matter of commitment and of the punishment to which offenders are exposed as a matter of censure. They are bound to adopt an internal perspective on the norm under which it assumes a normative status. This result is exciting in itself but it assumes a particular significance in view of the range of cases over which it applies. It turns out that the commitments people have to recognize in the course of honest

---

4   It will not be enough to say that I believe that Jones is trustworthy, rather than simply saying that he is trustworthy. Shared contextual expectations will mean that even then I am going to be taken to be expressing the belief, not just reporting it. I would be laughed out of court if I claimed, in explaining behavior which did not reflect the belief, that I had only expressed the higher-order belief that I believe that Jones is trustworthy, not the ground-level belief that he is.

communication, and the forms of censure that they are bound to license, extend over all forms of attitude and action, not just over beliefs.

5.1 Commitments to Attitude

Commitment, by our account, is a form of self-representation in which a speaker forgoes an otherwise available excuse for self-misrepresentation and does so as a matter of shared awareness with the audience. But commitment in this sense need not be limited to the case of belief. A participant in an exchange may commit to any of a variety of attitudes, not just to the attitude of belief. And equally, as we shall see, such a participant may go further and commit to one or another specific course of action.

Questions and requests and orders, as we saw earlier, involve the expression of attitudes, among them attitudes other than belief, not their descriptive attribution. The question expresses the wish to know whether something is the case together with the background belief that things are otherwise thus and so. The request expresses the desire that the addressee do something or other and the belief that this is possible. And the order expresses the act of giving a command as well as the associated belief that the speaker has the requisite authority to do so.

In each of these cases the speaker might have resorted to an excuse-allowing way of communicating the relevant attitudes, though that would have required a good deal of circumlocution. Instead of playing safe, however, the speaker opts for an excuse-excluding form of expression, thereby engaging a commitment and inviting censure for misrepresentation. No one will think that speakers should be censured if they make false background assumptions in asking questions, making requests, or giving orders. But everyone will think that they are subject to censure if it turns out that the attitudes they expressed were not actually in place: that the speaker was insincere or deceptive, for example, in pretending to a wish to know something, or pretending to a desire that something be done.

But it is not just in non-assertoric speech acts that speakers commit to attitudes other than belief. Suppose, using an apparently descriptive idiom, that I say 'I approve of white lies in politics'. I will certainly have expressed and committed to the belief that I do indeed hold that attitude of approval. But in normal contexts I will also be taken to have expressed and committed to that attitude of approval itself—and this, again, as a matter of shared understanding (Jackson/Pettit 1998; 2003). I will have put myself in a position where I cannot excuse myself evidentially if it turns out that I don't actually hold the attitude of approval ascribed. I will have expressed both the belief that I hold an attitude of approval towards political white lies and the attitude of approval itself.

The reason why this is so derives from the principles that govern conversation, and in particular from the principle according to which a speaker is expected to choose words that do not understate or overstate the information to be communicated (Grice 1989). When it comes to communicating your attitude of approval, you

33

might have done so in a clearly descriptive manner, expressing your belief that you approve, while indicating that that belief may be mistaken. Given that you do not opt for that manifestly available form of words you will be taken to be communicating something more—and this, as a matter of common awareness—in saying, baldly, 'I approve of white lies in politics'. The something more that you will be taken to communicate, plausibly, is that you are not hedging your bets on whether you have that attitude or not; you are staking your reputation on your proving to have the attitude, denying yourself access to an evidential excuse for any misrepresentation.

This commissive construal of your words fits with a broader sense of what you are doing in saying 'I approve of white lies in politics'. Why would you have any interest in telling us about your attitudes in a descriptive spirit? You might want to do that with your therapist or confessor. You might want to confess that you seem to hold an attitude of approval towards politically motivated white lies, you know not why. But in normal contexts such a confession would be out of place. And so the words you use are bound to be taken as a commissive expression, not just a descriptive report, of your attitude.

There is another, even better established way in which people commit to attitudes of approval and disapproval, apart from resorting to self-ascription. That is by means of employing evaluative terms, positive and negative. These would include stock examples like 'kind' and 'cruel', 'generous' and 'selfish', 'good' and 'bad'. And, within the practice of commitment, they might also include 'censurable' and 'not censurable'. Even if predications of evaluative terms are used to commit to beliefs, as I take them to be generally used (Pettit 2001), they serve at the same time to commit to attitudes of approval and disapproval. You would not count as understanding such a term, if you did not understand that to use it of something is to represent yourself as having an attitude of at least qualified approval or disapproval towards the item evaluated. And this self-representation will count as commissive, not just descriptive. If the self-representation proves to be inaccurate—if it turns out that you do not actually have the associated attitude of approval or disapproval—the misrepresentation will not be explainable and excusable by appeal to misleading evidence; it will be subject to censure.

5.2 Commitments to Action

Not only do we routinely commit to attitudes, however, in cooperating with one another conversationally. Even more importantly, we commit with equal regularity to performing specific actions. The point is best demonstrated by considering the contrast between my telling you what a third party is going to do in the event that you make a certain choice and telling you what I am going to do in that event.

Suppose that I tell you in consultative mode that somebody else intends to reward you for choosing A rather than B in a choice that you currently face, indicating therefore that he or she will indeed provide a reward. I thereby express the belief that the person intends to provide the reward, so that I cannot excuse myself if I prove to have misrepresented the belief. But I merely report that the person intends to provide that reward and if I prove to have misrepresented his or her disposition, then I may well be able to explain and excuse the misrepresentation by showing that I had been misled by the evidence available. I may be able to show, for example, that I overheard the person express an intention to reward the choice of A in a context where I wrongly thought that you were the subject of discussion.

But what now if I tell you that I, and not another person, intend to reward your choice of A? In such an address I will have committed to the belief that I so intend, as in the other case; I will not be able to explain or excuse any misrepresentation of that belief. But will I have committed to a belief such that if it proves to be incorrect—if I prove not to have the ascribed intention—I can explain and excuse the misrepresentation of my intention? Will I have made a commitment that has the same thin profile as the commitment in the case with the other person?

Suppose that I tried to explain and excuse my failure to provide the reward for your choosing A, on the grounds that I had misread my own intentions. I made the attribution of intention sincerely, so I might say, and I do not count as insincere and dishonest just because it proved to be false. This explanation would have no plausibility whatsoever—it would make me a laughing stock amongst my audience—in view of considerations that we rehearsed in discussing the commissive aspect of self-ascribing an attitude of approval or disapproval.

With the self-ascription of an attitude there is a clear distinction between reporting, in a fallible spirit, that I think I have the attitude and ascribing the attitude without reservation. And in the same way there is a clear difference between reporting in a fallible spirit that I think my intention is to do such and such and ascribing that intention without qualification. Under standard principles of conversation, therefore, the choice of the unqualified words means that there is more information to be communicated than what the qualified statement would have conveyed. And that information, plausibly, is that I am committed to the intention. I have put aside appeal to any evidential excuse for misrepresenting the intention, if I prove to have misrepresented it. I have locked myself in.

That makes for a first disanalogy between reporting on someone else's intention to provide a reward and expressing my own intention to provide it. But, importantly, there is a second disanalogy too. This appears when we consider another way in which I might explain why I got the other person's behavior wrong and misled you about the prospect of a reward. This also is a form of explanation and excuse that is not normally available in the case where I say that I myself, not another person, intend to reward your choice of A.

Where I reported the intention of the other person, predicting a reward, it may be that I got the other person's intention right but that he or she failed to provide the reward because of a later change of mind. I may be able to show that the person gave up on the intention to provide a reward after I made my report to you but before you actually made the choice of A. Perhaps there is some collateral indication of that shift of attitude or perhaps the person is willing to confess that it did indeed occur. If I can explain the failure of my prediction on grounds of such a change of mind, then I will be able to excuse myself just as effectively as if I had been able to explain it on grounds of misleading evidence. Thus I will be able to continue to present myself to you as a sincere and honest interlocutor.

The second disanalogy between the first-person and the third-person case is that just as I cannot excuse my failure to provide you with a reward on evidential grounds, so I will not be able to excuse it on the grounds of a change of mind. I will be a laughing stock if I try to invoke this excuse just as I will be a laughing stock if I try to invoke the other. I will make a mockery of my words if I try to claim that while I ruled out the possibility of having gotten my intention wrong, I did not mean to rule out the possibility of changing my mind.

Why is this so? Arguably, once again, because of the principles of conversation. Instead of having said 'I will reward you for the choice of A', I might have said something much more qualified. I might have told you that I intended to provide you with a reward for choosing A but that there was a possibility that I could change my mind. In the absence of that qualification, the declaration of an intention to provide a reward, or the declaration that I will provide a reward, is bound to be construed as communicating something more. And the extra information that it is naturally taken to communicate is that I am committed to rewarding your choice of A in a way that denies me access, not just to an evidential excuse for not acting on such an intention, but also to the excuse that invokes a change of mind.

We saw earlier that there is very good reason why I might want to commit to a belief or other attitude, and not hedge my bets. Exposing myself to a penalty for any misrepresentation, I can make it much more credible thereby that I hold that attitude and I can hope to elicit an equally committal response in you. It should be clear on parallel grounds why I might want to commit to a certain action, not just commit to an intention to perform it while retaining the right to change my mind. By committing to the action rather than just the intention I expose myself to penalty for non-performance on even a wider front than before and I give you firmer grounds still for taking me at my word and responding in kind. I make a double commitment, renouncing the possibility of excusing misrepresentation of myself either on evidential grounds or on grounds of a change of mind.

This doubly strong commitment constitutes what we call a promise and is available with actions but not with attitudes. I can tie myself to doing something independently of how my mind changes in the meantime. But I cannot do this with attitudes, since it is of their nature that they are not subject to my decision or fiat. I cannot promise you to believe something, since belief is meant to reflect evidence and fact. I cannot promise you to desire something, since desire is meant to reflect how things appeal in light of my beliefs about them. And if it seems that I can promise you to intend to do something, that is because this is understood in a way that is not distinct from promising to perform the action itself.

Is there an ordinary term—other than the more or less technical word 'expression'—for the act that commits me to an attitude alone, be that attitude a belief or desire or intention? The word 'avowal' answers well to acts of attitudinal commitment, at least when they are made in assertoric mode. When I commissively assert that I believe something, or approve of something or intend to do something, then I may be said to avow the belief or approval or intention. And when I commissively assert that I am giving you an order or command, then I may be said to avow that I am doing so. In view of this sort of usage, we might use the word 'avowal' for attitudinal commitments, as we can use the word 'promise' for commitments to action.[5]

5.3 My Word is My Bond

Whenever I make a commitment, be it an avowal or a promise, I lock myself into a certain performance—I bind or obligate myself—by manifestly abjuring recourse to a certain excuse for not living up to the relevant self-representation. In commitment to an attitude I lock myself into continuing to display the attitude ascribed, putting aside the possibility of invoking an evidential excuse for having misrepresented myself. In commitment to an action I lock myself into actually performing that action, putting aside the possibility of invoking either an evidential or a change-of-mind excuse for proving to have misrepresented myself.

The binding of the self that commitment involves is not absolute, of course, even in the case of the promise. I may excuse self-misrepresentation in the case of an avowal—an attitudinal commitment—by appealing to a change of mind or by appealing to a change of circumstance; it is only the evidential sort of excuse that is set aside. And I may excuse self-misrepresentation in the case of a promise—a commitment to action—by appealing, if not to a lack of evidence or a change of mind, at least to a change of circumstance. I didn't keep the promise, I say, not because I got my intention wrong, nor because I had a change of mind. I failed to keep the promise, so the excuse will go, because circumstances changed from how we assumed in common they were, when I made the commitment: I believed that the change of circumstance effectively negated the terms of understanding on which the promise was made.

The binding aspect of commitment, notice, is always relative to another person. I deny myself access to a certain excuse for misrepresenting my attitude or action in the sense that I allow you, the addressee of my self-representation, to punish any misrepresentation. What denying access to the excuse means is that I deny myself the corresponding grounds for complaining about any punishment you might impose. When I lock myself into the attitude or action, I bind or obligate myself to you; I give you authority to demand performance or to exact redress (Darwall 2006).

This interpersonal aspect of the binding involved comes out in the fact that you can release me from the bond. You can release me from a promise, as I will certainly

---

5   There are lively debates about the nature of promising to which this discussion can be seen as a contribution. My approach rejects the broadly expectation-based approach defended in Scanlon (1998, ch. 7). It belongs with approaches that takes promising to involve a transfer of rights, though the rights invoked here—those associated with the practice of excusing oneself—are given a naturalistic explanation. See Thompson (1990).

expect you to do should circumstances change in a way that undermines the terms on which the promise was made. And while you cannot release me from an avowal, you at least have a unique authority—as you have with promises too—to forgive me any misrepresentation that I may have practiced.

6. Conclusion

As people seek to be honest with one another, they inevitably provide more than the benefits mapped in the counsel-and-consult model. The process of honest communication entails the formation of commitments to attitudes and commitments to actions among the parties; it leads them inescapably into making mutual avowals and promises. Thus it enables the parties to lock one another in various patterns of thought and action, on pain of a penalty against which they cannot complain—a penalty that counts as censure. And all this is so, no matter how naturalistic the basis on which the norm of honesty emerges and survives. Out of the naturalistic motions of prudential, norm-creating adjustment come the makings of normative obligation: the commitments that authorize claims and the censure that makes such claims effective.

Bibliography

Axelrod, R. (1984), *The Evolution of Cooperation*, New York

Bar-on, D. (2004), *Speaking My Mind: Expression and Self-knowledge*, Oxford

Brennan, G./P. Pettit (2004), *The Economy of Esteem: An Essay on Civil and Political Society*, Oxford

Coleman, J. (1990), *Foundations of Social Theory*, Cambridge/MA

Darwall, S. (2006), *The Second-Person Standpoint: Morality, Respect, and Accountability*, Cambridge/MA

Elster, J. (1999), *Alchemies of the Mind: Rationality and the Emotions*, Cambridge

Grice, P. (1989), *Studies in the Ways of Words*, Cambridge

Hardin, R. (1982), *Collective Action*, Baltimore

Hart, H. L. A. (1961), *The Concept of Law*, Oxford

Jackson, F./P. Pettit (1998), A Problem for Expressivism, in: *Analysis 58*, 239–51

— / — (2003), Locke, Expressivism, Conditionals, in: *Analysis 63*, 86–92

Jarvis Thompson, J. (1990), *The Realm of Rights*, Cambridge

McAdams, R. H. (1997), The Origin, Development and Regulation of Norms, in: *Michigan Law Review 96*, 338–433

McGeer, V. (1996), Is 'Self-knowledge' an Empirical Problem? Renegotiating the Space of Philosophical Explanation, in: *Journal of Philosophy 93*, 483–515

— (2005), Out of the Mouths of Autistics: Subjective Report and Its Role in Cognitive Theorizing, in: A. Brook/K. Akins (eds.), *The Philosophy and Neuroscience Movement*, Cambridge, 987–127

— (2008), The Moral Development of First-Person Authority, in: *European Journal of Philosophy 16*, 81–108

Milinski, M./D. Pfluger/D. Kuelling/R. Kettler (1990), Do Stickelbacks Cooperate Repeatedly in Reciprocal Pairs?, in: *Behavioral Ecology and Sociobiology 27*, 17–21

Miller, D. T./D. A. Prentice (1996), The Construction of Social Norms and Standards, in: E. T. Higgins/A. W. Kruglanski (eds.), *Social Psychology: Handbook of Basic Principles*, New York, 799–829

Moran, R. (2001), *Authority and Estrangement: An Essay on Self-knowledge*, Princeton

Nowak, M./K. Sigmund (1993), A Strategy of Win-stay, Lose-shift That Outperforms Tit-for-tat, in: *Nature 364*, 56–58

Pettit, P. (1990), Virtus Normativa: Rational Choice Perspectives, in: *Ethics 100*, 725–55; reprinted in: P. Pettit (2002), *Rules, Reasons, and Norms*, Oxford

— (1995), The Virtual Reality of Homo Economicus, in: *Monist 78*, 308–29. Expanded version in: U. Maki (2000) (ed.), *The World of Economics*, Cambridge; reprinted in: P. Pettit (2002), *Rules, Reasons, and Norms*, Oxford

— (2000), A Sensible Perspectivism, in: M. Baghramian/A. Dunlop (eds.), *Dealing with Diversity*, London, 60–82

— (2001), Embracing Objectivity in Ethics, in: B. Leiter (ed.), *Objectivity in Law and Morals*, Cambridge, 234–86

— (2006), Error-dependent Norms, in: G. Eusepi/A. Hamlin (eds.), *Beyond Conventional Economics: The Limits of Rational Behaviour in Political Decision-Making*. Essays in Honor of H. G. Brennan, Cheltenham, 108–24

— (2007), Joining the Dots, in: M. Smith/H. G. Brennan/R. E. Goodin/F. C. Jackson (eds.), *Common Minds: Themes from the Philosophy of Philip Pettit*, Oxford, 215–344

— /M. Smith (2004), The Truth in Deontology, in: R. J. Wallace/P. Pettit/S. Scheffler/M. Smith (eds.), *Reason and Value: Themes from the Moral Philosophy of Joseph Raz*, Oxford, 153–75

Richerson, P./R. Boyd (2005), *Not by Genes Alone: How Culture Transformed Human Evolution*, Chicago

Seyfarth, R. M./D. L. Cheney (1984), Grooming, Alliances and Reciprocal Altruism in Vervet Monkeys, in: *Nature 308*, 541–43

Sober, E./D. S. Wilson (1998), *Unto Others: The Evolution and Psychology of Unselfish Behavior*, Cambridge/MA

Sugden, R. (1986), *The Economics of Rights, Cooperation and Welfare*, Oxford

Ullmann-Margalit, E. (1977), *The Emergence of Norms*, Oxford

Wilkinson, G. S. (1984), Reciprocal Food Sharing in the Vampire Bat, in: *Nature 308*, 181–84

— (1990), Food Sharing in Vampire Bats, in: *Scientific America 262*, 64–70

Winch, P. (1963), *The Idea of a Social Science and Its Relation to Philosophy*, London

Thomas Spitzley

The Importance of Being Honest
A Comment on Philip Pettit

Even though it may be possible that the emergence of (most) norms can be explained in a naturalistic way, there are norms where a further explanation is needed, viz. as to why on the one hand people conform to them because they *ought* to conform and on the other hand compliance is enforced because non-compliance *ought* to be punished. It must be explained, that is, why some norms "gain a normative status in the minds of those who implement them" (19), why compliance is supplemented by commitment and enforcement by censure. In his article Philip Pettit tries to show that "there is at least one plausible, naturalistically explicable norm in the implementation of which commitment and censure *inevitably* make an appearance and play an important role. This is the norm of honesty in communication, which rules out any form of deception between interlocutors." (20, my emphasis)

To put it in a nutshell: the basic idea is fascinating, but I think the argument fails. To support this claim I shall make some remarks on three topics: 1. the key concept 'honesty', 2. the essential premise, and 3. the alleged consequence.

1. The Key Concept

In trying to explain the meaning of 'honesty' Pettit treats dishonesty on a par with deception. "It is in virtue of the *intent* of a communication, not its content", Pettit claims, "that a report counts as non-deceptive or deceptive" (23, my emphasis). It is not quite clear, though, whether that might not be too restrictive: A speaker might be known to a hearer not only as a notorious liar, but also as a deceiving person; at a certain occasion the speaker says exactly what she believes to be true, what she says *is* even true, and she also has no intention to deceive the hearer; however, since the hearer does not trust the speaker, she therefore gets deceived. In such a case it is neither in virtue of the *intent* of the communication nor in virtue of its *content*, but rather in virtue of its *context* that the report is deceptive. To be sure, considering what follows later, Pettit must be more interested in cases in which the speaker intentionally deceives the hearer, but it seems as if his explication is somewhat made-to-measure.

1.2

There are two key sentences which sum up Pettit's explanation of the meaning of 'honesty': "[W]hat is required for non-deception or honesty is not accuracy or adequacy—if you like, truth—but rather sincerity" (23) and "What honest, non-deceptive assertion requires, then, is that it be sincere" (24).[1] For either sentence the obvious interpretation is that it states only a *necessary* condition for honesty, viz. sincerity, but then it remains an open question which further conditions must be satisfied for a sincere assertion to be an honest one. If that interpretation were adequate, Pettit would thereby not have pointed out the meaning of 'honesty'.

According to a more charitable interpretation Pettit provides more, viz. something like 'That an assertion is honest means that it is sincere'. If that were so, two questions arise, to which as far as I can see Pettit does not provide an answer: a) Is this explication informative?[2] b) Why is the relevant norm expressed in terms of being honest and not in terms of being sincere?

2. The Essential Premises

2.1

Pettit is not interested in honest assertions tout court, but only in honest belief expressions. Expressing a belief is different from reporting on a state of affairs, Pettit claims. Obviously, one difference lies in what is represented. When I report on a state of affairs, I represent *the environment* as being in a certain state, yet when I express a belief, I represent *myself* as holding that belief. One might ask, however, why one should not say that one reports on a belief, too. According to Pettit the decisive feature by which this question can be answered seems to be that every genuine report is based on evidential grounds, yet in cases of belief expression I neither have nor need any evidence for representing myself as believing something—at least in normal cases. In those cases a misrepresentation of oneself as believing that p can therefore not be explained on evidential grounds.

For an expressive self-representation of a belief to be *sincere*, Pettit claims, it "must be accurate and adequate to the facts; the speaker must actually have the belief expressed [...]" (24). This is reminiscent of a famous passage in Hume's *Treatise*: "For since all actions and sensations of the mind are known to us by consciousness, they must necessarily appear in every particular what they are, and be what they appear." (Hume 1978, 190) If Hume were right, then, indeed, a speaker who

---

1 Cf. also 29: "honesty requires sincere communication".
2 I should be inclined to answer 'no', but I do readily admit that some subtleties of the English language may have escaped me here.

expresses her beliefs inaccurately and inadequately to the facts would be insincere. But is he right? There is plenty of reason to doubt that.

Indirectly, Pettit makes use of the traditional view that we have a special access to our present states of mind: while you need to rely on evidence if you want to attribute to me the belief that p, I don't. I can, so to speak, read my beliefs off my mind, they are transparent to me. If this picture were correct then, indeed, my incorrectly representing myself as believing that p could only be due to my being insincere.

Granting that a speaker's misrepresentation concerning his beliefs or other attitudes cannot be explained on evidential grounds as it is possible in the case of reports on the environment, might there not be other explanations for why I misrepresent myself as having a certain belief? Pettit does not discuss this question. However, may I not assert something which I take to be a true expression of my belief (cf. 23), even though it is not? And if so, would this assertion not be sincere? What, e.g., if I am a victim of what we ordinarily call self-deceit? When in such a case I represent myself as having the belief that p and that is not adequate, am I then being insincere or dishonest? I don't think so. Am I deceiving (or trying to deceive) the hearer? Since according to Pettit the intent of the communication is decisive, the answer here, too, must be 'no'. When I am deceiving myself, I don't have an intention to deceive anybody, not even myself—at least not in normal cases. Such an assertion may only count as deceptive if one allows its deceiving power to be due to its context cf. above, 19. In any case, an explanation why such an assertion may have a deceiving effect on a hearer may make use of the very feature Pettit draws attention to: since in cases of belief expression one cannot go wrong because one's evidence is misleading, a hearer may expect that what the speaker sincerely expresses must be correct. If, therefore, a hearer has no reason to doubt a speaker's sincerity, she will rely on the speaker's belief expression, and therefore she will sometimes get deceived.

2.2

Pettit claims that we can conclude to a person's being insincere and dishonest from her asserting that she believes that p yet not acting accordingly (29f.). This makes clear that what he understands by 'belief' is a behavioural disposition, something which ceteris paribus influences how one acts. However, the expression 'belief' is ambiguous; it may also mean "a belief whose relational object is occurring to the subject" (Davis 2003, 322), i.e. a belief that p so that the subject is currently thinking that p. My behaviour is, e.g., influenced by my belief that $2 + 2 = 4$, yet in most situations the relational object of this belief, viz. that $2 + 2 = 4$, is not occurring to me, it is not present to my mind. It is much easier to argue (and it has been argued) that I am in a privileged position concerning the beliefs which are present to my mind, i.e. my occurrent beliefs, that with respect to them I don't need any evidence, but only need to express them. Pettit, however, needs the stronger thesis according to which we can (simply) express our dispositional beliefs, a thesis for which he does not offer any arguments.

Pettit maintains that at times one does not represent one's belief expressively but does so "just descriptively" (30). In the latter case I say what I believe "so far as I can tell", I say "what I find myself inclined to say" (cf. 30) at the specific moment. To my view, Pettit here makes implicit use of the distinction just mentioned, yet his illustration of the situation is misleading. The clause "so far as I can tell" suggests that I am not sure, that I happen to have insufficient evidence, or that relevant evidence is necessarily inaccessible for me. Yet what I'm not sure about and what this evidence is needed for is whether it is really true *that p*, and not whether *I believe* that p.

In such a case I could at least sometimes easily express my occurrent belief, but since I'm only *at present* inclined to say that p and since it might be that tomorrow or in one week's time I shall no longer be inclined to say that p, neither a hearer nor even I myself have a guarantee as to how I shall then behave. Alternatively, and this seems to be a situation which Pettit has in mind, I could be described as somebody who doesn't believe anything with respect to whether p is the case or not, or who doesn't know what to believe. If that is true, there would be no belief to express—as long as one understands by 'belief' something which is usually relatively stable, but only with respect to a belief thus understood my later behaviour may belie my report.

How would we react to a person who every other day expressed her liking for something else? Take books: first she would, e.g., express her really special liking for Jane Austen, then for Jerry Cotton, after that for Shakespeare and then for Truman Capote. True, we would have a hard time to understand her, and maybe we would even claim not to understand her, but would she be insincere or dishonest? Would such a person be adequately described as somebody who changes her mind every other day? I don't think so. That sounds too 'active', whereas the truth may be that it sort of happens to her. In any case, this example, too, makes it clear that it is much too strong a claim that we can conclude to a person's being insincere and dishonest from her asserting that she believes that p yet not acting accordingly.

3. The Alleged Consequences

3.1

"With the appearance of [the] notion of an excuse, the concepts and the practices of both commitment and censure will also become available." (29) For the sake of the argument I grant that. However, since the notion of an excuse is strongly connected with the notion of an exculpation it is clear that it is a moral notion itself, and so it is little wonder that one moral notion brings other moral notions in its wake. When Pettit claims "The concept of an excuse may not be strictly definable on the basis of the naturalistic concepts introduced in this story", it becomes clear that he is aware of the problem just mentioned, yet it seems as if he underestimates the consequences of using this terminology.

A better, not so morally laden term would have been 'explain'. In case of need a speaker who asserted that p could easily *explain* why he asserted something which turned out to be false. He could, e.g., say that all the relevant evidence which was available to him at the time of his assertion pointed to the truth of *p*. Yet that the notion of explaining should carry with it commitment and censure is not at all plausible. If there is a norm of honesty in communication, it is, therefore, understandable that there will be a demand for a speaker to explain why she made a false assertion, but it is not "inevitable that the notions of excuse, commitment and censure will make an appearance too" (31).

3.2

Pettit talks about "[t]he welcome character of honest communication" (25), and claims that all of us would gain benefits from a norm of honesty (ibid.). He also maintains "it should be no surprise if each of us is disposed to pronounce on how all of us in the society welcome honesty" (25, fn. 1). I do not in the least want to doubt that, yet I should like to emphasize that honesty is only second best. Arguably, the best would be a norm of truth in communication.[3]

Interestingly enough, there is such a norm, at least according to Donald Davidson. In a nutshell, the reasoning goes like this: When we want to ascribe propositional attitudes to a creature we must presume that it is largely rational, i.e. we must take its reasons for acting to be understandable and its language to be translatable into our language. If a speaker utters 'It's raining', she thereby expresses a belief. As a rule she has this belief *because* it is raining, since beliefs are not independent of the state of the world. Because beliefs are causally determined by the state of the world, and because the hearer and the speaker share the same world, the hearer may presume that to a large extent her beliefs correspond to the speaker's beliefs and are also true.

In interpreting a speaker the hearer must observe the principle of charity, according to which as much as possible of what a speaker takes to be true is indeed true, and sentences which a speaker takes to be true are in general consistent in itself as well as with each other. To be sure, a speaker may have false beliefs, but "[i]f we cannot find a way to interpret the utterances and other behaviour of a creature as revealing a set of beliefs largely consistent and true by our own standards, we have no reason to count that creature as rational, as having beliefs, or as saying anything" (Davidson 2001, 137).

---

3 Arguably, because there are some good reasons for claiming that (some) dishonesty may be merciful, that complete truth in communication would neither be in the interest of the speaker as well as of the hearer and that it would not always be beneficial for a partnership or a society.

So first of all, Davidson proposes a norm for hearers, viz. 'Presume that most of what a speaker asserts is true!'. However, a corollary of that norm is a norm for speakers: if a speaker wants to be understood, she must behave in a way that makes her utterances interpretable in the first place. Therefore, ceteris paribus, she had better a) apply the words she uses always to the same things, and b) say what she takes to be true.

If everything we say were true, we would do best as far as our interpretability is concerned. Alas, since we don't always know what is true, we are in no position to make sure that all our assertions are true. Yet if that isn't possible, the second best is not to lie or otherwise deceive our hearers. In short, mutual understanding, in the literal sense of interpreting someone's utterances correctly, is best made possible if the speaker is honest and sincere in what she asserts.

If Davidson is right, nearly everyone conforms to this norm. In addition, all other conditions for something's being a norm which Pettit sums up (cf. 21) seem to be fulfilled. Therefore, 'Be interpretable!' or, alternatively, 'Tell the truth!' or, more modestly, 'Be honest!' may rightly be called a social norm. What is more, however, is that we here seem to have naturalistic explanation for the rise of the norm of honesty in communication, which is an alternative to the one given by Pettit.

Accepting the Davidsonian account I just sketched would also explain why there is no real escaping from such a norm. Anybody who tried doing this would thereby put himself definitely and in the true sense of the term outside of society. We could not understand her, and this covers her linguistic as well as her non-linguistic behaviour. We could neither communicate with her nor could we make any sense of what she does, and therefore we could not treat her as a full member of our society. That we follow the norms 'Presume that most of what a speaker asserts is true!' and 'Be honest!' is therefore a condition of the possibility of mutual understanding.[4]

Independently of what one may think about the rival explanations concerning the rise of the norm of honesty in communication, and independently of how one evaluates Pettit's attempt to bridge the norm-normative gap, the following is certainly not in dispute between the two of us: the importance of being honest.

Bibliography

Davidson, D. (2001), Radical Interpretation, in: D. Davidson, *Inquiries into Truth and Interpretation*, Oxford, 125–139

Davis, W. A. (2003), *Meaning, Expression and Thought*, Cambridge

Hume, D. (1978), *A Treatise of Human Nature*, ed., with an analytical index, by L. A. Selby-Bigge, with text rev. and var. readings by P. H. Nidditch, Oxford

---

[4] It is not quite clear what kind of explanation Pettit is looking for when he wants to explain the emergence of the norm of honesty. Is it supposed to be a historical explanation? And what are its conditions of adequacy or correctness?

Robert Sugden

Is There a Distinction between Morality and Convention?

1. Introduction

I first read David Hume's *Treatise of Human Nature*, with its analysis of justice as an 'artificial virtue', about twenty-five years ago. I immediately felt that I was learning deep truths about the social world and about the human sense of justice. Ever since then, I have retained the conviction that Hume's analysis is essentially correct, and I have used it as a starting point in my attempts to model the emergence and stability of ideas of justice and reciprocity. Recently, however, I have come across findings in developmental psychology which, if taken at face value, seem to cast doubt on the Humean analysis. Conversely, if that analysis is correct, standard interpretations of the psychological evidence may be in error.

In Hume's account, human beings have natural sentiments of sympathy. These sentiments are directly responsible for the 'natural virtue' of benevolence, but are only indirectly implicated in the sense of justice. Justice originates in conventional solutions to conflicts of interest in human interaction. Initially, each person's motivation to act in accordance with such a convention is merely self-interest. Once a conventional practice is in place, however, mechanisms of natural sympathy come into play. Their effect is to induce, among those people who participate in the practice, a sense of general approval for actions which accord with the convention and of disapproval for actions which do not.

My book *The Economics of Rights, Cooperation and Welfare* (*ERCW*) develops a theory of the emergence of social norms which integrates Hume's ideas with Adam Smith's account of fellow-feeling and with the twentieth-century game theory of Thomas Schelling in economics, David Lewis in philosophy and John Maynard Smith in biology. *ERCW* was first published in 1986. In the second edition, published in 2004, I reviewed its arguments in the light of subsequent developments in economics, philosophy and psychology, and concluded that they remained fundamentally sound. But shortly after completing the second edition, my confidence was somewhat shaken. I discovered that there is a literature in developmental psychology which treats 'morality' and 'social convention' as distinct domains of reasoning and judgement.

According to this literature, moral and conventional rules are categorically different. Moral rules deal with issues of welfare, fairness and trust. These rules are perceived as objectively valid, independently of particular social practices and sources of authority (for children, typically parents and teachers). Conventional rules specify how interactions are to be structured within a given social system. These rules are perceived as socially contingent; the wrongness of violating them is removed if persons in authority give their permission, or if one moves to a social system in which they are not operative. There is a well-developed experimental protocol, the *moral/conventional distinction task*, for testing whether a subject can recognise this distinction, and this is standardly used to assess psychological development. Normal children can recognise the moral/conventional distinction from about the age of three or four. For young children, typical examples of moral transgressions include hitting another child, stealing another child's property, and breaking promises; typical examples of conventional transgressions include talking in class without first raising one's hand, undressing in the playground, and going into toilets designated for the opposite sex. However, there is a significant exception to this finding: children with psychopathic tendencies have difficulty in making the moral/conventional distinction, as do psychopathic adults.

From a Humean perspective, the whole idea of a moral/conventional distinction is problematic. One might expect *natural* virtues to be supported by rules with the characteristics that have been attributed to the moral domain, but many of the rules that supposedly fall on the moral side of the moral/conventional distinction (for example, rules against stealing and promise-breaking) are, in a Humean analysis, paradigm cases of convention. Viewed through the lens of this analysis, conflicts over the use of physical goods (which supposedly belong to the domain of morality) are not different in kind from conflicts over who speaks and who listens (which supposedly belong to the domain of convention). In most societies, each of these conflicts is resolved by rules whose precise specifications are arbitrary; these rules work because, in a given society, most people understand them in the same way and accept the normative obligations they impose. Such rules are not objective moral truths that are independent of social contingencies. But neither are they the commands of some constituted authority that is empowered to waive them at will. If it is true that a moral/conventional distinction is salient for children, it is tempting to interpret that fact as evidence of moral naïveté. Perhaps, as the Humean analysis maintains, principles of fairness and trust *are* fundamentally similar to conventional rules such as 'drive on the left', but this truth of social theory is too subtle for children (and probably most adults) to recognise. But for we Humeans, the anomalous behaviour of psychopaths gives pause for thought. It would be disturbing to have to conclude that psychopaths have a better understanding of the nature of morality than psychologically normal people do.

In any case, a naturalistic theory of morality should be capable of explaining how moral concepts are learned. It is clear that the moral/conventional distinction task has revealed empirical regularities in people's perceptions of social and moral rules. A reader of *ERCW* is entitled to ask whether these regularities are consistent with the hypotheses advanced in that book.

Among psychologists who discuss the moral/conventional distinction task, there is disagreement about how far the distinction between morality and convention is innate. Some commentators interpret the evidence from this task as supporting the very general hypothesis that human beings are innately equipped with the capacity to reason morally, and that moral reasoning uses distinct systems or 'modules' of the mind. This idea has been put forward particularly forcefully by Marc Hauser (2006) in a book whose title encapsulates his central claim: *Moral Minds: How Nature Designed Our Universal Sense of Right and Wrong*. If Hauser is right, there is a further problem for the Humean account of justice. According to that account (and as I shall explain in more detail later), rules of justice can begin as unintended regularities in human behaviour. Gradually, these regularities evolve into conventions and then into moral rules. The first stage in the emergence of a convention occurs when an individual begins to recognise that other people's behaviour shows some pattern, whether intended or not, and that his self-interest is served by aligning his own behaviour with that pattern. At this stage, many of the mechanisms of rule-recognition and rule-following may be common to the learning and following of straightforwardly prudential rules. And even when conventions have become moralised as rules of justice, there is considerable overlap between the dictates of morality and of prudence (as expressed by the proverb that honesty is the best policy). It is difficult to reconcile this analysis with the hypothesis that the human mind uses different processes for moral and non-moral reasoning.

My aim in this paper is to investigate the moral/conventional distinction, as discussed by developmental psychologists, in relation to the Humean theory of justice I present in *ERCW*.

2. A Humean Model of the Emergence of Rules of Justice

In *Leviathan*, Thomas Hobbes imagines a state of nature in which men are permanently at war with one another. One of the forms that this warfare takes is that

> ... if any two men desire the same thing, which nevertheless they cannot both enjoy, they become enemies; and in the way to their end, which is principally their own conservation, and sometimes their delectation only, endeavour to destroy, or subdue one another. (1651, chapter 13)

Hobbes's conclusion is that the only way to escape this state of war is by the creation of a 'common power' which can force individuals to respect property rights. But one might think that this kind of conflict could be resolved without needing to call on an external enforcer. That is what Hume claims. After discussing the problems that are caused by the lack of property rights in 'external goods', Hume argues that the solution is 'a convention enter'd into by all the members of the society to bestow stability on the possession of those external goods'. But:

> This convention is not of the nature of a *promise*: For even promises themselves, as we shall see afterwards, arise from human conventions. It is only a general sense of common interest; which sense all the members of the society express to one another, and which induces them to regulate their conduct by certain rules. I observe, that it will be for my interest to leave another in the possession of his goods, *provided* he will act in the same manner with regard to me. He is sensible of a like interest in the regulation of his conduct. When this common interest is mutually express'd, and is known to both, it produces a suitable resolution and behaviour. ... Nor is the rule concerning stability of possession the less deriv'd from human conventions, that it arises gradually, and acquires force by a slow

progression, and by our repeated experience of the inconveniences of transgressing it. (489–490)

In *ERCW* I develop a family of models of Hobbes's case of the two men who desire the same thing, and show how conventions of the kind described by Hume can emerge spontaneously in from recurrent human interaction. Much of my analysis is adapted from models used by theoretical biologists to investigate the behaviour of animals of the same species which come into conflict over resources, such as nesting sites or mating opportunities. I now describe the simplest of these models.[1]

Consider a large human population in which pairs of individuals recurrently come into conflict over valuable resources. Each individual faces such conflicts many times, but against different opponents. Each such interaction is represented by the *Hawk-Dove game* shown in Table 1; payoffs can be interpreted as measures of individual self-interest. In each game there are two roles. One player, the *Possessor*, is in possession of the resource when the interaction begins; the other, the *Challenger*, is not. Each player has two alternative pure strategies. The *Hawk* strategy is to act with increasing aggression until the other contestant backs down or until one contestant is seriously injured; the *Dove* strategy is to back down at the first sign of aggression by the other contestant. V is the value of the resource and D is the cost of injury to the loser of a fight; $D > V > 0$, implying that *Hawk* is the best response to *Dove* and vice versa. The symmetry of the payoff matrix represents the assumption that the asymmetry between *Possessor* and *Challenger* is uncorrelated with payoffs or fighting ability; it is assumed that if both contestants choose *Hawk*, each is equally likely to win the fight, and that if both choose *Dove*, each has an equal chance of getting the resource without having to fight.

Table 1: the Hawk-Dove game

		Challenger	
		Dove	Hawk
Possessor	Dove	$V/2, V/2$	$0, V$
	Hawk	$V, 0$	$(V-D)/2, (V-D)/2$

$D > V > 0$

The asymmetry between the roles of *Possessor* and *Challenger* is arbitrary as far as payoffs are concerned, and one might think that it could have no significance for how the game is played. But, as I now show, that would be a mistake.

First, suppose that no one is conscious of the asymmetry between the two roles, and that individuals learn which strategy is better for them by trial and error. Then

---

1 The analysis summarised in the following three paragraphs is presented in more detail in Sugden (2004, 58–107); it is adapted from the model of asymmetric animal contests presented by Maynard Smith/Parker (1976).

the only equilibrium is one in which, in the population as a whole, *Hawk* is played with probability *V/D*. (There cannot be an equilibrium in which *Hawk* is always played, since every individual would do better by unilaterally deviating to *Dove*; and vice versa. So equilibrium requires a mix of *Hawk* and *Dove* play, such that each strategy has the same expected payoff. This implies a probability of *V/D* for *Hawk*.)

But now suppose instead that individuals recognise the asymmetry between the roles and entertain the possibility that behaviour might be role-dependent. In this case, the game has two additional and stable equilibria—one in which everyone follows the rule 'If *Possessor*, play *Hawk*; if *Challenger*, play *Dove*', and one in which everyone follows the opposite rule 'If *Possessor*, play *Dove*; if *Challenger*, play *Hawk*'. These equilibria can be interpreted as de facto property rules for resolving conflicts over resources. Each rule is arbitrary; but each has the property that if everyone can expect everyone else to follow it, everyone has an incentive to follow it himself. Such a rule is a *convention*. Further, and crucially, the mixed-strategy equilibrium is now unstable. There can be a mixed-strategy equilibrium only if *Hawk* is played with probability *V/D*, not only by individuals in the aggregate, but also by *Possessors* and *Challengers* separately. If, for any reason, the probability of *Hawk* rises above *V/D* for, say, *Possessors* and falls below *V/D* for *Challengers*, then every individual has an incentive to play *Dove* as *Challenger* and *Hawk* as *Possessor*. Such deviations from the mixed-strategy equilibrium are self-reinforcing. The implication is that recurrent play of the game can be expected to lead to the eventual emergence of one or other of the conventions.

It is essential to Hume's argument that conventions are prior to the sense of justice: "Without such a convention [of property], no one wou'd ever have dream'd, that there was such a virtue as justice, or have been induc'd to conform his actions to it." (498) This is the point of his distinction between natural and artificial virtues. A natural virtue such as sympathy induces actions whose value is immediately evident to the actor, independently of social context. (Consider a mother who hears her baby crying with hunger, and feeds him. If the mother is motivated by natural sympathy, her sense of the baby's contentment on being fed is an immediate emotional reward, and confirms the value of her action. She does not need to think about what other mothers do.) But the rules of justice are too arbitrary for individual actions to have this kind of direct emotional feedback. Indeed, as Hume points out, individual acts of justice, considered in isolation, often have adverse effects on general welfare (his example is a beneficent man who repays a large debt to a miser [497]). The moral value of justice can be perceived only if justice is understood as a set of rules that are followed *generally*. But if that is so, the rules must be in operation *before* they are perceived as morally obligatory. According to Hume, the emergence of rules of justice is to be explained by 'interest', as it is in the Hawk-Dove model. The question of why we 'annex the idea of virtue to justice' requires a separate analysis.

In *ERCW* I present such an analysis. This is not exactly that of Hume, since it draws on Smith's later analysis of fellow-feeling, but it is Humean in spirit.[2] The essential idea is that human beings tend to feel resentment when they are conscious of being harmed by other people's unexpected actions. Resentment is a negative emotion which is directed against another person; it compounds disappointment that an expectation has been frustrated with anger towards the person who has frustrated it. I postulate that this is a primitive emotion, prior to any sense of moral entitlement. I suggest that the evolutionary value of resentment might be as a cue for aggression in situations in which this is likely to pay. Think of the Hawk-Dove game. Suppose the convention 'If *Possessor*, play *Hawk*; if *Challenger*, play *Dove*' has become established. Then individuals must be motivated to act accordingly—to be aggressive in the role of *Possessor* and submissive in the role of *Challenger*. In other words, the perception of being *Possessor* must cue a desire to fight against any *Challenger* who tries to take the disputed resource. Is there a general emotional mechanism that would generate such a specialised desire, irrespective of the nature of the dispute and of the convention that is being violated? One obvious answer is a mechanism which responds to the frustration of an expectation by directing aggression towards the person who has frustrated it.

Some philosophers have criticised this part of *ERCW* on the grounds that the emotion of resentment has moral content: for you to feel resentment against another person, they argue, you must be conscious that he has *wronged* you, or at least that he has deliberately and knowingly frustrated your expectations. I can accept that these factors tend to increase the anger and aggression of resentment, but (for the reasons I have already given) I maintain that resentment does not require them. In any event, it should be clear why a Humean analysis needs an assumption of this kind. The aim is to show that the *prior* existence of a property convention *subsequently* induces a moral sentiment of justice. If a moral sentiment is to emerge, it must surely do so as the transformation of some prior emotion; and to require that prior emotion to be itself moral would lead to an infinite regress.

If my argument so far is correct, a property convention will tend to be associated with regularities in people's emotional repertoires: people will predictably feel resentment when they are harmed by other people's deviations from that convention. This is where Smith's mechanism of fellow-feeling takes effect. Smith's hypothesis—one that has been confirmed by recent psychological and neurological research—is that emotions are contagious.[3] If person A's action in breach of a convention provokes person B's resentment, then A's consciousness of B's hostility towards him will tend to induce a negative affective response in A. Further, if person C observes A's action and B's response, she can be expected to experience some reflection of B's resentment. (The reader might ask why C sympathises with B's

---

2 Hume postulates that our moral approval of justice derives from "sympathy with public interest" (499–500). Smith ([1759] 1976, 85–91) thinks this psychologically implausible, and I agree. The following analysis is presented in more detail in Sugden (2004, 218–223).

3 For more on Smith's hypothesis and the evidence which supports it, see Sugden (2005).

resentment rather than with A's aggression. If C normally conforms to the convention, she will find it easier to imagine herself in B's position than in A's. Again, it is necessary to assume the prior existence of the convention in order to explain the emotions it induces.) Thus, A's breach of the convention will have a general tendency to induce negative emotions directed at A, which in turn will induce unease in A. And this, according to Smith, is just what morality *is*. Morality is a system of rules specifying the propriety of emotions. To judge that an emotion has propriety is to approve it as appropriate to the circumstances in which it is experienced. And, as Smith puts it: "To approve of the passions of another ... as suitable to their objects, is the same thing as to observe that we entirely sympathise with them." ([1759] 1976, 16) Morality is just the generalisation of fellow-feeling.

Notice how, in this account, the sense of justice is an emergent property of a social process; it is not a property of the individual human mind. Notice too that in the earlier stages of this process, the relevant interactions are between individuals engaging in non-moral reasoning. Because of this, the rules of justice inherit properties of non-moral conventions. In particular, they inherit whatever properties favoured the emergence of the conventions from which they have grown. For example, suppose there is some small asymmetry in the Hawk-Dove payoffs, so that the role of *Possessor* confers a marginal advantage in a fight. This will favour the emergence of the convention 'If *Possessor*, play *Hawk*; if *Challenger*, play *Dove*' rather than its opposite.[4] Once the convention is fully established, this asymmetry in fighting ability is irrelevant, since fights do not occur. Nevertheless, its effects are imprinted on the convention and hence on the sense of justice that is induced: people come to feel that possession is associated with moral entitlement.

This sense of moral entitlement may be generalised beyond the cases in which following the convention is prescribed by self-interest. For example, if the Hawk-Dove payoffs vary across games, an individual may sometimes find himself as *Challenger* in situations in which he can take the resource at minimal cost to himself (say, because the *Possessor* is unusually weak). Although self-interest dictates *Hawk* in this non-standard case, this motivation may be inhibited by the perception that *Challengers* who play *Hawk* are generally the object of disapproval—and that he himself disapproves of such behaviour on the part of others. This inhibition is a form of fellow-feeling. In this sense, natural sympathy plays a part in the moralisation of rules of justice. But it remains true that, in standard cases, the actions prescribed by justice are also in the self-interest of the person to whom they are prescribed, given that other people can be expected to follow the convention. Thus, even when the sense of justice has emerged, it has a belt-and-braces relationship with prudential reasoning.

A somewhat similar analysis can be made of principles of reciprocity, such as promise-keeping, mutual aid, and playing one's part in the provision of public goods. In these cases, it is necessary to analyse *repeated* interactions among indi-

---

4   This mechanism is explained in Sugden (2004, 93–95), which again adapts an earlier argument by Maynard Smith/Parker (1976).

viduals who can recognise one another and can remember who did what in previous interactions. In small groups of individuals who interact relatively frequently, conventions of reciprocity are likely to emerge. Mechanisms of resentment and fellow-feeling then induce a corresponding system of interrelated sentiments of approval and disapproval. This is what we (as members of such groups) perceive as the morality of fairness and reciprocity. Thus, in the small groups in which practices of reciprocity first emerge, reciprocity is supported by motivations of both interest and morality.[5] These practices may then spread to larger groups of potential cooperators, or persist as initially small groups increase in size. Large-group cooperation usually requires institutionalised systems of incentives, for which the morality of reciprocity is merely a back-up;[6] but occasionally moral sentiments alone may provide sufficient motivation.

So, if the Humean analysis of justice and reciprocity is correct, there is no discontinuity between the domains of prudential and moral reasoning. There seems to be no role for mental modules dedicated to the processing of moral reasoning. We do not need moral minds, only prudence and fellow-feeling.

3. The Moral/Conventional Distinction

The moral/conventional distinction, as a concept in developmental psychology, seems to have been first proposed by Elliot Turiel; other major contributors to the topic (and sometime collaborators with Turiel) include Larry Nucci and Judith Smetana. My principal sources are Turiel et al. (1987), Smetana (1993) and Nucci (2001). It seems that the distinction was discovered when developmental psychologists investigated a stage-based theory of moral development proposed by Jean Piaget (1932) and Lawrence Kohlberg (1969). According to that theory, young children (up to the age of about ten) treat all rules as stemming from the commands of authority, and so have no sense of morality as an autonomous domain. However, the moral/conventional distinction task revealed that children as young as three or four were capable of distinguishing between authority and morality.

Smetana gives the following summary of the moral/conventional distinction, as it is understood by its proponents. She begins with two prototypical scenarios of events in a daycare centre for pre-school children. In 'Event A', Lisa, Michael and David are rocking in a rocking boat and Jenny is waiting for her turn. As the rocking boat slows down, Jenny (presumably out of frustration at waiting) bites Lisa. In 'Event B', the children are being taken to a pool. Jason has forgotten his bathing costume and is asked to choose one from a communal stock. He insists he wants to

---

5 These mechanisms are explained in Sugden (2004, 108–182).
6 Compare Hume's ([1739–40] 1978, 538–539) account of how two neighbours with a common interest in draining a meadow can achieve their objective by voluntary action, while a thousand people with a similar common interest will fall foul of the free-rider problem.

wear a pink costume even though the teachers tell him that the pink ones are for girls. Smetana says:

> Event A is an example of a *moral* transgression. Moral rules pertain to issues such as others' welfare (or harm), trust, or the fair distribution of resources. ... Moral knowledge is thought to be constructed from the intrinsic consequences of acts for persons. Because moral events have consequences for others' rights and welfare, moral rules are hypothesized to be obligatory, non-alterable, and applicable across situations, and the wrongness of moral acts [i.e. transgressions of moral rules] is thought to be non-contingent on specific social rules or authority dictates. ... In contrast, Event B is an example of a *social convention*. Conventional knowledge is constructed from an understanding of the social system and refers to the arbitrary and consensually agreed-upon behavioural uniformities that structure social interactions within social systems. ... In contrast to moral rules, conventional rules are hypothesized to be contextually relative, arbitrary and changeable, and the wrongness of conventional acts is hypothesized to be contingent on the rules and dictates of authority. Morality and social convention are hypothesized to be distinct types of social knowledge that develop in parallel out of different types of social interaction. (1993, 112–113)

Smetana uses a three-way classification of social rules, in which the third type is *prudential* (for example: do not touch the electricity outlets, do not jump from a moving swing); but most work has focussed on the distinction between moral and conventional rules.

Notice that Smetana is classifying rules along two conceptually independent dimensions. One dimension concerns their *content*. Here the distinction is between rules that deal with welfare, fairness and trust and rules that deal with "arbitrary and consensually agreed-upon behavioural uniformities". I take it that Smetana is defining the first class of rules as 'moral' and the second as 'conventional', and I will follow this practice when discussing the moral/conventional distinction. The second distinction concerns the *structural properties* of rules. Rules in one class, which I shall call *non-contingent*, are perceived by individuals as "obligatory, non-alterable, and applicable across situations". Rules in the other class, which I shall call *socially contingent*, are perceived as "contextually relative, arbitrary and changeable".

Smetana is proposing two empirical hypotheses. The weaker hypothesis is that, within any given social group, psychologically normal individuals recognise a distinction between non-contingent and socially contingent rules, and their categorisations of specific rules as one or the other are in broad agreement. The stronger hypothesis is that the content-based distinction between moral and conventional maps onto the structural distinction between non-contingent and socially contingent: moral rules are non-contingent while conventional rules are socially contingent. This mapping is hypothesised to hold across all societies.

The most common mode of investigating the moral/conventional distinction is to take some act which transgresses a rule, to describe this to subjects, and then to ask subjects to express certain judgements about it. In the case in which the subject is a child or adolescent and the act occurs at school, typical questions have the form:

Q1. Would it be all right to commit the act if there were no school rule against it?

Q2. Would it be all right to commit the act at home, or in a different school?

Q3. Would it be permissible to change the rule?

Q4. Would it be all right to commit the act if the teacher gave permission?

Q5. How serious is the transgression?

Q6. How much punishment does the transgressor deserve?

The usual finding is that moral rules (that is, rules that are classified by investigators as being concerned with welfare, fairness or trust) elicit 'No' answers to Q1–Q4, while conventional rules (that is, rules intended to secure coordination in social organisation) elicit 'Yes' answers to the same questions. Q5 and Q6 elicit a less sharp distinction. There is some tendency for moral transgressions to be judged more serious and more deserving of punishment than conventional transgressions, but there are some conventional rules, in particular ones concerned with decency, sexual behaviour and gender roles, that subjects construe as socially contingent (i.e. answer 'Yes' to Q1–Q4) while treating transgressions as serious.

Another mode of investigation is to ask subjects to justify the judgements expressed in answers to questions such as Q1–Q6. Moral rules are typically justified by appeals to fairness and the welfare of others, while conventional rules are justified in terms of the commands of authority, the threat of punishment, social expectations or the need for social coordination.

The proponents of the moral/conventional distinction point to a very large number of investigations which have found the regularities summarised in the preceding two paragraphs. There have been several studies of American children who have had devout religious upbringings—as Catholics, Mennonites or Conservative or Orthodox Jews. These children generally differentiate between the standard 'moral' rules (not hitting, not stealing, and so on) and the specific rules prescribed by their religion; they perceive the former as universally obligatory, but are more likely to judge the latter to be alterable by religious authorities and obligatory only within the relevant community. Although most studies have used Western populations, a considerable number of studies have been made of children and adolescents in other cultures, often with similar results. However, some investigations have produced apparently conflicting findings. It seems that subjects in many non-Western cultures have a stronger tendency to justify rules by appeal to customs and traditions, and to perceive those rules as non-alterable. This tendency is more marked among groups of relatively low socio-economic status (perhaps because those groups have had less exposure to 'Westernising' influences). In some cultures (for example, in Korea) subjects are more likely to offer justifications which appeal to social status, social roles and courtesy.[7]

---

7   My source here is Nucci (2001, 11–13, 21–51, 94–97).

Turiel et al. (1987, 172–174) summarise the findings of this line of research by presenting lists of rules that have been classified as non-contingent or socially contingent through use of the moral/conventional distinction task, and by claiming that this classification separates moral from conventional rules. The list of non-contingent (and moral) transgressions includes hitting, name-calling, stealing, destroying another's property, breaking a promise, and not taking turns. The much longer list of socially contingent (and conventional) transgressions includes chewing gum in class, undressing in the playground, calling a teacher by her first name, dressing casually in a business office, public nudity, swearing and cross-gender dressing.

Psychopaths and individuals diagnosed as having antisocial personality disorders give anomalous responses to the moral/conventional distinction task.[8] Their judgements of the relative seriousness of moral and conventional transgressions are similar to those of normal populations, but when justifying why moral transgressions are bad they are much less likely to refer to the effects of the transgression on the victim, and much less likely to judge that moral transgressions would remain wrong if rules prohibiting them were removed. James Blair, Derek Mitchell and Karina Blair (2005, 59), in an authoritative discussion of psychopathy, treat this anomaly as an "impairment in moral reasoning": even when adult, psychopaths are unable to perform a reasoning task that is within the capacity of pre-school children. It seems that psychopaths can understand social rules, but lack a normal understanding of morality.

Blair et al relate this phenomenon to other known characteristics of psychopaths. Psychopaths have impaired ability to recognise and to respond empathetically to other people's sadness or fear (but have normal responses to anger, happiness and surprise). They also show abnormally weak emotional responses to anticipations of threats and punishments. Since the imagination of one's own future emotions may use similar mental processes as the imagination of other people's emotions, this is further evidence of a failure of empathy. Psychopaths are also deficient in the capacity to understand situations which, for normal individuals, would induce guilt, even though they have a normal understanding of embarrassment. Presumably guilt is more dependent than is embarrassment on the perception of others' sadness and fear. Blair et al argue that empathetic responses to others' sadness and fear are crucial for socialisation. In the playground, for example, a normal child is conditioned not to make unprovoked attacks on other children by responding empathetically to the emotional reactions of children who are attacked. I take Blair et al to be suggesting that this form of aversive conditioning is implicated in children's perception that rules prohibiting harm are independent of context and authority.

---

8   This paragraph relies on Blair et al. (2005, 47–66, 124–128).

4. Is the Moral/Conventional Distinction Conventional?

According to the standard interpretation of the moral/conventional distinction, the distinction between rules that are perceived as universally obligatory and rules that are perceived as socially contingent maps onto the distinction between rules that pertain to welfare, fairness and trust and rules that do not. I am not fully convinced about the reliability of this mapping.

In part, my scepticism arises from my work as a social theorist of morality. The methodology of social theory is very different from that of developmental psychology, and each approach focuses on some explanatory mechanisms at the expense of others. I acknowledge that social theory in the tradition of Hume and Smith, Schelling and Lewis, uses simplifying psychological assumptions that specialists in the field will see as naïve. But, in compensation, it has a much richer analysis of the mechanisms by which social conventions and moral rules emerge and become self-sustaining as unintended consequences of human interaction. In the light of this analysis, the idea that rules of welfare, fairness and trust can be defined independently of convention seems equally naïve.

A further ground for scepticism is the reflection that welfare, fairness and trust are central components of *liberal* morality. This is a morality that is probably accepted by most developmental psychologists and perhaps also by most teachers in the schools that have been studied. In some work on the moral/conventional distinction, there seems to be a political subtext of secular liberalism, viewed in opposition to the politics of identity. Thus, Nucci (2001, 50–51) presents his findings in support of a proposal that moral education in the (American) public school system should cover those elements of substantive morality that are "central concerns" of all religious and ethical systems, without "hiding behind a smoke screen of value relativism", but should exclude all teaching of "particular doctrinal values". I cannot help feeling that it is too neat, too suggestive of wishful thinking, to suppose that a universal property of developmental psychology maps on to one's own particular moral code.

In my (admittedly superficial) reading of the relevant literature, I have come across various discussions which articulate, and provide supporting evidence for, my initial reservations about the objectivity of the moral/conventional distinction. I now turn to these.

A number of writers have raised doubts about the hypothesis that context-independence and authority-independence are attributed to, and only to, rules concerned with welfare, fairness and trust. Rules of other kinds have sometimes been found to be perceived as universally obligatory. For example, Jonathan Haidt, S. Koller and M. Dias (1993) have found that actions that evoke feelings of disgust tend to be perceived as universally prohibited. Examples include incest (even under conditions in which there is no risk of procreation), sexual intercourse with dead animals, and (for Americans) cutting up the American flag and using the pieces as rags to clean the bathroom. The flag example is interesting because of the way it evokes ideas of sacredness and pollution in a particular Western population. As

Mary Douglas (1966) has argued, the symbolism of purity and pollution seems to be universal to human societies, even though different societies have different systems of symbols. Richard Shweder, Manamohan Mahapatra and Joan Miller (1987) investigate the moral/conventional distinction in a population of Brahman and Untouchable individuals in Bhubaneswar, an old temple town in Orissa. They find that Brahmans perceive many rules of purity and pollution as universal, and treat transgressions of these as much more serious than everyday cases of hurting, stealing or breach of trust. For example, Brahman children perceive as universally obligatory the rules that women must not cook during their menstrual periods (children know about women's recurring periods of 'uncleanness', even though they do not know about menstrual bleeding) and that women must change clothes between defecation and cooking.

It seems that in just about all societies, *gratuitous* hurting of others is perceived as non-contingently wrong. That is surely not surprising: it is hard to see how any social organisation could function effectively if all its members were allowed to assault one another at will and without reason. And since sadness and fear are strongly susceptible to emotional contagion, one would expect a general, cross-cultural tendency for hurting to be disapproved of, *other things being equal*. But once one goes beyond trivial cases, one finds many cultures and social organisations in which specific kinds of physical assault are permitted in specific circumstances. One finds too that the rules that delimit legitimate assault are socially contingent.

The Brahman children studied by Haidt et al saw no transgression in a scenario in which a husband beats his wife for repeatedly going alone to movies without his permission, or in one in which a father canes a son who repeatedly truants from school. Up to the nineteenth century, flogging was routinely used as a punishment for adult workers on naval ships and on slave plantations, and in many Western countries, harsh physical punishments of children and adolescents continued to be considered normal well into the twentieth century. Within certain boundaries, violence between children was accepted too. For example, I went to primary school in the 1950s in a predominantly working-class area of northern England. If one child reported to a teacher that, in the playground, he or she had been hit by a child of the same age and sex, the standard response was: 'Hit him (or her) back'. I now think that this attitude expressed concepts of honour and respect. A child who had to appeal to a teacher to deal with a dispute with another child was showing himself to be 'soft', and would lose the respect of his fellow-children. By teaching children to stand up for themselves, teachers were inculcating what were generally seen as morally appropriate standards of behaviour. My guess is that, in this culture, most children judged 'hitting back' as universally permissible (and perhaps even obligatory), and not something whose rightness was dependent on authority. Similarly, perhaps, the men of Bhubaneswar who beat their wives for disobedience perceived themselves as upholding their respect as husbands.

It is also interesting to look at the issue of socially accepted violence from the opposite side. In societies in which most forms of physical violence are no longer seen as acceptable, how do people think about practices of violence that are accepted in other societies, or were accepted at other times? This question has been investigated by Daniel Kelly, Stephen Stich, Serena Eng and Daniel Fessler (2007), using a web-based questionnaire with adult (and mostly American) participants. Respondents were asked to consider various scenarios of non-gratuitous violence. In one example, an officer on a ship finds a subordinate sailor drunk on watch and punishes him with five lashes with a whip. In one version, the event took place three hundred years ago; in another, it takes place on an American cargo ship in 2004. In another example, a sergeant in charge of training American commandos subjects them to serious physical abuse in simulated interrogations, to prepare them to deal with interrogation by enemy forces. In one version, this practice is not prohibited by army regulations and is approved by the sergeant's superiors. In another, the Pentagon has just issued new regulations prohibiting this previously common practice. Respondents were much more likely to say that the violent act was 'OK' in the first version of each scenario (that is, in which violence is socially accepted or approved by authority) than in the second (in which it is not). The implication seems to be that, for adult Western subjects, prohibitions on non-gratuitous violence are context- and authority-dependent.

I was particularly struck by a critique of the moral/conventional distinction by Carolyin Pope Edwards (1987), based on fieldwork among the Oyugi people of Kenya, carried out in the 1970s. Edwards argues that, from an early age, Oyugi children have a strong sense of the wrongness of transgressing rules which structure social interaction—rules of politeness, respect, etiquette, the division of labour and the performance of work tasks. They perceive these rules as just as obligatory as rules concerning care for others and the control of aggression. Edwards explains this difference between Oyugi and American children as the result of differences in their experiences of economic and social organisation:

> The African children described in this study live in large, rural households that are economic as well as social units; children are given responsibilities at an early age that may increase their identification with social rules and help them appreciate their value. In such a cultural context, the distinction between the obligatory/ interpersonal and organizational/ regulatory domains may be less prominent than in American classrooms where 'school rules' so obviously come 'from outside'. (126)

> The 'good purposes' or 'reasons for' many kinds of rules can be made comprehensible to young children. Just as a child who receives a hit or kick can directly experience the purpose of rules prohibiting aggression, so too a child who experiences a delay in her supper because her older sibling did not collect the firewood can see for herself the inherent 'rightness' of rules about obedience to parents. Similarly, just as a child who cares for an infant can apprehend the purpose of moral rules prescribing nurturance, so too a child who tries to control an unruly, unhygienic, and unmannerly toddler can construct the inherent need for cleanliness and etiquette standards. (139)

Edwards's argument, as I understand it, is that breaches of social conventions typically *are* harmful to others, but the mechanisms which generate this harm are not always transparent. A child who has been brought up in a small nuclear family and who has not taken part in cooperative productive labour has an impoverished understanding of the implications of 'conventional' transgressions. It is only because the modern child's realm of experience is so restricted that the moral/conventional distinction is so salient for her.

The proponents of the moral/conventional distinction recognise some of the problems exhibited by examples such as these, and try to deal with them by using the idea of 'rule overlap'—the idea that a rule or action may be *both* moral *and* conventional. Smetana (1993, 119), following Turiel (1983), describes three kind of overlap.

The first type of overlap occurs when "conventional concerns for social organization entail injustices (such as in a caste system)". The implication seems to be that there can be arbitrary rules of social organisation and stratification that are in some sense functional, while also being unjust. But what is meant by saying that, say, the rules of a caste system are unjust? If the claim that the caste system is unjust is made from the external viewpoint of a theorist, then that seems an irrelevant interjection: we are supposed to be investigating people's perceptions of rules, not moralising about them. Alternatively, if people in the caste-based society *perceive* these rules to be unjust, then (according to the proponents of the moral/conventional distinction) they should also perceive that injustice to be independent of authority and social contingency; and so "conventional concerns for social organisation" should have no force in legitimising it. (Compare the case of the teacher who says that it is all right to steal.)

The second type of overlap concerns "second-order events in which a violation of a convention results in psychological or physical harm to others adhering to the convention"; Smetana's example is driving on the left when it is conventional to drive on the right. This example illustrates perfectly why, from a Humean perspective, the moral/conventional distinction is problematic. Whenever a convention of justice or reciprocity is in operation, an individual who deviates from it will tend to harm others. That is not an exceptional case in which harm and convention happen to overlap; it is a characteristic property of rules of justice and reciprocity. Of course, the harm caused by unilateral deviations is not always immediately obvious. For example, it may be difficult for young children to understand the purpose of a rule requiring them to ask the teacher's permission before speaking in class; such a rule may be *perceived* as an arbitrary regulation, imposing a pointless form of social order. It requires some degree of moral maturity to understand how conventions work. (Recall Edwards's interpretation of the differences between American and Oyugi children: according to this account, the Oyugi children are more mature.)

The third type of overlap consists of what Smetana calls "ambiguous multidimensional events, where individuals make different domain attributions about the same event". I take her to mean that there can be rules that some people perceive as moral (that is, as pertaining to welfare, fairness or trust) but which others perceive as merely conventional. Smetana suggests that debates about abortion and homosexuality provide "examples of such multifaceted issues". Turiel et al. (1987, 212–215) use this concept of multidimensionality to try to counter Shweder et al's interpretations of the Bhubaneswar data. Discussing the scenario in which a husband beats his disobedient wife, Turiel et al. say:

> It is likely that Indian subjects view the maintenance of familial role differentiations as a matter of great importance, permitting the use of corporal punishment to ensure its enforcement. ... [The] finding that Indians did not view the act as a transgression suggests that they judged the moral feature of physical harm as subordinate to the social-organizational consideration of authority and maintenance of sex-role differentiations.

Well, yes, but how does that support the hypothesis of a moral/conventional distinction? Turiel et al seem to be saying that, in this case, the perception of a moral prohibition against harm is overruled by the perception that wife-beating is a socially approved practice which maintains the family as a form of social organisation. But that should not happen if moral prohibitions are perceived as independent of social contingencies.

Turiel et al. introduce a different form of argument when they discuss the scenario of the father who canes the son. In this case, they suggest, respondents who see nothing wrong in the father's action may be evaluating the event "on the basis of naive theories of child-rearing and discipline practices", according to which physical punishment is in the long-term interest of the child, and so not really a case of harm at all. Similarly, they offer instrumental, welfare-based rationalisations for such Brahman customs as the rule that widows should not eat fish. Here the claim is that we are dealing with an "unearthly-belief-mediated moral event": the widow who eats fish is believed to be offending the spirit of her dead husband and so causing harm (207).[9] I have to say that these explanatory manoeuvres read like ad hoc attempts to reformulate a hypothesis so as to avoid disconfirming evidence. (I wonder what instrumental reasons Turiel and Nucci would find to rationalise the rule against using the American flag to clean the toilet.)

In a more general manoeuvre of retreat, Turiel et al. claim that their position is misrepresented by critics who assume that the distinction between moral and conventional rules is 'objective'. The correct reading of their position, they say, is that the concepts of welfare, fairness and trust which define the moral domain have to be interpreted subjectively, with "consideration to context, circumstances, or interpretations and meanings given to them by individuals" (205–206). But if one takes this line, the moral/conventional distinction starts to dissolve. We still have a distinction between rules that are perceived as non-contingent and rules that are perceived as socially contingent. But if the concepts of 'welfare', 'fairness' and 'trust' are themselves subjective and context-dependent, how does a person's knowledge of rules about welfare, fairness and trust differ from her knowledge of consensually agreed-upon behavioural uniformities that structure interactions within social systems? Turiel et al. seem to be saying that the central 'moral' concepts of welfare, fairness and trust may, after all, be conventional.

---

9   See also Nucci (2001, 102–104), who discusses a similar range of what appear to be counter-examples to his hypothesis, and uses very similar arguments to try to eliminate them.

5. Conclusion

So what implications can be drawn from the study of the moral/conventional distinction? Does this research cause problems for the Humean analysis of the emergence and stability of rules of justice?

I think there can be no doubt that the moral/conventional distinction task has identified systematic patterns in the human understanding of morality. In particular, it has established that, from a very young age, normal children acquire the subjective perception that some of the rules of behaviour that they learn are 'objectively' or 'universally' moral, while others are socially contingent, or contingent on the commands of authority. The fact that children can distinguish between these two categories is evidence that they are developing the ability to engage in a simple but significant form of autonomous moral reasoning: they have a concept of moral obligation that is not merely a reproduction of commands from adults.

The evidence from psychopaths strongly suggests that emotional empathy plays a crucial role in our learning of (what we perceive as) non-contingent obligations. In the classroom and playground settings of a modern primary school, it is not surprising that the most salient emotional cues are associated with actions by which one child hurtfully contravenes the expectations of another, for example by hitting her, or taking or damaging her property. Such actions naturally induce immediate and transparent responses of fear and sadness, and those emotions are particularly susceptible to emotional contagion. Thus, normal children gradually internalise rules which prohibit these kinds of harm. At the same time, children are being made aware of various rules which they are expected to follow, but whose function is not so transparent. If breaches of these rules do not seem to hurt anyone very much, the obligation to follow them is not internalised.

However, emotional contagion need not be restricted to actions which cause 'objective' harm. Take the case of disgust. If a child behaves in a way that a parent thinks of as deeply disgusting, the parent's negative emotional response is likely to be easily perceived by the child, and liable to emotional contagion. The point is not that the disgusting action causes offence and that offence is a form of harm (thus belonging to the domain of morality). Rather, disgust—just like the fear felt by someone who has been assaulted—is a negative affective state which can be perceived by empathy. If certain kinds of action reliably induce disgust, and if children are sufficiently exposed to experiences of that regularity and sufficiently insulated from contrary experiences, we should expect rules against those actions to be internalised and to be perceived as universally obligatory.

Relative degrees of insulation may be significant in explaining the apparently conflicting evidence about whether rules that are specific to particular religions are perceived as non-contingent. I conjecture that, in contrast to the Brahmans of Bhubaneswar, even the most devout religious communities in America are insufficiently insulated for their rules to have this property. Thus, the Orthodox Jewish child in America does not learn that transgressions of religious rules induce emotions of disgust; he learns that transgressions of Orthodox rules by Orthodox Jews induce emotions of disgust in Orthodox Jews.

As we get older, and as we get more experience of the diversity of forms of social organisation, we may come to realise that many of what at first sight seem to be arbitrary conventions serve useful functions, and that each of us tends to be harmed when other people unilaterally deviate from such practices. One form that this understanding takes is illustrated by the Oyugi children who understood the function of hierarchical authority structures in organising cooperative work tasks. Another form is illustrated by the adult respondents who recognised that flogging as a punishment on board ships can be morally prohibited in one culture and morally permissible in another.

I see no fundamental tension between what is known about the moral/conventional distinction and the Humean theory of justice and reciprocity as moralised convention. To the contrary, that distinction is the product of an essentially Humean form of moral learning, in which moral rules are codifications of predictable emotional responses to recurrent stimuli, and are learned by empathic contagion. The psychopath who cannot perceive morality as autonomous, who cannot see the difference between an internalised moral sentiment and an external regulation, is not a person who has a better understanding than the rest of us of the true nature of moral rules. He is someone whose capacities for learning moral rules is impaired.

Bibliography

Blair, J./D. Mitchell/K. Blair (2005), *The Psychopath: Emotion and the Brain*, Oxford

Douglas, M. (1966), *Purity and Danger: An Analysis of Conceptions of Pollution and Taboo*, London

Edwards, C. P. (1987), Culture and the Construction of Moral Values: A Comparative Ethnography of Moral Eencounters in Two Cultural Settings, in: J. Kagan/S. Lamb (eds.), *The Emergence of Morality in Young Children*, Chicago, 123–151

Haidt, J./S. Koller/M. Dias (1993), Affect, Culture and Morality, or Is It Wrong to Eat Your Dog?, in: *Journal of Personality and Social Psychology 65*, 613–628

Hauser, M. D. (2006), *Moral Minds: How Nature Designed Our Universal Sense of Right and Wrong*, New York

Hobbes, T. ([1651] 1962), *Leviathan*, London

Hume, D. ([1739–40] 1978), *A Treatise of Human Nature*, Oxford

Kelly, D./S. Stich/S. Eng/D. Fessler (2007), Harm, Affect, and the Moral/Conventional Distinction, in: *Mind and Language 22,* 117–131

Kohlberg, L. (1969), Stage and Sequence: The Cognitive-developmental Approach to Socialization, in: D. Goslin (ed.), *Handbook of Socialization Theory and Research*, New York, 347–380

Maynard Smith, J./G. Parker (1976), The Logic of Asymmetric Contests, in: *Animal Behaviour 24*, 159–175

Nucci, L. (2001), *Education in the Moral Domain*, Cambridge

Piaget, J. ([1932] 1965), *The Moral Judgment of the Child*, New York

Shweder, R./M. Mahapatra/J. Miller (1987), Culture and Moral Development, in: J. Kagan/S. Lamb (eds.), *The Emergence of Morality in Young Children*, Chicago, 1–83

Smetana, J. (1993), Understanding of Social Rules, in: M. Bennett (ed.), *The Child as Psychologist: An Introduction to the Development of Social Cognition*, New York, 111–141

Smith, A. ([1759] 1976), *The Theory of Moral Sentiments*, Oxford

Sugden, R. (2004), *The Economics of Rights, Co-operation and Welfare. Second Edition*, Basingstoke

— (2005), Fellow-feeling, in: B. Gui/R. Sugden (eds.), *Economics and Social Interaction*, Cambridge, 52–75

Turiel, E. (1983), *The Development of Social Knowledge: Morality and Convention*, Cambridge

— /M. Killen/C. Helwig (1987), Morality: Its Structure, Functions, and Vagaries, in: J. Kagan/S. Lamb (eds.), *The Emergence of Morality in Young Children*, Chicago, 155–243

Geoffrey Brennan

Hume's/Sugden's Psychopathy?
A Comment on Robert Sugden*

1. Introduction

The point of departure for Sugden's paper is that *"certain findings in developmental psychology, if taken at face value, seem to cast doubt on the Humean analysis"* of morality (47). Those developments depend on a distinction between morality and convention; and indeed advance the claim that the incapacity to make this distinction is a feature of *"psychopaths and individuals diagnosed as having antisocial personality disorders"* (57).

These developments are—at least *prima facie*—problematic for the Humean account, Sugden thinks, because Hume's is ultimately an account of morality *as* convention. Moreover, since Sugden rather enthusiastically supports the Humean account, the developments, by extension, represent a problem for Sugden. Hence the title of this commentary.

Now, Sugden's anxiety in this matter turns out not to be an especially serious one, because his ultimate conclusion is that there is *"no fundamental tension between what is known about the moral/conventional distinction and the Humean theory of justice and reciprocity as a moralized convention"*. On the contrary, the distinction *"...between an internalized moral sentiment and an external regulation"* is, on Sugden's view, something that emerges quite naturally from Hume's account *"in which moral rules are codifications of predictable emotional responses to recurrent stimuli, learned by empathetic contagion"* (64). Besides, no-one, as far as I know, has ever accused Hume of having psychopathic tendencies (with the possible exception of Rousseau—and there one might think that the boot was on the other foot); and nothing in my associations with Bob Sugden over the years would suggest anything of the kind in relation to him, either. So, the convention/morality distinction really operates for Sugden here less as a serious challenge and more as a kind of trope around which he can rehearse a description of the Humean/Smithian account of morality that he favours.

Actually, as far as I know, no-one else has taken particularly seriously the idea that the morality/convention distinction, as mobilized in the developmental psychology literature that Sugden cites, is at all problematic for the Humean account. But this is not to say that the Humean account—or the specific version of it that Sugden

---

* I am grateful to Michael Baurmann for comments on an earlier draft. Remaining errors are my own entirely.

offers—might not be questionable on other grounds. And my main object here is to raise some of these other questions.

2. Convention vs. Morality?

However, let me offer, at the outset, some remarks about the morality/convention distinction directly. The first of these is a purely logical point. Suppose the set of conventions includes conventions that are not moral conventions—the laws of logic, perhaps. If this were so (and it seems self-evident to me that it *is* so), then to say that moral conventions are conventions is not to say that there is no distinction between moral and non-moral conventions. It is *that* distinction presumably which psychopaths have trouble with. But failure to make that distinction does not in any way commit you to the notion that moral conventions are not conventions. I take it that this is what Sugden himself believes and what he takes Hume to believe. But if this is all that is at stake, it is difficult to take seriously the possibility that there is any challenge at all—even a 'face value' one—in the developmental psychology claims. Everything collapses to a mere verbal play.

The second is a methodological issue about 'distinctions'. Often, what is expressed as a categorical distinction is better represented in terms of a spectrum: appeal to 'distinctions' suggests that there is a knife-edge categorization (rather like 'true' and 'false'). But the distinction between moral and non-moral conventions may not be like that: it may be a matter of degree. And indeed, the relevant spectrum may have a number of dimensions. That is, there may be a number of properties that are in play, some or all of which can come in degrees. And so there may be lots of 'difficult cases'. But the fact that there are lots of difficult cases does not mean that the relevant dimensions of the spectrum are not well-defined: any conceptual problems that arise may reflect the determination to characterize cases in terms of a simple 'dichotomy' (e.g. moral/non-moral) rather than anything deeper.

I think Sugden is himself guilty of some ambiguity in this connection. He identifies a number of writers who point to the complexity of the distinction between moral and non-moral ('mere') conventions and to the possibility of overlap in categories. What he says of these writers is that, in pointing to certain ambiguities, they are retreating from claims "*about the* **objectivity** *of the moral/conventional distinction*" (58). Now, I am not entirely sure what Sugden means by "objectivity" here; but I do not see how questions of overlap (for example as discussed in pages 58–62 of his paper and 60–62 especially) bear on objectivity under any standard meaning. For example, I take it that the concept of "tallness" is objective in the sense that we can distinguish which of any two people is the taller. But when we describe a person as 'tall' in abstraction, there is clearly a contextual and interpretative element: tallness is comparative, and categories overlap. But this does not I think bear on the objectivity of tallness.

John Broome (1999) makes the point that philosophers tend to think categorically and economists to think comparatively and he thinks that (in ethics at least) economists have the better of that difference. He thinks that 'betterness' is a better concept than 'goodness'.[1] But I take it that to think that 'betterness' is a more useful or fundamental concept than goodness/badness does not commit you one way or the other to a meta-ethical position as to whether your conception of betterness is 'objective' or not. My point here is not meant to be an especially deep one. It is just to emphasize the difference between two questions:

- Is the distinction between moral requirements and mere conventions a knife-edge matter (like true/false, under certain readings)?
- Are the differences to which that distinction points 'objective' ('real') or something else?

On this basis, let me push the 'false dichotomy' aspect here a little harder. Sugden, following Hume as he interprets him, seems to want to push accounts of morality into two mutually exclusive categories: the 'conventional account' in which convention is made to account for everything of importance; and an imagined opposed account (I suppose some kind of 'natural law' account) in which convention plays no role at all. However, I imagine that even 'natural law' theorists (the sensible ones anyway) would concede that there is a significant conventional aspect in much morality. They would also presumably want to claim that there is a critical 'unexplained residual' in the purely conventional account. Suppose for example that a natural law theorist holds there to be a natural law against murder. There would remain issues about how exactly murder is to be defined. Is killing in self-defense (or killing an enemy soldier; or terminating an unwanted pregnancy) 'murder' (but possibly excusable) or is it not murder at all (but perhaps nevertheless culpable)? This natural law exponent may well think that *these* matters of definition in the natural law are mainly matters of convention. But the underlying moral norm against murder, she presumably thinks is not a convention. Or suppose that there is a natural law against theft. The general rule—'don't take things that belong to someone else'—requires a more detailed specification of the property rights structure, many of which details (perhaps all) the natural law theorist might regard as essentially matters of convention, without retreating from the idea that theft is wrong *per se*.

I suppose that one kind of partial 'natural law theorist' would be one who claims that there is an ineluctable genetic element in the evolution of morality—that actual moral codes come to us as 'co-evolved' with a directly evolutionary and a purely conventional component. I confess that I do not see how Hume (or Sugden) could deny *any* role for genetic evolution on the basis either of *a priori* theorizing or of the observations that Sugden makes. Actually, I would have thought that current accounts of the evolution of 'co-operation' in the animal world would have given extrapolations to the human domain some presumptive plausibility. To say this of course is not to deny an extensive role for convention in the determination of actual moral systems; it is just to say that the moral/non-moral distinction remains. And it

---

[1] Actually, he thinks 'goodness' is "fully reducible" to 'betterness' which is an additional and distinct claim.

is not obvious that that distinction doesn't remain 'all the way down' the explanatory chain.

Let me put my anxiety a different way. I think Hume establishes that one *can* logically separate the question of how rules emerge (the convention account) from the question of how they take on moral force (Sugden's Smithian gloss). I don't see that he establishes that any satisfactory explanation of 'justice' *must* observe this separation. I do not see, for example, how anything that he or Sugden says disposes of the 'co-evolutionary' account.

3. Hume/Sugden's Morality

Suppose we set these issues aside, accept the broad convention story, and just focus on the distinction between moral and non-moral conventions. This distinction certainly requires that we identify a 'moral' element applying in some cases and not in others, and it is on Hume's/Sugden's account of this element that we ought to focus attention. That would constitute the account of 'morality' as such.

The critical feature, as Sugden sees it, in the moral case appears to be the presence of certain distinctive emotions, triggered routinely by certain kinds of stimuli, and "*learned by empathetic contagion*". Someone who has internalized the moral code feels guilty when he himself does something immoral and feels moral outrage when he sees someone else doing that thing. 'Guilt' here is to be distinguished from mere regret at having made a miscalculation—or perhaps at having been found out; and 'moral outrage' is to be distinguished from aesthetic distaste or disgust. The person with psychopathic tendencies cannot make this distinction, or so the story goes.

Again, first, a logical query: is it *really* the absence of the ability to make this distinction that is critical? After all, that category includes the person who treats *all* conventions as moral—who exhibits moral outrage when the forks are not placed correctly on the table and feels deep guilt when she makes a mistake in her sums. This kind of 'uni-moralist' fails to make the relevant distinction—but her internal emotional repertoire is such that she has fully 'internalised' the moral code. Her failure seems to be that she has swallowed too much. This excess may in certain conditions lead her to act immorally. She might do something truly bad, so as to prevent a lapse in etiquette, for example; and she will be excessive in her responses to such lapses by others. But she does not fail to feel guilt when she does something morally wrong: the internal incentives to behave as the moral code requires will be broadly intact. The incapacity to have moral emotions at all is not the same as the inability to distinguish moral from non-moral cases. And the psychopath seems to fit better the former case than the latter.

But what of Sugden's account of what bridges the convention-morality gap? He grounds this aspect of his account in the fact (let us take it to be a fact) of a certain contagion in emotions. Take his example. A breaks a convention and thereby B's interests are affected negatively. This fact induces resentment in B. Observer C 'sympathizes' with B's resentment. So C approves of B's resentment regarding it as 'proper to the circumstances' and so (?) disapproves of A. It is important here that C sympathizes more strongly with B's resentment than with any emotions that A might have—and Sugden thinks that this bias is explained by the fact that C is (by the fact of the relevant convention) more often in B's predicament than in A's—more often complying with the convention than breaking it. It is also important to the account that B's resentment is entirely non-moralized—because otherwise one would be helping oneself to a moral element in the *explanans* as well as the *explanandum*. Finally, it is important that A desires the good regard of others so that when A finds that others share B's resentment of his action A feels at least shame and possibly guilt.

I confess that I don't find this account entirely persuasive. I think firstly that Smith's account of the 'moral sentiments' is more moralized than Sugden seems to imply. I do not deny that, for Smith, approval of a passion as suitable to its object is equivalent to fully sympathizing with it; but in Smith's account, such 'approval' involves consultation with the 'sympathies' of the *impartial spectator*—and that consultation is itself a moral exercise. To reverse the order of operations, to say that C 'fully sympathizes' with B's response, is to say C must 'approve' of that response. Only if C approves of B's response, does C disesteem A. And this 'approval' (and disapproval) is not just a matter of B's perception of B's own interests. It is an independently moral matter.

Secondly, it is an unexplained feature, lying 'outside the model', why A breaks the convention in the first place. If the convention is genuine, then A's self-interest is sufficient to assure compliance. It seems as if the equilibrium in the prior convention game must allow for a minority of back-sliders. Note that the back-sliders have to be in the minority in order to ensure that the balance of observer sympathy goes the right way. So, for example, in n-person prisoners' dilemma interactions where most people are 'defecting', there can be no moral rule against such defection: all the observers on Sugden's analysis will sympathize with rule-breakers, because they are rule-breakers themselves. But that doesn't seem right. Moral norms concerning things like carbon emissions or giving to third-world charities or joining the bush-fire fighting team do emerge, even where they are more honoured in the breach than in the observance.

But thirdly, and perhaps most importantly, it seems to me that there is a more plausible account of the emergence of morality that starts in a different place. Consider the case of 'trust'. The trust predicament involves sub-game imperfection. Everyone will have predictable prudential reasons to fail to fulfill the terms of voluntary agreements; but they also have prudential reasons for being able to credibly pre-commit. If 'trustworthy types' can be identified by others (with appropriately high probability), then it will be advantageous over some range to be a trustworthy type—that is, to be a locally irrational fulfiller of commitments made to others. Obtaining the advantages of fulfilling commitments is one of those things that Elster (1983) describes as a necessarily unintended by-product. That is, if you form an intention to be trustworthy because increasing the likelihood that you will be trusted will increase your objective pay-off, then you are likely to break with your intention once the opportunity to fulfill your intention comes: the same motive that induces you to form the intention induces you to break with that intention in the arena of action.[2] Morality must be binding *for its own sake* to get the behaviour right.

So, if your parents wish to bring you up in a way that will make life go maximally well for you, they may well seek to instill in you certain beliefs and inculcate in you thereby certain 'moral' attitudes—ones such that you will feel decidedly uncomfortable if you break with certain stipulations. Call this the 'potty-training' account of morality. It is doubtful whether you could instill such beliefs in yourself, even recognizing that having them would be good for you.[3] But anyone who is benevolent towards you, and has the power to influence your beliefs, will have an incentive to induce in you beliefs of this kind. It may take more than one generation for such beliefs to become fully inculcated. Generation 1 in educating their children will be motivated solely by benevolence; generation 2 in educating their children will be motivated by a (perhaps weak) belief in the intrinsic truth of moral strictures, plus benevolence; generation 3 by a somewhat stronger belief plus benevolence and so on. Some such account suggests both why morality might be connected to self-interest; and why it must transcend self-interest to do its work.

In the Humean account, one might wonder whether, since agents are presumed to comply with the convention from self-interest, what exactly morality adds. Morality seems to appear like an optional extra—a kind of fifth wheel in the overall account. In the 'trust' account of morality, by contrast, the internalization of morality is crucial because it operates against prudence at the point where trustworthy action is called for: in this sense, the first of the 'moral sentiments' is guilt, and guilt stands locally *against* prudence!

These moral attitudes, once in place, can do double duty. They can both motivate directly. And they can motivate indirectly via the esteem (and disesteem) of others—as in the broadly Smithian manner.[4] Here, there is no problem explaining the approval and disapproval of norm violators—anyone who possesses a 'moral sense' will have a disposition to approve of people who behave morally and a disposition to disapprove of people who behave immorally. So if people care about approval, esteem effects will boost purely internal moral ones.

There is of course nothing 'social contract'-y about all this. Everything is built up from individual rationality, broadly construed. But compliance with conventions emerges essentially because every agent will have an interest in interacting with others who are more reliable followers of conventions—and this may include

---

2 A more extended treatment of these issues can be found in Güth/Kliemt (1994) and in a slightly different mode, Brennan/Hamlin (2000).
3 One of John Broome's parables involves the patient who is recovering from an operation, whose rate of recovery is a positive function of his confidence about it. If he believes he will get better in n days, he will get better in (n + 1) days. This gives him reason to believe that he will get better tomorrow (assuming n > 0). But he can't believe that for the reason that this will ensure he gets better in two days, because the reason for the belief involves its negation.
4 For an extended treatment see Brennan/Pettit (2004).

'norms' that deal with public goods provision. If contributing to public goods supply is a signal of a 'good, trustworthy citizen', then individuals may have an incentive to contribute—even though the structure of the 'contribute' rule would not *be* a 'norm' in the absence of moral motivations. (Since lots of recently emergent 'environmental' norms seem to have precisely this public goods character, they would seem to represent an explanatory problem for the Humean account.)

Hume famously thought[5] that, in relations with peoples who could not do you harm, considerations of justice would not apply—only considerations of benevolence. (He seems to have had relations with the American native peoples in mind.) That observation suggests that something like the Sugden/Skyrms account of 'justice' might well be what Hume intended. But it is notable that, on the alternative view that I am advancing, norms of justice might apply when people *cannot* do you harm. Observers may well say: well, if he does not fulfill his undertakings with Indians (or does not observe their property conventions) then he is more likely to be unreliable in fulfilling commitments to *us* (and/or observing *our* property rights). In this way, extending considerations of justice to the American Indians (even if they could not in any way defend their 'rights') can be entirely congruent with the requirements of prudence. To my mind, this kind of account provides a more plausible conception of "the inconveniences of transgressing … the rule concerning stability of possession". But it is non-Humean in that the reasons for my observing the relevant norms do not depend on any *reciprocal* observance. On my reading, my interest "to leave another in possession of his goods" does not depend on a belief that doing so will induce him to "act in the same regard toward me". It does depend on the fact that my failing to observe conventions of property will induce others at large to be reluctant to truck with me, and that this reluctance will be costly to me. But this is a different story. And it is one that, for reasons already explained, seems to require an element of moral motivation more or less from the ground up.

One final observation. Sugden may claim that my rival account may be acceptable for some aspects of the emergence of morality, but is less well-targeted on the question of property rules specifically—which for Hume is the central content of 'justice'. I am not persuaded of that claim; but perhaps it has some validity. However, any argument to this effect is a two-way street. Sugden extrapolates from the case of property to morality more generally—in a manner, incidentally, that seems to me distinctly under-argued. In fact, it is not clear to me that it can even be entirely Humean. After all, Hume's isolation of justice as an 'artificial' virtue is presumably designed to distinguish justice from the natural virtues (like benevolence)—which suggests that these natural virtues (morality?) could play a foundational role in other cases. If justice is special in the relation that it posits between morality and prudence, then Hume would presumably find extrapolation from justice to morality *tout court* problematic—and it ought to be, by extension, problematic for Sugden.

---

5   Smith disagreed with Hume on this matter.

4. Bottom Line

In the foregoing, I have drawn a distinction between two questions:
- Does the developmental psychology distinction between morality and convention raise any deep problem for Hume's 'conventional account' of morality?
- Is Hume's account (or more accurately, Sugden's version of Hume's account) of the emergence of justice and morality more generally totally persuasive?

Sugden and I are agreed that the answer to the first question is no—indeed, obviously no. My inclination is to see the distinction between morality and convention as a false dichotomy: that distinction is best rendered as one of degree, not of substance, and could with serious loss be recast as a distinction between moral and non-moral (or 'mere') conventions. It may be stating the obvious, but there can be little doubt that there is a conventional element in all morality. To concede this is not to provide any intellectual succor to the 'psychopath': the psychopath's failure is the incapacity to recognize any moral element in norms at all.

Sugden and I are also agreed that any account of morality must be 'evolution-compatible'. That is, it must be the case that agents who are moral have some survival advantages—otherwise morality would presumably have long since died out. Those survival advantages almost certainly connect positively with prudential considerations for the agents concerned—in some fashion, and at some level.

But the possible connections are many. Hume insists that, in relation to the specific virtue of 'justice', the exercise of explaining the emergence of the convention that underlies justice can—and he thinks should—be divorced from the question of how that convention acquires its normative force. That convention, in the Sugden interpretation, is a practice of fighting more vigorously to defend what one possesses in the status quo than when one attempts to acquire what others possess. This interpretation is certainly consistent with Hume's thought that we cannot owe obligations of justice to people who cannot harm us when we threaten to take their possessions. In cases like this, Hume thinks, we can only owe obligations of benevolence.

This claim seems false to me, as a description of how most people think of justice. In any event, I think a better account of the emergence of morality and its relation with prudence is given via the analysis of trustworthiness and the capacity of morality to solve problems of sub-game imperfection in individually rational strategies. Virtue is prudentially valuable because others are more inclined to cooperate with those who can be recognized as virtuous. And as economists have recognised since Adam Smith, man in civilized society is more dependent on the cooperation of his brethren than he is apt to realize. The hawk-dove game might well explain the emergence of territoriality among animals; but, as Smith insists, cooperation of the kind characteristic of human society is quite a different phenomenon from anything we observe among animals. And it is in the human setting that morality and the norms of justice need to be explained. For that purpose, I think there is at least one account on offer (following Güth/Kliemt 1994) that is more convincing than the Humean one that Sugden advances.

Bibliography

Brennan, G./A. Hamlin (2000), *Democratic Devices and Desires*, Cambridge
Brennan, G./P. Pettit (2004), *The Economy of Esteem*, Oxford
Broome, J. (1999), *Ethics Out of Economics*, Cambridge
Elster, J. (1983), *Sour Grapes*, Cambridge
Güth, W./H. Kliemt (1994), Competition or Cooperation: On the Evolutionary Economics of Trust, Exploitation and Moral Attitudes, in: *Metroeconomica 45(2)*, 155–187

Nicholas Southwood

Norms, Laws and Social Authority[*]

1. Introduction

It is often observed that there are salient *contrastive questions* that explanations, to be fully adequate, must be capable of answering.[1] That is, it is appropriate to test an explanation E of some fact or phenomenon X by asking whether E is capable of answering certain questions of the form, 'why X, rather than (some alternative fact or phenomenon) Y?'[2]

Consider a candidate explanation of why cows have four stomachs—say, that it allows them to digest efficiently certain sorts of grasses. In order for the explanation to be adequate, it must be capable of answering questions such as: (i) Why do cows have *four* stomachs, rather than more or less than four? (ii) Why do cows have four *stomachs*, rather than four digestive organs of some other kind? (iii) Why do *cows* have four stomachs and donkeys not have four stomachs? What constitutes an adequate answer to one of these questions will not necessarily constitute an adequate answer to the others.

Though it has not been widely appreciated, I believe that there are also a number of salient contrastive questions that arise for the question of what explains the existence of *social norms*. My aim in this paper is to focus on one of these in particular, namely, 'why social norms, rather than (regulatory) laws'?[3] The question is particu-

---

[*] Earlier versions of this article were presented in the Philosophy Department Faculty Colloquium at the University of Leiden in April 2008 and at the conference *Norms and Values: The Role of Social Norms as Instruments of Value Realisation* at the *Centre for Interdisciplinary Research* at the University of Bielefeld in May 2008. I am grateful to audiences on those occasions for their useful feedback and especially to my commentator on the latter occasion, Stefan Huster, for his insightful remarks. The article emerged out of many hugely profitable and enjoyable discussions with Geoff Brennan, Lina Eriksson and Bob Goodin, and forms part of a larger collaborative project in which we are engaged on normative explanation. Research for the article was carried out under ARC Discovery Grant DP0663060.

[1] Some philosophers go further and hold that this is just what an explanation *consists* in, namely, an answer to a salient contrastive question. For the locus classicus, see Van Frassen (1980, ch. 5). See also Lipton (1990).

[2] Which contrastive questions are salient may well be thought to be somewhat context-sensitive, depending on, amongst other things, the goals and interests of the explainer, the explainee and the appraiser.

[3] As should be obvious, I am interested here only in regulatory laws, not constitutive laws, since it is only the former that constitute a genuine competitor (or at least alternative) to social norms. I am very grateful to Michael Baurmann and Ruth Zimmerling for forcing me to clarify this point.

larly challenging since social norms and laws are *similar* in many important respects; they share many essential properties in common. The differences, on the other hand, are quite subtle. For an explanation of social norms to be able to offer an adequate answer to the question 'why social norms, rather than laws' therefore demands a fairly high level of explanatory fine-grainedness. It is a demand that, I suspect, many common explanations of social norms—such as those that seek to explain social norms in terms of their serving our interest in being able to coordinate and cooperate with others—will turn out to be ill-placed to meet.[4]

The paper is in two main parts. In the first part, I shall provide an account of what social norms are and how they are different from laws, focusing on three important respects in which they differ. In the second part of the paper, I shall then propose and defend a certain hypothesis about what explains why there are social norms, namely, that they serve what I shall call our *social authority* interest. I shall argue that the hypothesis does a good job of rendering intelligible each of the three differences between social norms and laws and hence answering the question, 'why social norms, rather than laws'.

2. Distinguishing Social Norms and Laws

I have already noted that social norms and laws share many important similarities. My aim in this section will be to show how they differ. Before doing so, however, it will be instructive to say something briefly about what I take social norms to be.

Here is a quick and straightforward answer. Social norms are simply *general social rules or requirements*. They are *rules or requirements* inasmuch as they *require* things of people: new acquaintances to shake one another by the hand; women to wear headscarves; guests to bring a bottle of wine when they are invited to dinner. To say that 'it is a social norm in Germany that one shake the hand of anyone to whom one is introduced', for example, implies that there is a requirement in Germany to that effect, a requirement that one might intentionally or accidentally flout by, for instance, turning one's back on one's new acquaintance and ignoring her. They are *general* requirements inasmuch as they make general rather than merely particular demands; they require the performance of certain *types* of acts by certain types of individuals in certain types of circumstances, rather than merely the performance of particular token acts. And they are essentially *social* requirements inasmuch as they are requirements that are inherent in, and that only make sense relative to, particular groups of communities. A requirement is always a social norm in or of a group of community. It makes no sense to inquire whether any given requirement—the requirement that women wear headscarves, say—is a social norm

---

4 Other salient contrastive questions include: 'why social norms, rather than individual norms', 'why social norms, rather than customs or conventions?' and 'why social norms, rather than moral principles?'

simpliciter. Rather, social norms are essentially tied to the particular groups or communities in which, or of which, they are norms.

This quick answer to the question of what social norms are has the virtue of neatly distinguishing them from a number of other phenomena with which they might otherwise be confused. The fact that it conceives of social norms as requirements serves to distinguish them from conventions and other kinds of behavioural regularities, since the latter, unlike the former, do not entail (though they are frequently accompanied by) requirements to behave in the conventional way.[5] The fact that it conceives of social norms as general requirements serves to distinguish them from requirements that are particular in application, such as the (moral-cum-prudential) requirement that I meet a particular deadline. And the fact that it conceives of them as essentially social requirements serves to distinguish them from other kinds of norms or normative principles, such as norms of morality, rationality, prudence and epistemic justification, which, at least on standard ways of conceiving of these phenomena, do not seem to depend for their existence on, or to be tied essentially to, particular groups of communities.[6]

Unfortunately, however, the quick answer is of quite the wrong kind for our purposes. For recall that we are interested in the question, 'why social norms, *rather than laws?*'. The problem is that laws also fit the account of social norms that we have given. Laws, too (whatever else they are), are general social rules or requirements. They are rules or requirements—requirements to honour contracts, vote, refrain from driving with a blood alcohol reading in excess of .05, and so on. They are general rather than particular in application, attaching to act-types rather than act-token. And they only make sense relative to particular groups of communities. We cannot ask whether a requirement R—the requirement that citizens over the age of 18 vote in general elections, say—is a law simpliciter but only whether it is a law in or of a particular political community.

In order to distinguish social norms from laws, what we need instead, then, is a characterisation of social norms that sheds light on the particular kind of general social requirements they are. I shall say that for a (suitably general) requirement R to be a social norm in or of a particular group or community is for R to be *accepted* within that group or community. For R to be 'accepted within a group or community' is for R to be such that a sufficient number[7] of the members of the group or community have *internalised R*, where the fact of common acceptance (or internalisation) is a matter of common knowledge among a sufficient number of the mem-

---

5   For the opposing view that conventions entail requirements, see Lewis (1969) and Gilbert (1989).
6   There are, of course, proponents of non-standard accounts that would dispute these claims, for example, proponents of relativist accounts of morality such as Harman (1975).
7   It might be objected that talk of a 'sufficient number' is vague, and hence that the analysis implies that whether a requirement R is a social norm in or of a particular group or community will also be a vague matter. That is quite correct but not an objection. On the contrary, it is a virtue of the analysis.

bers of the community.[8] Saying just what it takes for an individual to 'have internalised a requirement' is a hard issue. But I take it that internalising a requirement R involves a complex of attitudes such as (i) believing R^9, (ii) being disposed to disapprove of those who violate R, (iii) being disposed to encourage others to comply with R, and (iv) believing the aforementioned attitudes to be justified.[10]

To illustrate the account, take a putative social norm, such as the social norm in Saudi Arabia that women wear headscarves. According to my proposal, to say that the requirement that women wear headscarves is a social norm in Saudi Arabia is just to say that two conditions are satisfied. First, a sufficient number of Saudi Arabians must (i) believe that women are required to wear headscarves, (ii) be disposed to disapprove of any woman who doesn't wear a headscarf, (iii) be disposed to encourage the wearing of headscarves by women and (iv) believe the aforementioned beliefs and dispositions to be justified. Second, that a sufficient number of Saudi Arabians satisfy (i)–(iv) must be a matter of common knowledge among a sufficient number of Saudi Arabians. That is to say that a sufficient number of Saudi Arabians must know that a sufficient number of other Saudi Arabians have internalised the requirement, know that the others know it, know that the others know that they know it, and so on.

We saw that the first answer to the question of what social norms are—that they are general social requirements—fails to distinguish social norms from laws. By contrast, the second answer—that they are *commonly accepted* general requirements—will allow us to appreciate that there are three crucial respects in which social norms and laws differ. The first concerns the kinds of sanctions they involve. The second concerns the kind of internalisation. And the third concerns the kinds of objects to which they may attach. Let us look at each difference in turn.

2.1 Sanctions

Social norms are commonly accepted general requirements. By contrast, being a commonly accepted general requirement is not sufficient for being a law. This is because laws entail that there are generally accepted state-based *sanctions* that apply to those who violate the requirements that constitute them (Bicchieri 2006, 8). Take any law you like: the law in Australia forbidding motorists from driving with a blood alcohol level in excess of .05; the law in California requiring parents and guardians to send their children to registered state schools; the law in France forbidding landlords from evicting their tenants in winter. In order for these to be laws,

---

8   Compare the quite different account of social norms offered by Christina Bicchieri (2006, 8–28).
9   This assumes that the requirements that constitute social norms are deontic propositions. If instead they are non-propositional—e.g. imperatives—then obviously the appropriate attitude would be some other mental state.
10 This is based on the account offered in Hooker (2000, 75ff.).

there must be generally accepted state-based sanctions that attach to those who violate them. This is not to say that anyone who violates the laws will, in fact, be sanctioned. The legal system is, after all, an imperfect one. Violators may elude detection. Insufficient evidence may exist to find them guilty. Moreover, the costs involved in actively pursuing violators may be thought not to warrant it. Nonetheless, unless there are generally recognised state-backed sanctions that attach to the violation of the law, it simply ain't a law.

Two features of these legal sanctions are especially worth noting. The first is a matter of who is responsible for meting them out. A crucial aspect of law—an aspect that distinguishes it from more primitive forms of justice—is that responsibility for sanctioning rests with a higher authority, namely, the state. Rather than leaving the matter in the hands of individual citizens, responsibility for sanctioning is, as we might say, centralised. The second is a matter of the character of the sanctions themselves. These vary dramatically, of course, depending on the nature of the law that has been violated and the legal system in which it exists. Nonetheless, sanctioning tends to involve the public imposition of tangible sanctions: fines, incarceration, other kinds of restrictions, even death.

Social norms, by contrast, do not necessarily (or even typically) involve these kinds of sanctions. They certainly do not entail generally accepted *state-based* sanctions. It may be a social norm in the football team of which one is a member that players not flirt with one another's girlfriends. For this to be so, the requirement that players not flirt with one another's girlfriends must be commonly accepted. But it does not follow that players would accept that it is the state's business—or, for that matter, the business of, say, the president of the club—to impose any sanctions on those who deviate from this norm. Or again, it may be a social norm in Germany that one shake the hands of anyone to whom one is introduced. But I take it that no German would accept that the state is entitled to impose any sanctions on those who fail to shake the hands of someone to whom they are introduced.

Nor do social norms need involve *public or tangible* sanctions. Violations of social norms *sometimes* incur public and tangible sanctions, of course. Thus, I might see my neighbour throwing litter over my fence and, being the peace-loving chap that I am, send my buddies around to smash up his car or scrawl 'Keep Cronulla Beautiful' on his front door. Less dramatically, I might gossip loudly about him to other neighbours, or just cast a disapproving look in his direction. But public and tangible sanctions such as these need not—and in many cases will not—attend to known violations of social norms. For, as has been repeatedly emphasised, such sanctioning is costly (Buchanan 1975; Axelrod 1984). Smashing up one's neighbour's car may result in his smashing up one's face. Gossiping about him may result in his spreading malicious lies about one in turn. Even simply making one's displeasure known may result in retaliation. Moreover, all these things take a certain time and energy and emotional zeal.

Social norms, then, do not necessarily involve the kinds of generally accepted sanctions that laws do. Does this mean that social norms don't necessarily involve *any* kinds of generally accepted sanctions? Following Brennan and Pettit, I want to suggest that social norms do indeed entail certain kinds of generally accepted sanctions. Recall the definition of social norms I gave above, as commonly accepted general requirements. And recall that I took certain attitudes to be partly constitutive of internalising a requirement. Of particular relevance is the disposition to disapprove of those who violate a requirement. In order for a requirement to be commonly accepted, it must be the case that there is a general tendency to disapprove of those who violate it.

This opens up the following interesting possibility. What if, following Geoffrey Brennan and Philip Pettit, we think of this disapproval as itself constituting a kind of sanctioning (Brennan/Pettit 2004)? Notice that such *normative sanctions*, as we might call them, are quite different in kind from legal sanctions. First, unlike legal sanctions, responsibility for doling out normative sanctions rests solely with the individual members of the groups or communities in which the requirements that have been violated are social norms. There is no centralisation of responsibility for sanctioning, no higher institutions apart from, and over and above, ordinary individuals like us. In this sense, normative sanctioning works more like the more primitive forms of justice to which I alluded above. Still, unlike many primitive forms of justice, there is nonetheless a *generalised* disposition to disapprove. Rather than the responsibility for sanctioning resting with the individual who has been directly harmed, responsibility for normative sanctioning is everyone's business. There is a shared responsibility for looking down our noses, scorning, being contemptuous of those who have violated requirements that we accept, even if the violations have not affected us directly.

Second, though shared, normative sanctioning is essentially private and intangible.[11] It is a matter of people having the experiences constitutive of the attitude of disapproval. And such experiences occur within their heads. This is important, since it allows a solution to the sanctioning problem that I mentioned above. Being private (and also generally involuntarily exhibited), disapproval is relatively uncostly. The intangible-ness of the sanctions may lead some to doubt their efficacy. But that would be patently absurd. We are social beings. We care about what others think of us. We like being liked, approved of, respected and dislike being disliked, disapproved of and scorned. So, to heap disapproval on someone is precisely to impose on her something that she takes to be unpleasant, something that she has reason to want to avoid.

2.2 Internalisation

What of the second difference between social norms and law? Very briefly, social norms entail that the requirements that constitute them are commonly accepted within the groups or communities in which they are social norms, where this is under-

---

11 Brennan and Pettit speak of the "intangible hand" of approval and disapproval (or esteem and disesteem).

stood as meaning that the requirements have been *internalised* by a sufficient number of the members of those groups or communities. Take the requirement that beachgoers not leave rubbish behind. If this requirement is *not* internalised by a suitable majority of persons within a particular group or community—if, say, there is no general propensity on the part of the members of the group or community to accept that beachgoers are required not to leave rubbish behind, to disapprove of those who do, and so on—then it simply cannot be a social norm in or of that group or community.

Laws, by contrast, do *not* seem to entail that the requirements that constitute them have been internalised in this way by a suitable majority of the members of the groups or communities in which they are laws. Of course, *many* laws *do* involve requirements that have been internalised by a suitable majority.[12] Laws forbidding people to engage in murder, rape, assault, prejudicial deception, and so on, presumably all involve requirements that have been internalised. Nonetheless, not *all* laws are like this. The requirements that constitute laws *need not*, as a matter of logic, be internalised.

What are examples of non-commonly internalised laws? One interesting candidate is *obscure laws*. These include laws of such complexity that they are hard for the non-legally-trained majority to grasp. It seems highly unlikely that a sufficient number of the citizens or residents of any country will have internalised all the requirements that constitute the administrative law, for example, of that country. Internalisation, as we have seen, involves a disposition to disapprove of anyone who violates the requirement. But it seems rather incredible to suppose that many citizens would have any attitudes at all concerning those who violate the more abstruse requirements of administrative law. It would presumably be a matter of supreme indifference to them.

It might be said that, even if individuals, as they actually are, would not disapprove of those who violated obscure laws, they would do so if they were to understand the requirements that constitute the laws. Is this not enough for a requirement to be said to be internalised? Let us say, in a concessive spirit, that a requirement is *strongly internalised* by an individual if the individual actually accepts the requirement, is disposed, given her actual understanding of the requirement, to disapprove of anyone who violates the requirement, and so on; and *weakly internalised* if it is only true that she would accept the requirement, be disposed to disapprove of anyone who violates it, and so on, *were* she to understand it. It suffices to note that social norms entail strong internalisation. Laws do not entail strong internalisation. Even if laws entail weak internalisation, there remains this difference between social norms and laws.

As it is, however, I am not inclined to think that laws entail either strong or weak internalisation. To see this, consider another category of laws, unpopular laws—say, laws that are generally taken to be outmoded or unfair or otherwise immoral or

---

12 That is just to say that there is considerable overlap between the laws and social norms of particular communities.

unjust. Take laws forbidding homosexuality, for example. Such laws will doubtless often exist in homophobic societies, societies where there is a general acceptance that homosexuality is wrong and a general tendency to disapprove of homosexual behaviour. But we can also easily imagine a tolerant society in which the laws regarding homosexuality are drastically out of step with the attitudes of the populace. Thus, even if homosexuality is unlawful, the majority of the citizens may not accept that men are required to refrain from homosexual acts or to disapprove of those who do. This need not be a matter of their not understanding the requirement that constitutes the content of the law. They may understand it all too well. They may simply not accept it. Nor need we assume that they would accept it if they were to think about it carefully. On the contrary, we can imagine that the more they were to think about it, the more resolutely opposed to it they would become.

Laws, then, don't appear to entail the kind of internalisation that social norms entail. However, there is a stronger claim with which this claim must not be confused, namely, that laws don't entail any kind of internalisation at all. Those who are attracted by a particularly virulent brand of positivism may be inclined to endorse the stronger claim. However, as H. L. A. Hart famously argued, it sits awkwardly with the putative normativity of law. Laws seem to have some kind of grip on us that makes them importantly different from, say, mere commands backed by brute force (Hart 1961). Saying exactly what this comes to is not obvious. But the key, it seems to me, is that the state's right to create, administer and enforce the relevant requirements must be commonly accepted, that is, accepted by a suitable majority of citizens or residents. We might call this *procedural* internalisation and distinguish it from *substantive* internalisation, whereby the substance or content of the requirement itself has to be internalised. It is this feature of law, I believe, that makes it normative, rather than merely coercive.

It might be objected that the concession that laws entail procedural internalisation is inconsistent with my earlier insistence that laws do not entail commonly accepted requirements. For, on the one hand, it might be said that the state's enjoying a commonly accepted entitlement to create, administer and enforce laws entails common acceptance of a requirement to obey the law. And, on the other hand, for there to be common acceptance of a requirement to obey the law appears to entail that any law within the political community in question must be such that the requirement that constitutes it be commonly accepted.

The argument, however, only possesses a semblance of plausibility because of an equivocation with respect to the notion of 'a requirement to obey the law'. Either this is understood as a requirement to obey the law in each and every case, or it is understood as a requirement to obey the law in most cases. If it is understood as a requirement to obey the law in each and every case, then it does not follow from the state's enjoying a commonly accepted entitlement to create, administer and enforce laws that there must be common acceptance of a requirement to obey the law. For it is perfectly possible for a majority of persons to accept the right of the state to create, administer and enforce laws, while insisting on their own right to resist certain of these laws, say, those that they regard as unfair or unjust or contrary to underlying principles inherent in the fabric of the political community. This simultaneous acknowledgement of the legitimacy of the state's power to govern and trenchant insistence on one's right to resist particular laws is precisely what characterises civil disobedience and renders it distinct from revolution, anarchy and mere petulance (Rawls 1971, 299). Suppose, on the other hand, that we understand the requirement to obey the law as a requirement to do so in most cases. In this case, the presence of such a requirement obviously does not entail that, for any law, the requirement that constitutes that law must be commonly accepted. At most, it entails that, for most laws, the requirements that constitute the laws must be commonly accepted. Either way, it does not follow that laws entail substantive internalisation.

2.3 Objects: Actions and Attitudes

The third difference between social norms and laws concerns the *objects* to which the requirements that constitute them apply. The account of social norms I have sketched just says that they are commonly accepted general requirements; it leaves open the kinds of things to which these requirements may apply. And indeed, there is some plausibility to the thought that social norms do not apply solely—or, as I should say, purely—to actions, but also to attitudes.[13] The requirements that constitute laws, by contrast, seem to apply only to actions.

That laws apply only to actions is, I take it, reasonably uncontroversial. The claim can easily be misunderstood, of course. First, I certainly do not want to deny that attitudes are relevant to many actions—including many actions to which laws apply. A court can hardly determine whether an individual is guilty of murder or manslaughter without taking account of her intentions. Second, attitudes are also relevant in many jurisdictions when it comes to legal sentencing. The presence or absence of remorse, for example, may have a bearing on a judge's estimation of the character of the defendant, which in turn may sway her when it comes to the nature of the sentence. Neither of these points, however, undermines the claim that laws themselves only attach to actions.

What about the claim that social norms also attach to attitudes? I am unsure about whether there are *pure attitudinal social norms*—generally accepted requirements simply to have or not have certain attitudes. I shall not try to decide that question here. But there do seem to be *impure attitudinal social norms*—social norms that have an essential attitudinal dimension. The first are requirements to express certain emotions—negative emotions such as grief (when something unpleasant happens, such as a death in the family), or positive emotions such as joy (say, at the birth of a child). It does not seem that this is simply a matter of acting—say, acting as if one is experiencing grief or joy. Rather, it seems to be in part a matter of experiencing certain emotions. The second are requirements involving action/motive pairs—

---

13 The following has benefited greatly from discussions with Geoff Brennan. Indeed, it was Geoff who initially convinced me that social norms do not apply solely to acts.

acting for a particular reason. Are there not social norms that consist of requirements to do or not to do things for a certain reason? For example, is there not a social norm in many contemporary societies that one not marry solely for pecuniary gain? Third, there are taboos. What distinguishes taboos from other social norms, it seem to me, is that the requirements that constitute them attach not just to the forbidden act but to the contemplation of the act. Take incest taboos, for example. An incest taboo is not just a requirement not to have sex with one's close relatives. It is a requirement not to entertain the possibility of doing so, not to think about it, not even to ask oneself the question.

This concludes my discussion of how social norms and laws differ. Notice that we are now in a better position to understand just what the question, 'why social norms, rather than laws?' amounts to. What we are asking, in effect, is, 'why requirements that entail normative sanctions and substantive internalisation and that attach to attitudes as well as to actions, rather than requirements that entail legal sanctions and procedural internalisation and that attach only to actions?'

Putting things this way makes particularly clear the inadequacies of certain common hypotheses about the explanation of social norms. Consider, for example, the hypothesis that the explanation of social norms lies with their serving our interest in being able to coordinate and cooperate with others (see, for example, Ullmann-Margalit 1977; Coleman 1980; Bicchieri 2006). The problem is that from the perspective of our coordination and cooperation interests, the distinctive features of social norms that we have enumerated have no obvious rationale. To the extent that social norms serve these interests, it seems that laws would serve them just as well if not better. In the remainder of this paper, I shall present and defend a very different hypothesis about what explains social norms that I shall argue is not susceptible to this worry.

3. The Social Authority Account

Here, in essence, is the hypothesis I shall defend. Social norms exist because they serve what I shall call our '*social authority interest*'.[14] By 'social authority' I mean

---

14 It might be objected at the outset that the social authority account constitutes an instance of the kind of objectionable "functionalism" that Jon Elster (1982) warned us against. This is not right. The social authority account, unlike the forms of functionalism with which Elster was taking issue, is based on the idea of individual interests and is not inconsistent with methodological individualism. It may nonetheless be objected that the account conflates explanation and justification and that, in the absence of an appropriate feedback mechanism, it cannot be genuinely explanatory. This last point is controversial for reasons famously presented by Cohen (1982). Even if Elster is right and Cohen wrong, however, it seems that at most this would show that the account is incomplete. Moreover, identifying such a mechanism does not seem an insurmountable task. Finally, to the extent that the objection holds against the social authority account, it seems to hold equally against the kinds of rational choice theoretic explanations we mentioned above. I am grateful to Lina Eriksson for this point.

the shared authority we possess as individual members of a group to determine how other individuals are to live.[15] To say that we have a social authority *interest* is to say that social authority is something we have reason to want. Moreover, I believe that this is not reducible to other things we have reason to want. So, social norms exist because they serve a non-reducible interest we have in having this kind of shared authority over others.

3.1 The Social Authority Interest

In order to clarify just what our social authority interest amounts to, it will be useful to contrast it with several other interests we have. First, it must be contrasted with the interest we have in possessing certain kinds of *power*. To have power is, roughly, to have the ability to exercise *effective control* in determining that certain things will happen.[16] Most relevant for our purposes is power *over others*, namely, the ability to control how others live their lives—what they will and won't do, perhaps even what they will and won't think and feel.[17] Our social authority interest, by contrast, is an interest we have in having a certain kind of *authority* over others. Authority, unlike, power is an essentially normative notion. Whereas to have power is to have the ability to exercise *effective control* in determining that certain things will happen, to possess authority is a matter of having a recognised *right or entitlement* to expect or demand that certain things will happen. Authority and power can, of course, come apart. We can have authority without power, since our authority may not be respected in each and every case. Think of the teacher whose students recognise his right to expect and demand what happens in the classroom, but who also get great amusement out of violating this right by pulling faces at him when he's not watching. And we can have power without authority, since the ability to determine what happens need not be accompanied by any recognition of one's right to do so. Think of the kidnapper who can determine whether his hostages live or die but who does not enjoy a recognised right to end any life.

Second, our social authority interest must also be contrasted with our *individual authority* interest—the interest we have in having a recognised right to determine how we ourselves, as individuals, are to live. This is an interest that underlies many important rights such as the right to freedom of movement, conscience and associa-

---

15 The social authority account draws inspiration from the individual authority account of promises advanced by David Owens (2006).
16 Many considerations afford us such power: physical strength, intelligence, knowledge—to mention just a few.
17 I take for granted that we often have an interest in having such power. Power over others may even be an intrinsic good—something worth having for its own sake—but it is certainly an instrumental good. It helps one to protect oneself against others. There can be little worse than being powerless in the face of others. If one has power over others, then this renders one immune from troublesome interference. More nastily, it also allows one the opportunity to interfere with them in ways that may be personally advantageous.

tion. Indeed, it may, with justification, be regarded as one of the fundamental tenets of a liberal society that individuals have a recognised entitlement to a sizeable sphere of freedom to live their lives as they see fit, even where the choices they make and the beliefs they have are not the ones they ought to make and have, objectively considered. Our social authority interest by contrast, is an interest in having authority over others—a recognised entitlement to have *others* do things.

Third, our social authority interest can also be usefully contrasted with our *collective authority* interest—the interest we have in groups or collectives to which we belong having authority over individuals (including perhaps us). Unlike collective authority, social authority is a kind of shared authority that we possess *as individuals*, albeit as individual members of groups, not a kind of authority that is had by the groups themselves.

So much for what social authority is. But what is valuable about it? Why think that we have a social authority *interest*? Part of the answer is doubtless that having social authority helps to realise *other* interests we have, including the three other interests that I just mentioned. It helps serve our power interest since, although power and authority can come apart, having social authority can obviously be itself a source of power. The power of parents does not consist merely in the fact that, being older, stronger and hopefully wiser, they are *able* to make choices for their children, but also in the fact that the children typically acknowledge their *right* to do so. We are creatures for whom the presence of relations of authority can be a powerful motivator. To violate a right that we acknowledge others to have is often something that we are not prepared to do.

Having social authority is also importantly related to our ability to effectively realise our individual authority interest. On the one hand, there is the familiar point that enjoying a certain sphere of social authority seems to be a conceptual prerequisite for enjoying individual authority. It simply makes no sense to talk of our having a recognised right to determine how we shall live without others recognising our right to determine that others don't interfere with how we choose to live. Thus, for example, our having a recognised right to determine our religious beliefs seems to entail having a recognised right that others not interfere with our determination of our religious beliefs. On the other hand, as David Owens points out, our individual authority interest, like many other important interests, "is best served by a bit of give-and-take":

> [S]omeone motivated to insist on the right to decide for themselves what they are going to do will also be motivated to seek the right to require another to behave in a certain way, where their own decisions depend on the actions of that other person. And, in return for receiving this right, they may be willing to sacrifice their own freedom. (2006, 70)

Having social authority can also obviously help buttress our collective authority interest. A soccer referee is generally going to have an easier time having his right to punish any player who violates a particular rule of the game (the tripping rule, say) recognised if the players recognise one another's right not to trip one another. This point can perhaps be grasped even more clearly if we suppose that this is not so. Suppose, then, that the players don't recognise one another's right not to trip one another. Perhaps they think it's a stupid rule, evidence of the 'cissification' of the code. Perhaps they played most of their football in an era before the rule was introduced. Perhaps they have recently decamped from some other code, which does not contain such a rule. Under these circumstances, the referee is going to have a much harder time having his right to enforce the rule recognised.

So having social authority is valuable in part because it helps us to realise effectively these and other related interests. Still, I don't think this exhausts the ways in which social authority is valuable, or even captures what is most valuable about it. Rather, I think we also have reason to want social authority because it is deeply implicated in—indeed a constituent of—another important value, namely, the value of *community*. I take it that communities are partly constituted by relationships that exist between their members, and relationships of any kind are in turn partly constituted by relations of recognised entitlement and accountability. To be someone's friend is in part a matter of your recognising that you are entitled, as friends, to expect things of one another and hence accountable to one another to that extent. If you did not recognise this kind of mutual entitlement and accountability, this you simply couldn't be friends. Similarly, for there to exist a community is in part a matter of the members of the community recognising entitlements that others have of them, as fellow members of the community, and hence recognising a kind of common accountability that obtains between them. Absent this kind of acknowledged entitlement and accountability, we simply couldn't enjoy the value of community in the full-fledged sense.

I happen to think there is some plausibility to the thought that being a member of a community and the various things that are part of that—a sense of belonging, being able to identify as a member of a community and have common values qua members of the community, a common history, etc—are things we have reason to want for their own sake. But all that I am committed to saying is that our interest in being part of a community and through it our social authority interest cannot be *reduced* to these further interests. The different interests that will be served by different people being part of different communities in different circumstances will be massively diverse. Our social authority interest hence provides a kind of unifying higher-order umbrella interest that contains and makes sense of all these divergent lower-order interests.

2.2 Why Social Norms, Rather than Laws?

I have been trying to say what our social authority interest amounts to and to make plausible that we have such an interest. Let us now consider the hypothesis that our social authority interests explains why there are social norms, that social norms exist because they serve our social authority interest. Why should we accept this hypothesis? Notice, first, that the hypothesis seems capable of explaining why we might expect there to exist *general social requirements*, a category to which, as we have seen, social norms belong. That there exist *requirements*, rather than, say, mere regularities, is readily explicable, since my having a right to expect others to X entails that others are required to X. That there exist *general* rather than merely particular requirements is also readily explicable, since this seems to be the only of doing justice to the fact that social authority is both possessed by, and wielded over, the same individuals. That there exist essentially *social* requirements is readily explicable, since social authority involves a shared right that is only recognised within, and hence only meaningful relative to, particular groups or communities. The social authority hypothesis therefore appears to be well placed to answer certain important contrastive questions: Why social norms, rather than conventions? Why social norms, rather than particular requirements? Why social norms, rather than moral principles?

But we are interested here in a different kind of contrastive question, namely: Why social norms, rather than laws? We saw above that there are three key differences between social norms and laws that any adequate answer to this question must be capable of explaining. Can the social authority account interest explain these differences?

Consider, first, the different kinds of *sanctions* that social norms and laws involve. As we saw above, normative sanctions differ from legal sanctions both in respect of who is responsible for meting out the sanctions and in respect of the nature of the penalties imposed. Whereas legal sanctioning is a matter of bringing to bear the coercive apparatus of the state and imposing penalties of a tangible kind, normative sanctioning is principally a matter of our subjecting those who have violated social norms to the more intangible forces of social disapproval. The social authority hypothesis offers a relatively straightforward explanation of both these differences. Regarding who is responsible for the sanctioning, it is clearly crucial that this responsibility be borne by the individual members of the groups. If we were simply to surrender all responsibility for sanctioning to some higher authority such as the state, this would amount to surrendering social authority itself. Inasmuch as they entail sanctions that are maintained by the members of the groups, social norms therefore constitute exactly the right kind of tool for realising our social authority interest, whereas laws simply don't.

What about the intangible, rather than tangible nature of the sanctions? One thing to say here is that it is a matter of what is universally feasible. Even if more tangible sanctions are feasible in particular cases—the disapprover is in a position of strength relative to the disapprovee, say—it is plainly unrealistic to suppose that this will always be so. But in order for authority to be genuinely shared, it must be the case that the sanctions that members are entitled to impose on others are of the same kind. Disapproval is arguably the only kind of sanction that will satisfy this condition of universal feasibility. A second, related idea would be that our social authority interest is shaped by other interests that compete with it. Since to possess social authority is to possess a shared entitlement to sanction, it had better not involve an entitlement to sanction any old how. More tangible sanctions bring with them familiar dangers. It is not clear that our social authority interest extends that far. A third thing to say would be that since disapproval constitutes a mode of sanctioning that seems sufficiently robust for what is required to serve our social authority interest, any more robust mode of sanctioning is, even if not antithetical to social authority, simply unnecessary for it.

But I think we can and should go further than that. The role of disapproval as a way of realising our social authority interest is not exhausted by these kinds of practical considerations. A way of bringing this out would be to say that, even if all practical obstacles to the imposition of more tangible sanctions were removed, it would remain the case that disapproval had a privileged and non-dispensable role in the achievement of social authority. I would want to argue that this role is traceable back to the value of the relationship of community in which social authority is crucially implicated. Simply put, a relationship without a disposition—and a claimed right—to disapprove of others for doing and not doing certain things is not a relationship in the full-blooded sense in which I am interested here.

This brings us to the second difference between social norms and laws, namely, the kinds of *internalisation* that they entail. Social norms, as we saw, entail a kind of substantive internalisation such that the requirements that constitute them have been internalised by a sufficient number of the members of the groups in which they are social norms. Laws, by contrast, entail only a more modest kind of procedural internalisation, namely, that the right of the state to enforce the requirements that constitute them be generally accepted.

Can thinking of social norms as serving our social authority interest help explain this difference? I think it can. On the one hand, the kind of procedural internalisation associated with law is obviously incapable of generating social authority. For one, as we have already seen, it involves bestowing authority in the wrong place. The existence of social authority requires recognising a right on the part of the individual members of a group, whereas laws involve recognising a right on the part of a higher authority in the form of the state.

For another, the content of the right we recognise is also of the wrong kind. What we recognise, in the case of law, is the right to enforce the requirements that constitute laws by encouraging compliance and punishing non-compliance. We do not necessarily recognise the requirements themselves; we do not accept that we are required to obey the law, at least not in each and every case. But social authority involves more than a recognised right to enforce requirements. It involves, in addition, a recognised right to *demand and expect* certain things of others. Once again, this follows from the kind of interest that I argued we have in social authority, an interest in having a certain kind of relationship with others. Consider the analogy with friendship. We would be odd friends indeed if we merely accepted that our 'friends' were entitled to get us to do things and, if we failed to do them, to punish us (with tangible or intangible sanctions). To be a friend in the full sense, and to enjoy the value that is associated most centrally with it, is to accept that we are required to do those things. Similarly, to be a member of a community in the full sense is to accept the requirements that individual members have the right to expect others to comply with, that is, to accept the requirements themselves.

On the other hand, whereas this is precisely what is lacking in the modest kind of internalisation associated with law, this is not true of the richer kind of substantive internalisation entailed by social norms. Rather, the latter is of exactly the right kind for our social authority interest. When we internalise a requirement in the substantive way, we do not merely accept the right of others to try to get us to comply with the requirement, or, if we don't comply, to sanction us. Rather, we accept the requirement itself. In doing so, we necessarily regard ourselves as accountable to others so far as complying with the requirement is concerned.

Finally, what about the different *objects* to which social norms and laws apply? Laws, I suggested, apply only to actions, whereas social norms may also apply in part to attitudes. Can the social authority hypothesis explain this apparent difference? Once again, I think the key lies with appreciating the essentially relational value of social authority. Attitudes are, as I observed above, central to any kind of relationship. It is not enough, in order that we are friends, lovers and so on, that we behave in certain ways, but also that we have certain attitudes concerning the individuals with whom we enjoy the relationships. But attitudes also play a normative role in our relationships. To become friends with someone is to take oneself to be required to have certain attitudes: to feel (and not to feel) certain feelings; to think (and not to think) certain thoughts; to be moved by certain considerations. We doubtless only ever imperfectly fulfill these attitudinal demands. We sometimes feel feelings that we recognise we ought not to feel and fail to feel feelings that we recognise we ought to feel. We think thoughts that we recognise we ought not to think and fail to think thoughts that we recognise we ought to think. We are moved by considerations we recognise we ought not to be moved by, and are not moved by considerations that we recognise we ought to be moved by. For all that, we acknowledge the legitimacy of the attitudinal demands, as can be witnessed by the guilt we feel for having or failing to have the relevant attitude.

If we think of social norms as a tool for realising our social authority interest, the idea that they can apply in part to attitudes as well as actions begins to make perfect sense. For we would expect the requirements that constitute social norms to have an attitudinal dimension, given the essentially relational nature of the value of social authority. Indeed, it would be rather strange that they did not apply to our attitudes. Whereas any requirements that applied exclusively to actions, like laws, would seem to be of the wrong kind to serve our social authority interest.

To be sure, we should not normally expect the requirements to apply so *extensively* to our attitudes as in the case of more intimate relationships such as friendship and various forms of love. Indeed, part of the difference between these more intimate relationships and most kinds of community seems to be a greater range and intensity of attitudes both present and required in the case of the former. This seems to correspond to what we typically see. Once again, then, a central difference between social norms and laws that initially looked rather surprising begins to look perfectly comprehensible on the assumption that social norms exist to serve our social authority interest.

4. Conclusion

I began this paper with a challenge: How are we to explain the existence of social norms in a way that is capable of answering the question, 'why social norms, rather than laws?' I have offered a certain hypothesis about the explanation of social norms—that they exist because they serve our social authority interest—and suggested that the hypothesis appears to offer a compelling solution to the challenge. Key differences between social norms and laws are thereby rendered readily comprehensible. If we were to want a tool that serves our social authority interest, we would want it to have the features that social norms have, rather than the features that laws have. This provides some reason to believe that the hypothesis is true.

Bibliography

Axelrod, R. (1984), *The Evolution of Cooperation*, New York

Bicchieri, C. (2006), *The Grammar of Society: The Nature and Dynamics of Soial Norms*, New York

Brennan, G./P. Pettit (2004), *The Economy of Esteem*, Oxford/New York

Buchanan, J. (1975), *The Limits of Liberty: Between Anarchy and Leviathan*, Chicago

Cohen, G. (1982), Reply to Elster on 'Marxism, Functionalism and Game Theory', in: *Theory and Society 11(4)*, 483–95

Coleman, J. (1980), *Foundations of Social Theory*, Cambridge/MA

Elster, J. (1982), The Case for Methodological Individualism, in: *Theory and Society 11(4)*, 453–82

Gilbert, M. (1989), *On Social Facts*, London/New York

Harman, G. (1975), Moral Relativism Defended, in: *Philosophical Review 84(1)*, 3–22

Hart, H. L. A. (1961), *The Concept of Law*, Oxford

Hooker, B. (2000), *Ideal Code, Real World*, Oxford

Lewis, D. (1969), *Convention: A Philosophical Study*, Cambridge/MA

Lipton, P. (1990), Contrastive Explanation, in: D. Knowles (ed.), *Explanation and Its Limits*, Cambridge/New York, 247–66

Owens, D. (2006), A Simple Theory of Promising, in: *Philosophical Review 115(1)*, 51–77

Rawls, J. (1971), *A Theory of Justice*, Cambridge/MA

Ullmann-Margalit, E. (1977), *The Emergence of Norms*, Oxford

Van Fraassen, B. (1980), *The Scientific Image*, Oxford

Stefan Huster

Social and Legal Norms
A Comment on Nicholas Southwood

1. Introduction

Nic Southwoods illuminating paper tries to explain the existence of social norms by contrasting social and legal norms (in his terminology: 'laws'). My remarks will concern his definition and explication of the concept 'social norm' (2.) and his explanation for the existence of these norms (3.).

2.

In Nic Southwoods account, social norms are not laws, meaning they are not elements of the legal system. Furthermore, they are, however, neither conventions nor other normative principles, such as norms of prudence or moral norms. After that, it becomes a little bit mysterious, what kinds of general requirements are left, that should count as social norms. Therefore the examples for social norms given by the paper have to be looked at:

- The following principles are presented as social norms: 'to shake the hand of anyone to whom one is introduced' and 'guests to bring a bottle of wine when they are invited to dinner'. It is implausible why these principles could not be qualified as norms of convention instead.
- The specific requirement 'that beachgoers are not leave litter behind' is seen as a social norm as well. But is this not a norm of fair cooperation and, therefore, a moral norm?
- The same could be said about the Saudi-Arabian norm that obliges women to wear headscarves. Most people supporting this norm view it as a quasi-moral norm, based on their religious beliefs. Of course, one could argue this moral norm to be wrong, but this would, as a matter of fact, have no impact onto its character as a moral norm—as seen from the perspective of this community.

To summarize: Social norms always contain an obligation of some kind or other. This becomes evident, when the paper says that we disapprove the violation of a norm, that we sanction this violation and so on. This obligation may have weak ramifications, as in the case of conventions, or a strong impact, as in the case of the requirements of core morality. In every of these cases, there is an obligation, and that obligation must be based upon something—morality (even the particular morality of a certain group), convention or something else. A norm that is just and merely social can hardly ever be imagined. There are always reasons for norms—may they be good or bad—and these reasons can be described as reasons of convention, of morality and so forth.

It would therefore be much more plausible to not try to make a distinction between conventions and other normative principles on the one hand and social norms on the other hand, but instead to accept the term 'social norm' as subordinate concept that describes different kinds of general social requirements.

3.

My second annotation concerns the correlation of norms and laws in the process of constituting a community and in their effect in serving our—as Nic Southwood calls it—social authority interest. In this respect, the paper points out a very sharp distinction between social norms and legal norms. In my view this distinction is exaggerated. Let me highlight two points that are in turn connected to each other.

a) The paper considers the law to exclusively be as a system of rules that are enforced by the state and implemented by external sanctions. Because of that, laws allow neither to express disapproval nor to create mutual obligations. This seems to me a description of the law that is a little too mechanical. If, for instance, someone is sentenced under the German criminal law, this does not entail an external sanction only (that he has to go to prison), but also a 'sozialethisches Unwerturteil', which translates to: a social-ethical judgement about his behavior being morally wrong. This demonstrates that law does in fact entail normative sanctions. And, in this way, we as a political body or as a law community have the potential to express disapproval.

b) It may be argued that the fact remains that not the individual but the state sanctions violations of the law, which brings me to my second point. As the paper states: We devolve all responsibility for sanctioning to some higher authority.

Again, that seems to me to be a simplified picture of the law, especially in a democratic system. When someone is convicted in Germany, the judge starts his verdict with the words 'im Namen des Volkes' ('in the name of the people'). In a democratic system, the citizens are not only the recipients of laws, but also their authors (Habermas 1992). The state is not only 'some higher authority', but also an instrument of the people to express their common goals and values. The state and its law are elements of our 'social authority interest', to determine how other individuals should live.

c) To summarize: It seems evident that the law also has the function to create and stabilize the community. In modern pluralistic societies where opinions and values differ, the law is perhaps the sole medium to get a nation-wide sense of community (Huster 2002, 673 ff.).

As conclusion I therefore want to recommend another explanation for the relationship of laws and social norms: In pluralistic societies the law can only apply to the normative fundamentals, the basic principles of our living together, the so-called "ethical minimum" (Jellinek 1908, 45). The fact that a lot of social norms beside the law exist, finds its explanation in the deep disagreement concerning the question how to live. In a free society we can let this question to be answered by different social groups, their beliefs and their particular norms. Then it is up to the individual citizen to decide, which social norm he wants to follow.

Bibliography

Habermas, J. (1992), *Faktizität und Geltung*, Frankfurt/M.

Huster, S. (2002), *Die ethische Neutralität des Staates*, Tübingen

Jellinek, G. (1908), *Die sozialethische Bedeutung von Recht, Unrecht und Strafe*, 2. ed., Berlin

Bernd Lahno

Norms of Evaluation vs. Norms of Conduct

1. Introduction

The concept of a norm primarily refers to rules, standards or principles, which state what individuals should do, must not do or are allowed to do (in some wide sense). In a second sense it may also refer to a certain sort of social fact—a 'social norm'. In this second, descriptive use of the term, a norm is a behavioral regularity with certain characteristics such as normative expectations and social sanctions. Norms as social facts are fundamentally related to norms in the first sense. The behavioral pattern of a social norm is to some extent the result of the fact, that at least some people acknowledge a rule or standard as a guide of conduct with a certain amount of authority. At least some people must take an internal point of view (Hart 1961, 86f.) towards the norm; otherwise what we have is just a behavioral regularity, not a social norm. Now, the object of the internal point of view is, of course, the norm in the first sense, not the behavioral regularity.[1] So the concept of a norm as a rule or standard is prior to the concept of a social norm.

I will be concerned here with norms in what I take to be the prior sense of the word: rules, standards or principles, which assert some demand on individual conduct.[2] I shall focus on what can be called 'prescriptive norms', i.e. norms, which can—roughly—be stated in the form 'Under condition C one should ϕ'. There are, of course, norms which are not prescriptive, such as some technical norms or power conferring norms.[3] Thus I am not claiming here that all norms are prescriptive. But it seems fair to say, that prescriptive norms are at the core of most normative systems, and, thus, a primary—if not the primary—object of any attempt to analyze the character of norms and normative systems.

I shall distinguish two forms of prescriptive norms, namely norms of conduct, which directly tell us what to do under certain circumstances, and norms of evaluation, which tell us what to value (2.). In general, moral norms, whether they are norms of evaluation or norms of conduct, have both, an action guiding and an evaluative aspect. Moral norms of evaluation make a demand on our conduct mediated by

---

1 For Raz (1990, 53ff.) this is an important reason, why Hart's 'practice theory' of norms is fundamentally flawed as a general theory of norms.
2 Some of the arguments put forward here are explored in the context of social norms in Lahno (2009).
3 Even those norms that can in general be stated by a deontic sentence are not necessarily prescriptive norms. A permission in a strong sense is not equivalent to any prescription (cf. von Wright 1963, 85ff.).

instrumental rationality. Moral norms of conduct demand that we should evaluate acts in a certain way (3.). Norms of evaluation relate to the concept of the good, norms of conduct to the concept of the right. Consequentialism holds that norms of evaluation are fundamental in morality, whereas deontological ethics is characterized by the fundamental conviction that the moral quality of an act is solely determined by the fact that it is motivated by respect and acceptance of the right principle of conduct (4.). I will argue that morality cannot be reduced to a demand on the evaluation of states of affairs paired with instrumental rationality. Consequentialism is wrong, because it cannot provide a sufficient basis as a moral guide of conduct (5.). Still, norms of evaluation do have moral significance. Deontological ethics are wrong because they cannot account for the role that consequences and their evaluation play in ethical judgment (6.). I conclude with some tentative remarks on the tendency to frame moral demands in consequentialist terms.

2. Prescriptive Norms

A prescriptive norm is characterized by the fact that it can be stated in the form: 'If condition C applies every person should ϕ!', or more formal:

$$\forall x\, O(\phi(x); C(x)).$$

For all individuals x it is obligatory to ϕ if condition C applies. I will refer to x as the *addressee* or the *norm subject*, to C as the *condition* (of application) and to ϕ as the *object of the norm*.

C(x) may refer to any state of affairs. It can be complex in the sense that it may be the conjunction or disjunction of other more simple conditions. The argument x is added to C to indicate that the condition might be dependent on x. To give an example, C(x) might state that x stands in a certain relation to another person such as 'x is the father of person a'. It may also refer to some property of x such as 'x is rich' or 'x is ten feet tall'. Thus, although the general form of the norm is universal, i.e. the domain of x is the set of all individuals, any restriction of the group of individuals the norm effectively addresses can be incorporated by giving suitable conditions C(x). It may be the case that all moral norms (or all valid moral norms) are universal in some wider sense, but this is a matter of normative discourse, which I will not discuss here. The concept of a prescriptive norm as analyzed here is, in principle, applicable to universal norms (in any sense) as well as to norms that address only a restricted group of individuals.

What are the kind of things that a norm tells us we ought to? What is the domain of ϕ? A first answer seems to be: the set of all actions, which an individual may perform. A typical example of a prescriptive norm would be: 'If x is the father of person a and a is a minor without sufficient monetary resources at his disposal, then x should pay the tuition fee for a!' In this case ϕ is the act of paying the tuition fee for a. But many norms do not only refer to a particular act or to a particular type of act—a generic act.

A more common norm is: 'A father should pay for the education of his child!' While the condition of this prescriptive norm can be given in the same form as before, the object here is of a different kind. The norm does not tell me that I ought to pay the fee of some specific primary school that my son wants to attend; nor can I meet the demands of the norm solely by paying the fee of any primary school. The norm demands more: I have to agree on some scheme of education for my son and I am obliged to bear all the expenses that are connected to the realization of such a scheme. So paying the tuition fee for some specific school may be part of the realization of the scheme and, thus, part of observing the norm. But, although I do follow the norm by acting this way, I have to do other things according to the scheme as well to actually abide by the norm.

So the object of the norm is not necessarily a particular (generic) action. It may rather be a certain (generic) scheme of action, a way of conduct. I will call any prescriptive norm whose object is some generic action or some generic way of conduct *a norm of conduct*.

Rather than prescribing certain actions many norms are negative in that they prohibit to act in a certain way. These can be understood as norms of conduct by allowing ϕ to refer to 'negative' ways of conduct: If ϕ is some scheme of conduct that can in principle be the object of a norm of conduct, then $\neg\phi$ is (to be understood) also (as) a way of conduct that can be the object of a norm of conduct.[4] Following this line of argument I will use the concept of a norm of conduct in a way that it may refer to positive precepts as well as to prohibitions.

Although norms of conduct form an important part of prescriptive norms there are other possible objects of prescriptive norms. An example is given by the norm: 'If a person x has sufficient evidence that p is true and no evidence to the contrary, x should believe that p!'

Obviously, anything that can be demanded of a person or anything a person can be held responsible for may be the object of a (prescriptive) norm. As Michael Smith notes (2005, 10), among the things we can be held responsible for are our beliefs and our desires. However, we do not choose our beliefs or desires—at least having a desire or a belief is not the direct result of a decision in the way an action is. One may argue, therefore, that it is principally inadequate or unjustified to be held responsible for our beliefs or desires. I think this argument is unsound, but it is beside the point anyway. It misinterprets the 'can' in 'can be held responsible'. I do not intend to make a normative claim about the justification of demands here. All I am saying is that there are such demands in the sense that they are intelligible and regularly made.

My main interest here is in norms that may be used or are offered as a guide to individual action and, in particular, in moral norms. Norms of rationality as the one given above are—if at all—only indirectly related to action. They are, also, usually not regarded as moral norms. This is different with prescriptive norms whose object

---

4 Note that the correct logical form of 'You shall not do ϕ if C applies!' is $\forall x\, O(\neg\phi(x); C(x))$, not $\forall x\, \neg O(\phi(x); C(x))$.

is a desire of the addressee of the norm (at least in some wide sense of desire). A good example is the 4th commandment of the Decalogue:[5] 'Honor your father and your mother.' No doubt, this commandment demands that we should act in some certain way: we should treat them as honorable. But this is not the core of the norm. Merely treating them as honorable is not enough. We have to actually honor them, i.e. we have to develop and cultivate certain feelings toward them. We have to give sufficient value to their life, interests and feelings. So the norm essentially aims at our feelings, our ways to evaluate things, at our preferences. That we act in certain ways is just a result of abiding by the norm, an (insufficient!) indicator that we actually do abide.

I will call prescriptive norms whose object is a certain way or scheme to evaluate things *norms of evaluation*. Norms of evaluation are quite common in morality. In fact, half of the Ten Commandments are norms of evaluation while the other half consists of norms of conduct.[6]

3. Moral Norms

Morality is generally considered to be concerned with the characteristics and the rules of right conduct. Therefore the paradigmatic form of a moral norm may seem to be the form of a norm of conduct. But as we have seen before, norms of evaluation also relate to action.

Norms of conduct tell us how to act directly while norms of evaluation do so indirectly. If a moral norm tells us to value a certain state of affairs, then—as a moral norm—it tells us also that we should act in ways such that this value is adequately respected. The relationship between norms of evaluation and action is given by instrumental rationality. An instrumentally rational individual will act in a way that the consequences of her actions will have optimal value according to her preferences, i.e. according to her scheme of evaluation. Thus, if an instrumentally rational person abides by a norm of evaluation she will act such as to optimize according to the evaluative scheme of the norm. A moral norm of evaluation will typically demand not only that we evaluate states of affairs in a certain way, it will also demand that we act accordingly—and that means: act as is instrumentally rational in view of the given scheme of evaluation. Thus, it is not enough to develop and cultivate certain feelings toward parents to abide by the 4th commandment. We also have to actually treat them honorably.

It is not only the case that moral norms of evaluation involve some demand on our conduct, it is also true that moral norms of conduct are essentially connected with evaluative demands. Take for example the moral norm 'One should not hurt another person!' It primarily demands, that I should not do anything, which may hurt another person. But as a moral norm it does more than this. It demands that I

---

5   According to the Roman Catholic/ Lutheran Division of the Ten Commandments.
6   Norms of evaluation are: the 1st, 3rd, 4th, 9th and 10th commandment.

should devalue all sorts of acts insofar and inasmuch as they cause harm for other persons. To see this, imagine a person who actually acts in a way that no other person is hurt. So her behavior is consistent with the norm. But, imagine that her reason to act in this manner is that she (mistakenly) thinks that any harm she does to anybody else will cause the same harm being done to her. Although this person externally acts in line with the norm, we would not say that she follows the norm in the deserved correct way.

Moral norms of conduct demand that we should act in certain ways; but this is not all they do. They also demand that we do it for the right reasons. By telling us what we ought to do they implicitly give us an evaluative scheme for actions and they demand that we adopt this scheme and act upon it.

Not all norms of conduct necessarily include such a demand on evaluation. But moral norms do. David Hume gives an explanation why this is so. Any singular moral judgment is, according to Hume, primarily directed to the person acting not to the single act. That this is so is a consequence of all moral judgments being rooted in moral passions. One characteristic of moral passions is, that they are—as Hume calls them—*indirect* passions (Hume 1978, 276ff.). Indirect passions are intentional in character. Their decisive property is that their object does not coincide with their cause. Moral passions are generally elicited if we observe some state of affairs, which we appreciate or disappreciate. These feelings of approbation are then transformed into similar moral passions, which are directed to the person, who brought the state of affairs about. This is only possible if the person and the related state of affairs are suitably connected: there must be some causal connection between the state of affairs and the acts of the person; and the acts must be actually attributable to the person, i.e. they must be sufficiently grounded in her character traits and preferences.

> The external performance has no merit. We must look within to find the moral quality. This we cannot do directly; and therefore fix our attention on actions, as on external signs. But these actions are still considered as signs; and the ultimate object of our praise and approbation is the motive, that produc'd them. (Hume 1978, 477)

One may reject Hume's moral psychology and his emotivism. Still, his analysis exhibits a fundamental insight into the nature of morality. The same insight can be found in Kant's distinction between acts that are merely "pflichtmäßig" ("in accordance with duty") and acts "aus Pflicht" ("out of duty", Kant 2002, 199; 1986, 23). As far as acts are merely in accordance with what duty says, as far as they are "pflichtmäßig", they bear—as Kant says—no moral value. Moral value is attached to the act only insofar as it is chosen "aus Pflicht", i.e. as far as it is actually motivated by duty.

Although morality is practical, moral judgments are not primarily judgments about acts; the crucial object of a moral judgment is rather the individual as a person, which is the source of its actions. Thus, moral judgments are primarily judgments about the character traits, the inclinations and aims of a person. Morality can, therefore, be understood as a second order evaluation: an evaluation of our evaluations.[7] If that is true, any moral norm makes a demand on our evaluations. But notice that the evaluative demand that is involved in moral norms of conduct is a demand on our evaluation of acts, whereas norms of evaluation as introduced above demand a certain evaluation of states of affairs. Acts generally bring about certain states of affairs but they are usually not considered to be states of affairs. So a crucial difference remains. To keep the two forms of prescriptive norms apart I shall reserve the term 'norm of evaluation' to those norms whose object is an evaluative scheme of states of affairs (not including acts). Nevertheless, I emphasize that some norms of conduct (and in particular moral norms of conduct), while not being norms of evaluation, do include a demand concerning the evaluation of acts or schemes of conduct.

4. The Right and the Good

One of the most prominent distinctions in ethical theory is the distinction between the right and the good. As Rawls says:

> The two main concepts of ethics are those of the right and the good; the concept of a morally worthy person is, I believe, derived from them. The structure of an ethical theory is, then, largely determined by how it defines and connects these two basic notions. (Rawls 1971, 24)

The distinction between norms of evaluation and norms of conduct is obviously related to the distinction of the right and the good. By making certain demands on our actions, moral norms of conduct express what is right. By making certain demands on our evaluations moral norms of evaluation express what is good. As I argued above, both types of moral norms make a demand on evaluation. Norms of conduct demand that we consent with an evaluative scheme of acts, i.e. an evaluative scheme in terms of the right, whereas norms of evaluation demand approval of an evaluative scheme of states of affairs, i.e. an evaluative scheme in terms of the good.

The problem of the relationship between the right and the good within moral theory has often been considered to be mainly a conceptual problem, the main question being whether either of the two concepts is definitionally prior to the other (see, e.g., Smith 2005). But this is beside the point. Rawls raises a substantial, not a linguistic problem. The problem is how the morally decent person is essentially characterized. A moral person will act in a certain way. But, as Hume and Kant argue, acting in a certain way is only a necessary, not a sufficient condition of being a morally decent person. A moral person must act from the right reasons, and these reasons are essentially determined by the evaluational schemes of the person. As both sort of evaluational schemes—evaluation of states of affairs as well as evaluation of

---

7   This is related to Sen's proposal to define a moral view as an "ordering of orderings" (Sen 1982, 80). But Sen restricts the range of the first order orderings to consequences of acts.

acts—may play a decisive role in decision-making, is any of the two more fundamental with regard to morality?

A consequentialist or teleological theory holds that *only* the evaluation of states of affairs is fundamental to morality. The evaluation of acts is derivative in that the value of an act is to be assessed according to the value of its consequences. Therefore, a morally decent person is completely characterized by her preferences (on states of affairs). This accords with the concept of a moral actor as often used in rational actor theory. Morality is usually incorporated into rational choice models of interaction by modifying the utility function in suitable ways.

From a consequentialist point of view, then, norms of evaluation form the core of morality, whereas norms of conduct merely express what we should do as instrumentally rational beings if we abide by the norms of evaluation. This does not make norms of conduct superfluous or non-moral norms. They are (morally) valuable just as all (valid) instrumental rules or hypothetical imperatives are valuable with regard to their particular aim. And so a moral system will typically include such rules. But if a person transgresses such a rule while abiding to all moral norms of evaluation, she is acting instrumentally irrational. So from a consequentialist point of view she is making a mistake, which points to a deficiency of rationality, not to a moral deficiency.

Note that the concept of consequentialism as introduced here refers to what is traditionally called act-consequentialism. The reason is that instrumental rationality relates single acts to their consequences only. The consequences from all (or sufficiently many) people following a rule cannot directly motivate a (solely) instrumentally rational individual, as it cannot bring about the social fact by its individual action. Therefore, the evaluation of the expected consequences of a norm being in rule cannot translate into a normative demand of conduct. In fact, rule-consequentialism may be a deontological ethical theory, which assesses the moral excellence of a person solely on her evaluation of acts according to norms of conduct.

In contrast to a consequentialist theory a deontological theory holds that only the evaluation of acts is fundamental to morality. It does not claim that the evaluation of states of affairs is in any way derivative on the evaluation of acts, it just states that only the evaluation of acts is morally significant, whatever the relationship of the evaluation of acts and state of affairs may be. So from a deontological point of view the core of morality is given solely by norms of conduct. In fact, the deontological theorist holds that only norms of conduct have genuine moral value. Norms of evaluation may have moral content only insofar as they are understood and used as a guide to action, i.e. insofar as they are read as norms of conduct. Kant is very clear on this. The merchant who acts honestly because he expects this to have the best consequences, the person who does not hurt another because he just cannot bear seeing another person suffer, the good Samaritan who helps other people because he partakes in their happiness, they all do the right thing. It may even be the case that they deserve our admiration or love for how they are. But as long as they act for the given reasons, as long as they do not act from general principles of conduct, their action has no moral content and our positive feelings toward them do not indicate moral quality. Kant's reason is that as long as somebody is just driven by his desires he is heteronomously determined. As he cannot actually choose his desires we cannot make him (morally) responsible on this behalf. He is acting autonomously only if he is acting from principles that he chooses, i.e. if he is acting from norms of conduct that he accepts as valid.

The deontological theorist does not necessarily claim that there are no valid norms of evaluation; he just thinks that they are not essentially moral. Nor does he claim that the evaluation of acts is necessarily independent of any evaluation of state of affairs. As a matter of fact, Kant's first formula of the categorical imperative indicates some relationship between a valid moral norm of conduct and the evaluation of states of affairs: "Act only on that maxim by which you can at the same time will that it should become a universal law." (Kant 2002, 222; 1968, 51) The phrase 'which you can at the same time will' points to some connection to the desires of a person. There are those maxims, which for logical reasons cannot be universal laws such as the maxim 'Do not keep your promises if that is to your advantage!', and which for this reason cannot coherently be wished to become a universal law.[8] Kant characterizes the related duties as "unnachläßlich" (Kant 1968, 55).[9] But other 'meritorious' duties ("verdienstliche Pflichten", Kant 2002, 225; 1968, 55) are grounded in the fact that some maxims, which are intelligible as general laws in principle, cannot be wished as a law, simply because we would not like to live in a world with such a law in force. These duties, therefore, have a fundament in our evaluations of states of affairs. One of Kant's examples is the duty to help people in desperate need. It is, argues Kant, of course possible that a general law were in force prescribing every person to act on behalf of her own advantage only. But we cannot wish this to be the case, as we have to face the possibility that the law turns against our own interests (Kant 2002, 224; 1986, 54).[10]

So what is substantially our duty may depend to some extent on the evaluations we (contingently) share as human individuals. Nevertheless, the crucial point for the deontological theorist is that the moral quality of an act is solely determined by the fact that it is motivated by respect and acceptance of the right principle of conduct—whatever his evaluations of states of affairs may be. The essence of deontological ethics does not seem to lie in any specific conceptual, logical or justificatory relationship between the good and the right but rather in the firm conviction that it is only by the acceptance of norms of conduct as authoritative, by acting from principles, that acts can possess moral quality.

Notice that consequentialist and deontological theory as defined above are just two extremes of a whole range of possibilities. The first holds that the evaluation of

---

8   If such a maxim were a universal law, the promising convention could not exist. So promises—and with them the proposed law—would be meaningless.
9   The English edition ignores this term; the related duties are just characterized as "strict or narrow" (Kant 2002, 225).
10 It is from examples as this that some interpreted Kant's practical philosophy and the categorical imperative as essentially rule-consequentialist. I do not think that this is adequate, but it seems fair to say that Kant did in fact accept some rule-utilitarian arguments.

states of affairs is fundamental to morality, whereas the second claims that only acting in accordance with norms of conduct can have moral quality, and, thus, an evaluation of acts is fundamental. But morality may actually have a richer structure with both, norms of conduct *and* norms of evaluation, as essential elements. I do believe that something like this must be true. In the next two sections I will argue that neither consequentialism nor deontological ethics can give a satisfying account of the way our life is influenced and determined by morality. So both must be wrong.

5. *Consequentialism*

The consequentialist holds that the evaluation of states of affairs is fundamental in morality. Acts are evaluated according to the evaluation of their consequences. Every act is conceived of as a poiēsis (Aristotle, NE, 1140a), a making or bringing about something, which has no intrinsic (moral) value apart from the value it produces. Norms of evaluation then suffice as a guide to (morally) right conduct. Because she aims at the good a morally decent and instrumentally rational person acts rightly.

But consequentialism does, in fact, not provide a sufficient basis as a moral guide of conduct. The reason is simply that not every act can be conceived of as a bringing about of something. This is in particular true in social interaction. Consequences are often not determined by single acts, but by the interplay of several acts done by different individuals only. In social interaction no person can typically bring about what she aims at on her own. Therefore her evaluation of possible consequences may not suffice to determine what to do. As I will argue now, consequentialism fails because it miscomprehends and simplifies the relationship between what we should do and what we aim at.

My argument will be based on a simple game theoretic analysis. Game theory provides an appropriate framework to analyze the strategic interdependencies of social interaction. It also fits neatly to the fundamental assumptions of consequentialism. Within game theory a rational individual is completely characterized by its options, its beliefs and its preferences, which are usually represented by a utility function. Consequentialism also holds that a morally decent person is characterized by her preferences. Moreover, what a person should do is, according to the consequentialist, determined by what an instrumentally rational individual with moral preferences would do. Game theory analyzes the implications of instrumental rationality in social interaction.

Thus, in order to explore the implications of consequentialism we have to do two things. First we have to consider how morality may be incorporated in the utility function of a rational individual. Then we can, secondly, use game theoretical methods to find out how rational individuals would act in typical situations. If consequentialism is right, then all moral norms of conduct should be explicable as the demand of instrumental rationality based on moral preferences.

Such an attempt to analyze morality in a rational choice framework is, of course, quite common. A prominent example is Harsanyi's utilitarianism, which characterizes a moral individual by its social welfare function (e.g. Harsanyi 1986). Sen (1986) introduced an account of morality based on moral preferences and—in part following Sen—Hegselmann, Raub and Voss (1986) explored some of the consequences of different accounts of moral preferences determined by different transformations of utility functions.

Consider a situation with two individuals, none of which has full control over the results of his action, such that a mutually advantageous result can be realized only if both are guided by a norm. One may think, for instance, of two scientists working on similar problems, who might exchange information on their findings. Each may profit from the progress of his partner. But at the same time, sharing private information on scientific progress with another person before publishing means investing time and effort in communication and—what is probably more important—it may mean running the risk of being outperformed by the other and losing some or all of the benefits of authorship. So, there is an incentive to minimize on the amount and quality of information given away. Moreover, if one does in fact decide to hide crucial information, the other will not instantly be in a position to know that this is the case. Nevertheless, as both are aware of the possible mutual gain they agree on working together.

To keep things simple, suppose that the situation is conceptualized as a strategic interaction, in which both individuals have two options, namely either to cooperate, that is, to share all relevant information, or to defect, that is, to give away only minor or defective information. The situation as described has, of course, the structure of a Prisoners' Dilemma and it shares this general structure with most other situations of mutual exchange. Table 1 gives a conceivable representation of the situation in strategic form.

Table 1: Prisoners' Dilemma

		C_B	D_B
A	C_A	3, 3	-2, 5
	D_A	5, -2	0, 0

The entries in the table should be read as payoffs; they represent external incentives, which are supposed to be common knowledge. If both actors are solely motivated by external incentives, then game theory predicts that both would defect. Defection is their strictly dominant strategy and (D, D) the only equilibrium of the game. Of course we know that cooperation is in fact possible in situations with a Prisoners' Dilemma incentive structure as the one described. One of the reasons for that is that we are moral beings. There is a very strong intuition that morality demands cooperation in such a situation. Any moral theory that cannot account for such a demand at least in some of these situations must seem inadequate. In fact, as far as I know, all moral theorists that have been confronted with such situations have been engaged in justifying cooperation and some even claim that it is one of the most prominent social functions of morality to secure cooperation in dilemma situations (e.g. Gauthier 1986).

The consequentionalist will point to the fact that the numbers in the table represent payoffs only, not the actual preferences of the individuals. Preferences are formed by morality and should be represented by effective utilities. These utilities will be dependent on payoffs to some extend, but they might well be ordered differently. So the actual game played is different from the one given in Table 1. There is an additional difficulty here in that one cannot directly observe the moral properties of an individual. Actors will typically not know how the preferences are actually formed by morality. So the game will probably be one of incomplete information. To keep things simple, suppose that this is not the case. Both actors are moral actors and this (including the effective utility functions) is common knowledge.[11] How would morality transform the given payoffs into moral utilities?

The transformation that would most certainly secure cooperation would make cooperation the dominant move. Both should prefer mutual cooperation to exploiting the respective other and both should prefer being exploited to mutual defection. But this is certainly inadequate. If there are any at all, very few individuals will actually evaluate the results of a cooperative project in this way; and this is also true for those individuals that understand themselves as a moral person (or those that are perceived as being a moral person by others). Moreover, if morality worked that way, it is hard to see, how it could survive. A moral person would be an easy victim of exploitation. But it does not work that way. We just do not like to be taken advantage of, and, what is more important, as we understand it, morality does not demand that we should like it better than mutual defection. So this transformation does not mirror actual moral evaluations. Neither does it reflect our firm moral intuitions.

Hegselmann, Raub and Voss call effective preferences, which accord with the transformation just described, Kantian preferences (1986, 160). But this is a misinterpretation of Kant's theory. At best the transformation describes the preferences a consequentionalist would prescribe his individuals if he wanted them to act in the same way as individuals do that internalized Kantian Ethics. But Kant was not a consequentialist. He thought that the evaluation of acts was (at least relatively) independent of the evaluation of their consequences. So he thought we could prefer an act to another although we would not prefer its consequences. His point was precisely that we should cooperate even though there is a chance—maybe a good chance—to be exploited and even though we would hate this to happen.

What I think is true is that a morally decent person will actually prefer the results of mutual cooperation to being favored by a one sided defection. A moral person will feel very uneasy with an advantage at the cost of another who trusted her. But

---

11 The following argument does not depend on this simplifying assumption.

she will also prefer mutual non-cooperation to being the victim of exploitation. If that is true then the effective preferences of moral individuals in a situation as the one given will form an Assurance or Stag Hunt Game. The game actually played could e.g. be the one in table 2.

Table 2: Stag Hunt

		B	
		C_B	D_B
A	C_A	3, 3	-2, 2
	D_A	2, -2	0, 0

It may seem reasonable that both actors should and would cooperate in a situation like this. (C_A, C_B) is not only the unique efficient equilibrium it also promises the overall best result to each of the individuals. What seems reasonable, however, does not necessarily coincide with the demands of instrumental rationality. We may take a closer look at the situation from the viewpoint of rational actor A.

What A should do depends on what B is going to do. If B cooperates, instrumental rationality requires that A cooperates, too. But if B defects, A should also defect. As was assumed, A is perfectly informed about the options and preferences of his partner B. Can rational A on the given information reasonably expect rational B to cooperate? What reason can he have for such an expectation? As B is in the same position he will cooperate if he expects A to cooperate. So A should have a reason to expect B to have the expectation that A will cooperate. But, again, since B is in the same position B can have a reason for such an expectation only, if he expects A having the expectation that B cooperates. Obviously such reasoning can go on endlessly without ever reaching solid ground. There is no independent reason for any expectation of any order available. Any solution of the problem must presuppose that either one of the actors acts in some way or other for no decisive reason or that at least one of them does perform some acts on behalf of expectations that he cannot decisively substantiate.

Note that the problem does not arise due to a lack of information. In fact, both actors have all the available information, which could be relevant for choice from a Rational Choice point of view, at their disposal. There simply is no such information that could solve the problem except the information that one of the actors solves the problem in some peculiar way. So, there is no information to induce rational cooperation unless there is already cooperation for other reasons.

One might want to point to (C_A, C_B) being the efficient and unique overall best outcome (see, e.g., Gauthier 1975; Taylor 1987). But note that although a cooperative move may lead to the most preferred outcome, it may also lead to the least preferred. Defection is the maximin strategy (and in the given case it is even risk dominant). If there is doubt, defection may be preferable. Well, this is the very seed of doubt. How can anyone be sufficiently sure that his partner will cooperate under such conditions? One can only be sure if there is sufficient reason to believe that the other can be sure that oneself will cooperate. But the other one—again—is in the same position. Obviously the bottomless pit of arguments starts over again.

That Rational Choice theory cannot account for coordination even in very simple settings has been noticed and analyzed by different scholars, most notably by Margaret Gilbert (1989; 1990) and Robert Sugden (1991; 1993; see also Lahno 2007). My point here is that moral preferences (on state of affairs) cannot solve the problem of cooperation on the basis of instrumental rationality alone. They may weaken the problem by transforming a dilemma situation into a coordination problem. But instrumental rationality does not suffice to do the rest of the job, as the consequentialist would have to maintain.

It should be obvious how the problem is actually solved. In situations of the given form we usually share the opinion that the right thing to do is to cooperate, i.e. we accept and follow a norm of conduct. As the argument shows this norm of conduct cannot be reduced to rational decision-making based on instrumental rationality and moral preferences. It cannot be reduced to norms of evaluation in the way the consequentialist proposes.

Still, abiding by the norm of conduct is not completely independent of our preferences on outcomes. After all most people will believe that by following the norm they also serve their ends in optimal ways. And they are right. Once there is cooperation because some individuals abide by the cooperative norm of conduct and once this becomes apparent, it is finally rational in the pure sense on instrumental rationality to cooperate; and this is true not only for those abiding by the norm—those who thus gave the initial impulse for cooperation—but also for the others. A rational individual not committed to the norm but living in a society with some normative consensus that cooperation is the right way to act in situations as the one described will cooperate. This is his optimal answer to the way others act.

However, even if all individuals possess moral preferences instrumental rationality cannot on its own justify following the norm of conduct for every individual. It can, at least, not be a shared conviction (it cannot be common knowledge) that all individuals are solely motivated by moral preferences and instrumental rationality. By some the norm has to be perceived as non-instrumental, as a categorical rather than a hypothetical imperative. Some individuals must follow the norm independently of whether it is individually useful to follow the rule or not, because they think it is right, or sufficiently many individuals must believe that there are some such non-instrumental norm followers, or sufficiently many must believe that there are sufficiently many who believe ... If no such condition applies, there will be no fundament of instrumentally rational compliance with the norm. Cooperation is instrumentally rational because there is adherence to the norm; the reverse—that there is adherence to the norm because cooperation is instrumentally rational, as the consequentialist would claim—is not true.

Still, morality may very well be perfectly consistent with instrumental rationality.[12] And I think it must be—at least in the long run; otherwise it would go extinct. But this is not my point here.

As the argument shows there is no adequate account of morality based on norms of evaluation and instrumental rationality alone. Morality has to incorporate, and actually does incorporate some norms of conduct that are perceived as categorical imperatives, as committing independently of the given aims of a person. Morality needs such norms at least to solve the coordination problems that moral actors inevitably face.

6. Deontological Ethics

Consequentialism is wrong because it cannot account for the fundamental role of norms of conduct in moral life. Deontological ethics, now, hold that *only* norms of conduct have moral significance. Whatever the evaluation of states of affairs of an individual may be, according to deontological ethics it is irrelevant from a moral point of view. The moral quality of a person is exclusively determined by the rules of conduct that she accepts and complies with. I think deontological ethics are also wrong. My argument here will be rather tentative. I will argue, first, that deontological ethics give an insufficient account of our actual moral evaluations, and, second, that consequences do play a non-neglectable role in determining whether a norm of conduct is in fact binding.

One of the most disturbing aspects of deontological ethics is that it disregards many human qualities, which we usually hold of high moral esteem. Mother Theresa is the standard example. The person that we know as Mother Theresa is of the highest moral regard because she devoted her life to the well being of others. She was full of love and care for all her fellow human beings and invested all her efforts in their support. To most of us, the seemingly boundless affection for others makes a considerable—if not the essential—part of her moral excellence.

In contrast, it has no moral quality whatsoever from a deontological point of view. It may even devalue her conduct in moral terms. Somebody who acts from benevolence may do the right thing; she may act "pflichtmäßig". However, that doesn't make her a morally good person. She is only following her inclinations. What she does has moral value only in so far as it is motivated by duty rather than inclination.

Mother Theresa might in part act from duty. But her sense of duty will strongly depend on her affection for others. Because she cares for the well-being of her fellow humans she feels obliged to help them. But in the eyes of the deontological theorist this renders her sense of duty dubitable. Her acceptance of the norm of con-

---

12   Compare on this also Gilbert (1990, 12ff.).

duct is motivated by her evaluation of states of affairs. The norm is, in a sense, accepted only as a hypothetical imperative.

It seems to me that this is a misconception of what we usually mean by moral excellence and morality. Of course one can define morality such that acting from inclination is principally a-moral by definition. But morality such defined is essentially different from morality as we usually understand the concept. There are different kinds of inclinations, good and bad. And they may very well be good and bad in a moral sense,—at least as the word is usually understood. A person, who is inclined to help if she sees somebody suffer, is perceived as a morally good person. Another person may probably enjoy watching somebody suffer. Something is wrong with that person. And as long as we cannot or do not trace his strange desire back to a physical defect, we will blame her morally: she is just evil.

That we do actually evaluate others morally according to their inclinations is shown by the importance we attach to norms of evaluation and by the effort that we invest in that part of moral education of our children. We want our children to have the right attitudes. So we try hard to convey a certain perspective of the world to them. We want them to learn what is valuable and what and who is to be respected. We do not merely tell them what they should do or what is forbidden to do, we make great efforts to make them experience what is worthwhile to be striving for.

My second argument is related to Max Weber's argument against an ethics of principled conviction (Weber 1994, 359–369). Weber characterizes an ethics of principled conviction ("Gesinnungsethik") as an ethical theory that derives norms of conduct from ultimate values and then demands absolute obedience to the norms. Confronted with social reality an adherent to such an ethical theory will regularly be confronted with a fundamental problem. His morals command to reject all unethical conduct. But at the same time he is urged to do everything to worship his ultimate values even if his individual effort will have no effect on actually furthering the realization of these values. Too often he will stick to an unquestioning devotion of his values, no matter what the consequences are. The reason is simply that in his devotion to absolute ultimate values he is disposed to ignore the consequences of individual acts. If consequences are bad, it is not on his fault. After all he is striving for the good. If that has bad consequences the wickedness of the world is to blame: "If evil consequences flow from an action done out of pure conviction, this type of person (the adherent of an ethics of principled conviction, B.L.) holds the world, not the doer, responsible, or the stupidity of others, or the will of God who made them thus." But an "ethics of responsibility" ("Verantwortungsethik") demands that we should not neglect the actual consequences of our acts in favor of following abstract principles derived from idealizations that do not in fact apply: "A man who subscribes to an ethics of responsibility, by contrast, will make allowances for precisely these everyday shortcomings in people. He has no right, as Fichte correctly observed, to presuppose goodness and perfection in human beings." (Weber 2004, 262) Weber's problem with an ethics of conviction is a general problem for any deontological ethics. Because individual consequences are morally insignificant in deontological ethics moral action may produce the most terrible consequences, consequences, in fact, which we detest for moral reasons. And the moral actor may be completely aware of this.[13]

The categorical imperative tells us that we should act only according to those maxims, which we can will to become a universal law. But what if we realize that, given the world as it actually is, our will turns out to be just wishful thinking? What if we very well know that the maxim is by no means and—in view of how things actually are—cannot be a (socially realizable) law? What if an individual act according to the maxim will not only not help realizing the law, but will in fact have consequences, which we cannot will? Kant will answer, that our (good) will is directed to right conduct only, not directed to consequences, which are the objects of our desires only. So consequences are irrelevant. But he is certainly wrong.

I believe that Kant borrowed the idea of the categorical imperative from Hume's analysis of artificial virtues (Hume 1978; see also Lahno 1995). Acting according to an artificial virtue has the decisive property. It is acting irrespective of individual consequences. The norm of conduct is accepted not because the according act is individually advantageous but rather because we appreciate the general practice according to the norm. Kant found that acting from such norms was the essence of morality thereby neglecting Hume's natural virtues. What he overlooked is that Hume's artificial virtues have an empirical grounding. They are not just schemes of conduct that we would will to come generally true, they are firmly rooted in existing—at least in evolving—social conventions. They are true or at least possible to become true.

In the last section I argued that in a coordination problem we need some individuals who are willing to do the right thing irrespective of the individual consequences of their act. But, of course, if there was no actual chance that coordination could be achieved by doing what is supposed to be the right thing, then it would not be the right thing. We may still wish that the norm of conduct would be established, we may even have the duty to do everything to make it become generally accepted. But as long as there is no chance for sufficient compliance and no chance to raise the chance by individual action, nobody can be obliged to act according to a norm of conduct that is suitable to serve as a coordination guide in principle only, but cannot in fact do so.[14] Norms of conduct may fail to gain or loose their normative power for empirical reasons. If the general conditions are such that the norm of conduct is lacking committing power, then, of course, consequences of individual acts must matter. If this is true then there is an essential role of evaluative schemes of consequences in morality and deontological ethics must be wrong.

---

13 Kant gives an impressive and—to my mind—repulsive example in his reflections on the (not existing) right to lie (Kant 1977).
14 Hobbes uses a similar argument in a somewhat different context, when he argues that in the state of nature (which is a state without any chance of coordination) the Laws of Nature oblige in foro interno, but not in foro externo (Hobbes 1968, 215; cf. on this also Kliemt 1985, 27f.).

7. Conclusion

Morality encompasses both, norms of conduct that tell us directly how we should act, and norms of evaluation that only indirectly do so by telling us what we should value. If my arguments are sound, then both sorts of norms are essential to morality in theory and practice. Consequentialism holds that only norms of evaluation are essential to morality. From this perspective all norms of conduct can be understood as hypothetical imperatives to promote the good as defined by the valid moral norms of evaluation. However, consequentialism is wrong. It ignores the crucial role that moral norms of conduct actually play in coordinating social life, a role that they can play only if understood and acknowledged as categorical imperatives. By contrast, deontological ethics claim that only norms of conduct are morally significant. This is, however, also wrong. It misconceives our actual practice of moral judgment. And it cannot account for the crucial role that consequences and the evaluation of consequences may play in moral deliberation, especially when social coordination on a norm of conduct is not achievable.

There seems to be some tendency in common sense morality to frame moral demands in consequentialist terms. One reason for this may be that norms of evaluation are often a more general guide of action: They are applicable to many different sorts of situations generating the appropriate norm of conduct in each of them. Thus consequentialist ethical theories usually exhibit a remarkably clear and compelling structure. Very few general principles of evaluation suffice as a common ground of moral deliberation.

But some norms of conduct prescribe acts that cannot properly be identified by their consequences; so there is no grip for norms of evaluation. A typical reaction seems to be to define new sorts of consequences that consist basically in the fact that some norm of conduct is being observed or violated. It seems to me that the concept of dignity has such a source. It is very hard to say what the dignity of a person consists in. It is not a thing we can add to a person or take away from her, it is also not a genuine property a person has, nor does 'having dignity' characterize a specific state of affairs. Still, it is easy to see what it means to have dignity: It is just shorthand for saying that a person has certain rights, that others ought do treat her in specific ways. Someone's dignity is preserved if those norms of conduct are observed; it is affronted if they are infringed. The concept of dignity obtains its meaning essentially from these norms. Take the norms away and the concept becomes empty. So, the concept of dignity serves to group certain norms together. It frames these norms of conduct by bringing them under the heading of a norm that has the form of a norm of evaluation: You ought to respect the dignity of another person! But this norm does not tell us to bring about something particular. It is in fact a general norm of conduct. It tells us that we ought to treat the other in certain ways (whatever the consequences are).

There are other concepts like liberty, which, I tend to think, should be analyzed in similar ways. There is nothing wrong with such concepts. We should just avoid being deceived by the form of the related norms. Morality cannot be reduced to norms of evaluation. Neither can it be restricted to norms of conduct. Morality is just not as uniform and simple as we might wish or some might think it is.

Bibliography

Aristotle (1998), *The Nicomachean Ethics*. Translated with an Introduction by D. Ross, Oxford
Gauthier, D. (1975), Coordination, in: *Dialogue 14*, 195–221
— (1986), *Morals by Agreement*, Oxford
Gilbert, M. (1989), Rationality and Salience, in: *Philosophical Studies 57*, 61–77
— (1990), Rationality, Coordination, and Convention, in: *Synthese 84*, 1–21
Harsanyi, J. C. (1986), Individual Utilities and Utilitarian Ethics, in: A. Diekmann/P. Mitter (eds.), *Paradoxical Effects of Social Behavour*, Heidelberg, 1–12
Hart, H. L. A. (1961), *The Concept of Law*, Oxford
Hegselmann, R./W. Raub/T. Voss (1986), Zur Entstehung von Moral aus natürlichen Neigungen, in: *Analyse & Kritik 8*, 150–177
Hobbes, T. (1986), *Leviathan*. Edited with an Introduction by C. B. McPerson, London
Hume, D. (1978), *A Treatise of Human Nature*, Oxford
Kant, I. (1968), *Grundlegung zur Metaphysik der Sitten*, Frankfurt/M.
— (1977), Über ein vermeintes Recht aus Menschenliebe zu lügen, in: *Werkausgabe Bd. VIII (Die Metaphysik der Sitten)*, Frankfurt, 635–643
— (2002), *Groundworks for the Metaphysics of Morals*. Translated by A. Zweig, edited by T. E. Hill Jr. and A. Zweig, Oxford
Kliemt, H. (1985), *Moralische Institutionen. Empiristische Theorien ihrer Evolution*, Freiburg-München
Lahno, B. (1995), *Versprechen. Überlegungen zu einer künstlichen Tugend*, München
— (2007), Rational Choice and Rule-Following Behavior, in: *Rationality and Society 19*, 425–450
— (2009), Norms as Reasons for Action, in: *Archiv für Rechts- und Sozialphilosophie 95*, 563–578
Rawls, J. (1971), *A Theory of Justice*, Cambridge/MA
Raz, J. (1990), *Practical Reason and Norms*, Princeton
Sen, A. (1982), Choice, Orderings and Morality, in: A. Sen (ed.), *Choice, Welfare and Measurement*, Cambridge/MA, 74–84
Smith, M. (2005), Meta-Ethics, in: M. Smith/F. Jackson (eds.), *The Oxford Handbook of Contemporary Philosophy*, Oxford, 3–30
Sugden, R. (1991), Rational Choice: A Survey of Contributions from Economics and Philosophy, in: *The Economic Journal 101*, 751–785
Sugden, R. (1993), Thinking as a Team: Towards an Explanation of Nonselfish Behavior, in: *Social Philosophy and Policy 120*, 69–89
Taylor, M. (1987), *The Possibility of Cooperation*, Cambridge
von Wright, G. H. (1963), *Norm and Action. A Logical Enquiry*, London
Weber, M. (2004), The Vocation of Politics, in: *The Essential Weber*. Edited by S. Whimster, London, New York

Michael Baurmann

Categorical Commitment and the Emergence of Norms
A Comment on Bernd Lahno[*]

1. Norms of Evaluation and Norms of Conduct

Lahno differentiates between two kinds of prescriptive norms: *norms of conduct* and *norms of evaluation*. Norms of conduct "tell us what to do under certain circumstances"; norms of evaluation "tell us what to value" (95). Both kinds of norms are related to specific conceptions of morality: consequentialism holds that norms of evaluation are the fundamental moral norms, deontological ethics in contrast stipulates that principles of conduct are the basis of morality. However, *both* concepts claim that they could direct us in certain situations, therefore consequentialism too must lead to normative guidelines of conduct. The crucial difference is that in consequentialism the moral norms of conduct are *hypothetical imperatives* merely expressing "what we should do as instrumentally rational beings if we abide by the norms of evaluation" (101), whereas in deontologism a moral norm of conduct is "perceived as non-instrumental, as a categorical rather than a hypothetical imperative" (107).

Lahno argues that both kinds of norms are needed in morality. Moral norms of evaluation alone "cannot provide a sufficient basis as a moral guide of conduct" (96). This is especially true for situations with interdependent social interaction in which the positive evaluated outcome is "not determined by single acts, but by the interplay of several acts done by different individuals" (103) as it is paradigmatically the case in situations with the notorious Prisoners' Dilemma. In dilemma situations a norm of evaluation that creates a preference for the cooperative outcome would transform the dilemma problem into a less severe coordination problem. But even a common preference for mutual cooperation cannot by itself determine a specific way of acting, because the actors have no definite basis for reciprocal expectations: "even if all individuals possess moral preferences instrumental rationality cannot on its own justify following the norm of conduct for every individual." (107)

To overcome this stalemate and to facilitate the emergence of the required norm of conduct at least some "non-instrumental norm followers" are necessary who "follow the norm independently of whether it is individually useful to follow the rule or not" (107). Therefore "to solve the coordination problems that moral actors inevitably face", morality "has to incorporate, and actually does incorporate some norms of conduct that are perceived as categorical imperatives, as committing independently

---

[*] I am indebted to Margaret Birbeck who helped to make my English readable.

of the given aims of a person" (108). However, moral norms of evaluation are not irrelevant or superfluous: the moral reason to be committed to a categorical norm is not independent of the possibility that this commitment could bring about a morally valuable state. It follows that "both sorts of norms are essential to morality in theory and practice" (111).

In my comment I will not contest the quintessence of Lahno's analysis. Instead I will take it as a starting point, try to extend its scope and to argue that the results reach beyond the norms of morality and are relevant to our understanding of social and legal norms as well. But I will approach the issue from a sociological point of view meaning that I am not tackling the—ethical—question of how actors can justify conformity to certain norms of conduct by moral or non-moral reasoning but the question as to the empirical conditions under which actors will conform to certain norms of conduct—the question of justification still being relevant as a possible factor for motivation. Thus, the insights of Lahno's analysis are not only normatively but also empirically important.

In the following I will differentiate between conditions for norms to *exist*, and conditions for norms to *emerge*. Applying Lahno's insights makes clear that there is a crucial difference between these two seemingly similar sets of conditions and that to concentrate only on conditions of existence bears the risk of ignoring relevant aspects of an empirical theory of norms. I will discuss these issues with regard to moral, social and legal norms in turn.

2. Moral Norms

Lahno poses the question: under what *conceptual* conditions can moral norms provide a sufficient basis for a guide of conduct? My question is: under what *empirical* conditions can moral norms adopt this function? The two questions are closely connected: given that Lahno proves that moral norms provide an efficient guide of conduct if they prescribe certain preferences and/or certain actions then the empirical conditions for these norms to exist are those under which actors factually *accept* and *follow* these norms. Therefore Lahno's analysis can be used as a blueprint.

I will begin by exploring the conditions for a moral norm to exist. As I am interested in norms that are effective guides of conduct, I am interested in the existence conditions for moral norms of *conduct*—whether they are derivative and deduced from norms of evaluation or not. I will follow Lahno in focussing my analysis on norms that serve the crucial function of prescribing cooperation in dilemma situations like they do paradigmatically in a Prisoners' Dilemma. That is not the only function of moral, social or legal norms—but an essential function that surely deserves special attention.

The first step will be an itemization of the existence conditions of a moral norm of conduct which is based on a moral norm of evaluation.[1]

Empirical conditions for a moral norm to exist

Let N be a norm of conduct that prescribes cooperation in dilemma situations. N exists as a *moral norm* in a group G if for each individual i of G:
1. i conforms to N;
2. i conforms to N because i believes that
    (a) for moral reasons i should prefer all members of G to conform to N;
    (b) all other members of G conform to N.

Conditions 1 und 2 should specify conditions under which a moral norm exists in a group as a 'social fact'.[2] Condition 1 states that the members of a 'moral community' actually conforms to the norm in question—although 'conformity' should be understood in a wide sense, not excluding partial deviation from a norm. Condition 2 typifies the *moral dimension* of the norm N. It presumes that N can be designated as a moral norm because its followers conform to it on the basis of moral reasons. It is left open here what kind of reasons moral reasons could be. As the empirical existence condition 2(a) states that i as a matter of fact believes that these moral reasons are salient and that i is effectively motivated to act on the grounds of this belief. Again it is left open why i has this belief and why i has the disposition to be effectively motivated by it. But note that the moral reasons in 2(a) are not initially referring to N as a norm of conduct but to a separate norm of evaluation that requires i to adopt a certain *preference*: the preference for a situation in which all relevant members of a group uniformly cooperate. Condition 2(b) reflects Lahno's qualification that a "morally decent person will actually prefer the results of mutual cooperation" to one-sided defection but "she will also prefer mutual non-cooperation to being the victim of exploitation" (106). Therefore, i is a morally motivated *conditional norm follower*: i will follow a norm on the condition that the other addressees of a norm obey this norm as well and—together with i—can bring about the desired state of affairs.

If these conditions prevail, the existence of a moral norm is an equilibrium. All members of a group will conform to the norm because they want to maintain the preferred state of mutual cooperation and because they rightly believe that the other members of their group do so as well. They all have rational reasons on the basis of their preferences to follow the norm. Under these conditions N is a hypothetical imperative that is required by instrumental rationality and derives from a norm of evaluation as implied by 2(a). The conformity to this norm of evaluation *transforms*

---

[1] My analysis is partly influenced by the concepts developed in Bicchieri (2006) and Hart (1994); I discuss Hart's practice theory of norms in Baurmann (2009).
[2] I do not mention the possible impact of social sanctions because individuals in a dilemma situation have no incentives and/or no options to sanction defectors. The picture may change if we consider that sanctions may be imposed categorically. But this would fit into the general line of argumentation which is developed here.

the initial dilemmatic situation into a situation with a coordination problem; the actual conformity to the derivative norm of conduct *solves* this coordination problem: the expectation that the other members conform to the norm is a self-fulfilling prophecy under these conditions.

This result does not contest Lahno's central thesis that moral norms of evaluation are not a sufficient basis for guiding conduct. On the contrary, this thesis is in fact reinforced if we consider the empirical conditions for a moral norm *to emerge,* meaning those conditions under which a moral norm can be established in a situation in which this norm is not yet existent and in which, therefore, nobody already conforms to this norm. In such a situation, as Lahno argues, even if all members of a group would actually prefer the whole of the group—including themselves—to conform to a norm, they would have no rational reason for actual conformity because they can not solve the involved coordination problem. The disposition to conditional norm following that derives from the acceptance of the norm of evaluation in the sense of condition 2 is not sufficient for the empirical emergence of a norm of conduct. This becomes apparent if we delete the actual conformity to a norm from our scheme:

Empirical conditions for a moral norm to emerge I

Let N be a norm of conduct that prescribes cooperation in dilemma situations. There is a group G such that, for each individual i of G:
1. i conforms to N on the condition that i believes that
    (a) for moral reasons i should prefer all members of G to conform to N;
    (b) all other members of G conform to N.

It could be assumed that condition 1(a) is fulfilled under the same presuppositions as in the case of an existing norm. To believe 1(b), however, can not be rationally justified even if condition 1(a) is fulfilled and all members of G would prefer all of them to conform to N. Therefore N is not a hypothetical imperative for i which i could accept on the basis of instrumental rationality alone. Conditional norm conformity as expressed in condition 1 is not sufficient to bring about the emergence of N as a moral norm in G. It remains true that a disposition to conditional norm conformity which is based on a norm of evaluation transforms the original dilemma situation into a less demanding coordination problem. But more than a norm of evaluation and instrumental rationality is asked for to solve this remaining problem.

As Lahno claims, the gap could be filled if N existed (also) as a categorical norm: this would be the case if at least some members of the group conformed to N irrespective of whether conformity to N promotes their personal aims *and* irrespective of whether the other members of the group obey N or not. This, in turn, could be the case if some members of the group believed that moral reasons demand unconditional commitment to N. These moral reasons could—and should as Lahno argues—include a proviso that the overall result of norm conformity is appreciated and that there is a chance that a general practice of norm conformity is achieved (110). If such an unconditional norm commitment is exercised to a sufficient extent, it could provide an initial impulse for cooperation and also trigger norm conformity in the conditional norm followers who accept N only as a hypothetical imperative. Consequently, the empirical conditions for a moral norm to emerge must be complemented:

Empirical conditions for a moral norm to emerge II

Let N be a norm of conduct that prescribes cooperation in dilemma situations. N emerges as a *moral norm* in a group G only if there is a sufficiently large subset of G such that, for each individual i of the subset:
1. i conforms to N;
2. i conforms to N because i believes that for moral reasons
    (a) i should prefer all members of G to conform to N;
    (b) i should conform to N.

3. Social Norms

As in the case of moral norms, the focus is on social norms in their role as instruments to overcome cooperation problems in situations with dilemmatic structures. The difference is that, firstly, it is excluded from the outset that social norms may be norms of evaluation that prescribe certain kinds of preferences; social norms are considered only as norms of conduct that prescribe cooperation in the face of incentives to defect. Secondly, it is assumed that conformity to a social norm is not based on a disposition to accept moral reasons but on a disposition to conform to a norm on condition that other members of a group demand this conformity. Once again, the scope and possible origins of such a disposition are not discussed here. Against this background the existence conditions for a social norm can be characterized in the following way:

Empirical conditions for a social norm to exist

Let N be a norm of conduct that prescribes cooperation in dilemma situations. N exists as a *social norm* in a group G if there is a sufficiently large subset of G such that, for each individual i of the subset:
1. i conforms to N;
2. i conforms to N because i believes that a sufficiently large subset of G
    (a) prefers i to conform to N;
    (b) conforms to N.
3. i prefers the other members of G to conform to N.

Moral norms are *personal norms* and their existence is exclusively connected to people who accept these norms as orientation for their own behaviour. In contrast, a social norm is a result of normative expectations which are directed to *other* people. Therefore, we can already speak of a social norm existing merely if a 'sufficiently large subset' of a group accepts and endorses this norm. Normative expectations could be formative for a whole group even if not all of its members hold and express these expectations. Likewise, the social efficacy of a norm does not presuppose that all members of a group obey. However, as norm existence in the case of social norms should be used as a gradual concept, there is no need to define a crucial numerical threshold.

Condition 2(a) articulates the essential difference between a moral norm and a social norm by stating that an individual does not conform to a norm for moral reasons but because other members of a group demand conformity to the norm. Condition 2(b) reflects again the preference for not becoming a sucker and be exploited by defectors. The fulfillment of the third condition is a straightforward result of dilemma situations in which cooperative behaviour at least of others is preferable for each actor; its fulfillment also ensures the fulfillment of condition 2(a).

As in the case of a moral norm, it is easy to see that according to these conditions an existing social norm constitutes an equilibrium. The disposition to conditional norm conformity as expressed in condition 2 transforms the initial dilemma situation into a situation with a coordination problem because i prefers mutual cooperation over unilateral defection. And the—rationally justified—belief in a sufficiently high level of conformity of the other members of a group solves the coordination problem and makes conformity to a social norm an instrumentally rational strategy.

If we, on the other hand, consider the empirical conditions for a social norm *to emerge,* it comes as no surprise that also the same obstacles arise. Even if all members of a group actually would prefer all other members to conform to a norm and would be ready to conform themselves under this condition, they would have no rational reason to conform because of the intractable problem to mutually adjust their empirical expectations. The disposition to conditional rule following that derives from the acceptance of the *normative* expectations of the other members of a group is not sufficient for the empirical emergence of a social norm. That becomes obvious if we delete the actual conformity to a norm from our scheme.

Empirical conditions for a social norm to emerge I

Let N be a norm of conduct that prescribes cooperation in dilemma situations. In a group G there is a sufficiently large subset of G such that, for each individual i of the subset:
1. i conforms to N on the condition that i believes that a sufficiently large subset of G
   (a) prefers i to conform to N;
   (b) conforms to N;
2. i prefers the other members of G to conform to N.

Also in this case the disposition to conditional norm conformity transforms the original dilemma situation into a coordination problem. But even if the subset of G comprises all members of G, the disposition to conditional norm following is not sufficient to facilitate actual conformity to N. Though i can rationally believe 1(a), which means i can rationally believe that enough other members of the group demand i's norm compliance (because of condition 2), for well-known reasons i cannot rationally believe that the condition 1(b) is fulfilled.

From this follows that also in the case of social norms the gap has to be bridged by at least some members of the group conforming to a norm unconditionally, without aiming at the realization of an appreciated state of mutual cooperation and therefore without reference to the behaviour of the other group members. And as in the case of moral norms this requirement can be satisfied if conformity to N is perceived by some group members as a categorical demand which is independent of instrumental reasoning. But contrary to the case of moral norms the content of such a categorical commitment can have two different specifications:

Empirical conditions for a social norm to emerge II

Let N be a norm of conduct that prescribes cooperation in dilemma situations. N emerges as a *social norm* in a group G only if there is a sufficiently large subset of G such that, for each individual i of the subset:
1. either
    (a) i conforms to N;
    or
    (b) i conforms to N on the condition that a sufficiently large subset of G prefers i to conform to N;
2. i prefers the other members of G to conform to N.

Both variants of norm commitment can solve the coordination problem because both variants are independent of the norm conformity of other group members. And both commitments *can* be the result of moral reasons: in regard to 1(a) N could be a moral norm for i on the basis of moral reasons which categorically prescribe conformity to N; in the case 1(b) i may be ready to conform to N because i may accept a 'secondary' norm which prescribes conformity to a 'primary' norm if conformity to this norm is preferred by a sufficiently large subset of the members of a social group. Conformity to this secondary norm can again be motivated by moral reasons which demand subordination to the 'collective will'. Therefore, moral norms can play an important role as pillars for social norms. But whether i has moral reasons for norm commitment or whether other reasons or factors are effective, the relevant aspect is the fact that the empirical emergence of a social norm is dependent on the condition that at least some members of a group are committed categorically to this norm.

4. Legal Norms

The third variety of norms which are examined here are *legal norms* (or legal *rules* as is the linguistic convention in an Anglo-Saxon context). Again, we pick out the possible role of legal norms to facilitate cooperation in dilemma situations. Legal norms just as social norms are not norms of evaluation but norms of conduct. What distinguishes legal norms from moral norms and from social norms is that conformity to legal norms *as legal norms* is not based on a disposition to accept moral reasons or social expectations but on the disposition to conform to a norm on the condition that the 'legitimate' legal authority of a group demands conformity to this norm. In this case too, the exact content and basis of such a belief in the 'legitimacy of legality' is not discussed here. It should only be registered that this characterization of legal norms does not exclude the fact that a legal norm can be accepted by some or many people primarily as a social or a moral norm. The existence conditions for a legal norm can be stated accordingly:

Empirical conditions for a legal norm to exist

Let N be a norm of conduct that prescribes cooperation in dilemma situations. N exists as a *legal norm* in a group G if there is a sufficiently large subset of G such that, for each individual i of the subset:
1. i conforms to N;
2. i conforms to N because i believes that
   (a) the legal authority of G prefers i to conform to N;[3]
   (b) a sufficiently large subset of G conforms to N;
3. i prefers the other members of G to conform to N.

Condition 2(a) involves the *differentia specifica* of a legal norm: it is defined by a particular type of conditional norm conformity that refers to a legal source. Condition 2(b) once more corresponds to the preference not to be mistreated by defectors and free-riders and the third condition expresses again the dilemma situation in which each actor has a preference for the cooperative behaviour of others. Likewise, as in the case of moral and social norms, an existing legal norm transforms a dilemma situation into a coordination problem and enables an equilibrium of mutually adapted expectations.

The analogue to moral and social norms carries over to the empirical conditions for a legal norm *to emerge*. Even if all members of a legal community were actually ready to follow the will of a legislator and to conform to the legally enacted norms, they would have no reason to actually do so as long as all members of the community make their conformity conditional on the conformity of others. The disposition to conditional rule following that is based on the acceptance of the will of a legislator is not sufficient for the establishment of a legal norm.

Empirical conditions for a legal norm to emerge I

Let N be a norm of conduct that prescribes cooperation in dilemma situations. In a group G there is a sufficiently large subset of G such that, for each individual i of the subset:
1. i conforms to N on the condition that i believes that
   (a) the legal authority of G prefers i to conform to N;
   (b) a sufficiently large subset of G conforms to N;
2. i prefers the other members of G to conform to N.

---

3   I do not refer to legal sanctions as a possible incentive, because this would only shift the problem to another level: to legal norms that prescribe sanctions. At the ultimate level, conformity to the norms of a legal system cannot be based on legal sanctions (cf. Hart 1994).

There is no need to repeat the arguments to discover that an intractable coordination problem is again present and that the disposition to conditional norm conformity is not sufficient to produce actual conformity to a legal norm. Therefore, also for legal norms the gap must be bridged by at least some members of the legal community conforming to N categorically and unconditionally, without reference to the behaviour of the other members of their group. However, in the case of legal norms a commitment to a norm can have three different variants:

Empirical conditions for a legal norm to emerge II

Let N be a norm of conduct that prescribes cooperation in dilemma situations. N emerges as a *legal norm* in a group G only if there is a sufficiently large subset of G such that, for each individual i of the subset:
1. either
   (a) i conforms to N;
   or
   (b) i conforms to N on the condition that a sufficiently large subset of G prefers i to conform to N;
   or
   (c) i conforms to N on the condition that the legal authority of G prefers i to conform to N;
2. i prefers the other members of G to conform to N.

All three kinds of commitment solve the coordination problem because they are independent of the norm conformity of other group members. And in each case moral reasons can be the motivating factor: norm commitment according to 1(a) could be based on moral reasons which unconditionally prescribe conformity to N; in case 1(b) i's norm commitment may be the result of a moral norm prescribing conformity to norms on the condition that this norm is advanced by other group members; 1(c) refers to a secondary norm which prescribes conformity to a primary norm if conformity to this norm is the will of a legislator: conformity to this secondary norm can be motivated by moral reasons that claim a moral duty to conform to legally enacted norms. These findings can be summarized by saying that the emergence of a legal norm can be backed either by the fact that the legal norm is also accepted as a moral norm, as a social norm or is deduced from a moral principle of law obedience.

5. Conclusion

The main result of the foregoing considerations is the contention that moral, social and legal norms cannot emerge as pure conventions providing we understand by a convention an equilibrium of mutually adjusted behaviour that is based on instrumental rationality alone. If the conclusions we drew are correct, the existence and sufficiently wide distribution of categorical norm commitment is a necessary condition for the emergence of moral, social and legal norms. In the case of social norms these categorical norms can be moral norms, in the case of legal norms they can be moral and/or social norms. The theoretical insight that moral norms can provide a necessary ingredient for the existence of social norms and that moral and social norms in turn can support the existence of legal norms is in accordance with well-known facts. We know from experience that social norms are often combined with moral beliefs and that legal norms are embedded in social norms and fostered by moral convictions. But the relationship is valid also in the other direction: effective legal norms can provide a supportive context for the emergence of social norms because they can safeguard against free-riders and defectors, effective social and legal norms together can serve the same function for moral norms. Morality can thrive if morally motivated individuals can expect people without such a motivation to comply with moral norms for other reasons. A minimum of norm conformity guaranteed by social and legal norms can trigger norm conformity in morally motivated norm followers that, in turn, can support the social and legal norms of a group. Unfortunately, this mutual interdependence can not only result in a productive equilibrium and virtuous circle of effective moral, social and legal norms—it can also produce a vicious circle of norm erosion and decline.

Bibliography

Baurmann, M. (2009), The Internal Point of View as a Rational Choice? An Empirical Interpretation of the 'Normativity' of Social and Legal Rules, in: *Rationality, Markets and Morals 1*, 25–47

Bicchieri, C. (2006), *The Grammar of Society. The Nature and Dynamics of Social Norms*, Cambridge/MA

Hart, H. L. A. (1994), *The Concept of Law*, 2nd ed. with a postscript, Oxford

Edna Ullmann-Margalit

Surveillance, Privacy, Sanctions, Cleanliness: Norms and Values in the Kitchen-Camera Case[*]

1. The Incident

In the summer of 2007, a senior member of the Center for the Study of Rationality at the Hebrew University of Jerusalem arranged for the installment of a closed-circuit TV camera in the Center kitchen. An email went to all the members, explaining that the camera was installed to solve the problem of cleanness in the kitchen.

Within minutes, a response was circulated, expressing dismay: "I find this very offensive! [—] What kind of idea is this??" This message was the first in a torrent of emails: within a week, some 120 emails were circulated, using the internal mailing list of the Center.

A week later, I, as the director of the Center, ordered the removal of the camera. I should mention that my position—as well as that of the first email writer, just quoted—against the camera was, and remained, a minority position in the Center. In what follows, I make my case against the camera. Still, I attempt to canvass the set of issues involved in an even-handed manner.

Here is a sample of some of the main theses, in a condensed form:

- Surveillance for security reasons is different from surveillance for other concerns (such as cleanness).
- The problem with surveillance is not the fact that everything you do may be watched by someone, but rather the fact that there may be someone who is watching everything you do.
- There is more to privacy than wanting to hide.
- Confronting kitchen transgressors with proof of their misdeed is an act of shaming. Shaming sanctions involve a problematic set of costs: to the culprits, to the individual enforcers, and to the community as a whole.
- Zero-tolerance toward cleanness offenders is unacceptable within the context of an academic community.
- The tendency to under-discuss norms of cleanliness and to undervalue them is, in part, gender related, as cleaning activities are generally associated with women.

---

* Gil Kalai assisted me in writing this article. I wish to acknowledge my large indebtedness to him. I also want to thank Maya Bar-Hillel, Michael Biggs, Avishai Margalit, and Cass R. Sunstein for helpful comments on earlier drafts. A partially overlapping article, "The Case of the Camera in the Kitchen: Surveillance, Privacy, Sanctions, and Governance", is in *Regulation and Governance 2008/2*, 425–444.

- The kitchen camera affair touches upon a basic chord in many people's minds. This chord seems connected to some basic sensibilities determining people's life choices and core convictions.

The incident of the kitchen camera affords us a valuable, and in some respects hilarious, opportunity to reflect upon a large set of normative issues, exemplifying debates about norms, clashes of norms, trade-offs between norms, norm-related emotions, and more. It is the smallness, concreteness and seeming triviality of the incident that helps bring this large set of vexing normative concerns into a sharp relief.

I regard the incident as a sort of peeping-hole through which a large canvas, richly painted, reveals itself. In this essay, I try to delineate the main contours of the intricate painting that emerges, while constantly remaining aware of and referring back to the peeping-hole itself—namely, the kitchen-camera case—that gives us the particular perspective from which this exploration is undertaken.

The extensive email exchange among the members of the Center that took place during the week between the installation of the camera and its removal, serves me as an invaluable resource. I scatter quotes from it throughout the article, under fictitious names.

2. Background: The Center

The Center for the Study of Rationality is an academic research center within the Hebrew University of Jerusalem. It has about forty members (note: 'members', in what follows, are professors, as distinct from 'staff'), who come from more than ten different departments of the university. The members are bound together by their interest in interactive, strategic behavior and by loose adherence to the conceptual framework and methods of Game Theory (for more about the center see: www.ratio.huji.c.il).

The Center occupies the top floor of a lovely building on campus. Its premises include office space and public spaces such as a lecture hall, a seminar room, a common room etc. One of the Center facilities, and a hub of activity in its own right, is a well-equipped little kitchen. Much beloved by all, it is primarily frequented for its excellent espresso machine and a more or less constant supply of cookies. The maintenance staff of the HU cleans the kitchen every morning, five days a week. Otherwise, the upkeep of a clean kitchen throughout the day is up to its users. Most users clean up after themselves, most of the time. Occasionally, however, a crisis episode occurs in the kitchen: it becomes messy and dirty, sometimes quite seriously so.

3. Surveillance

The real discussion should be about why a bunch of intelligent, well educated, and probably well-meaning people in the center of rationality (no less!) cannot run their affairs without surveillance. I find it remarkable. [Jonathan, 5 Jul 2007, 20:46]

In recent years, people are growing increasingly accustomed to public surveillance. At airports and malls, in banks and supermarkets, in trains and subways, at the entrance to office buildings and to apartment buildings, closed-circuit television cameras are everywhere. Many of our daily steps are being watched and recorded; our private lives may be reconstructed to an unprecedented degree of accuracy and detail.

What is the appropriate reaction to the circumstance of near-ubiquitous surveillance?

Here are two contrasting possibilities. First, it seems reasonable to say that if we are becoming increasingly used to being increasingly watched by cameras, why should we care if we are being watched by one more camera. Seen in this light, a monitoring camera in a university-center kitchenette seems hardly a reason to get incensed. All-the-more-so since the camera is meant to serve the indisputable good purpose of keeping the kitchen clean and to help eradicate a-social free riding behavior.

The second, converse, reaction is at least as reasonable. It asserts that, given the unfortunate circumstance of almost ubiquitous cameras, we should do everything in our individual power to draw some lines wherever possible: we should fight a rear-guard battle to protect as much as we can of the shrinking private space around each of us.

To get a handle on this, let us focus on the purpose of the surveillance. After all, the reason we accept the ever stepped-up surveillance around us is that it is supposed to be in the service of enhancing our security. The protection of life and property is a purpose with which we do not wish to argue.

A camera in an academic center's kitchen, however, is a different story altogether. The very first email that protested the installment of a camera in the Center kitchen as "very offensive", went on to explain: "Especially since this is meant to promote neatness, rather than to prevent theft." [Miri, 28 Jun 2007, 12:59]

The distinction between criminal and non-criminal activities seems to carry weight here. Objecting to surveillance that is meant to help catch people engaged in criminal activities, such as planting a bomb or robbing the cash register, is different from objecting to surveillance that is meant to help catch people engaged in non-criminal activities. This remains true regardless of how obnoxious these activities may be, at least in the eyes of some—whether because of their free-riding nature or because of their intrinsic messiness.

"Little objection should be raised", said one email writer, "if someone were hired to sit all day long in the kitchen—for two shekels a day—in order to modify the colleagues' behavior." [Joel, 29 Jul 2007, 10:05] How does being watched by a

125

person, while you prepare your coffee, relevantly compare with on-screen monitoring?

Before addressing this question (in section 6 below), I note that visual Surveillance raises many questions. What is the relevant difference between the case in which the camera only transmits its pictures to computer screens in real time, and the case in which it records the images? Related to this is the question of whom to charge with the task of monitoring the screen, or with viewing the recorded tapes. How comfortable are the Center members with assigning this task to the Director (or to some other members on the Director's behalf) as compared, say, with charging the administrative staff with this responsibility? And how comfortable will he (or she or they) be with this task?

One interesting suggestion in this context that came up in the exchange was to connect the computers of all of the members of the Center to the closed-circuit television camera in the kitchen. The thinking behind this suggestion is that in this way the surveillance will be carried out by all (or by some or none) of the members themselves, but not by any 'central' authority, nor by the administrative staff.

If filmed, you may have further questions. You do not quite know what the camera caught, or how it will be interpreted or by whom. You also do not know whether there will be 'secondary use' of these images without your consent,[1] or when, by whom, or for what purpose. Finally, what is the line separating surveillance from voyeurism, anyway?

4. 'Reasonable Expectations of Privacy'

Altogether, I don't understand how the matter of privacy applies to a common kitchen. What would one want to do there 'privately'? [Isaac, 4 Jul 2007, 00:19]

An academic kitchenette is not a private space in the sense in which one's own kitchen in one's own home is. American law has a doctrine about 'reasonable expectations of privacy', according to which unless there exists a 'reasonable' expectation that what one does or says in a certain place will not be seen or heard by someone else, no warrant or court order is required for conducting a surveillance operation by law enforcement authorities in that place.[2] The question therefore turns on how one establishes whether, in a given instance, one's expectation of privacy is 'reasonable'.

---

1 'Secondary use' refers to the use of data obtained for one purpose for a different and unrelated purpose without the person's consent.
2 This doctrine was developed in connection with the Fourth Amendment's protections (enacted in 1791) against "unreasonable searches and seizures". For more see LaFave (1996), Nissenbaum (2004, 112, 117–8), Katz v. United States, 389 U.S. 347, 360–61 (1967), and also http://www.notbored.org/privacy.html.

Given the four criteria laid down by US law for establishing reasonable expectations of privacy (which I shall not elaborate here), expectations of privacy are not reasonable in the Rationality Center's kitchen. Hence, strictly speaking no violation of privacy occurs when the kitchen is monitored by closed-circuit television.

Yet, one may still reasonably object to the surveillance on broader privacy-related grounds. One objection, for example, is based on the chilling and inhibiting effects of the camera. 'Chilling effects' is a legal term used mostly in the US to describe a situation where conduct in general, and speech in particular, is self-suppressed for fear of being penalized.

Surveillance of any sort can create chilling effects on people's conduct, inhibiting them from acting spontaneously and unselfconsciously. Surveillance cameras are interventionist measures: their introduction affects people's behavior (like a thermometer whose insertion into the liquid might affect its temperature). Such effects are acknowledged as harmful in the political context, where free speech and other liberties essential for democracy might be chilled. The harmful effects will surely be at least as obvious and immediate in an academic context, where spontaneity, mutual trust and the free flow of ideas are all-important; and in the normally friendly, informal environment of an academic kitchen, especially so.

The basis for another objection will be a recent theory, labeled 'contextual integrity'. Its starting point is the observation that public surveillance seems to fall outside the range of the traditional approach to privacy protection that dominates contemporary legal and public discussion (see e.g. Gavison 1980), and it undertakes to explain why the commonly accepted theoretical and legal approaches to privacy fail to yield satisfactory conclusions in the case of public surveillance.

Introduced by Helen Nissenbaum (2004) and further developed by her and others, the theory of contextual integrity aims to offer a model of informational privacy.[3] When the machinery of this theory is applied in detail to the Rationality-Center kitchen, it appears to yield the conclusion that the installment of a closed-circuit television camera in it does constitute a violation of relevant informational norms; whether or not this constitutes violation of privacy depends, in the last analysis, on one's chosen definition of privacy.

---

[3] See, e.g., The Logic of Privacy, in: *The Economist,* January 4, 2007.

5. 'Nothing to Hide'

I see no reason for people to object to the camera in the kitchen, UNLESS THEY HAVE SOMETHING TO HIDE. And if they have something to hide, it should not be done in the common area. [Alex, 4 Jul 2007, 12:42]

The idea that the people who object to the camera have something to hide is so preposterous that it could only cross the mind of one who thinks everything in life is a simple strategic game. [Miri, 4 Jul 2007, 18:06]

As it turns out, the argument that a person who has nothing to hide should have no problem with surveillance comes up frequently in discussions of privacy issues. It is one of the primary arguments made when balancing privacy against security. "In its most compelling form, it is an argument that the privacy interest is generally minimal to trivial, thus making the balance against security concerns a foreordained victory for security." (Solove 2007)

In truth not only privacy in the kitchen, but also cleanness in the kitchen, are rather trivial concerns, at least in comparison with the Global War on Terror. Still, in non-security contexts, people come up with a number of instinctive retorts in response to the seemingly compelling 'If you've got noting to hide, you've got nothing to worry about' argument. Among the typical examples: 'This is not about something I want to hide: this is about it being none of your business', or 'If you had nothing to hide you would not have curtains'.[4]

Concealment pertains not only to criminal acts. People are much preoccupied with concealing wrinkles on their faces or their loss of hair. Elton John had a perfectly just complaint against the paparazzi who showed him to the world without his wig. People's attitude to their private parts, intimate relationships, serious illnesses or the details or their bank accounts makes them want to shield all these from anyone's uninvited gaze.

'Something to hide' is obviously taken by most people as a much broader category than wrongful doing or something to be ashamed of;[5] and what people want to protect as *personal* goes beyond what is strictly defined as *private*. The concept of intimacy indeed presupposes concealment: where everything is known and revealed to all, intimacy is precluded.

"We don't want to expose ourselves completely to strangers even if we don't fear their disapproval, hostility or disgust", says Thomas Nagel, in his insightful chapter on the larger topic of what he takes to be the importance of concealment as a condi-

---

4   Some guidebooks to Amsterdam, in their section about the famous Red Light District, talk of Calvinist open-curtain culture proclaiming to the world that nothing untoward is happening behind their front doors; the architecture of many Dutch houses indeed allows for an uninterrupted view from front to back.
5   For an opposite view, consider Richard Posner's ([1973] 2007), according to which privacy consists of a person's right to conceal discreditable facts about himself.

tion of civilization. "The boundary between what we reveal and what we do not, and some control over that boundary, is among the most important attributes of our humanity." (Nagel 2002, 4) "The 'nothing to hide' argument … forces the debate to focus on its narrow understanding of privacy." (Solove, 23) There is more to privacy than wanting to hide.

6. Being Watched

Cameras are feared more than people because people are there and you adjust your behavior. [Rachel, 30 Jun 2007, 08:12]

What difference does it make whether we are being watched by a person or by a camera?

One difference concerns symmetry. When a person watches you, you can watch him or her back. When you know that you are being watched but cannot watch back, an asymmetrical relationship is initiated, leading to an asymmetrical power relationship with the potential to engender feelings of humiliation.

The one-sided mirror—say between an employer's room and the employees'—provides an example. Or think of that quintessential scene from war movies, where the sergeant major inspects the new recruit, moving his eyes over the rooky from top to bottom and back and forth, while the new recruit has to fix his gaze straight ahead (Margalit 2001). The asymmetry of gaze strongly attests to the asymmetry of power. Movies by directors like Kieslowski or Egoyan come to mind too for exploring with detail and fascination the theme of voyeurism, or the uninvited asymmetrical gaze, and its ramifications.

When you are in the public space, say when you walk about in the mall or the municipal park, you know that every step you make may be watched by someone. There is no problem here. There *is* a problem, however, when one particular person is or may be watching your every step. This can be sinister: you are being followed, or stalked, or worse.[6]

The problem with surveillance, then, is not the fact that everything you do may be watched by someone—but rather the subtly different fact that there may be someone who is watching everything you do. This, to me, is the heart-of-the-matter, one of the main insights I have come with from researching this issue: that so much hangs on the switch in the order of the quantifiers.[7] And the corollary problem with video

---

[6] Consider the lyrics of the well-known song of the *Police*: "Every breath you take / Every move you make / Every bond you break / Every step you take / I'll be watching you." The beauty of Sting's song notwithstanding, the situation it describes is uncomfortably close to stalking.

[7] The benign case is 'For every step s that you make, there is, or there may be, person P, such that P is watching s'. The sinister case, in contrast, is 'There is, or there may be, person P such that, for every step s that you make, P is watching s'.

monitoring is that it is a setup that in principle makes it possible that there should be someone who is, or may be, watching you all the time.

In addition, it is often the case that the video monitoring is equipped with a recording device as well, without warning anyone about it. Also, once captured on tape, you may be watched over and over again. All of these elements are serious aggravating circumstances that go beyond the mere asymmetry of the gaze.

Much attention was given in recent years to Bentham's quaint notion of the *Panopticon*—a type of prison building whose design allows a God-like overseer to observe all prisoners without being seen by them. Foucault, famously, used the idea of the Panopticon as a formative metaphor of the project of modernism, highlighting the total loss of individual privacy—equated with the total loss of protection from centralized systems of unwanted gaze. Indeed Foucault took the idea of the Panopticon an important step further by talking about the drive to *self*-monitoring through the belief that one is under constant scrutiny (Wood 2003).

In the long subtitle to his treatise *Panopticon or the Inspection House*, Bentham mentions a list of establishments other than prisons, "in which Persons of any Description are to be kept under Inspection". Among them hospitals, madhouses, schools, and various work places. As the proverbial locus of privacy, the home of course provides the starkest contrast to the Panopticon and to the other 'inspection houses': home is meant to provide protection from any, and all, unwanted gaze. Where on this spectrum should we locate an academic research center within a university? Do we want to see it as a 'work-house' in Bentham's sense, thus closer to the penitentiary end of the spectrum, or rather as closer to the home end?

I take this occasion to note that the interface between my discussion of general issues raised by the kitchen camera case on the one hand, and their relevance to the specific case of the kitchen camera on the other, is delicate, indeed sometimes tenuous. Of course, the kitchen in the Rationality Center would not have become a panopticon had the camera remained, so it may strike one as an over-exaggeration to bring up the notion of the panopticon in this context. A similar feeling of disconnect may occur with regard to the discussion (above) of the chilling effects of the camera, or to the problem of shaming sanction discussed below, and possibly to further issues as well. I therefore reiterate the peeping-hole simile mentioned at the outset and point out that, rather than arguing for direct relevance, I take the incident of the kitchen camera as an opportunity to reflect upon a wide set of normative issues and to suggest some normative conclusions.

Here is a different tale about a camera in another academic kitchen. It might throw different—and helpful—light on our case.

"If I remember correctly, the first web-cam was used exactly to monitor a shared coffee room in a university. It involved computer science students who didn't want to walk to a different floor to get coffee if the pot was empty. So they set up a camera via the Web, to be able to see whether the coffee pot was full. This didn't cause any discussion of privacy." [Ofer, 4 Jul 2007, 18:48] The email message concludes: "It seems to me that the problem with the camera is not really the issue of privacy but rather of being 'checked upon'."

This is a correct insight. It looks as if the mere idea that one's image and activities are projected onto a screen is not what one objects to in general; it also looks as if the violation of one's privacy is not what one objects to in particular. What people find objectionable in the case of the Rationality Center kitchen camera is 'being checked upon'. People object, first, to the disciplinary purpose behind the installment of the camera. Secondly, people seem to be sensitive to the grotesque disproportionality of the surveillance device, relative to the purpose behind its installment.

7. Disciplining Behavior

Confronting people who were spilling coffee and sugar or not cleaning their cups based on video records is not going to be a lovely scene. [David, 29 Jun 2007, 09:25]

Suppose the closed-circuit television is connected to the computer screens of all members of the Center, so that anyone can watch what goes on in the kitchen in real time. No 'central agency' is charged with the disciplinary action: rather, the charge is equally distributed among all Center members.

This idea of peer discipline may appear attractive but its effectiveness is dubious. When it is everyone's responsibility to catch transgressors, it ends up being the responsibility of no one. Depending on who happens to be watching their screens at the relevant time, catching the culprits becomes a matter of happenstance.

If people do not make it their habit to connect to the closed-circuit television, the solution offered by it is ineffective. If they do, and they happen to see a colleague messing up the sink, or leaving the milk outside the fridge and the foam pipe un-wiped, what exactly are they supposed to do? Whatever they do, they might find themselves dealing with phenomena such as recrimination, badmouthing, rumor spreading, whistle blowing, or shaming.

All of these constitute part of the price that the Center community might have to pay for the methods it chooses to use for catching the culprits, and for punishing them. The adverse effects on the working atmosphere within the Center, and the possible damage to the values essential to the fabric of the Center community, need to be balanced vis-à-vis the value to the Center community of a clean kitchen.

Suppose, next, that a taped record is kept of all images transmitted from the camera to the monitors. Surely, the potential effectiveness of the camera for disciplinary purposes in this case increases significantly. Not only is it possible to discover who was remiss, but it is also possible to confront the wrongdoers with 'proof' of their misdeeds.

However, the very existence of the taped record cannot be taken lightly. Some rules and regulations have to be decided upon ahead of time, regarding questions like who can see the tapes, how to prevent their misuse or abuse in general—and access to them by non-approved parties in particular, how long they are to be kept, and more. Moreover, some second-order questions need to be addressed: what are the correct procedures to settle the procedural questions just posed (e.g., who decides who can see the tapes, etc.). I am not suggesting that these issues are insurmountable; but I am saying that they are delicate matters, to be addressed with tact, and with due transparency.

Let us now consider the act of confronting the transgressors with on-camera proof of their misdeeds, reminding ourselves that the transgression in question is not a criminal offense or felony. Nor is it even a disciplinary offense in the usual sense (like cheating in an exam, or plagiarism) but rather a misdeed of a different, 'softer' nature.

The idea of using surveillance cameras (or polygraphs, for that matter) within the family is, to most people, unthinkable. When you find a dirty sink, or un-wiped coffee stains on the floor, at home, you may tell your children off, even punish them. But already when it comes to your spouse, the question of confronting him or her is not an altogether simple matter. Family politics and issues involving baggage from the past are often complicating factors (Ullmann-Margalit 2006).

When the culprits are one's colleagues, the issues are comparably complex, perhaps even more so. In analogy to the case of the family, it may be better, and wiser, to hold back. Moreover, it may be wrong to see the act of confronting a transgressor with proof of his or her misdeed as a triumphal act, parallel to the clinching climax of a criminal court case: we must see it, rather, in the different light of an act of shaming.

8. Shaming and Shaming Sanctions

We also need a mechanism to deal with those who are 'caught'. I suggest that the first step will be a discreet conversation with [the Director] or somebody. [Rachel, 30 Jun 2007, 14:25]

To treat a person who forgot to return the milk to the refrigerator as someone who is 'caught' and who will, 'as a first step', be summoned to a 'discreet' conversation the Director, is mind boggling. [David, 30 Jun 2007, 21:59]

Shame is a private emotion. I am ashamed when I realize that what I said or did diminishes me in my own eyes; when I privately experience embarrassment and loss of self-respect (Williams 1993, 89). Shaming is a social act; one person putting another person to shame. It can also be public, when the act of shaming occurs in the presence of an audience, or of witnesses. Shame induced by a second party intrinsically involves elements of derision and contempt, and hence loss of dignity and humiliation (Nussbaum 2004; Margalit 1996).

In the Jewish sources, 'whitening' someone's face in public, namely shaming them, is likened to spilling that person's blood. The commandment not to shame is comparable in its importance to 'Thou shall not kill'.

The theme of shame sanctions has gained growing presence in the legal literature since the mid-1990's (e.g.: Kahan 1996; Massaro 1997; E. Posner 2000). Shame sanctions have a strong element of spectacle for the spectators, and shame for the offender. Their effects on the public can be politically dangerous; their effects on the offender violate human dignity.

Public punishments (whipping, flogging, dunking, branding) used to be an integral part of the old punishing traditions but have largely faded away. The current American practice "takes milder forms, such as requiring offenders to wear shirts describing their crimes, publishing the names of prostitutes' johns, or making offenders sit outside public courthouses wearing placards" (e.g. 'I am a Drunk Driver') (Whitman 1998).

Caught by a closed-circuit television camera, offenders are exposed red-handed, or actually dirty-handed. The exposure here is quite literal: one is seen misbehaving; perhaps one's misconduct is even broadcast on tape in the presence of others. The very exposure is meant to be, and to do, the condemnation.

Informal shaming sanctions may comprise scolding and rebuking, and also ridicule contempt, avoidance, shunning, and more. Of their several idiosyncratic features, one is that people's reaction to them is extreme: either one finds them easy to ignore, or one finds them particularly harsh and cripplingly diminishing of self-esteem. The effectiveness of such sanctions on people of the first sort is nil; with respect to the second sort, the effect is likely to be overkill, and hard to predict (Whitman 1998, 1091).[8]

Also, shaming sanctions seem particularly vulnerable to the phenomenon of diminishing effects. So, while the administering of a shaming sanction for the first time may have overkill effect, with consequences that are difficult to control and predict, its repeated use may prove ineffectual (cf. Harel/Klement 2007).

Stigmatization imposes costs on the enforcers too. In order for it to work, stigma relies on the active cooperation of individuals who must incur costs in privately sanctioning the offenders: the effectiveness of private sanctions is based on the willingness of individuals to incur such costs.

> Other things being equal, the larger the costs private enforcers incur in the imposition of private sanctions, the less the willingness of private enforcers to stigmatize, and consequently, the less effective stigma becomes. (Harel/Klement 2007, 358)

Assessing the costs borne by private enforcers is crucial therefore for predicting the effectiveness of the proposed scheme of stigmatization.

An academic center like the Rationality Center, as a community, must face the consequences for its morale and esprit de corp once it becomes a surveillance community. It must face the possibility that some of its members will become peeved, even humiliated, by the effects of shaming. It must also be concerned with the question of whom to charge with delivering the rebuke, whether this charge is fair, and what its costs might be. (And how about the idea of a camera recording the sanctioning proceedings too, in the spirit of 'guarding the guardians'?)

---

8 Kahan and E. Posner (1999, 386) also make the point that the stigmatizing effects may often be too large or too small, and thus they do not render themselves easily to achieving the desired results.

9. Changing People's Behavior

Game theory teaches us that one can modify people's behavior with the right incentives. [Alex, 6 Jul 2007, 10:51]

We put the camera, and if that does not work, then I suggest a high voltage fence as the next step... [Andre, 3 Jul 2007, 10:23]

The camera as such does not clean the kitchen. But can it guarantee a clean kitchen? Evidently some in the Center not only hoped it will, but were convinced it will. Why?

One line of thinking is, surely, that the camera deters potential transgressors from transgressing. The complementary line of thinking is, presumably, that if transgression does occur, then the camera enables catching the culprits. Once the culprits are caught and punished—and the news goes around—deterrence kicks in again and transgression stops.

Deterrence can work—up to a point. It is clear that sustained cleanness in the kitchen cannot rely on the camera's deterrence effect alone. Incidentally, for partial deterrence the camera may not in fact be necessary. As one contributor to the email exchange pointed out, "in some experiments by behavioral economists, merely having a poster of a face with big eyes on the wall markedly improved compliance".[9]

So far for deterrence. Let us now probe the complementary argument, about catching the culprits. What is the causal chain that supposedly connects the catching of the culprits with a clean-kitchen-forever? With what degree of confidence can we expect people's behavior to improve as result of disciplining measures?

Changing people's behavior is a notoriously complex business. Much of social science—and most of education—is about this. Psychologists and priests, criminologists and political activist, sales persons and advertising agencies—all of these and many others attempt to affect and change people's behavior. The methods they come up with range widely over persuasion, propaganda, brainwashing, coercion, conditioning, manipulation, formal and informal sanctions, incentives and disincentives, carrots and sticks. In an open society, the choice may be somewhat restricted.

Confronting a person with evidence of his wrongdoing and punishing him for messing up the kitchen may have the desired effect of 'teaching him a lesson'. But then, it may not. Or it may have the desired effect for a while and then wear off. When his colleagues hear about this, some may indeed improve their behavior in the kitchen. But then, some may not.

Why do some people react one way and others the other? Under what conditions is one reaction likelier than the other one and by how much? This is the stuff of complex social science. The puzzling point to me was realizing that for several of the participants in the exchange, the full success of the surveillance device was a

---

9   Bateson, Nettle and Roberts report an elegant study that backs up this statement, with regard to norms of generosity (2006).

sure thing. In their minds, the installment of a camera amounted—as a matter of necessary truth and logical certainty—to the achievement of one hundred per cent cleanness in the kitchen. Consider: "The dichotomy is not a false dichotomy; it's a real, practical one. If we want to keep the kitchen open—AND I DO—we either have the camera, or the administrative staff keeps cleaning it." [Isaac, 5 Jul 2007, 17:46][10]

In fact, the unbearable lightness of accepting this means-end connection was characteristic of the proponents of the camera, who saw the chain as an ultimate winning argument. Strikingly, this was not the case for the camera opponents, who had qualms with the normative aspects of the means-end chain. Here is a particularly telling comment, revealing how people's views regarding the anticipated efficacy of the camera device intertwine with people's views about its normative acceptability: "I suspect that the people who think this measure [i.e., the camera] is repugnant also don't think it will work, and the people who think it WILL work, don't find it repugnant." [Miri, 30 Jun 2007, 17:17]

One factor the proponents of the camera did not consider, but we surely must, is that the presence of the camera may start altogether unanticipated chain reactions, bringing about unintended consequences. For example, people may wish to avoid any encounters with the camera, and hence leave their dirty coffee cups all over the place rather than return them to the kitchen—thus raising the general messiness level at the Center, not reducing it.

The point is that people do not always respond in the way that somebody intended them to respond. Their reaction to the camera may diverge from the causal chain meant to improve their cleanness behavior in the kitchen. The design of human response to a novel technical device has its limits; sometimes it even backfires.

An attempt by a respected Los Angeles medical doctor to improve his colleagues' cleanness-related behavior was reported not long ago by Stephen J. Dubner and Steven D. Levitt (of *Freakonomics* fame).[11] Many medical studies have shown, they say, that hospital doctors wash or disinfect their hands "in fewer than half the instances they should". The story highlights how hard it is to change people's entrenched habits and how much effort can be required to solve the seemingly simple problem of changing people's hand-washing behavior. (See also section 10.3 below.)

---

10 Note, too, that the causal (not logical) means-end connection here is not free of potential obstacles and glitches of a technical nature. We might think, for example, of the possibility that the view of the camera is blocked, supposing two or more people are in the kitchen at the same time, or that someone obstructs the view on purpose. Again, the quality of the tape might be bad, or nobody is monitoring the closed-circuit television when a transgression occurs (assuming no recording takes place), and so on.

11 Stephen J. Dubner and Steven D. Levitt, Selling Soap, *The New York Times (Magazine)*, September 24, 2006.

10. Cleanness

Cleaning kitchens—or bathrooms, or other peoples' tushies—is not a violation of 'all notions of human dignity and decency and fairness'. [Miri, 5 Jul 2007, 22:16]

In contrast to the hospital case, cleanness in the Center kitchen serves no distinct instrumental purpose. Nobody is going to die because of a sub-standard level of cleanness in the kitchen. (Besides, the following morning the cleaner arrives.)

In the hospital, a policy of zero-tolerance toward transgressors is instrumentally justified; not so in the case of an academic kitchen. Bluntly put, I believe that zero-tolerance toward cleanness offenders is intolerable within the context of an academic community.

Even if insistence on an impeccably clean kitchen at the center serves no distinct instrumental purpose, habitual free riders and offenders should not be tolerated. Members of the community known habitually not to clean after themselves should not expect to be able to get away with this behavior. But occasional lapses and instances of absent-mindedness should be tolerated. A machinery of spying, catching, confronting, shaming and sanctioning—all in the name of reaching one hundred percent cleanness in an academic kitchen—is in my view unacceptable.

10.1 Is Cleaning Humiliating?

Let us distinguish between cleaning after others and cleaning after oneself. Cleaning after other people as part of one's job, or cleaning after babies, the sick, or the elderly of one's own family, involve no humiliation. When casual guests leave your bathroom-sink somewhat stained, you may barely register this. But if they are house-guests for several days and expect you to constantly clean after them, then you may well feel annoyance, irritation, aggravation and even insult and, on occasion, humiliation.

Humiliation occurs when loss of dignity is involved. Whether loss of dignity occurs does not depend on the act of cleaning itself. It depends largely on the intentions and expectations involved: on whether or not you perceive that the other person expects and intends you to clean up after them, and even more so when these intentions and expectations are systematic. To intend and to expect others to clean after you (when it is not their job to do so) is to indicate that you do not consider them your equals, or that you hold them in disregard. In normal circumstances, this is humiliating (Margalit 1996).

It so happens that in the Rationality-Center kitchen, (a) the three secretarial staff persons quite routinely perform little cleaning-up chores upon entering the kitchen (like wiping off the sink or the coffee-machine steaming pipe, etc); (b) most Center members know this; (c) it is not an explicit part of these staff persons' job description to do this; and (d) these staff persons are women.

In the email exchange following the installment of the camera, members on both sides of the argument expressed discomfort with this state of affairs. Many expressed the view that, regardless of how the camera dispute is resolved, the Center's secretarial staff should not be *expected* to clean up after messy members. (For fairness, however, I note that, occasionally, several Center members also perform such clean-up acts.)

10.2 The Social Norm of Cleanness

The norm of cleanness, simply stated, is as a social norm that enjoins us to leave a place no less-clean than it was when we entered it. As such, the cleanness norm is a special case of the norm of considerateness, which generally enjoins us to take other people into account when we act, so as to decrease the discomfort to them that our own presence or behavior might entail.[12] The note in the gym saying "Be considerate of others: wipe down the machines after use" is an example of the cleanness norm qua special case of the considerateness norm.

Some people, sometimes, go beyond the call of the considerateness duty and act in a supererogatory way: they go out of their way to help others or do others a favor. Regarding the cleanness case, such people would leave a place positively cleaner than it was when they entered it. In choosing to act this way, no loss of dignity is involved.

One of the participants in the Kitchen Camera exchange said the following: "I publicly pledge to always clean up after myself, and my guests, in the Center kitchen. I personally am adding the following, too: I will also clean the kitchen when necessary even if it is not my own mess." [Miri, 5 Jul 2007, 22:16] The first part of this statement Miri explicitly framed as a challenge to every Center member to undertake the same pledge; indeed as put, it recapitulates the cleanness norm. It is a pledge to do one's part in what is essentially a mutual, semi-contractual community-wide norm of behavior. The second part is different. In committing to clean up not just after herself but after others too, she pledges to go beyond the call of duty and expresses a personal choice, possibly implying the hope that the force of the personal example will impress the others and that they will follow suit.

Taken conjointly, both parts of this statement serve to make a further point, namely, that cleaning up after others, when it is one's own choice to do so, does not have to be degrading or humiliating. As is the case with many Good Samaritan-like acts, this is a supererogatory act and, as such, it is commendable.

---

12 Edna Ullmann-Margalit, *Considerateness* (unpublished manuscript).

10.3 Personal Cleanness

'Cleanliness is next to Godliness', goes a famous proverb. Cleanliness is a heavily laden notion in our culture, invoking ideas of moral cleanness, of uprightness, and of sexual and religious purity; extensively written about, inter alia, by such eminences as Norbert Elias and Mary Douglas. Dirt is equated with sin and defilement; cleanness with purity.[13] "Reflection on dirt involves reflection on the relation of order to disorder, being to non-being, form to formlessness, life to death", says Mary Douglas, and continues: "This is why an understanding of rules of purity is a sound entry to comparative religion." (2002, 7)

Disregarding the religion-related connotations, I note that norms of personal cleanness relate to the way we look and dress, to our habitual behavior at table, or in the bathroom, kitchen and bedroom—whether in our own home, in the homes of others, or in public places too.

There can be no question that, regarding norms and standards of personal cleanness, huge differences exist synchronically, between cultures, and diachronically, within our own culture at different historical periods. Just think of the counterculture of the 1960s and 1970s, with its substandard, 'non-bourgeois' norms of appearance and cleanness.

Even here and now, there are significant individual differences that are by-and-large tolerated within the vague boundaries of what our society considers socially acceptable cleanness. If challenged, each of us will be able to think of examples from our own circle of acquaintances, of meticulously clean people as opposed to substandard ones. We all know that within the family, too, standards may vary: spouses find themselves clashing over toothpaste stains in the bathroom sink, and adolescent kids often direct their rebellion at the home's cleanness standards. Ultimately, our cleanness standards are a highly personal matter, having much to do with our upbringing and parental home model.

It is difficult to change adult people's cleanness-related behavior and standards, perhaps even more difficult than to change people's behavior in general. Personal cleanness is entrenched in habits, which are "sort of second nature" (Ryle 1949, 41–42) and notoriously difficult to alter.

Private employers may set their own standards for their employees' appearance and personal cleanness; in the public sector, this is more complicated. As for the university, in principle it should serve as a model of toleration regarding faculty's idiosyncrasies and non-conformist behavior, including colleagues' deviation from prevailing standards of personal cleanness in particular. Still, the questions of how to handle those who breach the *social* norm of cleanliness (namely, cleaning after one-

---

13 It is no accident that the Boy Scouts' tenth law "A Boy Scout is clean in his thoughts, words, and deeds" was originally phrased by Baden-Powell as "A scout is pure in thought, word and deed", with unmistakable sexual connotations regarding the dread sin of "self-abuse". (See Rosenthal 1984)

self), what sanctions to impose and who should impose them—these, in the academic setting, are delicate matters indeed.

10.4 Gender Issues

Gender stereotypes inevitably loom large when dealing with issues of cleanliness. So, too, does the question of how high, or how low, are the stakes involved. To be sure, compared with the stakes involved with national security or personal safety, the stakes in connection with kitchen cleanness are lower. It would be a mistake however to infer from this that matters of cleanness, in and of themselves, are trifle and that the stakes they involve are inherently low. It may well be the case that the importance of cleanness in general and of cleanness-related norms in particular, is often overlooked precisely because of the tendency to associate cleaning activities with women (DeVault 1991).

In the case of the Rationality Center, the gender connection had to do less with the members (i.e. the professors) and more with the administrative staff. Over the years, the staff members did pick up the cleaning slack whenever the occasion arose and, over the years, the members of the Center had come to take this as quite natural. These states of affairs would never have taken place had not the staff members in question been women.

11. Governance and Process

Let me suggest to conclude this lengthy and sometime heated debate by casting a vote (electronically) among the Center's members. [Benny, 5 Jul 2007, 12:22]

Who, and how, should have made the decision about the kitchen camera? Should it have been a management decision, or rather a democratic, Center-wide decision? If the latter, then do all members have equal weights, or do the kitchen users and coffee drinkers have weightier votes? Should the non-kitchen users vote at all?

Furthermore, if only a minority of members object to the camera, but they feel very strongly about this, basing their objection on deeply held principles—ought the case still to be decided by majority vote? Or is this a case in which veto power might be granted to the opposition, no matter how small?

I do not have a proper grip on arguments that might justify vetoing rather than voting. Nevertheless, I find this question, as well as the previous ones, troubling. I conclude that, on the rare occasion that an academic community must make a decision that touches upon deeply held beliefs of some of its members, the question whether majority rule ought to prevail remains open.

12. Epilogue

I don't think that Rabelais or Swift or Waugh could have invented something as hilarious as the discussion that took place here. Keep the good work, folks. [Jonathan, 1 Jul 2007, 10:00]

What are my lessons from this incident?

One lesson has to do with the notion of solution. As noted by one email, "a dirty kitchen is disgusting. A camera-surveyed kitchen is repugnant. On balance, I am not sure the solution is better than the problem." Reflecting on the matter, I realize that a lot hangs on what one means by a solution here. Is it appropriate to strive for a solution that guarantees 100% cleanness, such that no dirty episode occurs in the Center kitchen, ever?

If we focus on the notion of the 'problem' rather than on the 'solution', perhaps we shall come to realize that this may be one of those cases (familiar to clinical therapists), in which a solution—or a resolution—is achieved largely by learning to accommodate to, and to live with, the problem. Namely, perhaps the solution here lies with teaching ourselves to live with somewhat lower standards of cleanness than what some of us expect at home, and with wiping up after others, occasionally. In any case, we can comfort ourselves with the thought that by the next morning the place will be clean again.

A second lesson derives from a striking observation about the email exchange. It is that most Center members made up their minds about the issue instinctively and instantaneously: their instincts were made up before their minds were. This contrasts with the attitude of many people to moral dilemmas, where they find themselves agonizing long and hard about what their opinion should be.

The corollary observation is that most of the participants in the exchange felt that the natural light of obviousness is on their side; they seemed not to recognize the potential validity, or even legitimacy, of the opposite attitude. People on each side of the argument tended to see the alternative to their own view as ridiculous, disingenuous, and even perverse.

So I gained the insight that cases of public surveillance are troublesome because they seem to "drive opponents into seemingly irreconcilable stances" (Nissenbaum 2004, 101). The new methods of gathering information drive some people into indignation, while others remain unconvinced and even puzzled by what they consider a mere dislike of new technologies and practices. It seems that traditional theoretical frameworks fail to handle these conflicting attitudes and stances.

I share with you, then, the speculation that the kitchen camera affair, its triviality notwithstanding, touches upon a basic chord in many people's minds. This chord, moreover, seems connected to key sensibilities determining our essential life choices and core convictions about broad social issues.

In the months following the Kitchen Camera incident, I had occasions to tell various people the story of the Curious Incident of the Camera in the Kitchen. The idea of an academic community acting as its own Big Brother in the name of kitchen cleanliness variously regales and appalls the listeners. But I am also invariably asked how clean is the kitchen now. Well, the answer is that, overall, it has been kept reasonably clean, thank-you-very-much.

This is of course partly attributable to the effect of the email exchange itself, which helped heighten people's awareness of their personal responsibilities in the kitchen. Also, a number of additional measures were taken. For example, the doorstopper was removed, so that the kitchen door now slams shut and can only be opened with a key, thus reducing the chance that unauthorized persons will use the kitchen and, again, serving as a reminder.

Finally, in a brilliant move, one Center member put up a big sign next to the electric fan on the kitchen wall (where the camera was), proclaiming "CLOSED-CIRCUIT fan IN OPERATION". In doing so, he succeeded in artfully reminding people of the note about the camera that was there before and thus, vicariously, in gently nudging them to clean up. He thereby also succeeded in producing some good-natured smiles—which may well be the appropriate response to the Curious Incident of the Camera in the Kitchen anyway.

Bibliography

Bateson, M./D. Nettle/G. Roberts (2006), Cues of Being Watched Enhance Cooperation in a Real-World Setting, in: *Biology Letters 2*, 412–414

Bentham, J. ([1787] 1995), Preface to Panopticon or the Inspection House, in: M. Bozovic (ed.), *The Panopticon Writings*, London, 29–95

Braudway, B. (2004), Scarlet Letter Punishment for Juveniles: Rehabilitation through Humiliation?, in: *Campbell Law Review 27*, 63–90

DeVault, M. L. (1991), *Feeding the Family: The Social Organization of Caring as Gendered Work*, Chicago

Douglas, M. ([1966] 2002), *Purity and Danger*, London and New York

Gavison, R. (1980), Privacy and the Limits of Law, in: *Yale Law Journal* 89, 421–471

Harel, A./A. Klement (2007), The Economics of Stigma: Why More Detection of Crime May Result in Less Stigmatization, in: *Journal of Legal Studies 36*, 355–378

Kahan, D. M. (1996), What Do Alternative Sanctions Mean?, in: *Chicago Law Review 63*, 591–653

— /E. A. Posner (1999), Shaming White-Collar Criminals: A Proposal for Reform of the Federal Sentencing Guidelines, in: *Journal of Law and Economics 42*, 365–91

LaFave, W. R. (1996), *Search and Seizure: A Treatise on the Fourth Amendment (3rd edition)*, St. Paul/Minn.

Margalit, A. (2001), Privacy in a Decent Society, in: *Social Research 68*, 255–269

— (1996), *The Decent Society*, Cambridge/MA

Massaro, T. M. (1997), The Meanings of Shame: Implications for Legal Reform, in: *Psychology, Public Policy and Law 3*, 645–704

Nagel T. (2002), *Concealment and Exposure*, Oxford

Nissenbaum, H. (2004), Privacy ad Contextual Integrity, in: *Washington Law Review 79*, 101–139

Nussbaum, M. (2004), *Hiding from Humanity: Disgust, Shame and the Law*, Princeton

Posner, E. A. (2000), *Law and Social Norms*, Cambridge/MA

Posner, R. A. ([1973] 2007), *Economic Analysis of the Law (7th edition)*, New York

Rosenthal, M. (1984), Recruiting for the Empire: Baden-Powell's Scout Law, in: *Raritan: A Quarterly Review 4*, New Brunswick

Ryle, G. (1949), *The Concept of Mind*, Harmondsworth and Middlesex

Solove, D. J. (2007), 'I've Got Nothing to Hide', and Other Misunderstandings of Privacy, in: *San Diego Law Review 44*, 1–23

Tönnies, F. ([1887] 2001), *Community and Civil Society* (ed. J. Harris), Cambridge

Ullmann-Margalit, E. (2006), Family Fairness, in: *Social Research 73*, 575–596

Whitman, J. Q. (1998), What is Wrong with Inflicting Shame Sanctions?, in: *The Yale Law Journal 107*, 1055–1092

Williams, B. (1993), *Shame and Necessity*, Berkeley

Wood, D. (2003), Foucault and Panopticism Revisited, in: S*urveillance & Society 1*, 234–239

Michael Biggs

Storm in a Teacup?
A Comment on Edna Ullmann-Margalit

Most of the conference was pitched at a high altitude of conceptual abstraction. This article is a refreshing descent to a specific example of norms and values. The insufficiency of social norms to maintain a clean kitchen led someone to install a closed-circuit television camera; subsequent debate over the legitimacy of surveillance illustrates how clashing values generate social conflict. The author provides a rich and detailed description of university life (and advertises culinary facilities that most academics will envy!). My comments are divided into three sections. The first analyzes the problem of keeping the kitchen clean within the familiar framework of collective action. The second section poses the challenge of explaining long-term transformations in values, focusing on the value of privacy. The final section emphasizes the importance of emotions.

At the most basic level, the author analyzes a problem of collective action. When a kitchen is used by many people, cleanliness is a collective good. Everyone benefits from a clean kitchen, but everyone also has an incentive to leave his or her mess for others to clear up. The problem of collective action is often invoked to explain the existence of norms. Such norms are christened 'Prisoner's Dilemma norms' in the author's classic discussion of *The Emergence of Norms* (1977). The norm in this case would be something like 'Clean up after yourself!' If everyone complied with the norm rather than succumbing to the temptation to free-ride, then the kitchen would have been perfectly clean. Needless to say, some people violated the norm. The resulting lapse in cleanliness led a frustrated academic to install the camera. With monitoring, free-riders would now face the threat of public shaming—and perhaps even material sanctions.

Monitoring was strongly opposed by a minority of academics. They did not want to shame their colleagues or even to contemplate any sanction from above. Unfortunately, the author does not use her ethnographic knowledge to investigate whether the opponents of monitoring tended to be those who left the kitchen in a mess. One suspects that the free-riders were especially likely to articulate principled objections to monitoring.

The reluctance to enforce compliance seems puzzling, assuming that it was not confined only to free-riders. If we consider the larger context, however, this becomes explicable. The university already pays maintenance staff to clean the kitchen every day. This means that the norm 'Clean up after yourself!' remains tenable even when some people violate it. Although the kitchen becomes messier over the course of the day (dirty cups accumulate in the sink and stains on the counter top), what is crucial is that it reverts to a sparkling condition next morning. This is suboptimal for those academics who have high standards of cleanliness, but it is manageable.

Consider the pure case of collective action, where the academics would really have to clean the kitchen themselves—as in a household or kibbutz. Then the norm of 'Clean up after yourself!' would be severely undermined by lack of compliance. Gradually the kitchen would become messier and messier. You could not simply ignore a dirty cup till next morning. Some people would have to clean up after the free-riders as well as themselves. The norm would thus become 'Clean up the kitchen (even if you did not make the mess)!' Now a colleague's failure to clean would force someone else to contribute more than their fair share. In this pure case—where there is a genuine collective action problem—I hypothesize that staff would be far more likely to support a camera for monitoring. To put this to the test, the author as Director of the Center could conduct an experiment: give the maintenance staff a holiday and tell the academics that they are entirely responsible for cleaning the kitchen. Does opposition to monitoring diminish?

Even in the pure case of collective action (without maintenance staff), monitoring can be separated from the specific technology of the closed-circuit television. There is no need for any technological solution. Create a roster where each academic is assigned to thoroughly clean the kitchen on a specific day, first thing in the morning. Now there are two complementary norms: 'On your assigned day, completely clean the kitchen by 9am!' as well as 'Clean up after yourself!' These norms are easily monitored. If at 10am you find the kitchen in a mess, you can identify with some confidence who has violated the norm—the person who was assigned to clean this morning. Moreover, whoever is rostered to clean tomorrow morning has a strong incentive to monitor and sanction violations of both norms (especially the first); any free-riding will make their task more onerous, as the kitchen will be in a worse state. Anyone tempted to violate the norm 'Clean up after yourself!' knows that their malfeasance will harm a specific person (the person who will clean tomorrow morning). I suggest that the identification of harm to a specific individual—rather than to a generalized collectivity—will make (at least some) people less willing to violate the norm, even if they could do so without being noticed.

The specific allocation of responsibility—with monitoring as a natural consequence—would not eradicate free-riding. Nevertheless, this institution plus the two complementary norms could prove resilient even in the face of a certain amount of shirking. Real problems of collective action, such as maintaining irrigation systems or preventing overfishing, have been solved in this manner (Ostrom 1990). When there is an incentive to free-ride, cooperative norms cannot survive solely by their motivational force; monitoring and graduated sanctions are also necessary.

By considering cleaning the kitchen as a problem of collective action, the vociferous opposition to monitoring and sanctions emerges as a puzzle. This puzzle is solved by examining the structure of the situation: the *deus ex machina* in the form of maintenance staff makes free-riding fairly tolerable to academics, even for those who follow the norm. Therefore academics have the luxury of articulating philosophical objections to the enforcement of the norm.

The debate over enforcement takes us to a second level of analysis. Here is it useful to distinguish norms from values (Parsons 1961). In this conception, norms are specific behavioral injunctions; values are abstract ends or goods which legitimize or justify norms. Some norms ('Drive on the left!') have no need of justification by values; some values (such as aesthetic values) have no close connection with norms. But there is usually a linkage between norms and values. In the case of the kitchen, the paramount values were cleanliness and privacy (equality was also a factor, though it was less salient). While we may agree that both cleanliness and privacy are valuable, the problem comes when the two conflict: how much of one are we willing to sacrifice to gain more of the other? Some participants in the debate gave primacy to cleanliness, others to privacy. The author suggests that women give greater weight to cleanliness. Because cleanliness (in regard to housekeeping) was traditionally women's work, it is 'devalued'—at least by men. Presumably women were more likely to favor the camera, but no data are presented to confirm this.

I will defer to the gender stereotype and focus entirely on the value of privacy. The author takes it for granted that privacy is something inherently valuable. The claim that 'this camera violates my right to privacy' is a compelling argument. Even those who disputed the conclusion had to accept the premise; they could argue that the right to privacy did not apply in this particular situation (the kitchen is not a private place) or they could argue that it was trumped by some other value. Presumably no one thought of questioning the value of privacy itself. What I want to argue is that the value of privacy demands explanation; it cannot simply be taken for granted as a universal good.

The valuation of privacy is a peculiar feature of contemporary Western societies. Obsession with privacy is especially notable in the United Kingdom, where it is enshrined in legislation like the Data Protection Act. While we are sharing anecdotes of university life, let me give a trivial but revealing example. When I joined one Department (not at my current university), naturally I was asked for a photograph to add to the notice board so that colleagues and students could identify me. I had to sign a release form, giving the university permission to display my likeness. By implication, my 'right to privacy' encompassed the right to keep anyone from seeing my face.

We know much less about values than about norms. Norms around collective action in particular have been extensively investigated; they are suited to experimental testing. With values, however, we are looking at historical-cultural change rather than recurring patterns of social interaction. This gives rise to a formidable methodological problem: there is essentially one 'case' where the value of privacy has come to prominence, namely the modern West. While there is some variations across countries (I suspect that it is especially pronounced in the United Kingdom), these cannot be treated simply as 'independent cases'. The European Union, for example, promotes privacy as a value and forces its institutionalization in member countries.

In the broadest view, the value of privacy is just the latest manifestation of a deep and powerful historical current: the increasing valuation of individual rights which has defined 'The West' since the late eighteenth century. One could argue that as more substantive individual rights—rights to vote, to free schooling, to decent housing, and so on—have become satisfied, then rights expand to encompass less significant domains. To put this another way, rights ascend up Maslow's hierarchy of needs. In this hierarchy, privacy seems to accord roughly with the level of esteem. The value of privacy fits well with Inglehart's (e.g. 1997) conception of a shift towards postmaterialism. This argument seems plausible; how it could be empirically tested is another matter.

Paradoxically, the value of privacy emerged when real life offered unprecedented levels of privacy. The platitude that the West is a 'surveillance society' is utterly false. Even leaving aside the totalitarian dictatorships of the twentieth century, surveillance was far more invasive in peasant villages or hunter gatherer bands. In the affluent West, children sleep in their own beds and often have their own bedrooms. A high proportion of adults live alone, without stigma; couples rarely live with their parents or other relatives. In cities, neighbors generally have little interest in what happens next door. The internet provides secret access to a world of information, allowing (for example) a teenager to enjoy explicit pornography or discover information on contraception or homosexuality. One might speculate that such high levels of privacy in everyday life help to explain the popularity of television shows like Big Brother; those shows tap a natural human interest in ferreting out (and gossiping about) 'discreditable' information pertaining to others, a desire frustrated by the extraordinary privacy granted by contemporary Western democracies.

Whatever its historical origins, the value of privacy is not simply an ethereal abstraction. Like any other potent value, it is institutionalized. The elevation of privacy as a value goes hand in hand with the creation of official positions dedicated to its promotion. At the governmental level, this post is often called a Privacy (or Information) Commissioner. Legislation or the threat of litigation forces organizations like firms and universities to create their own specialized positions—'data protection officers' and the like. People occupying those positions are then motivated to emphasize the value of privacy (and the prevalence and deleterious consequences of its violation), in order to increase their status within the organization and to swell their own budget.

These are some of the broader social forces that have made the value of privacy remarkably salient in modern Western societies—as illustrated by its frequent invocation in the debate over the camera in the kitchen.

The author concludes that participants in the debate "made their minds up about the issue at stake instinctively and instantaneously ... It may be said that people's instincts were made up before their minds were." (141) While the author suggests that this is somehow peculiar to issues of privacy, I argue that this is a general characteristic of debates over values and norms. One symptom is the uncanny coincidence of normative evaluations and instrumental assessments. (I owe recognition of this fact to Jervis 1976.) People who find a course of action to be normatively unjustifiable, because it violates cherished values, usually also assess that course of action to be instrumentally ineffective, in the sense that it will not achieve the desired results. Conversely, people who find a course of action to be morally justifiable usually also assess it to be instrumentally effective in bringing about the desired ends. In the case of the kitchen and the camera, I hypothesize that academics who expressed moral outrage at the violation of privacy also argued that surveillance would not actually produce a cleaner kitchen. And vice versa: academics who argued that surveillance would be effective also found it to be normatively justified.

If a person reasoned independently in positive and normative domains, then there should be as many cases of dissonance as consonance. Take a more dramatic question: whether we should torture suspected terrorists. One could evaluate torture as being normatively justified for gathering intelligence *and yet* judge torture as being less effective in this respect than humane treatment. Or one could judge torture as yielding valuable intelligence *and yet* evaluate torture as normatively unjustifiable. But these dissonant combinations are unusual: people tend to argue that torture is immoral and ineffective or they argue that it is morally permissible and effective. (Note that I am referring to the arguments of people who are not philosophers in debates outside the academic seminar.)

The consonance of normative evaluations and instrumental assessments could be explained by the pragmatics of rhetoric. If I really think that torture (or the camera in the kitchen) is immoral and therefore must be stopped, then I should argue publicly that it will also be ineffective—even if I secretly admitted its efficacy. My thinking would be as follows: if I fail to convince others with my normative argument, then I still have a chance to persuade them with an instrumental argument. Rhetoric may explain some part of the consonance, but it is implausible as a full explanation. Instead, I propose that normative questions provoke an emotional response (I would substitute 'emotions' for 'instincts' in the quotation above), which is then followed by a search for reasons to rationalize that response. In making sense of the emotional reaction to oneself, and in justifying it to others, one mentally 'recruits' as many reasons as possible: some involve values, others involve efficacy. Unless one is subject to conflicting emotions, all these reasons concur: either favouring or opposing a certain course of action.

We think that our reasoning explains our emotional response, but the causal order arguably runs the other way. I would end by emphasizing the importance of emotions (e.g. Prinz 2007). Emotions were almost entirely absent from the conference proceedings (from the content of the papers, I hasten to add, not the character of the discussion!), with the exception of Robert Sugden's contribution. Yet emotions such as anger, shame, and disgust underlay the debate over the camera in the kitchen: disgust at the dirtiness of the kitchen; anger towards those who disregarded the norm of cleaning up, or towards those who violated one's right to privacy; perhaps shame at being caught behaving discreditably. Further advances in our understanding of norms and values will require serious consideration of emotions.

Bibliography

Inglehart, R. (1997), *Modernization and Postmodernization: Cultural, Economic and Political Change in 43 Societies*, Princeton

Jervis, R. (1976), *Perception and Misperception in International Politics*, Princeton

Ostrom, E. (1990), *Governing the Commons: The Evolution of Institutions for Collective Action*, Cambridge

Parsons, T (1961), An Outline of the Social System, in: T. Parsons (ed.), *Theories of Society*. Vol. 1, New York, 30–79

Prinz, J. (2007), *The Emotional Construction of Morals*, Oxford

Ullmann-Margallit, E. (1977), *The Emergence of Norms*, Oxford

II. Epiricism and Efficacy

Cristina Bicchieri and Alex Chavez

Behaving as Expected: Public Information and Fairness Norms[*]

1. Introduction

Social norms are often invoked as explanations of pro-social behavior. Since norms are ubiquitous in society, it is important to be able to assess under which conditions individuals will be motivated to follow them, and to distinguish norm-motivated behavior from generic social preferences. To accomplish these goals, we need an operational definition of norms that allows us to make testable predictions about when norms will be followed, as well as to distinguishing norms from other concepts such as conventions or personal values. In what follows we adopt a definition of norms that is grounded upon individuals' preferences and expectations (Bicchieri 2006, 11).

For a social norm to exist and be followed, three conditions must be present. First, it is necessary that the individuals involved *believe* it exists and know the class of situations to which the norm pertains. This condition implies that individuals must be aware they are in a situation in which a particular norm applies, since lack of awareness may lead to non-compliance. We thus hypothesize that making a norm salient will lead, ceteris paribus, to more compliance (Cialdini et al. 1990). The second condition is that individuals must have a *conditional preference* for following the norm. Specifically, an individual will prefer to obey a given norm if she (a) expects other people to comply with it (empirical expectations) and (b) believes that other people expect her to obey the norm and may sanction transgressions (normative expectations). The third condition is the presence of empirical and normative expectations. It follows that an individual may not obey a norm she knows applies to a given situation if she fails to have the right kind of expectations. Transgressions may occur because one observes non-compliance, or alternatively normative expectations are absent, or they are present but one can violate them without being observed.

The conditional preference condition distinguishes social norms from personal values. In the latter case, one usually has an unconditional preference for following a

---

[*] We wish to thank the Goldstone Research Unit at the University of Pennsylvania for financial support, Werner Güth, Jonathon Baron, Robert Sugden, and seminar participants at the ZiF conference on Norms and Values and at the Universities of Michigan, CUNY, Yale, Milano, British Columbia, Alabama, Duke, Madrid, Texas at Austin, Arizona and the Wharton School for many useful comments and suggestions. We are grateful to Ryan Muldoon, Doug Paletta, and Giacomo Sillari for their assistance in data collection. Alex Chavez's work was supported by a National Science Foundation Graduate Research Fellowship.

certain rule, as expectations about others' compliance play little or no role in one's decision. Having a conditional preference for conformity also implies that one might follow a norm in the presence of the relevant expectations, but disregard it in their absence. We thus hypothesize that manipulation of expectations will produce major shifts in norm-abiding behavior. To test this hypothesis, we focused on a simple version of the Ultimatum game, in which one of the parties proposes a division of a fixed amount of money to another party who can then accept or reject the offer. If the offer is rejected, both parties get nothing. Experimental results show that participants' modal and mean offers are 40 to 50% of the total amount, and offers below 20% are rejected about half of the time (Camerer 2003). These results are generally interpreted as showing that subjects have a preference for fairness (Fehr/Schmidt 1999).

Our hypothesis instead is that subjects have a conditional preference for following fairness norms, and manipulation of expectations will lead to significantly different behavior among the same subjects in different conditions. These results cannot be explained by a fairness preference hypothesis, since the material consequences are the same across conditions, and the only difference between conditions is the level of information (and thus the expectations) of players. Furthermore, even if we were to modify the fairness preference hypothesis by making preferences conditional, it would remain to be explained under which conditions preferences would change. The theory of norms we adopt provides such a testable explanation.

To show that 'fair' behavior is dictated by norms that are conditionally followed, we manipulated both salience and expectations. In the salience treatment, we asked Proposers which of the options they thought Responders believed to be fair, thus focusing them on Responders' normative expectations. Our hypothesis was that making a fairness norm more salient would induce greater fairness on the part of Proposers. In both the salience and non-salience conditions, we asked Responders which of the Proposers' choice options they believed to be fair. The goal of this assessment was twofold. First, we wanted to check whether there was agreement in Responders' normative expectations. Agreement strongly indicates the presence of a shared norm of fairness. Second, we wanted to assess the agreement of Responders' normative expectations with Proposers' beliefs about them. It is significant that Proposers' answers (in the salience conditions) agreed with the overall Responders' answers, a fact that further indicates the presence of a shared norm.

What counts as fair may vary by context, and in a given context more than one fairness criterion might apply. Equity and equality considerations may coexist, and randomization is often perceived as a fair allocation mechanism, as when we use a lottery to allocate transplant organs. In our experiment, we added a choice option that randomized with equal probability between an equal and a very unequal share. Remarkably, a majority of Responders found this option fair, a finding also reflected in the Proposers' beliefs about Responders' assessments. Adding this option allowed us to check for *norm manipulation* (Bicchieri 2007). That is, when a norm can have several interpretations, individuals will tend to adopt the one most favorable to them. This form of self-serving bias has been studied in the context of equity vs. equality interpretations of fairness (Frey/Bohnet 1995; Hoffman/Spitzer 1985), and we show that we can elicit the same bias with a suitable random option, provided this choice option is common knowledge among participants.

To manipulate expectations, we changed the information conditions in three versions of the same division problem. We expected a change in normative expectations to affect Proposers' choices. We also predicted the occurrence of *norm evasion* (Bicchieri 2007): whenever it was possible for Proposers to defy normative expectations without Responders' knowledge, the proportion of unfair offers would be significantly higher. Due to the conditional nature of norm compliance, the more ambiguous the choice situation, the higher will be the proportion of individuals that flaunt the norm, since their behavior cannot be clearly interpreted as intentional, and thus no sanctioning is expected to occur.

Our paper is a contribution to a field that may be labeled *behavioral ethics*. It should be seen as a subfield of behavioral decision theory, taking into account social and psychological considerations in an attempt to understand pro-social, 'moral' choices. In this regard, we explore whether and why a pro-social norm will be followed, trying to gain insights about decision-making and motivation that are useful for further developing a behavioral account of moral choices.

2. Method

2.1 Participants

One hundred and six college-age subjects participated in our study across 11 experimental sessions. Advertisements specified that participants would earn 5 USD in addition to an amount that would depend on decisions made during the experiment.

2.2 Game Paradigm

Our experimental design employed a variant of the Ultimatum Game (Güth et al. 1982), in which one participant, the *Proposer*, provisionally received a sum of 10 USD—provided by the experimenter—and then proposed a division of that money with a *Responder*. The Responder subsequently decided to accept or reject the proposal. If the Responder accepted, both players received the amounts specified in the proposal. If the Responder rejected, both players received $0. The Proposer chose from one of the following options:

- (5,5) – to propose $5 for the Proposer, and $5 for the Responder;
- (8,2) – to propose $8 for the Proposer, and $2 for the Responder; and
- Coin – to let the outcome of a fair coin flip determine the proposal: heads corresponded to (5,5), and tails to (8,2).

153

2.3 Procedure

Upon their arrival, participants randomly drew ID codes labeled A1, A2, ... , An and B1, B2, ... , Bn, where n is twice the number of participants in the session, and proceeded either to Room A or B based on their codes. We distributed and read aloud a set of instructions, which explained the following:

- Based on random assignment, the participants in Room A were Proposers, and those in Room B were Responders.
- Participants would play three games,[1] each with a different person in the other room.
- By means of a public randomization device, we would select two of the three games at the end of the study to determine participants' cash payments.
- For each game, we would post on the blackboard the Proposer-Responder pairings using their ID codes, distribute instructions specific to that game, and then administer a short quiz to test their understanding of the instructions. By posting pairings publically, we maximized transparency and the likelihood that each participant would believe he or she actually was interacting with three different people in the other room.
- Subsequently, Proposers would be given a proposal form on which they would write their ID codes and choose one of the available proposals.
- After all Proposers completed their proposal forms, an assistant would take them to Room B, where the Responders would mark their decision to accept or reject the proposal.

2.4 Information

The proposal form that was used for each of the three games was determined by the information condition which we assigned to that game. Appendix B contains the proposal forms which differed slightly by information condition, as described below.

In the *full information* condition, the proposal form listed all three options: (5,5), (8,2), and coin. After Proposers completed their proposal forms, the experimenter in Room B flipped a coin in front of the Responders in case any Proposer had marked coin on her form. On any forms on which the Proposer chose coin, the experimenter then marked (5,5) or (8,2) based on the coin flip outcome. The instructions explained this, so that prior to making their decisions, all participants understood that Responders would know if the Proposers with whom they were paired chose coin.

In the *private information* condition, the Responder did not know that coin was available to Proposers, and Proposers knew this fact. To create this informational asymmetry, we left coin off of the proposal form. The experimenter in Room A

---

1 We described the games using the language of Hoffman et al. (1994).

explained to Proposers that they could indicate a coin choice by leaving both (5,5) and (8,2) unmarked; subsequently, the experimenter would flip a coin in Room A, and on any such forms, mark (5,5) if the outcome was heads, and (8,2) if the outcome was tails. Thus, Proposers understood that Responders were unaware that coin was an available option.

In the *limited information* condition, both Proposers and Responders knew that coin was available, but also that Responders would not be able to infer whether the Proposer chose coin or marked one of (5,5) and (8,2) directly. Specifically, the instructions explained that Proposers could indicate a coin choice by leaving both (5,5) and (8,2) unmarked on their proposal forms. The experimenter in Room B would flip a coin and mark (5,5) or (8,2) accordingly on any such forms. Crucially, he would flip the coin behind a small screen, so that no participant could see the outcome. Thus, all participants understood that the Responder would be unable to distinguish forms on which the Proposer chose (5,5) or (8,2) directly from forms on which the Proposer chose coin.

Finally, because Proposers did not receive feedback between conditions, and to minimize participants' confusion that occurred during a pilot study, we fixed the order of the information conditions as 1) full, 2) private, and 3) limited.

2.5 Salience

In each information condition, prior to making their choices, Responders completed a questionnaire that measured their normative expectations (see Appendix C).

The questionnaire asked whether the responder found each of the three choice options fair. The questionnaire was aimed at assessing whether there was an agreement in Responders' normative expectations, an indicator of (as well as a necessary condition for) the existence of a social norm. In addition, roughly half of our experimental sessions included an incentive-based questionnaire for both Responders and Proposers, which they completed in each information condition, following the quiz but prior to making their choices (See Appendices D and E).[2]

These questionnaires asked participants about their beliefs about the percentage of Responders who indicated (5,5), (8,2) and coin, respectively, as fair options. The questionnaires were designed to 1) make fairness norms more salient, and 2) test for an agreement between Responders' normative expectations and Proposers' beliefs about them. The other half of the sessions included no such questionnaires; they just included the first Responders' questionnaire (Appendix C). We distinguish salient sessions which included these two extra questionnaires from non-salient sessions which did not.

---

[2] For Responders in the salience condition, the second questionnaire in Appendix D was appended to the one in Appendix C.

2.6 Design and Analyses

The experiment used a 3x2 design, crossing three levels of a within-participant variable, information (full, private, and limited), with two levels of a between-participant variable, salience (non-salient and salient). The primary dependent variable was the Proposer's choice: (5,5), (8,2), or Coin.

We used a mixed-effects multinomial logit model to estimate choice probabilities. To determine the significance of information, salience, their interaction, and participant-level random effects, we used nested model comparisons based on the likelyhood ratio test statistic (LRT). Because small cell sizes made it inadvisable to base inference about the LRT on the chi-square distribution, we generated p-values for model comparisons using the non-parametric bootstrap. Bootstrap p-values lead to more accurate inference when cell counts are sparse. For the same reason, we generated p-values for the logit coefficients using the bootstrap. Appendix A contains additional details on the bootstrap methods we employed.

2.7 Hypotheses

We first hypothesized that, if there is a social norm, there must be agreement between Responders' normative expectations and Proposers' beliefs about them. We also hypothesized that choices would depend on information condition and salience. Based on the theory presented in the Introduction, we made several directional predictions by considering possible scenarios involving relevant fairness norms.

Firstly, we predicted that the proportion of coin choices would be higher in the full information condition than in the private or limited conditions. This follows because in the private information condition, there are no normative expectations for coin (as the availability of coin is unknown to Responders), and there should therefore be very few coin choices, since an outcome of (8,2) is likely to be rejected as unfair. In the limited condition, Responders could not determine whether the Proposer chose coin. Therefore the expected utility of coin is a combination of the probability of getting (5,5) or (8,2), and the probability that (8,2) will be accepted.[3] If the Proposer assesses a probability greater than 5/8 that (8,2) will be accepted, she will choose (8,2). If the probability is less than 5/8, the Proposer will choose (5,5). Only if the probability is exactly 5/8, the Proposer will be indifferent among the three options. Therefore, Proposers who believed that less than 62.5% of Responders would accept (8,2) would choose (5,5), since the expected value of choosing (8,2) would be less than 5. Proposers who believed that more than 62.5% of Responders would accept (8,2) would choose (8,2), since the expected value of choosing (8,2)

---

3   The expected utility of coin is equal to ½(5) + ½(8)p. p is the probability that the Responder will accept (8,2) because he believes that the Proposer is 'playing fair' and thinks coin is a fair choice. The expected utility of (5,5) is 5, and the expected utility of (8,2) is 8p. The value of p that makes one indifferent between the three options is 5/8, or .625.

would be more than 5. In either case, there will be few or no coin choices. Finally, in the full information condition, as long as there were Proposers who thought that choosing coin was perceived to be fair by Responders, the proportion of coin choices would be positive. This is because these Proposers believe that the expected utility of choosing coin is 6.5, while the expected utilities of choosing (5,5) or (8,2) are, respectively, 5 and 0. This is an example of *norm manipulation*; i.e., participants would adopt the (allegedly shared) interpretation of fairness that would benefit them the most. Indeed, coin maximizes expected monetary payoff without violating fairness.

Secondly, we predicted that there would be more (8,2) choices in the limited than in the full or private information conditions, because some Proposers would take advantage of the ambiguity of their choice. Specifically, if some Proposers believed that a large enough fraction of Responders thought that choosing coin was fair and that Proposers were playing fair by choosing Coin, then these Proposers could evade the norm and maximize their monetary expected value by choosing (8,2) in the limited information condition.[4] Thus, the proportion of (8,2) choices should be higher in the limited information condition than in the full information condition. In the private information condition, we expected the fraction of (8,2) choices to be low for reasons discussed below.

Thirdly, we predicted that there would be more (5,5) choices in the private than in the full or limited information conditions. Previous work has indicated that the proportion of (5,5) choices is around 70% when (5,5) and (8,2) are the only available options (Falk et al. 2000). Because the private information condition is most similar to this situation, and we expected (5,5) to be almost universally considered fair, we expected similar proportions of (5,5) choices. In the full information condition, because we expected a relatively larger number of coin choices (due to norm manipulation), we expected fewer (5,5) choices. In the limited information condition, because we expected a relatively larger number of (8,2) choices (as the ambiguity of choices led to norm evasion), we expected fewer (5,5) choices.

Finally, because we expected the questionnaire in the salient condition to focus Proposers on fairness—i.e., on choosing either (5,5) or coin, and not (8,2)—we predicted that the above effects would be amplified.

3. Results

3.1 Choices by Information and Salience

Figure 1 shows the choice proportions for each level of Information x Salience. As salience effects appeared to be small, we averaged across salience conditions in reporting the choice proportions below. 37.7% (20/53) of Proposers chose coin in

---

4 That is, p must be greater than .625 for a Proposer to choose (8,2) in the limited condition.

the full information condition, compared to 11.3% (6/53) in the private condition and 5.7% (3/53) in the limited condition, consistent with our first hypothesis. Consistent with our second hypothesis, more Proposers chose (8,2) in the limited condition (58.5% [31/53]) than in the full (24.5% [13/53]) or private (37.7% [20/53]) conditions. We observed the highest frequency of (5,5) choices in the private condition (50.9% [27/53]) relative to the full (37.7% [20/53]) and limited (35.8% [19/53]) conditions, consistent with our third hypothesis.

The primarily additive effect of salience combined with differences in choice proportions across information conditions suggests the presence of both main effects, but not their interaction. Indeed, nested model comparisons (see Table 1) confirmed that a model with main effects of information and salience—but not their interaction—fit the choice data the best. Participant-level random effects were not significant for any of the models in Table 1.

Table 2 shows the estimates for the model with both main effects of information and salience. Consistent with a norm-based explanation of choices, when normative expectations for coin are either absent (in the private condition) or can be defied without consequence (in the limited condition), the predicted probabilities of (5,5) and (8,2), respectively, are considerably higher than those of coin. This is indicated by the significantly positive coefficients. On the other hand, when normative expectations for coin are present and choices are transparent (in the full information condition), (5,5) is no more likely than coin ($p = .963$), whereas (8,2) is in fact less likely ($p = .038$). The substantial discrepancy between some of the maximum likelihood and bootstrap estimates of the standard error were due to right-skewed coefficients distributions; accordingly, we used percentiles of the bootstrap distribution to calculate p-values, instead of relying on the asymptotic normality of the coefficients.

Based on the model with both main effects, we performed formal tests of our first three hypotheses using bootstrapping to generate p-values (see Appendix A). As suggested by Figure 1, the probability of coin was significantly higher in the full information condition than in the private or limited information conditions ($p < .001$, for both the salient and non-salient conditions). (8,2), additionally, was more likely to be chosen in the limited condition than in the full or private information conditions ($p < .02$, for both the salient and non-salient conditions). (5,5), however, was not more likely to be chosen in the private condition than in the other two conditions ($p = .1$ and $p = .2$ respectively for the salient and non-salient conditions). Thus, we found support for our first two hypotheses but not for our third.

We found mixed support for our final set of hypotheses, that Proposers would be more focused on fairness in the salient condition and would therefore be more likely to choose (5,5) and coin, and less likely to choose (8,2). Respectively in the salient and non-salient conditions, there were 41 and 25 (5,5) choices ($p = .003$); 17 and 12 coin choices ($p = .2$); and 26 and 38 (8,2) choices ($p = .016$), where again we generated bootstrapped p-values using the model with both main effects. Because the interaction between salience and information was not significant (see Table 1), the norm-focusing effects reported above were limited to across information conditions.

3.2 Normative Expectations and Beliefs about Them

Table 3 reports the normative expectations of Responders. Clearly, almost all Responders considered (5,5) to be fair in all information conditions, and a majority of them also thought that Coin was fair. This may be surprising because the expected utility of Coin is only 3.5 USD for the Responder, whereas it is 6.5 USD for the Proposer. A possible explanation is that using a random device is perceived as a fair way to choose between alternatives. Responders might have compared Coin to the temptation of (8,2) and found the Proposer who refused to choose between (5,5) and (8,2) as one making a fair choice. Alternatively, some might have thought the Proposer, because of her role, had an entitlement to a greater share, and Coin seemed a fair compromise between five dollars and eight dollars.

Figures 2-4 show participants' beliefs about Responders' normative expectations for each information condition. There is a remarkable degree of agreement between Responders' and Proposers' beliefs about the normative expectations of Responders. Moreover, a comparison of Table 3 with Figures 2-4 shows that participants' beliefs about normative expectations are in agreement with the normative expectations themselves.

Such high degree of agreement is the strongest possible indication that there is a shared norm of fairness. Not only is (5,5) universally perceived as fair, but also Coin is thought to be fair by a majority of participants. This agreement explains the tendency to choose a self-serving interpretation of fairness (norm manipulation) in the full information condition, as well as the pattern of choices across information conditions, as we show in the following section.

3.3 Choices as a Function of Beliefs about Normative Expectations

A social norm explanation presupposes consistency between beliefs and behavior. In particular, it requires consistency between participants' beliefs about normative expectations and their subsequent choices. As we show below, the data show a high degree of consistency between beliefs and behavior.

We denote the Proposers' belief about the proportion of Responders who consider (5,5), (8,2), and coin, respectively, as being fair by $\varphi(5,5)$, $\varphi(8,2)$, and $\varphi(\text{coin})$. The distributions of these variables are summarized by Figures 2-4. To determine whether these beliefs could explain the variance in Proposer's choices, we fit a multinomial logit with information condition and the three questionnaire variables as predictors, based on a stepwise search.[5] The signs of the coefficients for the ques-

---

[5] We used a stepwise search that minimized Akaike's information criterion (AIC), a function of the likelihood which penalizes larger models (AIC = -2(log-likelihood) + 2k, where k is the number of parameters in the model that are being estimated). The scope of the model search were information, $\varphi(5,5)$, $\varphi(8,2)$, and $\varphi(\text{coin})$. When we expanded the scope to search amongst all two-way interactions as well, AIC selected a model which included $\varphi(8,2)$

tionnaire variables were in the appropriate directions (see Table 4). As the Proposer's belief that the Responder considered (5,5) to be fair increased, (8,2) became less likely relative to the reference choice of coin (p = .068). As φ(coin) increased, the odds of choosing coin over (5,5) increased as well (p = .048). For higher levels of φ(8,2), coin was less likely than (8,2) (p = .068).

Figures 5a-b show the predicted probabilities of (8,2) choices by condition as functions of φ(8,2) and φ(Coin), respectively. In the private information condition, for example, a Proposer who believes that no Responders find (8,2) to be fair (i.e., φ(8,2) = 0) has a predicted probability of .23 of choosing (8,2)—see Figure 5a.[6] However, a Proposer who believes that roughly 60% of Responders find (8,2) to be fair is more than twice as likely to choose (8,2), with a predicted probability of .55.

The strong dependency of (8,2) choices on the Proposer's belief that Coin is considered to be fair in the limited information condition (see Figure 5b) is also noteworthy. A Proposer who believes that no Responders find Coin to be fair has a predicted probability of only .10 of choosing (8,2). However, a Proposer who believes that all Responders find Coin to be fair has a predicted probability of .53 of choosing Coin, a five-fold increase. This occurs because the Proposer can choose (8,2) with impunity when the Proposer's estimate of the probability that Coin is considered fair by Responders is high. If the Proposer believes that a) the Responder thinks Coin is fair and b) the Responder believes that the Proposer is playing fair by choosing Coin, then (8,2) is expected to be accepted with high probability because it will be interpreted as the unlucky outcome of a coin flip. Moreover, as Figure 5b shows, the predicted probability of (8,2) choices in the limited information condition increases with the Proposer's estimate of the probability that Coin is considered fair by Responders. Whereas the existence of more than one interpretation of fairness leads to norm manipulation (i.e., the Proposer chooses Coin instead of (5,5) in the full information condition), the presence of ambiguity leads to norm evasion (i.e., the Proposer chooses (8,2) in the limited information condition because the source of the offer is not identifiable as being intentional or due to chance). Indeed, 76% of Proposers choose (8,2) in the limited information condition. And even when Proposers are focused on fairness in the salience condition, the proportion of (8,2) choices is relatively high.

Finally, Figure 6 shows the predicted probability of Coin choices as a function of φ(Coin) by condition. Clearly, the probability of choosing Coin increases with the Proposer's estimate of the proportion of Responders who consider Coin to be fair. As mentioned earlier, the Proposer's self-serving bias would lead to a greater frequency of Coin choices whenever it is clear that Responders know that Coin has been chosen and that they consider Coin to be fair. This can also be seen in Figure 1,

x φ(coin) in addition to the variables in Table 4 (AIC=158.61). However, we chose to present the simpler model without this interaction term, as it did not change our substantive results, and Figures 6-7 looked the same with or without it.

6   The other belief variables are held fixed at their median values for these predictions.

where the proportion of Coin choices in the full information condition is substantially larger relative to the other information conditions.

3.4 Responder Behavior

Table 5 shows that Responders discriminated between intentional offers and offers that were generated by a chance mechanism. In the full information condition, no (8,2) offers resulting from a Coin choice were rejected, whereas intentional (8,2) offers were rejected 23% of the time. Responders' rejection rates of (8,2) were also sensitive to the presence of an intermediate choice. In the private information condition, in which Responders believe the only choices are (5,5) and (8,2), the rejection rate is much higher than in the full information condition (40% vs. 23%), in which Responders know that the Coin choice is available. When there is ambiguity as to the source of the choice, as in the limited information condition, the rejection rate of (8,2) was low (16.1%). This suggests that the large majority of Responders who receive an (8,2) offer in the limited information condition believe both that it is the result of a Coin choice and that choosing Coin is fair. The large number of Proposers who choose (8,2) in the limited information condition seem to expect this low rate of rejections.

4. Conclusions

Having a well-defined, testable theory of social norms allows us to explain what would *prima facie* appear to be inconsistencies in individual behavior. Individuals choose to be fair on occasion, but revert to selfish behavior on others. The theory of social norms we adopt explains away these apparent inconsistencies. Compliance with a norm is conditional upon having the right kind of empirical and normative expectations. It is also important that individuals focus on the relevant norm in order for them to comply with it. The theory of we adopt (Bicchieri 2006) predicts that making a norm salient will tend to increase compliance and, even more important, that the presence of the appropriate expectations is crucial for attaining conformity to the norm. We thus expected that manipulating expectations by changing the information available to individuals would result in large shifts in behavior.

The data we presented highlight two important phenomena connected to norm compliance. The first is norm manipulation (Bicchieri 2007): when a norm can have several interpretations, individuals will tend to choose the interpretation that best serves their interests. This effect is evident in the choice of Coin in the full information condition. In this condition, the participants have common knowledge of the Proposer's access to the three choices of (5,5), (8,2), and Coin, as well as the Responder's ability to differentiate between an intentional unfair offer and an unfair offer resulting from a chance event. In the full information condition, the proportion of coin choices is the same as the proportion of (5,5) choices. Moreover, this manipulation of the fairness norm is made possible by the implicit and strong agreement among the Responder's normative expectations about the fairness of Coin choices and both Proposers' and Responders' agreement about such normative expectations. As we mentioned at the outset, such an agreement is a strong indication of the presence of a shared norm.

The second phenomenon is norm evasion. Norm evasion differs from norm avoidance, in which an individual avoids a specific situation to which a norm applies. A vivid example of norm avoidance is the behavior of the Iks described by Turnbull (1972). The Iks repaired their huts in the middle of the night so as to avoid their neighbors' offers of help, as such offers had to be accepted, and that involved incurring an obligation that the beneficiary wanted to avoid. Norm evasion, on the contrary, is the deliberate, private flouting of a norm even if one knows the normative expectations of the relevant parties. For many individuals, the presence of normative expectations without the sanctioning element weakens the grip of the norm. Such expectations can be violated at no cost, as the victim will not be able to distinguish an intentional action from a chance event. Norm evasion explains Proposers' behavior in the limited information condition, in which (8,2) was the most frequent choice.

Our work introduces the field of behavioral ethics and builds on the seminal work of Güth et al. (1982) and Hoffman et al. (1994), who showed the importance of context in games requiring the division of resources. We add to that work by showing that the effect of context is mediated by the role that normative expectations and shared norms hold in explaining behavior. Secondly, our measurement of first-order (Responders' fairness judgments) and second-order (Proposers' and Responders' beliefs about Responders' fairness judgments) beliefs is a highly useful but underused method in experiments on strategic interactions. Thirdly, our results potentially allow us to distinguish between different types of individuals. Future work will explore how a more fine-grained account of individuals' sensitivity to specific norms explains their choices, and whether there are correlations between sensitivities to different norms, such as those of cooperation, fairness, and reciprocity. Strong correlations would indicate the existence of a general disposition to follow social norms, whereas a low correlation would indicate that norm compliance is a local, norm-specific phenomenon.

Appendix A: Statistical Methods

Rationale for Statistical Methods

To evaluate our hypotheses and predictions, traditional approaches using the general linear model or the chi-square test for independence are inadequate for at least two reasons. Firstly, our data contain multiple responses from each participant. If these responses were substantially correlated, the standard error estimates produced by traditional methods would be too small. Secondly, four of the eighteen cells (3 choices x 3 information conditions x 2 salience treatments) in our data had counts of less than five, making inference based on asymptotic results unadvisable.

The Bootstrap

Asymptotically, logit coefficients and the LRT follow known distributions (under general regularity conditions). However, this is not true for small samples. The bootstrap distribution of a statistic can be used to check the validity of basing inference on asymptotic results. Roughly half of the coefficients in the multinomial logit models we estimated had right-skew (and hence, non-normal) bootstrap distributions, and the majority of the bootstrap distributions of the LRTs were not chi-square. Had we relied on traditional analyses based on the normal and chi-square distributions, our standard error estimates and p-values would have been too small. We provide details of our bootstrap methods below.

Let $y_{obs} = (y_1, y_2, \ldots, y_n)$ denote the vector of observed data, let $T(y_{obs})$ denote the *statistic* of interest, and let F denote the underlying distribution that generated the data. The bootstrap estimates F using y_{obs}, thereby producing an estimate, $F^{\wedge}$, of the distribution of $T(y_{obs})$. The *non-parametric bootstrap* estimates $F^{\wedge}$ as the distribution generated by random sampling with replacement from the set of observed data points, $\{y_1, y_2, \ldots, y_n\}$. The *parametric bootstrap* estimates $F^{\wedge}$ by estimating the model's free parameters and then sampling from the assumed distribution conditional on its parameters being fixed at their estimated values. Using either nonparametric or parametric bootstrap, one generates a bootstrap data set, y, by taking n draws from $F^{\wedge}$. The quantity $T(y)$ is the *bootstrap estimate* of $T(y_{obs})$, and the distribution of $T(y)$ is its *bootstrap distribution*. Letting $y_1, y_2, \ldots, y_n$ be n bootstrap data sets, the standard error estimate of $T(y_{obs,})$ is the standard deviation of $T(y_1), T(y_2), \ldots, T(y_n)$.

We produced each parametric bootstrap estimate based on the multinomial logit model by 1) fitting the multinomial logit model using maximum likelihood, 2) generating 159 draws from the multinomial distribution with its parameters fixed at their maximum likelihood estimates from step 1, and 3) computing and recording the bootstrap estimates of the statistic of interest. We then repeated the above steps 9,999 times to determine the distribution of the statistic. The procedure for generating non-parametric bootstrap estimates is similar: 1) randomly select 25 Proposers in the control and 28 Proposers in the salient condition, with replacement, 2) compute the statistic of interest, and 3) repeat the previous two steps 9,999 times.

To determine the p-value for each multinomial logit coefficient, we computed the smallest value of alpha for which zero was not contained in the confidence interval formed by the $(n*\alpha/2)$th and $(n*(1-\alpha/2))$th quantiles (sorted values) of the parametric bootstrap estimates of the coefficients, $T(y_1)$, $T(y_2)$, ..., $T(y_n)$.[7] The estimate of the p-value is the proportion of bootstrap estimates that fell strictly outside this interval, which estimates the probability of drawing a coefficient more extreme in either tail of its distribution than the observed value. Although the distribution of the coefficient divided by its estimated standard error converges in probability to the standard normal, this is not necessary true for small samples. Thus, computing a p-value based on quantiles of the bootstrap distribution is preferable. We determined the p-value for the LRT in the same way, except that we constructed a one-sided confidence interval by omitting the division of α by two, as we expected LRTs to be positive under the null hypothesis.

We also used the bootstrap to generate p-values for our hypothesis tests. For our first three hypotheses, we formed our test statistics by taking the predicted probability for the choice and information condition of interest, and subtracting from it the maximum of the predicted probabilities for the two other information conditions. For example, for the first hypothesis, that coin choices would be more likely in the full information condition than in the private or limited conditions, we subtract the maximum of the predicted probabilities of coin in the private and limited conditions from the predicted probability of coin in the full information condition. Because we expected this test statistic to be positive, the p-value was the proportion of bootstrap replicates that were negative. Test statistics for the last three hypotheses were formed analogously.

---

7   The decimal precision of this value is determined by the number of bootstrap replicates.

Appendix B: Proposal Forms

Proposal form for the first game (full information condition)

> (1) Identification number (Proposer fills this out): _____
> (2) Paired with (Proposer fills this out): _____
> (3) Proposer's choices (Proposer check one):
> ___ $5 for Proposer and $5 for Responder
> ___ $8 for Proposer and $2 for Responder
> ___ Let a coin flip decide which of the above choices will be made.
> (4) Responder's decision (Responder check one):
> ___ Accept   ___ Reject

Proposal form for second game (private information condition)

> (1) Identification number (Proposer fills this out): _____
> (2) Paired with (Proposer fills this out): _____
> (3) Proposer's choices (Proposer check one):
> ___ $5 for Proposer and $5 for Responder
> ___ $8 for Proposer and $2 for Responder
> (4) Responder's decision (Responder check one):
> ___ Accept   ___ Reject

Proposal form for third game (limited information condition)

> (1) Identification number (Proposer fills this out): _____
> (2) Paired with (Proposer fills this out): _____
> (3) Proposer's choices (Proposer check one):
> ___ $5 for Proposer and $5 for Responder
> ___ $8 for Proposer and $2 for Responder
> ___ Let a coin flip decide which of the above choices will be made.
> (4) Responder's decision (Responder check one):
> ___ Accept   ___ Reject

Appendix C: Questionnaire 1 for Responders

Item (3) of each block of questions was omitted for the private condition, because Responders did not know that the Coin option was available to Proposers.

Questionnaire

Your identification number: _____
Please guess how many Proposers will choose:
    (1) $5 for Proposer and $5 for Responder: _____
    (2) $8 for Proposer and $2 for Responder: _____
    (3) Let a coin flip decide: _____
If your guess is correct, you will earn a $1 bonus.

Please mark <u>any</u> options you believe are fair options. You are free to choose none of the options, one, or more than one option. Your answer will not affect your payment.
    (1) $5 for Proposer and $5 for Responder   [ ]
    (2) $8 for Proposer and $2 for Responder   [ ]
    (3) Let a coin flip decide   [ ]

Appendix D: Questionnaire 2 for Responders

Please guess how many Responders (excluding you) will select each of the options in the above question as fair options. For each line on which your guess is correct, you will earn a $1 bonus.
    (1) $5 for Proposer and $5 for Responder   _____
    (2) $8 for Proposer and $2 for Responder   _____
    (3) Let a coin flip decide   _____

Appendix E: Questionnaire for Proposers

The questionnaire item regarding the Coin option was omitted in the private condition, as Proposers understood that Responders thought the Coin option was unavailable in that condition.

Questionnaire

Your identification number: _____
Each Responder was asked to decide whether the '$5 and $5' option is fair.
Please guess how many Responders selected this option as fair: _____
Each Responder was asked to decide whether the '$8 and $2' option is fair.
Please guess how many Responders selected this option as fair: _____
Each Responder was asked to decide whether the coin flip option is fair.
Please guess how many Responders selected this option as fair: _____
Note that Responders may answer no to all questions or yes to one or more questions.
For each line on which your guess is correct, you will earn a $1 bonus.

Bibliography

Bicchieri, C. (2006), The Grammar of Society: The Nature and Dynamics of Social Norms, Cambridge
— (2008), The Fragility of Fairness: An Experimental Investigation on the Conditional Status of Pro-social Norms, in: *Nous (Philosophical Issues 18 Interdisciplinary Core Philosophy)*, 227–246
Camerer, C. (2003), *Behavioral Game Theory: Experiments on Strategic Interaction*, Princeton, NJ
Cialdini, R./C. Kallgren/R. Reno (1990), A Focus Theory of Normative Conduct: A Theoretical Refinement and Reevaluation of the Role of Norms in Human Behavior, in: *Advances in Experimental Social Psychology 24*, 201–234
Falk, A/E. Fehr (2000), *Informal Sanctions*, IEER Working Paper N. 59
Fehr, E./K. Schmidt (1999), A Theory of Fairness, Competition, and Cooperation, in: *The Quarterly Journal of Economics 114*, 817–868
Frey, B./I. Bohnet (1995), Institutions Affect Fairness: Experimental Investigations, in: *Journal of Institutional and Theoretical Economics 151*, 286–303
Güth W./R. Schmittberger/B. Schwarze (1982), An Experimental Analysis of Ultimatum Bargaining, in: *Journal of Economic Behavior and Organization 3*, 367–88
Hoffman, E./M. Spitzer (1985), Entitlements, Rights, and Fairness: An Experimental Examination of Subjects' Concept of Distributive Justice, in: *Journal of Legal Studies 2*: 259–297
Hoffman, E./K. A. McCabe/S. Keith/V. Smith (1994), Preferences, Property Rights, and Anonymity in Bargaining Games, in: *Games and Economic Behavior 7*, 346–380
Turnbull, C. (1972), *The Mountain People*, New York

Tables

Table 1
Model comparisons for information and salience. P-values are based on bootstrap quantiles (see Appendix A for details), and not the chi-square distribution.[8]

Null	Alternative	df	LRT	p
–	Null (N)	–	–	–
N	Information (I)	4	25.73	< .0001
N	Salience (S)	2	6.54	.05
I	I + S	2	7.05	.04
S	I + S	4	26.23	< .0001
I + S	I x S	4	3.67	.52

Table 2
Multinomial logit model of information and salience as predictors of choices. Maximum likelyhood (ML) and bootstrap standard error estimates are included. P-values are based on bootstrap quantiles (see Appendix A for details). The reference level for choice is Coin, for information is the full condition, and for salience is the salient condition.[9]

	Log-odds	ML SE	Bootstrap SE	p
(5,5)				
Intercept	0.02	0.37	0.39	.963
Limited	1.84	0.69	1.72	.0007
Private	1.50	0.55	0.72	.0009
Non-Salient	-0.07	0.48	0.48	.913
(8,2)				
Intercept	-0.89	0.45	0.47	.0380
Limited	2.83	0.71	1.73	.0001
Private	1.66	0.59	0.76	.0011
Non-Salient	0.86	0.50	0.53	.0777

---

8 The chi-square would have yielded the following less conservative p-values: respectively from top to bottom (see Table 2), $p < .0001$, $p = .04$, $p = .03$, $p < .0001$, and .45.

9 Thus, for example, the predicted probability of choosing (5,5) in the limited condition and salient treatment is $\exp(.02+1.84)/(\exp(0) + \exp(.02+1.84) + \exp(-.89+2.83)) = .45$.

Table 3
Normative expectations of Responders. Each cell contains the proportion (fraction) of Responders who indicated that the choice was fair.

	Choice					
Condition	5,5		8,2		Coin	
Full	96.4%	27/28	14.3%	4/28	64.3%	18/28
Private	96.4%	27/28	17.9%	5/28		
Limited	96.4%	27/28	14.3%	4/28	57.1%	16/28

Table 4
Multinomial logit model of information and beliefs about Responders' normative expectations as predictors of choices. The model was selected via a stepwise search (AIC = 166.83).

		Log-odds	p
(5,5)			
	Intercept	-13.34	.144
	Limited	0.86	.318
	Private	-0.03	.958
	φ (5,5)	14.99	.131
	φ (coin)	-2.33	.048
	φ (8,2)	0.89	.587
(8,2)			
	Intercept	4.95	.176
	limited	2.64	.002
	private	2.87	.05
	φ (5,5)	-7.21	.068
	φ (coin)	0.55	.663
	φ (8,2)	3.11	.068

Table 5
Rejection rates and frequencies by offer source, offer, and condition.

		Offer			
Offer:		(5,5)		(8,2)	
Full					
	Direct	0.0%	0/20	23.1%	3/13
	Coin	0.0%	0/16	0.0%	0/4
Private		0.0%	0/28	40.0%	10/25
Limited		0.0%	0/20	18.2%	6/33

Figures

Choice Proportions by Information x Salience

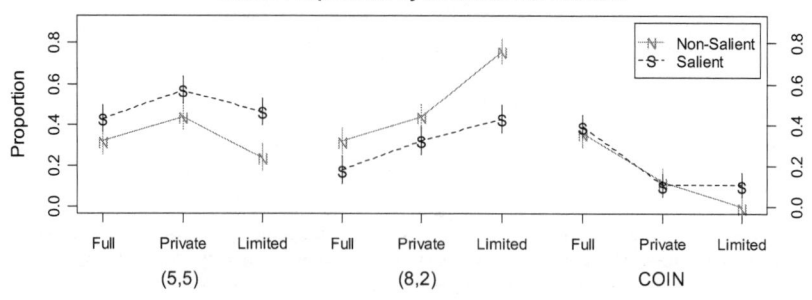

Figure 1. Choice proportions of (5,5), (8,2), and coin in each level of Information x Salience. Error bars are bootstrap estimates of one standard error of the choice proportion.

Full Information

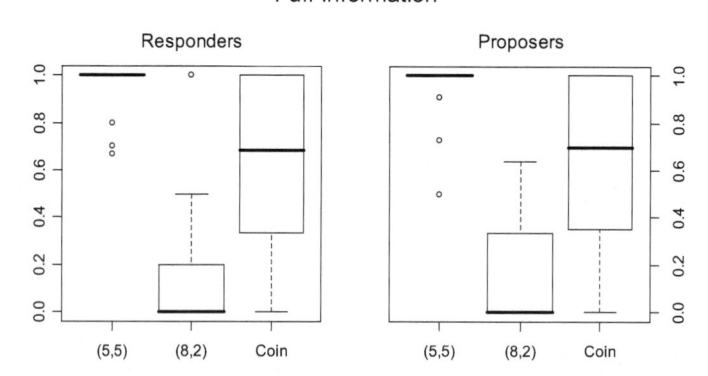

Figure 2. Boxplots of beliefs about normative expectations in the full information condition. Responders' mean beliefs were 97.0%, 12.6%, and 63.6%, for (5,5), (8,2), and Coin, respectively. Proposers' mean beliefs were 96.6%, 14.9%, 65.0%.

Private Information

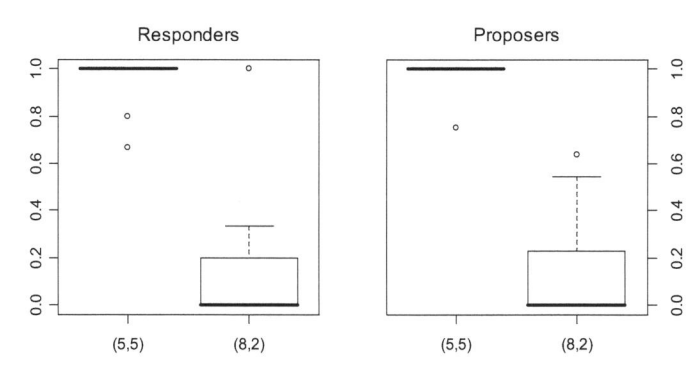

Figure 3. Boxplots of beliefs about normative expectations in the private information condition. Responders' mean beliefs were 98.1% and 16.0%, for (5,5) and (8,2), respectively. Proposers' mean beliefs were 99.1% and 12.5%.

Limited Information

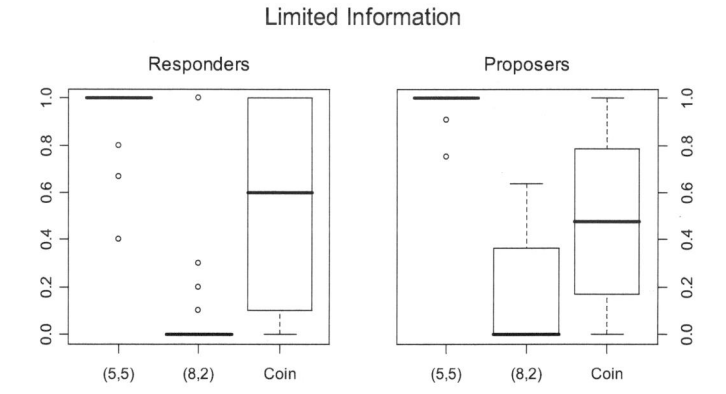

Figure 4. Boxplots of beliefs about normative expectations in the limited information condition. Responders' mean beliefs were 96.0%, 10.0%, and 54.4%, for (5,5), (8,2), and Coin, respectively. Proposers' mean beliefs were 98.8%, 17.6%, 49.3%.

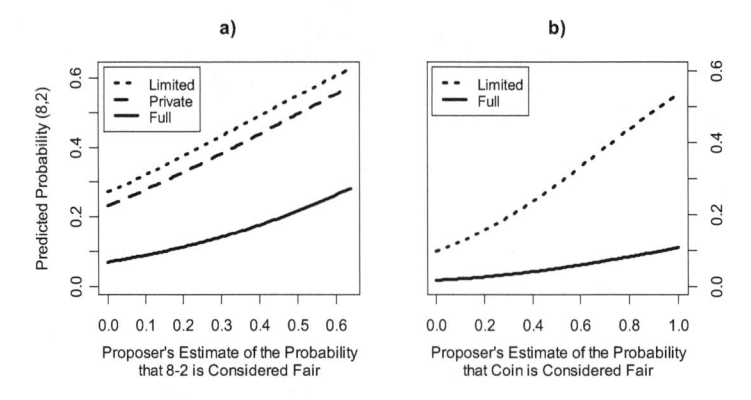

Figure 5. Predicted probability of (8,2) as a function of the Proposer's estimate of the proportion of Responders who considered a) (8,2) fair, and b) Coin fair, by condition. For each graph, the other beliefs are held fixed at their median values.

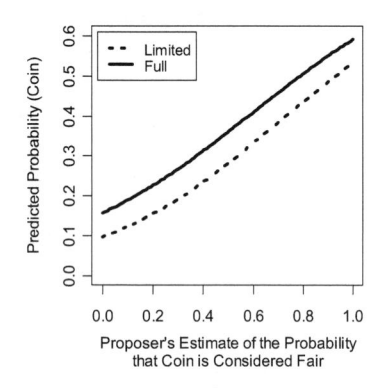

Figure 6. Predicted probability of Coin as a function of the Proposer's belief about Responders' normative expectations by condition. The other beliefs are held fixed at their median values.

Werner Güth and Hartmut Kliemt

Normative Expectations
A Comment on Cristina Bicchieri and Alex Chavez

1. Introduction

Cristina Bicchieri's and Alex Chavez's paper contains an innovative combination of information conditions and chance (coin flip) that we do like. To follow up on this basic idea might open up further interesting research prospects (see also related to this Bolton et al. 2005 who propagate 'random fairness'). Having paid that well-deserved tribute to the authors we see our task not as one of offering complimentary but rather complementary and critical comments. We will therefore probe into several aspects of the paper in form of critical remarks. In the next section (2) we will discuss the basic norm concept of the paper and whether the questionnaire provides convincing evidence for the existence of an inter-subjectively shared normative expectation. Then we take, not without a little aversion, to aversions as explanatory factors (3). This brings us to the point of discussing experimental methods (4) and results (5) and finally leads to our conclusions (6).

2. Questionnaire Response and Norm Existence

Providing criteria for the existence of norms is an old problem of what may be called the 'phenomenology of morals' (or what the authors call "behavioral ethics"). According to one strand of analysis it suffices for a norm to exist: a. that some individual x as a matter of fact desires that some other individual y acts in a certain way, b. that x intends to respond to the behavior of y with rewards or sanctions and c. that x can make his intentions as well as dispositions known to y. This seems to be the minimum for diagnosing the causal efficacy of some normative content. It captures how merely intended, imagined normative content becomes a real world causal factor: Individuals must bring the intended normative content to bear on the real world by their actions (in response to the actions of others).

It may be objected that what seems necessary and sufficient for some intrinsic 'normative motivation' to have real world causal effects is, however, not sufficient for the existence of a '*social* norm'. For that to be the case, it may plausibly be argued, many individuals in their separate capacities must happen to converge on the same normative content.

If individual behavior as shown in the different roles as specified by the normative content[1] converges we may state that we are dealing with some shared view of what 'ought' to be done. Like Bicchieri and Chavez we will use the term 'norm' from now on to refer to those norms that are widely shared in a population. We also agree that it is interesting to understand better what it implies in behavioral terms that normative orientations as a matter of fact express a shared view of what 'ought' to be done rather than idiosyncratic 'normative expectations' concerning the behavior of others. Whether the authors really capture a 'social norm' effect or merely the effect of making individuals alert with respect to a normative content, seems open though. More specifically asking proposers in the 'Salience' condition which allocation responders consider as fair clearly alerts them to the possibility that responders might be intrinsically motivated to reject certain proposals. But it does not necessarily follow that there needs to be a shared view of what ought to be done in situations like those of the mini-ultimatum game under study.

Furthermore, what they challenge by an 'ought' obligation is not at all inequ(al)ity aversion but rather let-down aversion (Charness/Dufwenberg 2006; Vanberg 2008) and the experimental method is somewhat flawed, e. g. by an inappropriate sequencing of treatments and by misleading participants without need.

3. Inequality-, Let-down-, and Aversion-aversion

In the tradition of psychological games (Geneakopolous et al. 1989), but often in less disciplined (by the so-called consistency requirement) ways, several authors have tried to account for experimentally observed prosocial behavior in terms of let-down or guilt aversion (Rabin 1993; Charness/Dufwenberg 2006; Vanberg 2008). The simple idea is to introduce expectations about what others expect 'me' to do as a factor of own decision utility in that disappointing others renders an option less attractive. To test this participants of experiments were asked about their first and second order behavioral expectations (i.e. were asked which choices were expected as well as which such expectations were expected).[2] Such a procedure can, of course, create serious demand effects.

Bicchieri and Chavez avoid to question self about behavioral expectations concerning other's behavioral expectations. They rather ask what self believes other would perceive as a fair choice. This addresses the effect of expectations concerning others' perception of fairness rather than actual choice behavior. This is a very subtle way of distinguishing 'ought'-obligations from purely idiosyncratic ethical concerns and, as we believe, a too subtle one. Moreover it misses out on crucial aspects of 'social norms' as postulated by the paper itself. We think that the 'ought' should and could have been induced in stronger ways, e. g., by one-sided contractual prom-

---

1   The content becomes causally effective by individual behavior as guided by individual perceptions of that content.
2   One could also ask for expectations concerning others' motives etc.

ises (Vanberg 2008) or by asking directly for the 'ought' rather than asking what one expects others think ought to be done.

Presumably the authors were to some extent misled by 'psychological game theory' (Geneakopolous et al. 1989; Dufwenberg/Kirchsteiger 2004; Falk/Fischbacher 2006), which they wanted to challenge, namely by capturing the 'ought' via second order beliefs. Presumably it would have helped also to take into account related experimental studies of

- Bolton et al. (2005) who propagate random fairness in case of unavoidable final allocative unfairness,
- Frohlich and Oppenheimer (1992) who explore behavior before and behind the veil of ignorance in order to compare the 'ought' (choices behind) with the more opportunistic (choices before) behavior,
- the random-pie ultimatum experiments where only proposers can judge fairness (similar to the 'Coin' condition of which only the proposer is aware) etc.

As far as the several aversions mentioned in the literature are concerned we are skeptical to the extent of almost developing an 'aversion-aversion' (see Güth 2008). The surprising popularity of a concept like 'inequality aversion' is certainly related to the fact that economists more often than not prefer theories that can be formulated exclusively in terms of consequences. The material payoffs and their distribution matter independently of factors that include the history, intentions etc. that led to the results. In fairness it should be said that the authors are not consequentialists of this rather simple minded kind nor are they adding another aversion to the list of aversions.

4. Experimental Method

The experimental workhorse is a mini-ultimatum game with two possible allocations of 10 units, namely

(5,5) or (8,2)

with the first (second) component specifying the proposer (responder) payoff. The proposer can either choose between the two allocations or rely on 'Coin' meaning that chance selects between the two allocations with equal probability. When 'Coin' is available but the responder is not aware of this possibility, the instructions specify merely two options for the proposer, namely (5,5) and (8,2). This is a slight violation of the experimentalists' norm not to mislead participants of experiments. If the authors would have said instead that

'the proposer can determine whether (5,5) or (8,2) is the allocation proposal'
or something similar, they could have avoided misleading their participants.

The '(No) Salience' treatment did (not) ask proposer-participants about their expectations concerning the number of responder participants who selected (5,5), (8,2) (or 'Coin') as fair (see appendix E of Bicchieri and Chavez). Although we do not deny that having to consider what responder participants view as fair will strengthen proposers' fairness concerns we have doubts that this is sufficient for the proposer to perceive the 'expected' as what 'ought' to be done. A proposer could be aware of such an expectation without accepting that it expresses more than a particular demand raised by other. There will be, so to say, an 'alerting' rather than an 'ought' effect. Bicchieri's und Chavez's question has, however, the advantage of capturing the possible heterogeneity of second order beliefs.

Whereas '(Non) Salience' was explored between subjects, the three information treatments

- 'Full' (the availability of 'Coin' and its choice is commonly known)
- 'Private' (only the proposer is aware of 'Coin')
- 'Limited' (the availability of 'Coin' but not its choice is commonly known)

were implemented in a within-subjects design. Specifically, each participant played all three information treatments in the order

'Full' → 'Private' → 'Limited'

constantly as proposer or responder (no role switching).

It seems very doubtful whether responder participants will be unaware of the 'Coin' option in 'Private' after having played 'Full'. The authors would have better explored also a sequence with 'Private' as the first game. If this would have resulted in too many treatments, one might have concentrated on just two information conditions, e. g. by neglecting 'Limited'. As far as this is concerned it seems that the study should best be treated as a pilot experiment for a larger experimental design. It is also unfortunate that the authors paid participants for two of the three information treatments as well as for the correctness of their beliefs what allows for diversification as in financial portfolio design (one insures against bad outcomes of one payment by hedging this risk via appropriate choices determining other payments).

5. Experimental Results

In case of 'Private' the direct choice of allocation (5,5) was clearly modal whereas 'Full' displayed a surprising share of 'Coin' supporting the 'random fairness' hypothesis of Bolton et al. (2005). 'Limited', however, crowded out such 'Coin'-choices by allowing proposer participants to hide their (8,2)-proposal as an unlucky random result of 'Coin'.

Responder participants (nearly) universally viewed the choice of (5,5) as fair and hardly ever that of (8,2). What is really surprising, however, is that in 'Full' and 'Limited' more than half of the responder participants judged 'Coin' as fair. This, however, may be simply a relative effect, namely of comparing 'Coin' with the direct proposal of (8,2). A control treatment could have checked how robust the fairness perception of 'Coin' is by allowing only for the direct choice of (5,5) as well as of 'Coin' by proposer participants. Still it is an intriguing result that random devices in determining allocations seem to be seen as fair and acceptable.

With respect to the allocation of organs by lottery that is mentioned by the two authors as an example of fairness by random choices the discussion at least among most ethical theorists seems to indicate otherwise. However the historical record of findings concerning the assignment of sailors for consumption after a shipwreck seems to suggest that allocation by lot is seen as fair under many circumstances (see Simpson 1997).

More basically, proposer participants who expect responders to view 'Coin' as fair propose more often the (8,2) allocation. Since such expectations render the (8,2) proposal less risky (at least in case of 'Private' and 'Limited'), this might be explained strategically. Another reasoning might be that someone who accepts 'Coin' automatically is willing to accept (8,2): so why don't I propose (8,2)?

The rejection rate (40 %) of the (8,2) proposal in 'Private' is in line with earlier findings. For 'Full' and 'Limited' it is 23.1 %, respectively 18.2 %. This, not altogether surprisingly, again casts doubt on the robustness of explanations based on fairness concerns. Most surprisingly, when resulting via 'Coin' in case of 'Full', the (8,2) allocation is never rejected. Apparently responder participants excused their proposer by arguments like 'at least (s)he gave me a chance'. The latter could support a more general intentionalist than consequentialistic approach (one punishes or rewards bad or nice intentions and not their (random) consequences, see Güth et al. 2001).

6. Summary

We completely agree with the authors that

- idiosyncratic other regarding concerns as, for instance, captured by let-down aversion are very dubious and
- 'oughts' as triggered by social norms or conventions or own promises or bilateral agreements are much more decisive.

'Salience' in the form of asking proposer participants about their beliefs what responder participants view as fair is, however, at best a poor substitute for testing such 'ought' effects directly. It should be compared with other 'ought'-inducements, e. g. by reviewing the experimental studies of norm enactment and norm compliance (e. g. Frohlich and Oppenheimer 1992; Büchner et al. 2005).

Enriching a mini-ultimatum game by including the 'Coin' option is definitely a very good idea, especially when varying what responders know about the availability and the choice of 'Coin'. But exploring 'Private' and 'Limited' only after 'Full' renders the results less compelling than they might be otherwise. Nevertheless the results are partly quite surprising and suggest follow up studies that would compensate flaws in the experimental design of this fine pilot study.

Bibliography

Bolton, G. E./J. Brandts/A. Ockenfels (2005), Fair Procedures: Evidence from Games Involving Lotteries, in: *Economic Journal 115*, 1054–1076

Büchner, S./W. Güth/L. M. Miller (2005), Conventions for Implementing Conventions—An Evolutionary and Experimental Analysis, in: *Working Paper Series of the Max Planck Institute of Economics Jena #21*

Charness, G./M. Dufwenberg (2006), Promises and Partnership, in: *Econometrica 74*, 1579–1601

Dufwenberg, M./G. Kirchsteiger (2004), Theory and Sequential Reciprocity, in: *Games and Economic Behavior 47*, 268–298

Falk, A./U. Fischbacher (2006), Theory of Reciprocity, in: *Games and Economic Behavior 54*, 293–315

Frohlich, N./J. A. Oppenheimer (1992), *Choosing Justice: An Experimental Approach to Ethical Theory*, Berkeley et al.

Geneakopolous, J./D. Pearce/E. Stacchetti (1989), Psychological Games and Sequential Rationality, in: *Games and Economic Behavior 1*, 60–79

Güth, W. (2008), (Non-)Behavioral Economics—A Programmatic Assessment, in: *Journal of Psychology 216*, 244–253

— /H. Kliemt/A. Ockenfels (2001), Retributive Responses, in: *Journal of Conflict Resolution 45*, 453–469

Rabin, M. (1993), Incorporating Fairness into Game Theory and Economics, in: *American Economic Review 83*, 1281–1302

Simpson, A. W. B. (1997), *Leading Cases in the Common Law*, New York

Vanberg, Ch. (2008), Why Do People Keep Their Promises? An Experimental Test of Two Explanations, in: *Econometrica 76*, 1467 – 1480

Lina Eriksson

Rational Choice Explanations of Norms: What They Can and Cannot Tell Us[*]

1. Introduction

Rational choice theory (RCT) explains norms in terms of individuals, their incentives and interactions, and in equilibrium terms. Since agents comply with a norm only if it is in their interest to do so, changing the incentive structure changes the norm. RCT analyses of norms often, but not inevitably, assume that norms are behavioural regularities sustained by sanctioning systems. They then go on to ask why and how it is that those norms exist. This question really consists of several different questions: why do norms exist, why does this particular norm exist, how do norms come into existence, why do norms continue to exist, why do norms change or not change, are dissolved or stable?

Most RCT analyses of norms answer questions about why norms exist in terms of functionalistic and rationalistic explanations: norms serve a function, they solve a problem people have, and therefore people create them to solve that problem. Usually, the problem is understood in game-theoretic terms: either it concerns the choice of one of the multiple possible solutions to a coordination game (in which case the norm will be self-sustaining once it exists) or ensuring cooperative behaviour in games of conflict like the Prisoners' Dilemma game (in which case the norm is not self-sustaining). This is however not functionalism as this view has been commonly known within social science. The rational choice version shares with traditional functionalism the emphasis on function, but differs in the focus on individual rationality: the function is sustained because it is in rational individuals' interests to sustain it, not because of some magical feedback mechanism. This is why the game-theoretic element is important. It is used to demonstrate a solution to an interaction problem—that is, a thoroughly *social* problem—in terms of individual rationality, not group rationality. According to this rational choice functionalism, people create a norm to solve a problem because it is in the interest of each, not because it is in the interest of all. However, as we will see further below, things are not quite this simple. Quite commonly, the analysis of norms is built on the idea of a *rational reconstruction*. A rational reconstruction is an explication (in game-theoretic terms) of what it is that norms *do*. This explication is then also taken to have some explana-

---

[*] I am grateful to Geoffrey Brennan, Robert Goodin and Nicholas Southwood for the great discussions that have inspired this paper, as well as to all the participants at the Bielefeld conference on norms, held in May 2008, and especially to Alan Hamlin for insightful and useful comments.

tory worth. In all fairness, I should immediately point out that not all RCT analyses of norms take such a rationalistic, functionalist approach, or a game-theoretic one, and that I will not discuss these other RCT analyses of norms.

The functionalist, game-theoretic approach, common as it is, gives rise to three worries:

1) There are many other functions that norms might (and do) serve, but which are not readily described in game-theoretic terms (or least they are not usually so described). A full account of norms must take into account this broader understanding of what it is that norms do.
2) In many cases when norms are needed, no norm arises magically to help solve the problem. So clearly the fact that there is a need for a norm is not enough to make one come about. Even if we accept the functionalist answer to the question of why norms exist in general, this answer does not suffice to explain why a particular norm exists.
3) Some norms do not seem to serve any functions: they seem neutral or outright harmful.

This paper is far from the first to criticize functionalism within RCT. Jon Elster, the critic of functionalism above all others, complains about Kenneth Arrow and James Coleman that they both "exemplify a mind-boggling combination of rational-choice individualism and society-wide functionalism" (Elster 2003, 303). And Eric Posner writes that "functionalism [...] is empirically false and methodologically sterile" (Posner 2002, 172). However, neither of them have discussed the functionalist argument for why social norms exist more than to point out that there are norms that do not seem to contribute to social welfare—that is, the third point above. But this point, I believe, is actually the weaker part of a proper argument against the functionalist analysis of why norms exist; as I will discuss below, the claim made against functionalism on the basis of the existence of 'bad' norms is not sufficiently developed, and is actually weaker than it is taken to be by, for example, Elster and Posner.

Before we turn to these problems, however, I must say a few words about what I take norms to be. Quite often a norm is taken to be only a behavioural regularity. This is clearly not enough: I seldom hang my clothes back in the wardrobe in the evening, yet there is no social norm that I should not. Another common suggestion (especially for RCT) is that norms are behavioural regularities sustained by informal sanctioning systems; often approval or disapproval, ostracism etc. This suggestion might however be too narrow on more than one account. First, we often call solutions to coordination games 'norms' but they do not rely on sanctions (indeed they are self-sustaining).[1] Second, some norms do not result in behavioural regularities

---

[1] Perhaps they should be called 'conventions' instead. But if there is a clear distinction between conventions and social norms, it is not clear that it has anything to do with which ones are self-sustaining. It seems reasonable, for example, that it has more to do with which ones have normative force and which ones seem completely ad hoc.

even though they do affect behaviour. For example, the most notable consequence of the very strong norm of reciprocity among the Ilk people is that they go to great lengths to avoid ending up in reciprocal relationships with others. Individuals have been known to mend their roofs in the middle of the night so as to not attract the 'help' of neighbours that then have to be helped in return (Elster 1989, from Turnbull 1972). Third, as many (for example Christina Bicchieri 1990) have argued, norms are characterized by expectations that most others will expect me to behave in a particular way, I expect them to behave in this way, they know that I expect them to and that I expect them to expect me to, and so on. Without these expectations social norms would not differ from rules enforced by others with force (which is one kind of sanctioning system that can give rise to behavioural regularities—if booing or waiving protest signs when the political leader drives down the street will result in people being sent to jail or beaten up, people will generally abstain from booing and waiving such signs). Fourth, many critics of RCT point out that one important aspect of norms is their normativity: people feel that they *ought* to comply with the norm in question, there is something *right* about it, something that gives others *legitimate* expectations that one will comply. This is not covered by the view that a norm is a behavioural regularity sustained by an informal sanctioning system. Since many RCT explanations of various phenomena consist in showing how the behaviours giving rise to these phenomena were in fact, contrary to appearance, in agents' self-interest, the focus of most RCT explanations of norms have understandably focused on showing why it would be in people's self-interest to comply, not why they would feel normatively compelled to do so. Normativity is, I believe, an important and insufficiently understood aspect of norms.[2] Although these and other issues are still unresolved matters of contention within RCT as well as between RCT and its competitors, RCT has nevertheless contributed impressively to our understanding of norms. This paper will concern issues that arise squarely within that framework, thus avoiding (as much as possible) debates about RCT versus its competitors and where the line between them should be drawn. For the sake of argument, I will therefore take norms to be behavioural regularities either self-sustaining or sustained by informal sanctioning systems, in both cases relying on expectations, expectations about expectations, and so on.

---

2 It might also be related to the backward-looking feature of norms that some, for example Elster (1990), have stressed. A norm is backward-looking if it states that a particular behaviour is called for because of what has happened before, not because of what consequences it will have. Hamlin comments that the backward-looking feature cannot be part of a definition of social norms if social norms are sustained by the fact that people comply to gain approval or avoid disapproval, since approval-seeking behaviour is forward-looking (Hamlin 1991). Nevertheless, many norms are also characterized by the notion of appropriateness; some actions are appropriate responses to certain other actions regardless of outcome. Or rather, perhaps, the *reason* why others approve or disapprove is sometimes at least partly that a particular response is considered appropriate given what has happened before. In that case, norms can be both backward-looking and forward-looking. Either way, the exact way this is to be resolved does not matter here.

2. Norms That Serve Functions

What I take to be the most common approach to why norms come into existence sees norms as solutions to various sorts of problems that arise because our actions affect others and we in turn are affected by theirs (see for example Ellickson 1991; Coleman 1990; however Coleman's rational choice account is usually not game-theoretic). Sometimes our mutual interdependence is bad news; the particular interaction effects make us all (or enough of us) worse off. Norms, on this account, are created or evolve to solve these problems. The approach is usually game theoretic, and the standard example is the coordination game. If we all agree to drive on the left hand side of the road, none of us will have any incentive to drive on the right hand side. Similarly, if we all agree to drive on the right hand side of the road, none will have an incentive to drive on the left hand side. The question is which one we choose, but once we are all coordinated, nobody will upset this equilibrium.

Some of these coordination games will be games with perfectly aligned interests. Others, like the Battle of the Sexes, will give asymmetrical payoffs, so that all players agree that coordination is first priority, but differ in their preferences over the possible solutions to the coordination problem. Solutions to coordination games, whether with symmetrical or asymmetrical payoffs, are special cases of solutions to a more general problem concerning externalities. When people's actions affect others, the affected people have an interest in regulating behaviour, either to ensure that actions with good externalities are performed or to stop actions with bad externalities.

Game theory also tells us that there is another important function that norms might serve, apart from being solutions to coordination games. In Prisoners' Dilemma type of games, it would be better for everyone if they cooperated, but since the agents have dominant strategies to defect, there will be no cooperation. If there was a norm to cooperate strong enough to change the underlying payoff matrix to make defection non-dominant, people would be better off, and it thus seems that here is a clear need for a norm.[3] The standard answer is that under some conditions, coordination around the cooperative behaviour is possible if agents play the game repeatedly: if cooperative behaviour now can ensure sustained cooperation in later rounds, the expected cooperation gains from future rounds can offset benefits from defection, as long as defection now brings about the opponent's defection later (Axelrod 1984). However, if the game is not repeated infinitely or at least indeterminately many times, social norms as cooperation-solutions to Prisoners' Dilemma games will often be in conflict with narrow self-interest. No matter what others do, it is better to defect, and a norm thus serves to realize cooperation benefits threatened by people's narrow self-interest. Many social norms seem to have this feature. It is

---

3 According to Bicchieri (2006), transforming Prisoner's Dilemma games and other similar games into coordination games is the sole function that social norms serve. She thus draws a clear line between conventions (solutions to coordination games) and social norms (cooperative solutions to Prisoners' Dilemma games).

clearly better to live in a society where people in general speak the truth than in a society where everyone lies, and yet best would be to live in a society where others are trustworthy and you yourself can lie when it is convenient. But without a norm against lying, everyone would lie, and nobody would be trustworthy. It is thus better to be bound by a norm against lying, even if it is inconvenient from time to time. Characteristic of this kind of norms is that they conflict with self-interest, at least narrowly interpreted. The norm will thus not be self-enforcing like a solution to a coordination game is.

Evolutionary game theorists have explored the conditions under which cooperation can evolve in a population in which agents play Prisoners' Dilemma games against each other. They typically assume that agents are of different types, some are cooperating and others defecting. The different behavioural types can be caused by people being genetically pre-programmed to behave this or that way, or because a part of the population follows a *norm* of cooperation. The question is then under what circumstances cooperators (for example, norm-followers) can do at least as good as defectors, so that they either stay a constant proportion of the population over time, or even spread. The literature suggests that the key factor is that cooperators interact with each other disproportionately often, either because they are surrounded by other cooperators (as might happen if cooperative behaviour is genetically transmitted and you live close to your family), or because they can tell who is a cooperator and who is not. The latter suggestion have given rise to theories about reputation effects and about costly signalling of cooperative dispositions, such as a tendency to blush when one is lying, emotional responses like rage at defection (see for example Frank 1988), or signals that one is prone to feel guilt when violating norms. We might signal group loyalties through choice of clothes, haircuts and music that cuts us off from all but one group, thereby showing our commitment to that particular group (see for example Posner 2002 for an account of norms as arbitrary signals of type; a rational choice account of norms that does not follow the lines described in this paper).

Another solution to how people come to cooperate in Prisoners' Dilemmas is to create that sanctioning system that has already been mentioned several times. Rational agents realize that they would be better off if they could all commit to cooperating. The problem is that they cannot make credible commitments, because whatever they say their opponents know that they have no incentive to cooperate. The classical solution is to create a Leviathan, a power that enforces promises to cooperate (or even just enforces cooperation, for that matter). Leviathan is often the state: the state enables people to enter contractual agreements with each other, safely assuming that the other part will fulfil their part of the agreement. The state thus creates a necessary condition for a well-functioning market economy. But social norms can (and often do) fulfil the same function: if a norm-violator is sanctioned heavily by either the person harmed by the violation (if anyone), oneself (by guilt over the violation), or—more typically—by third parties, people's incentive structure changes, and sometimes it changes enough that defection is no longer a dominant strategy.

3. Problems

The contributions of RCT to the theory of social norms are thus impressive (not an original observation). But there are some aspects of norms that the approach described above cannot account for. Three of these problems concern the claim that norms arise to solve problems. The first problem is that the functions that norms serve seem broader than what RCT, or more specifically game theoretic, analyses of norms acknowledge. The second problem is that some problems call for norms to solve them, and yet no norm has arisen to solve them. There must therefore be more to the explanation of why norms arise than the problems that need solving. Finally the third problem is that there are norms that do not seem to serve any functions at all; bad norms that make everyone worse off (as many others have pointed out).

3.1 Too Narrow a View of Functions

Enabling successful coordination and cooperation cannot be the *only* kind of function that norms serve. It might be that we are studying only norms of *cooperation,* as Bicchieri (1990) denotes them; this does seem to narrow down the focus to solutions to Prisoners' Dilemma games, but it does not address why these norms should be any different from other norms. A great number of social norms can be understood as solving a Prisoners' Dilemma game (which does not establish that this is the reason for why they exist), but if we are not clear why these social norms would differ from other social norms then neither can it be clear why we should group them together just because they happen to allow this interpretation.

Let us therefore look at other functions that norms serve. One is analogous to the one given to rules by rule consequentialism: what counts are good consequences of behaviour, but the consequences will be better overall if people follow rules instead of trying to maximize the good consequences in each decision. Similarly, by regulating our behaviour through norms we might achieve better consequences than if we try to assess consequences in every decision situation. If this is the case, clearly norms would serve a function, but one much broader than game theory specifies. In fact, norms can ease the burden of making decisions in general, by functioning as decision-making shortcuts. Not all such shortcuts are norms; as mentioned, social norms are characterized by a set of expectations and by an informal sanctioning system, and clearly not all rules of thumb share these characteristics. But some norms do help us make decisions. For example, consider what you should wear to a funeral. For most of us, the answer is 'black', and we do not waste any time choosing between the black suit and the red cocktail dress.

A further possible function of norms is to add a little extra motivation to do the right thing. Most of us are imperfect creatures, who are sometimes tempted to choose as we should not, even when we know it is not in our interest in the long run. Having a norm specifying that we ought to do that which we have reason to do means that the reasons we would have without the norm get a helping hand in motivating us by the extra reasons we have to avoid social disapproval and other sanctioning. It also helps others predict behaviour, because those who are not motivated to act as they have reason to will often be motivated by the threat of sanctions.

Finally, norms enable symbolic action. Norms create meaning, and this allows us to express attitudes through the use of symbolic actions. Consider again the norm to be dressed in black when attending a funeral. The norm makes it the case that one expresses respect through the choice of colour on one's clothes. Without the norm, we would not have been able to express respect through our choice of clothes: a Hawaii shirt with a sunset over a tropical beach would have been just as good—that is, just as devoid of either appropriate or inappropriate meaning—as a sombre black suit, but neither would express anything. To some, this might seem like a good thing. But expressing one's respect for the deceased and for the family and friends, signalling that one sees the death of their (or perhaps one's own) loved one as a tragic event, is something we have reason to want to be able to do. Doubtless we can do this in other ways, for example by saying so, but the norm about dress code adds one way in which we can do it.

Eric Posner rests his whole account of social norms as costly signals on what I call their role for symbolic action; norm compliance signals that we are of this or that type (Posner 2002). Norms then serve a *signalling function*. Norms in this way enable us to prove our group loyalties and create group identities. By violating norms of one group, thereby making me a less-preferred cooperation partner for members of that group, I show my commitment to another group. By wearing certain clothes, agreeing to certain rules or initiation rites, and so on I incur costs to show that I want to belong to a particular group and am willing to be a trustworthy member.

Generally, norms are part of a general shared culture that creates meaning and thus enables us to perform symbolic actions. To have such a culture can be seen as a coordination problem in itself. The ability to signal one's attitudes to others, to perform symbolic actions, is important in many aspects of our lives. What matters for the solution of the problem of how to create a rich enough layer of meaning to enable us to do what we need to do is not whether black clothes or Hawaii shirts signals respect and mourning, but that one of them does so. The person contemplating how to dress for the funeral must think that black signals the relevant attitude, he or she must know that others think so, it must be common knowledge that everyone thinks so and that everyone knows that everyone knows, and so on.

In an ideal world, maybe norms would not matter in this way: people could see what was in each others' minds, and could therefore directly discern everyone's attitudes. But expressive/symbolic action is not just about signalling to others: expressing our feelings and attitudes seem to fill a need in us regardless of others. We often perform some little ritual when we visit the grave of a loved one even when nobody else is there, and even when we believe the dead cannot see us. It might be the case that we have some imagined recipient for the signal in the back of our mind, but nevertheless expressive action is important even in cases in which the consequences of sending a particular signal to a particular audience do not seem to be what is important.

Norms might also serve several functions at the same time. Consider a norm for behaviour in a coordination game. It points out which of the possible coordination equilibria is chosen, thus enabling people to be successful in their attempts to coordinate. But norms might also serve a second function. If people are not perfectly rational—as, alas, at least the author of this paper is not—people can fail to act according to the coordination solution. They can fail to see their own interests in coordinating, or, as noted, they might be tempted to defect because of other, external, factors, even though it does mean losing the coordination benefits for this particular problem. Sanctions serve to add a little extra strength to the payoff of the coordinating behaviour, in some cases thereby helping people help themselves. If norms serve multiple functions at the same time, it is hard to determine *which* function is the one responsible for the norm's existence. Perhaps both are, or perhaps one is just a fortunate side-effect. But if we are content to consider one function obviously served to be a side-effect, why are we not equally content to consider both of them to be side-effects of some other mechanism that explains why norms exist?

3.2 Needs Not Satisfied

The too narrow view of what counts as a function was one problem. One could expect that all (or at least most) would be well if we analysed norms in terms of these broader functions. But unfortunately, as noted in the introduction, this is not the case, for two reasons. First, there is often a need to be filled and no norm arises to fill it: lots of coordination and decision-making problems go unsolved, in lots of cases we wish there was a simple way of expressing how we feel. Clearly we cannot take for granted that if the need for a norm arises, a norm will spontaneously be created to fill it. Second, there are several norms that do not serve any functions at all: inefficient or even destructive norms are far too common to be exceptions to a general rule about norms that serve important functions efficiently and well, leading to happiness and welfare for all (Elster 1990).

When discussing why some norms do not arise we need to distinguish between norms that solve Prisoners' Dilemma problems and those that solve coordination problems. The latter are characterized by the fact that it is in everybody's *individually rational* interest to coordinate with others, and that coordination is self-sustaining. As a result, it is rather puzzling that they often do not. Failure to solve Prisoners' Dilemma problems, on the other hand, is less surprising: after all, cooperating is only collectively, not individually, rational and creating a norm that will make cooperation individually rational requires the creation of a functioning sanctioning system, which is itself a Prisoners' Dilemma. Coordination problems, on the other hand, have none of these problematic features. They should therefore be easily solved, and it is puzzling that they are not.

Common understanding of coordination solutions is a necessary part of our lives. We know which side to drive on (coordination through law), we make plans about going to the movies and we implement those plans, showing up at the same movie at the same time and same day (coordination through explicit communication), we split money in half/half shares in coordination games where we lose all money if we fail to coordinate (coordination relying on focal points). Yet there are many cases where we need to coordinate and fail to do so. Consider the irritating swerve-with-the-shopping-trolley case: do you swerve to the left or the right when you meet another person with a shopping trolley turning into your aisle in the supermarket? Anyone who goes shopping with shopping trolleys in supermarkets have encountered this textbook example of a coordination problem at some point in their lives, and yet there is no clear norm about how to solve it, as we can all testify. Or consider the need for a norm that allows us to express what needs to be expressed when consoling a grieving friend: many who have lost somebody close to them have later told how their friends and colleagues shied away, not knowing what to say and do, and many of us have probably searched for words and actions that would express both our sympathy and willingness to help or listen if help or an ear is needed, while at the same time trying to discern whether the grieving person just wants to be left alone. Grief is part of life, none of us are strangers to it, and yet we lack simple ways of expressing what we want, both as sympathetic friends and when we are the ones grieving. We could try to make do without norms and just say what we think (which is what we do), but without clear norms care must be taken to formulate things exactly right and the effort and fear of failure keeps people apart when they want help or to help.

A need is clearly not enough for a norm to arise, because coordination around a particular solution does not become common knowledge automatically. So how does a particular solution become common knowledge? Sometimes functionalist, game-theoretic arguments seem to presuppose that a group gets together and talks it over: the explicit agreement points out the relevant coordination strategy. But this is often impossible because the number of people is too great, or people are too spread out—it might not even be clear who belongs to the group of relevant decision makers and who does not. Further, even if all relevant people *could* get together and make a collective decision, most norms do not originate this way; there is not even a clear time and place at which they came into existence. Rather they spread, perhaps slowly, to a population having originated in a subgroup. But even when subgroups form their own norms which could be extended to the whole group, these norms often fail to spread because of the common knowledge problem. Evolutionary stories of how norms spread in a bigger population usually rely on people being able to observe strategies' success rates (and able to imitate the good ones). In most cases, if you and I manage to both swerve left in the supermarket alley, nobody is there to watch. If they were, they might expect this strategy to be successful for coordination with others *who also observed* the solution. But if an observer goes around the corner into the next alley where she encounters a person who did not see the successful coordination, she will have no reason to expect this person to expect her to swerve left, and so will have no reason to play this strategy herself. They have to start from scratch. If she decided that since she had seen the strategy 'swerve left' being successful at least in one instance, she would always play that strategy and perhaps she would in the end affect others to adopt it too (after all, that would be the way to coordinate successfully with her). But she would have *no reason* to adopt this strategy in this unconditional way: if rational, she should adopt the strategy that she expects others to use too, and she simply has no reason to expect others to use this particular strategy just because *she* happened to observe it being employed successfully one time in alley number 12.

Admittedly, whether this evolutionary argument works depends on the norm in question and whether observation of one instance of successful coordination reasonably raises the expectation that the strategy played will be successful in other encounters; sometimes it will, sometimes it will not. Further, there are other evolutionary arguments, and some of them may be successful when the one discussed above is not. This said, however, it should be clear that it is not obvious how any given solution to a coordination problem spreads in a population. For cooperation solutions to Prisoners' Dilemma games, it should be even less so, given the added problem of conflict of interest.

The lack of a mechanism that ensures common knowledge is a common problem in real life. Quite often when we come to a new place or social context we deliberately and somewhat anxiously search for clues about what we are expected to do in that new situation. We know that others solve coordination problems differently, and that we need what we do not have: information about how those we will interact with expect us to solve it. That this information is not always easily accessible shows just how hard it can be to figure out what the favoured coordination solution is. Therefore it is surprising that not more attention has been paid to the role that common knowledge plays and how this knowledge can come about. (One of the early theorists to discuss it is Lewis 1969; see also Cubitt/Sugden 2003.)

3.3 Norms That Do Not Seem to Serve Functions

The problem with a functionalist account of norms is not just that there are needs unsatisfied, but there are norms that do not seem to serve any function at all, and even some that seem outright harmful. If all theory about why norms arise concern 1) demonstrating a need for one, and 2) that it could have originated from spontaneous interactions among boundedly rational agents, we will have excluded from the outset a complete theory of why norms come about, since we cannot address those norms that do not serve functions.

Such, or along similar lines, goes the usual criticism against functionalist analyses of norms. For example, Elster claims that norms of revenge cannot be analysed in functionalist terms because they lead to misery and death rather than to social welfare (Elster 1990). And Posner makes a point about how arbitrary many norms are, how unpleasant or harmful, and that we cannot take for granted that a norm is efficient (Posner 2002). However, Posner's own account of norms, according to which social norms are means for signalling what 'type' one belongs to and any behaviour that can be used for costly signalling will do, including those that on the whole have harmful effects on society, on the contrary illustrates how even 'bad' norms can be taken to serve a function; after all, they allow us to send credible signals. Posner argues that the effects of a norm are of two kinds: the internal effects concerning the cooperation or coordination benefits the norm allows, and the external effects concerning the effects on society of lots of people behaving in the way specified by the norm. This is true, but it does not work as an argument against functionalism: norms can still be understood in terms of their functions, not for the external effects on society but for the internal effects. If the mechanism that somehow caused the norm was sensitive to the function of the norm but not to interests of society of having the function served in this particular way, functionalism might still be useful for understanding why norms exist. Further, Posner argues that norms are not the only things that can solve a particular problem, and there is no reason to expect them to be the best solution to the problem. But in his signalling examples, the function norms really serve is not to increase general welfare but to enable credible signalling, and this they actually do just fine, even when the effects on the rest of society are less desirable. We must distinguish between whether a norm serves its function efficiently, and whether its serving this function is efficient for social well-being overall. The argument that functionalism is falsified through the existence of norms that do not serve functions is thus sometimes made too hastily. Even though I agree, ultimately, more care needs to be taken. In general, we must distinguish between norms that only serve a function for one group but not for others, norms that simply do not serve their particular function well, and norms that do not seem to serve any functions at all.

When evaluating norms we need to keep in mind the relevant reference group: if groups have conflicting interests, norms that serve the interests of one will not serve the interests of another. This can happen in at least two different cases. First, the society or wider group often has an interest in hindering a smaller subgroup from solving their coordination or cooperation problems, and norms that allow subgroups to solve such problems often cause problems for the wider population. For example, we do not want mafia groups to solve their problems of coordination, general cooperation and trust efficiently, because that would make them an even greater menace (see for example Ellickson 1991). Neither do we want companies to solve the problem of setting a joint high price, thus overcoming their problem that for any given sufficiently high price each company wants to undercut the others. An efficient solution to their price setting problem would mean the end of market competition—indeed, we even have laws against such solutions. Posner's own example of norms that discriminate against women or blacks are of the exact same kind: they serve the interests of white males in that they allow these people to signal that they are certain types. Norms among subgroups can serve the interests of the subgroups just fine, and still harm the society at large (or even just another group).

The other case is when a dominating group will benefit from everyone complying with a particular norm, and manages to impose this norm on the whole population even though it only serves the interests of a few.[4] The puzzle is then why those whose interests are not served by the norm would comply with it. To answer this question, we would have to say much more about how norms affect people's behaviour and about the motivation for norm compliance. Perhaps the stronger group can sanction behaviour of the weaker and therefore enforce norm compliance. Perhaps they have more subtle tools that work through the shared meanings and social identifications that everyone is affected by, and perhaps they can make the weaker group's members enforce their own compliance by making them accept the norm as legitimate or right, sanctioning violations with feelings of guilt. Whether these options would move us out of the realm of RCT is debated: it depends on whether one sees RCT as wedded to self-interest maximization and if so, if this includes the minimization of unpleasant feelings like guilt, regardless of the questionably rational standing of the psychological mechanisms that generate those feelings.[5]

So much for norms that serve the interests of some but not others. Let us turn instead to norms that do not serve the interests of any group well. Here one should caution against claiming that a norm does not serve a function at all, if all we mean is that it serves it badly. If norms are created by explicit agreement, it *is* puzzling why an inefficient norm would be chosen if another and better solution was available. But if norms evolve rather than arise as a result of an explicit decision, at least inefficiency can be explained as less-than-perfect rational choice functionalism: norms serve functions, but some factors might make them suboptimal.

One possible reason for such inefficiency is path dependency. If norms evolve, different individuals in the population must at some point have exhibited different behaviours. The behaviour that did best if everyone else was also behaving that way is not necessarily the same as the behaviour that does best against a variety of behaviours that people are trying when they are searching for a successful strategy. The result is that more and more people will learn to use the behaviour that does best

---

4   RCT has often been accused of ignoring power inequalities and asymmetric games, and even though an important literature discusses unequal bargaining positions and asymmetric outcomes (see for example Knight 1992), most focus on game-theoretic analyses of norms has concerned symmetric games although the Battle of the Sexes is an exception. But nevertheless the Battle of the Sexes game is a coordination game: both players prefer coordination over no coordination. The puzzle here are norms that seem to benefit *only* one group at another group's expense.

5   On the one hand, we could consider socialization to a norm irrational, since it hinders our rational calculations of consequences in particular situations in which we could do better had we violated the norm. Therefore perhaps internal sanctioning through feelings of guilt should not be included into a theory of rational choice. On the other hand, if we take for granted that we are guilt-feeling creatures, it seems rational for us to act so as to minimize these unpleasant feelings (or, on a more plausible account; if we the kind of creature that does think some actions normatively required and will therefore feel bad if we fail to perform them—and rightly so—it seems rational to act as we think we ought to). On the third hand, (if you have one) binding yourself to the mast by developing internal sanctions that will keep you on the straight and narrow path is clearly often beneficial, from a self-interest point of view, because it enables you to be trustworthy and make credible commitments.

in those varying circumstances. Once there has come to be coordination around this behaviour, nobody has an incentive to change unilaterally, and the optimal solution to the coordination game is not reached. An explicit agreement to switch to another behaviour that is recognized as better would get people out of the local optimum trap. But without such explicit agreement—or some other mechanism that changes the behaviour of most of the population at once—behaviour will stay inefficient. However, even when everybody could change simultaneously the costs involved in doing so can be high enough to deter change. For example, some countries that have considered changing their convention about which side to drive on have refrained from such change because of the high number of expected accidents and the costs associated with having a road network constructed for the 'wrong' convention.

Further, evolution is a *process,* and as such takes *time*. Even if the process is evolving towards an optimal state, there is no reason to believe that the state at any particular time is optimal. Yet another reason to expect inefficiency at any given time is that what state would be optimal depends on the circumstances and these have a tendency to change over time, thereby changing what the optimal state would be. Evolution is thus aiming for a moving target.

A more serious mismatch between behaviour and fitness can come about through the development of broad behavioural dispositions. A kind of behaviour that serves the person well in many situations in life can have bad consequences in one type of situation. But since the person has developed a disposition to behave in this way in general, the explanation for the unsuccessful behaviour in one type of situation can very well be that that kind of behaviour has good consequences in other situations. Biological evolution, where the variation stems from mutations and selection is on inheritance and reproductive fitness, is likely to give rise to this kind of phenomenon, because biological evolution cannot fine-tune our behavioural dispositions to particular circumstances. Cultural evolution, on the other hand, can be a little more fine-tuned to the problem at hand. First; since behavioural changes are not inherited and reproduced over generations but learned from more successful others, the time gap is shorter, so there is less risk that a particular behaviour was developed for circumstances that are no longer the case. Second, since people can acquire new behaviours during their lifetimes they have more resources than broad behavioural dispositions at their disposal. Because of our capacity to learn from each other, we do not have to develop dispositions that control our behaviour to the extent that a creature without ability to learn would have to. Therefore, when humans come across situations in which their previous strategies do not do well, they can deliberately set out to search for a new and better strategy, looking to others for more successful behaviours to imitate. The conscious search for more successful behaviours to learn from thus allows more fine-tuned behaviours. However, information cascades show that intentional adjustment to the behaviour of those one believes have more information can lead a whole group to adopt the behaviour of someone who did not really have a clue (Elster 2007, chapter 23). Further, the person whose behaviour is being imitated might feel that his or her views get confirmed by the number of others who seem to agree, thus lessening that person's own doubts.

So—have I really just managed to show that all norms do serve functions, after all? I hope not, for although I believe the denial of functionalism is made too hastily sometimes, I do not think all norms serve functions. Consider etiquette-rules. Sometimes it makes sense to see them as signalling devices, like Posner (2002) does: we signal that we care about what others think about us when we hold our cutlery in particular ways rather than in others. And sometimes the argument has been taken further; their function is to exclude those lower in the hierarchy from the group, so that the elite is forever designing new intricate ways of behaving, dressing and talking to distinguish themselves from others. But as Elster (1989) has pointed out, these rules work in the opposite direction as well: upper- and middle class members who wanted to join the working class for ideological reasons soon found out that they were excluded by rules for behaviour, talking and dressing. And yet clearly these rules cannot exist to protect the social status of the working class against those upper-and middle class people who might want to join.

It is possible that if we try really hard, we can find some sort of function—say, group identity—that the more absurd rules can nevertheless be said to serve *to some degree*, even if not efficiently. And yet, this only illustrates that the serving of functions is a continuum from 'not at all' to 'perfectly'; it can be true that even the absurd norms serve *some* function to *some* extent, and yet as that extent decreases, so does the usefulness of functionalism as a theoretical approach, and instead the more focus we need on how norms arise and thus what factors affect which norms are chosen out of all the possible ones that would serve the same function, many much, much better. If at the very end of that continuum there are norms that really do not serve any function at all, or only norms that serve their functions very, very badly, is less interesting. That far along the continuum, functionalism is not going to be of much use to us anyway.

4. What Exactly Are We Asking about Norms?

I have been careful to speak of analyses of *why* norms exist, not of *how* they have come to exist (except in the case of evolutionary arguments). The reason is that it seems so obvious that the rational choice functionalist, game-theoretic approach has nothing to say about *how* norms come about. The exact nature of the research question is however often a bit vague: is it really true that the functionalist game-theoretic approach tells us why norms exist but not how they come to do so? Or does it tell us why norms *persist* but not why they arose? Or why it is that norms in general exist, but not why any particular norm does so?

Many who use game-theory to understand norms choose to speak not of explanations of why norms exist or how, but of *rational reconstructions* of norms. A rational reconstruction of a norm is an explication of what it is that norms do, and of situations that are prone to generate norms.

A rational reconstruction of norms thus helps understand what norms are, *and how they are generated*. It is this latter point that is at the heart of my worries. Ullman-Margalit writes that:

> From this point the line of argument continues as follows: It is shown how, and in what sense, norms of specified types might solve each of these problems. It is then noted, on the one hand, that a large number of real-life situations reveal themselves on analysis as falling roughly under one of the three categories just mentioned and, on the other, that norms of the types suggested as solutions do in fact exist. The demonstration of this correlation between certain types of situational problems and certain types of norms which facilitate their solution is considered an account of the generation of these norms. (1979, 10)

But it's not quite clear what it means to give an account of how norms are generated, if we are not giving an explanation for why or how they exist. Clearly game-theory does not tell us *how* a norm comes into existence. It lacks all the necessary historical detail, and it is in general hard to specify a particular point in time at which a given norm was created. Most likely it has evolved over time, gradually becoming what it now is, as Ullman-Margalit herself points out. Equally clear is that Ullman-Margalit and others who use the rational reconstruction account of norms (for example, see also Skyrms 2004) do claim that the fact that norms often do happen to solve certain problems is not a mere coincidence. After all, this problem-solving function is "considered an account of the generation of these norms". Exactly how this works is not spelled out, but the following story is the most plausible I can come up with.

There are some problems, usefully characterized in game-theoretic terms, such that norms can solve them. This fact is part of *why* norms exist. But it is not an account of *how* norms come to exist, because they can come into existence in lots of different ways: people might get together and decide on a new norm to regulate their behaviour, or the norm might evolve through many interactions, or arise out of what used to be a mere behavioural regularity that happened to also solve what would otherwise have become a problem, or ... All of these different stories of *how* norms come into existence, however, have in common that *if these norms had not happened to solve a problem they would not exist*. Maybe, then, the right way to understand the rational reconstruction-account is as a counterfactual argument.

But this counterfactual argument is still vulnerable to the problems pointed out in this paper: that there are similar problems that are not solved, and that some norms do not seem to serve functions. The latter point I have made an effort to undermine myself, so perhaps I should not make too much of it. But the first one is important. In response, it can be (and has been) argued that the game-theoretic rational choice functionalist account is supposed to be an account only of a particular set of norms; those that solve Prisoners' Dilemma problems, coordination problems or, in Ullman-Margalit's case, problems of inequality. This response is unsatisfactory for two reasons. First, because not all real-world cases of these problems are solved, as we have seen. However, serving a function might still be a *necessary*, even if not *sufficient*, condition for the emergence of norms. Second, however, it is an unsatisfactory account because we then need an explanation of why some social norms should be

193

explained in a fundamentally different way than other social norms. Either you claim that all social norms fulfil these functions, in some way or another, or you accept that some social norms do and some do not. If you choose the latter route, why is it not most plausible that all social norms have the same basic explanation? That is, why should we believe that some norms can be explained game-theoretically even though nothing is said about how other norms are explained? We cannot judge whether the particularist, rationalistic functionalist story is more plausible than a general one if we are not given even a hint about how other social norms are to be explained. And this weakens the case for the rational reconstruction account. For example, Ullman-Margalit in fact does not attempt to prove that her three kinds of situations prone to generate norms are the only kinds of situations that do, but upon reflection she thinks they are. But if we claim that they are, we must also deal with the claim that there are norms that do not seem to fulfil these functions.

Further, I hope to have showed that the functionalist argument discussed above does a less than convincing job of telling us why norms exist: if nothing else, it cannot be the whole story because a) there are needs that go unsatisfied, and b) many norms, although they might be said to serve functions, do so badly and others would have done so much better (and the interesting questions is then why this norm and not a better one). Further it is not clear to me in what respect we really can separate the issue of *why* from *how*. There is nothing puzzling about claims that a particular group of people living in the same house adopted a particular norm about cleaning of the communal laundry room in order to solve a problem they were facing, and this is non-puzzling whether we are told the exact details about who said what at the meeting, or even whether there was a meeting and not just a rule somebody made up and then consolidated with the others one by one. But when a very inefficient norm with an origin in a distant and distinctly foggy past is claimed to exist in order to achieve a goal it miserably fails to achieve to any reasonable extent and with any reasonable efficiency, it is less obvious that it existed *in order to* achieve this goal. Why should we take the small degree of function to be evidence for why it exists, given the number of functions we can come up with, the variety of ways in which, say, group identity can be expressed, and the degree of inefficiency we allow? It seems no matter what norm, we can come up with some function that it serves, especially if it does not have to do so particularly well. And as mentioned above, if we acknowledge that any given norm often serves more than one function at the same time, it is not clear how we determine which function—if any!—was the reason for the norm.

A short detour is called for here: notice that evolutionary theories based on this approach actually *do* tell us something about *how* a norm has spread—namely, how it *could have* spread. These models can thus be taken to explore *possible* scenarios for the *origin* of the norm (Binmore/Kirman/Tani 1993). Game theoretic accounts that complement the static approach with an evolutionary story are thus, it seems, saying something about both the function *and* possible spread. What is the explanatory worth of this? That depends on the state of the field. If the existence of the phenomenon (in our case, norms) is very puzzling, and people are asking how on earth it can exist, then it can be very valuable indeed to show how it could have arisen. But if the literature is full of these 'how possible'-stories the addition of yet another is of much less value.

Back to the static game-theoretic story and its interpretation then. The less likely it is that a group of people got together and said 'let's solve this problem—suggestions anyone?', or that people at least recognized the same problem—and did so *as* the same problem—and set out to solve it, the less reason we have to think that there is a distinction between *why* and *how*. Perhaps norms arise out of accident, as unintended side-effects, etc. Maybe what we should focus on is not so much an imagined answer to *why they exist*—because there might not be one—but an answer to *why it is that they persist once they have come into existence*. Actually, Elster (2007) claims this is how economists usually think of the question. Why norms come into existence is a matter of historical accident, and beyond what the social sciences can tell us, the argument goes.

But if we take the static game-theoretic analyses to have no connection to questions of norm origin, there is no need for talk of functions at all. All the work is done by the *equilibrium*: nobody has an incentive to change their behaviour given either the coordination game equilibrium or the cooperative equilibrium induced by the informal sanctioning system. But equilibria can arise in all sorts of situations and have any kind of social well-being effects. So why so much talk about whether norms solve coordination or cooperation problems? The focus on functions thus makes sense only if we think we actually answer, at least partly, why it is that norms *exist*, not only why they *persist*.

Let us turn instead to the suggestion that the functionalist game-theoretic approach explains why norms in general exist but not why a particular norm exists. The fact that there are unsatisfied needs seem to support this. The claim could go like this: many interaction situations call for norms, and all norms have in common that they have arisen to satisfy this need, but it takes something over and above this need to create a norm, and therefore any particular norm can be explained only by reference to both the need for a norm and to this extra thing that brings the norm about. Thus, there is a *necessary* condition for norms (satisfy a need/serve a function) but this condition is *not sufficient* for a norm to come about. However, if we accept that there are norms that do not serve functions, the claim is false. If we instead believe that even harmful norms serve functions but do it very badly, most of the work is being done by whatever factor apart from function that is needed to bring a norm about: indeed, since the norm in question is supposedly so inefficient it would be really interesting to know why this one and not a more efficient one was selected.

5. Conclusions

The (particular) functionalist approach discussed here suffers from three problems. The first one is that norms obviously serve more functions than the ones captured by coordination games or Prisoners' Dilemmas (or Battle of the Sexes or ...). Of course, it is not necessary for RCT to focus on a narrow set of games for understanding norms. Further, many of the other functions I have been discussing may be cast as coordination game solutions; this, for example, may be the best way to understand the norm to wear black at funerals. But the standard functionalist game-theoretic RCT account of norms clearly leaves out many important functions that norms serve.

The second problem is that the functionalist story cannot be the whole story: in many cases when norms are needed to solve some problem or another, none comes to the rescue. Clearly it is not the case that if there is a need for a norm, one will arise. This problem might come down to the difference between giving necessary and sufficient conditions for the existence of norms (but as discussed above, it is not clear that this route is satisfying).

Third, some norms do not seem to serve any functions at all. Some have seemingly neutral consequences, others are outright bad for us. This, I argued, is however possible to account for quite readily within RCT: some of the suggestions were that norms can evolve in ways that get them (and us) stuck on local optima, and path dependency can result in less-than-optimal outcomes. Some norms that seem detrimental also are so for some people *but not for everyone*: the norm might serve some people's interests but not those of others, etc. However, the less efficient the norms, the less useful is a functionalist account for understanding them, regardless of whether they can be said to serve *some* function to *some* (small) degree.

Finally, it is unclear exactly what question the functionalist game-theoretic approach is supposed to answer.

Bibliography

Axelrod, R. (1984), *The Evolution of Cooperation*, New York

Bicchieri, C. (1990), Norms of Cooperation, in: *Ethics 100*, 839–861

— (2006), *The Grammar of Society – The Nature and Dynamics of Social Norms*, Cambridge

Binmore, K./A. Kirman/P. Tani (1993), Introduction: Famous Gamesters, in K. Binmore/A. Kirman/P. Tani (eds.), *Frontiers of Game Theory*, Cambridge/MA, 1–25

Coleman, J. (1990), *Foundations of Social Theory*, Cambridge/MA

Cubitt, R./R. Sugden (2003), Common Knowledge, Salience and Convention; A Reconstruction of David Lewis' Game Theory, in: *Economics and Philosophy 19*, 175–210

Ellickson, R. C. (1991), *Order without Law – How Neighbors Settle Disputes*, Cambridge/MA-London

Elster, J. (1989), Social Norms and Economic Theory, in: *Journal of Economic Perspectives 3*, 99–117

— (1990), Norms of Revenge, in: *Ethics 100*, 862–885
— (2003), Coleman on Social Norms, in: *Revue Française de Sociologie 44*, 297–304
— (2007), *Explaining Social Behaviour: More Nuts and Bolts for the Social Sciences*, Cambridge
Frank, R. H. (1988), *Passions within Reason: The Strategic Role of the Emotions*, New York
Hamlin, A. P. (1991), Rational Revenge, in: *Ethics 101*, 374–381
Knight, J. (1992), *Institutions and Social Conflict*, New York
Lewis, D. K. (1969), *Convention: A Philosophical Study*, Cambridge/MA
Posner, E. A. (2002), *Law and Social Norms*, 2nd edition, Cambridge/MA-London
Skyrms, B. (2004), *The Stag Hunt and the Evolution of Social Structure*, Cambridge-New York
Turnbull, C. (1972), *The Mountain People*, New York
Ullmann-Margalit, E. (1979), *The Emergence of Norms*, Oxford

Alan Hamlin

The Rationality and Functionality of Norms
A Comment on Lina Eriksson[*]

1. Introduction

Lina Eriksson raises three worries relating to the rational choice theoretic approach to norms: one concerning the limitations of game theoretic modelling as a means of identifying the functions that norms might serve; one concerning the explanation for the non-existence of norms in some situations that seem appropriate for norms to exist; and one concerning the emergence of norms which appear to play no useful function (and may even be harmful). Before commenting on these worries and their implications for both rational choice theory and the theory of norms, I will sketch out some more general comments on Eriksson's functionalist interpretation of rational choice theory and on the distinction between explaining *why* a norm arises and explaining *how* a norm arises.

2. Functionalist Rational Choice Theory—Choice or Emergence?

Eriksson identifies an approach to the explanation of norms as embodying both rational choice (game theoretic) and functionalist elements: "norms serve a function, they solve a problem people have, and therefore people create them to solve that problem." (179) At the same time she recognises that this interpretation of functionalism is "not functionalism as this view has been commonly known within social sciences. The rational choice version shares with traditional functionalism the emphasis of function, but differs in the focus on individual rationality: the function is sustained because it is in rational individuals' interests to sustain it, not because of some magical feedback mechanism." (179) So, what exactly are we to make of this combination of rational choice and functionalism?

First, I want to stress that while the rational choice approach to norms certainly focuses significant attention on the functionality of specific norms, it is not functionalist in any significant or deep sense—in that it does not seek to explain the existence of a norm primarily by reference to the claim that this norm would serve some particular overall function in society. I take it that this is a clarification of what

---

[*] I am happy to acknowledge the benefits of conversations with Lina Eriksson and other participants at the Norms and Values conference, ZiF, Bielefeld, May 2008—particularly Russell Hardin, Nic Southwood and Edna Ullmann-Margalit.

Eriksson means when she distances herself from "functionalism as this view has been commonly understood".[1]

The potential confusion here is understandable, there is a sense in which any rational choice theory might be considered to be 'functionalist': rational choice theory must be committed to the idea of purposeful behaviour (regardless of the detailed specification of individual motivation and 'purposes') and, if behaviour is purposeful, it might be said to be 'functional'. People act for reasons, those reasons can be construed in terms of ends-in-view and so actions serve the 'function' of attempting to achieve relevant aims. But this minimal 'functionalism' falls far short of what we have in mind when we speak of the functionalist model of explanation.

The rational choice approach, as Eriksson notes, "explains norms in terms of individuals, their incentives and interactions, and in equilibrium terms" (179), in most of her paper, Eriksson emphasises the elements of individual incentives and choice in the process of generating and sustaining norms—but here I want to shift the emphasis towards the idea of equilibrium. Thus where Eriksson writes that "people create a norm to solve a problem" (179), I would prefer to say that a norm emerges as part of an equilibrium that supervenes on individual choices, and that such a norm may solve a problem. The difference might seem pedantic, but I will suggest that the shift from direct choice to the indirect emergence of norms is important and helps us to address the three issues identified by Eriksson.

By focusing on equilibrium I would also hope to cast some light on the distinction between why norms emerge and how they emerge. Eriksson's position is that "it seems so obvious that the rational choice functionalist, game theoretic approach has nothing to say about *how* norms come about" (192). I would agree that the rational choice account has no detailed step-by-step account of the mechanism by which norms arise, but this fact should be seen in a rather different light—as an example of a more general claim about equilibrium analysis, and about the strategy of rational choice theory.

Whatever the setting, the idea of an equilibrium is a formal analytic construct specified in terms of a set of necessary and sufficient conditions.[2] In general, economists do not have a detailed account of how (or whether) equilibrium is reached—only a set of propositions about the properties of equilibria and the factors that might be expected to shift equilibria. For equilibrium analysis to be a useful guide to real world activity, there must be some presumption that the real world approximates to equilibrium (at least on average or in the longer term), but this presumption is not supported by a narrative account of the process leading to equilibrium, but rather by reference to the idea that any non-equilibrium situation must be such as to provide at least some (rational) individuals with an incentive to change

---

1 For a clear discussion which contrasts the rational choice approach with the functionalist approach see Harsanyi (1969).
2 This is true whether we are considering game theoretic settings (such as the idea of Nash equilibrium) or more traditional market settings (such as the idea of Walrasian equilibrium).

their behaviour.[3] So, it is the general background assumption of individual rationality that supports the relevance of equilibrium analysis.

Now, whether this provides an outline account of *how* norms come about (as well as how they persist) depends on the desired granularity of the explanation. At the coarse-grained level it seems reasonable to say that norms come about (and persist) as a result of the interplay of (more or less) rational behaviour, while admitting that, at the fine-grained level, we lack any specific story accounting for any particular norm since such a story could only operate in terms of the detailed analysis of each of a myriad of individual agents in particular settings at particular times. In this way, it seems to me that the important distinction is not between *why* norms come about and *how* norms come about, but between course-grained accounts of norms as social phenomena that necessary focus on general structural issues, and fine-grained accounts of specific norms that might offer forensic insights into particular issues. It seems clear that the rational choice theoretic strategy, here and elsewhere, is to attend to the general structural issues rather than the particularities.

3. Three Worries

Once one accepts that the rational choice approach to norms is coarse-grained and focuses on emergent equilibria rather than direct choice, some of Eriksson's worries may seem less pressing. I will briefly consider the three identified worries in reverse order.

The concern over the fact that some norms appear to be function-free or even dysfunctional is intended to raise the question of how such norms can be explained within a rational choice framework. But this explanation seems relatively straightforward from our course-grained, equilibrium perspective. We are well used to the idea that equilibria can be inefficient, and that in settings with multiple equilibria there can be no presumption that the more efficient equilibrium prevails. The same applies to norms. Equilibria (norms) are not directly chosen and, under some circumstances, those equilibria (norms) may not serve any particular interest or 'function'. Another way of pointing to the same idea is to refer to the idea of evolution—where the evolutionary process must be distinguished from some normative idea of progress. While evolution is driven by some selection mechanism, so that innovations are selected if and only if they satisfy some criteria, it is not the case that all evolved characteristics are necessarily 'functional'. There are at least two types of counterexamples—one where the selection criteria are not perfectly aligned with the criteria of 'functionality', the other where circumstances shift over time so that a characteristic that evolves under circumstance α and is 'functional' under that circumstance, might seem function-free or dysfunctional under circumstance β. So, the

---

3 This is most obviously true of the idea of Nash equilibria, but is also true of Walrasian equilibrium—where a disequilibrium situation (an imbalance of demand and supply) will lead to profitable opportunities for at least some agents.

worry of dysfunctional norms does not seem to raise any particularly deep concerns for a coarse-grained, equilibrium interpretation of rational choice theory—although I agree that it would cause deep concerns for any truly functionalist explanation of norms.

The worry concerning the non-existence of norms in circumstances where norms might appear to offer a potential solution to a social problem seems similar. Here again, the puzzle seems to be predicated on a direct choice view of the rational choice theoretic approach to norms—where it would indeed seem difficult to explain why we would not choose a norm in circumstances where that norm offers functionality. But the emphasis on emergent equilibria again helps to dispel this concern. Of course there are circumstances where some agents may have the option of direct choice—although here we tend to think not of norms but of laws. If it were the case that there was a situation such that the adoption of some norm would offer significant and widespread benefits, we might think that a political entrepreneur would face an incentive to propose a law (or policy) that might serve the identified function, since if the assumption of significant and widespread benefits is valid, such a policy would attract support. Similarly, some emergent norms might be codified and reinforced by choice of legislation or policy.[4] This points to the interaction between the rational choice theoretic approaches to politics and legislation and the approach to norms. Over at least some range, norms, policies and laws may be substitutes for each other and the emergence of each type of social structure will be connected through relatively complex mechanisms. While we might think of norms as emergent properties and laws as chosen objects, this is too simple a distinction, as is made clear by reference to the idea of laws emerging from political equilibria.

Having suggested that two of Eriksson's three worries might be laid at the door of functionalism rather than rational choice theory I would finally agree with Eriksson that the concern regarding the limitations of game theoretic modelling as a means of identifying the range of norms is real. Here then we have an issue arising out of a specific definition of a norm—largely built around the notion of a co-ordination equilibrium or equilibrium selection device. Eriksson is right to stress the fact that we often refer to 'norms' in a wide range of settings that do not seem to fit easily into this definition: norms as rules of thumb, norms that allow us to express our feelings in ways that will be understood, and so on. The question here then is whether rational choice theory can address these other senses of 'norm' or whether it is constrained from doing so—with a subsidiary question being whether these various types of 'norms' are sufficiently distinct to deserve different titles or whether they should all be accommodated under a more general definition of a norms.

On the first, substantive, question I would suggest that there already exists a rational choice theoretic literature devoted to at least some of these 'other' types of norms—certainly on both the rationality of rules of thumb, and on expressive ration-

---

4   The standard example of a norm associated with driving on the left/right provides a clear example of a norm that is typically reinforced in this way.

ality[5]—and I see no reason to suppose that rational choice theory (free of any deep commitment to functionalism) should not tackle the full range of such topics. On the subsidiary, terminological, question it is clearly the case that there currently exist a variety of formal definitions of norms and that each such definition will tend to be identified with a particular delimitation of the ordinary language usage of 'norm', and with a particular mode of analysis.[6] If we are operating within such a formal definition, we must stay within it—and use different language for cases that fall outside of the formal definition—not least for the sake of clarity. There can be no guarantee that we can find a suitably formal definition of a norm that is an exact match to our ordinary language usage of the word 'norm'. But none of this has any necessary implication for the substantive issue of constructing rational choice based understandings of whichever class of 'norms' might be of interest.

I will end by identifying two points that seem to me to be of major significance in any rational choice theory of norms, and which might be added to Eriksson's list of worries. The first relates to the normativity of norms and the worry concerns the extent to which rational choice theory can give an account of the motivating force of norms as norms. The issue here is that if rational choice theory is constrained to view individuals as narrowly self-interested, it is difficult to see how such a theory can accommodate the normative status of (at least some) norms. I take this to be an argument against the constrained view of narrow self-interested rationality. My second and final additional worry concerns situations in which norms conflict. To the extent that norms are intended to be read as proximate guides to action, we require an understanding of a calculus of norms that can be deployed when two (or more) relevant norms conflict. One possibility is that in such cases the norms themselves are discarded and the individual decision maker has to fall back on specific, detailed consideration of underlying reasons; another possibility is that norms have some in-built hierarchy such that some norms trump other norms. There are clearly other possibilities. But the point here is to highlight the fact that we live in a world of many norms, and that norm conflict can be expected to arise on a significant scale, so that we need some understanding not only of how such norms arise and persist, but also of how realistically rational agents operate in a world of both reasons and norms.

Bibliography

Brennan, G./A. Hamlin (2000), *Democratic Devices and Desires*, Cambridge
— (2008), Revisionist Public Choice Theory, in: *New Political Economy 13*, 77–88
Brennan, H. G./L. E. Lomasky (1993), *Democracy and Decision*, Cambridge

---

5   For example, on rules of thumb see Rubinstein (1998). On expressive rationality see Brennan/Lomasky (1993). Both are incorporated to some extent in: Brennan/Hamlin (2000; 2008).
6   Pettit (1990) provides a clear example.

Harsanyi, J. C. (1969), Rational Choice Models of Political Behavior vs. Functionalist and Conformist Theories, in: *World Politics 21*, 513–538

Pettit, P. (1990), Virtus Normativa: Rational Choice Perspectives, in: *Ethics 100*, 725–55

Rubinstein, A. (1998), *Modeling Bounded Rationality*, Cambridge/MA

Rainer Hegselmann and Oliver Will

Modelling Hume's Moral and Political Theory—
The Design of HUME$_{1.0}$*

1. Hume's Rich Informal Theory under the Principle of Suspicion

In *Of Morals*—that is part III of *A Treatise of Human Nature* (Hume 2007[1739f.])—and in *Enquiry Concerning the Principles of Morals* (Hume 1998[1751]) David Hume addresses a fundamental problem, the origin of justice and government. According to Hume, *both* are human *inventions*. They evolved and emerged in a long process that finally made it possible for us—i.e. mammal beings with a 'natural' nature that is more appropriate for living in *small* groups—to live together in *large* societies. Though there are no personal ties between most members of these large societies, huge indirect exchange networks emerged. Specialisation and division of labour are highly developed.

Compared with our prehistoric predecessors we enjoy an unbelievable wealth—not everywhere, not all the time, and not without setbacks, but in and for significant parts of the modern world and the modern times, at least of the last two centuries.[1]

The key components in Hume's theory are:

1. An *original human nature* that—if not transformed and modified—in a very literal sense, causes serious trouble in large groups (for instance, confined generosity, favouring the loved ones and a systematic short-sightedness).

---

* This work is part of the project 'Emergence in the Loop' (EmiL: IST-033841) funded by the Future and Emerging Technologies programme of the European Commission, in the framework of the initiative 'Simulating Emergent Properties in Complex Systems'. Many thanks to Marlies Ahlert, Eckhart Arnold, Werner Güth, Russell Hardin, Hartmut Kliemt, Bernd Lahno, and Martin Neumann for valuable input and discussion and to Matthew Braham who in addition helped us correcting our Teutonic English. Rainer Hegselmann started to model Hume's ideas 10 years ago as a fellow at the Center for Interdisciplinary Research, Bielefeld University, in the research group Making Choices, 1999–2000. This article was finished while he was visiting professor at the Catholic University of Leuven as a guest of the Formal Epistemology Project during the summer term 2009. Many thanks to both institutions for their hospitality.

1 Gregory Clark argues in Clark (2007) that up to 1800, there was basically a Malthusian economy in the world: For the average or median human being, wealth tends to be on the subsistence level. This diagnosis is not totally new. New is the—now fiercely debated—explanation that Clark gives: Due to lucky circumstances that prevailed in England since about 1250, capitalist attitudes spread socially and probably even genetically from the top of society to the middle classes. That, finally, created the conditions to escape the Malthusian trap—so Clark's argument goes.

2. The invention of *artificial virtues*, especially *justice*, that are acquired by some sort of character transformation and maintained by the practice of mutual approval and disapproval. *Artificial* means that justice is not a part of the original human nature. Hume's *justice* essentially is respecting property, transfer of property by consent, and keeping promises.[2] Hume's justice is not (re-)distributional justice or a kind of fairness.

3. A *division of labour*[3] with a corresponding development of special capabilities;

4. The invention of *central authorities* that monitor, enforce, and—eventually—punish behaviour.[4]

The question, how living together in large-scale societies is possible at all, puzzled already the ancient Greeks. In one of Plato's dialogues[5] the sophist *Protagoras* gives a very modern answer that—after some deciphering of the myth in which Prometheus and Epimetheus do some creation work—amounts to saying: A high blood toll was paid to learn the lessons. But then, finally, mankind invented both, *moral virtues* and *enforcement agencies*. That made it possible to live together co-operatively in comparatively wealthy large-scale societies where high proportions of interactions are no longer based on family ties or good personal acquaintanceship.[6] Obviously Protagoras' view is at least very similar to Hume's view.

Hume delivered a *rich informal* theory, at his time more detailed and thoroughly thought through than any other theoretical work in the tradition of Protagoras—but nevertheless qualitative, informal, and to a certain degree a draft. The last three decades have seen a lot of work on that conception: systematising assumptions, identi-

---

2 To avoid misunderstandings Hume states: "[...] I must here observe, that when I deny justice to be a natural virtue, I make use of the word natural, only as oppos'd to artificial. In another sense of the word; as no principle of the human mind is more natural than a sense of virtue; so no virtue is more natural than justice. Mankind is an inventive species; and where an invention is obvious and absolutely necessary, it may as properly be said to be natural as any thing that proceeds immediately from original principles, without the intervention of thought or reflection. Tho' the rules of justice be artificial, they are not arbitrary. Nor is the expression improper to call them laws of nature; if by natural we understand what is common to any species, or even if we confine it to mean what is inseparable from the species." (Hume 2007, 311)

3 Of course, the much more detailed analysis of division of labour is given by Adam Smith in the opening chapters of *An Inquiry into the Nature and Causes of the Wealth of Nations* (Smith (1979[1776])). But already in Hume's writings specialisation and division of labour is a central result and driving force in human history.

4 It is Hume's view that living in large societies requires something new: "But when men have observ'd, that tho' the rules of justice be sufficient to maintain any society, yet 'tis impossible for them, of themselves, to observe those rules, in large and polish'd societies; they establish government, as a new invention to attain their ends, and preserve the old, or procure new advantages, by a more strict execution of justice." (Hume 2007, 348) One should note that establishing an enforcement agency is a special type of division of labour.

5 See the dialogue *Protagoras* in Plato (1997).

6 If we trust Lucretius' *De rerum natura*, then Epicurus held a similar view as well; see Lucretius (1922).

fying inconsistencies, incoherences or theoretical tensions, putting it into a broader perspective, integrating new scientific insights from evolutionary biology and psychology. Major contributions are Baurmann (1996), Binmore (1994), Gibbard (1990), Hardin (2007), Kliemt (1985; 1986), Lahno (1995), Mackie (1980), Skyrms (1996), Sugden (2004) and Ullmann-Margalit (1977).

With $HUME_{1.0}$ we start to develop *a computational* model of that theory. *Why model Hume's theory?* If successful we get a model that allows us to study in detail the complex dynamical interplay of a bunch of mechanisms. We should be able to analyse systematically under specified assumptions in which regions of the parameter space virtues, specialisation, and wealth prosper; and how robust or how sensitive these processes are when parameters and/or mechanisms vary to some degree. Hume's theory is about fundamental processes in the evolution of societal life. However, it is a rich informal theory. As such it belongs under the *principle of suspicion* that says:

> Our intuitions about the often non-linear interplay of factors is very, very bad—and that even if only few factors are involved. Therefore: Do not trust rich informal theories unless the dynamics of their key components is at least partially checked by models that explicitly specify the central parameters, mechanisms and their interplay (***Principle of suspicion***).

Modelling Hume's theory contributes to a systematic *evaluation* of that theory. In a certain sense, *experimentation* with that theory will become possible. Under a hermeneutic perspective, the model is an *interpretation* or *reconstruction* of the theory. Admittedly, that reconstruction is very poor in terms of details: only a skeleton is left. However, abstracting away from almost all details is the precondition for a rigorous and explicit analysis of the dynamical interplay of the key components in Hume's theory.

The following is a description of the model $HUME_{1.0}$. That is a model, in which Hume's key components 1–3 and especially virtues play an important role. However, *central authorities*—key component 4—are *left out*. They will be included only in $HUME_{2.0}$. Thus, the model $HUME_{1.0}$ aims at an analysis of 'how far one can get' *without* central authorities.

In sections (2) to (7) the main components of $HUME_{1.0}$ will be described. In section (8) we put the pieces together and report some first results. To avoid disappointment, this paper does *not* present a thoroughgoing analysis of $HUME_{1.0}$. Rather it describes the components, solutions of design problems, and further research perspectives.

2. Component$_1$: Specialization and Division of Labour

We model specialization and division of labour in an abstract way. Assuming discrete time, $t = 0, 1, 2, \ldots$, in each period some of the agents get a *problem* of a certain type. The problem is characterised by a positive integer $k \leq K$, with K being the exogenously given number of different problems that might arise. K is constant over time. Among their characteristics agents have a *competence vector* with K components. The real valued kth component characterises the competence c_{ik} of an agent i to work on a problem of type k. The competencies are assumed to sum up to 1.

Initially, all agents are equally good or bad at solving certain problems, i.e. $c_{ik} = \frac{1}{K}, \forall i \forall k$. By working on a *certain* problem, agents improve their ability to solve the type of problem they have. However, at the same time their *other* competencies *deteriorate*. Formally, that can be realised by adding a certain Δ to the component in question and afterwards renormalizing the whole competence vector in such a way that $\sum_{k=1}^{K} c_{i,k} = 1$ holds again. By that procedure the competence vectors of agents become *time dependent*: If agents get the chance to work on those problems on which they are comparatively good, then the agents become better at solving them and that is what we mean by *specialization* (in the model this will be reflected in the distribution of the entries in the competence vector).

In a compact form the competencies of agent i at time t are given by

$$C_i(t) = \langle c_{i1}(t), c_{i2}(t), ..., c_{iK}(t) \rangle. \tag{1}$$

(In the following we often do not explicitly annotate the time dependency of the vector's components if misunderstandings are not possible.)

Depending upon the values in their competence vector, agents can be more or less competent in solving a problem of type k—and that has consequences. We assume that agent j's competence in solving problem k influences the *value* and the *costs* of a solution and thereby the *added value*. The latter is understood as the difference between value and costs of a solution.

It is very natural to assume that the *higher* the competence, the *higher* is the value of the solution. Infinitely many functions can be used to describe the intended effect. We use the very simple non-linear function

$$\text{VALUE}_{jk} = constant_{value} + c_{jk}^{\varphi}. \tag{2}$$

VALUE_{jk} is the value of the solution of problem k if agent j with the actual competence c_{jk} works on the solution. The exponent φ controls the strength of the *competence* effect: for $\varphi < 1$ the value of the solution increases steeply with increasing *low* competencies; for $\varphi > 1$ the value increases steeply with increasing *high* competencies; for $\varphi = 1$ the value is proportional to competence. The $constant_{value}$ shifts the function upward and downward. The left-hand side of Figure 1 shows the effects for different values of φ under the condition $constant_{value} = 1$.

It is again very natural to assume that the higher the competence, the lower are the costs to produce the solution. To determine costs we use the function

$$\text{COSTS}_{jk} = constant_{costs} - c_{jk}^{\sigma}. \tag{3}$$

It is now the exponent σ that controls the strength of an over- or underproportional competence effect, while $constant_{costs}$ moves the function upward and downward. The right-hand side of Figure 1 shows the *costs* for different values of σ, now under the condition that $constant_{costs} = 1$.

Subtracting the costs from the value gives the *value added*:

$$VALUE\_ADDED_{jk} = VALUE_{jk} - COSTS_{jk}. \quad (4)$$

To simplify the situation we will assume from now on that

$$constant_{costs} = constant_{value} = 1. \quad (5)$$

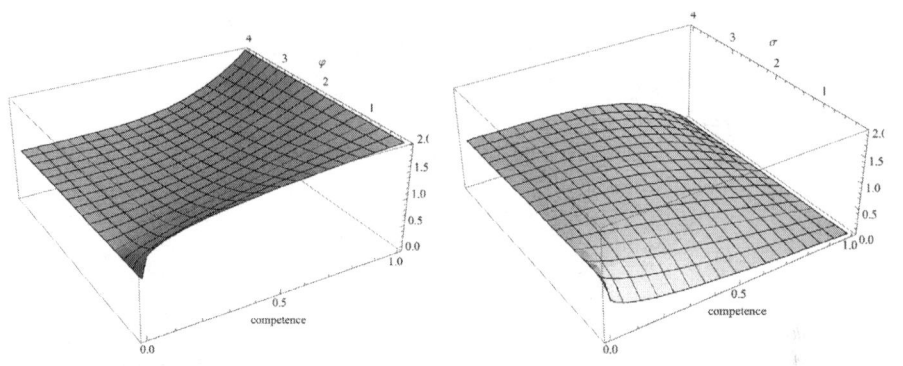

Figure 1: Competence dependent value of a solution (0.25 ≤ φ ≤ 4) under the condition *constant*$_{value}$ = 1 (left) and competence dependent *costs* of a solution (0.25 ≤ σ ≤ 4) under the condition *constant*$_{costs}$ = 1 (right).

Based on that we get

$$VALUE\_ADDED_{jk} = \left(1 + c_{jk}^{\varphi}\right) - \left(1 - c_{jk}^{\sigma}\right) = c_{jk}^{\varphi} + c_{jk}^{\sigma}. \quad (6)$$

The simplifying assumption has certain effects: positive competencies generate positive values. We avoid negative added values. For the worst possible competence, i.e. 0, the costs are 1 and the added value is 0. For the best possible competence, i.e. 1, the costs are 0 (but note that the dynamics of competencies as described above has the effect that a competence can go to 1 only if times goes to infinity). The maximum added value is 2. Figure 2 shows the *value added* for different competencies and values of φ given that $\sigma = 1$.

If all agents tend to get problems of all sorts, then within the framework as outlined above the agents could profit a lot from a functioning exchange system based on high specialization and division of labour.

3. Component₂: Exchange

Exchange tends to be risky (Hardin 1982). One or both partners may deviate from agreements, default on payment or delivery or defect from the agreement in some or even all of the many ways that exist. In HUME$_{1.0}$ it is not different.[7]

---

[7] Of course, there exist almost risk free exchange regimes, for instance via mediators. But that implies institutions and an already existing division of labour. In our pre-historical context such institutions not yet exist.

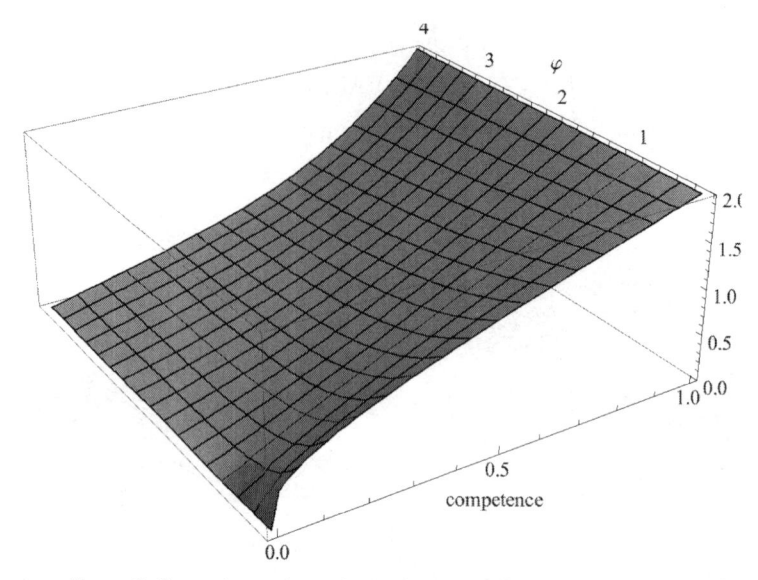

Figure 2: Competence dependent value added for $0.25 \leq \varphi \leq 4$ and $\sigma = 1$.

Modelling requires to make the exchange structures explicit. We suppose that in each period there are *two* types of agents or agent roles that are randomly assigned: *P-agents* are agents that have a randomly assigned *problem*. *S-agents* offer *solutions*. Later, by further specification, we will determine whether an agent can be both *or* is either a *P-* or a *S*-agent. Since we allow *do-it-yourself*-solutions, exchange in the usual sense takes place if and only if in a match the *P-* and the *S*-agent are not the same. Different structures of real exchange can be distinguished in answer to the question *who delivers/pays when*? Figure 3 gives an overview.[8]

The so called *trust game* (*TG*) captures the fundamental social predicament that co-operation (joint ventures, mutual exchange) is extremely difficult in situations in which one player has to move first *without any guarantee that the other player later reciprocates*. In its extensive form, the *TG* is given by the game tree in Figure. The payoffs for the two players are indicated at the three possible end results of the game. The upper payoff is the payoff for player 1; the lower payoff is the payoff for player 2. As usual, the payoffs are assumed to be given by a *von Neumann-Morgenstern utility function*. That implies they are unique only up to positive affine transformations. Therefore two payoffs can be set to 0 and 1 respectively. As a consequence, all possible *TG*s can be characterised by the two parameters a and b. To keep the characteristic rank ordering for the results of *TG*s, the restrictions are that a < 0 and b > 1.

---

[8] Here and in the following we often use a sort of monetary jargon. However, what we model is a prehistoric economy long before money was invented. Thus the model's real 'currency' is crop, prey, personal service, i.e. natural valuables of all sorts. To pay for something, baskets of valuables can be compiled.

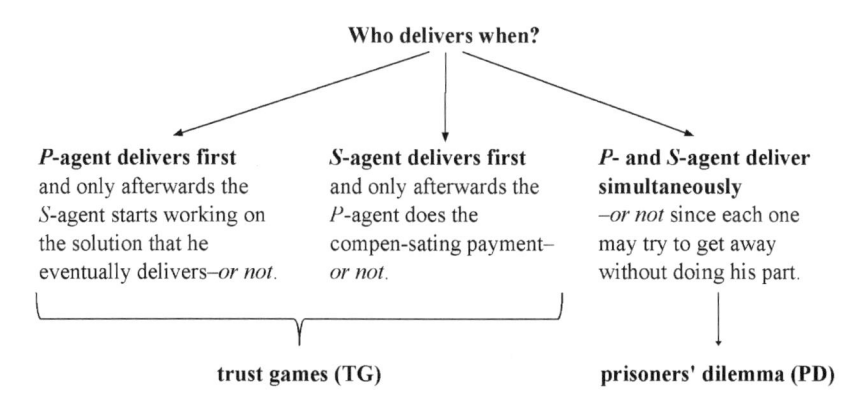

```
                        Who delivers when?
          ┌───────────────────┼───────────────────┐
P-agent delivers first    S-agent delivers first    P- and S-agent deliver
and only afterwards the   and only afterwards the   simultaneously
S-agent starts working on P-agent does the          –or not since each one
the solution that he      compen-sating payment–    may try to get away
eventually delivers–or not. or not.                 without doing his part.
└─────────────────┬─────────────────┘                         │
                  ▼                                           ▼
          trust games (TG)                          prisoners' dilemma (PD)
```

Figure 3: Three risky exchange structures

By backward induction, with *rational* players playing the *non-iterated, one-shot* TG there is only one solution—and that is an inefficient one: anticipating that player 2 will go for exploitation at his node, player 1 decides for no trust at his very first decision node. The result is the inefficient outcome with the payoff ⟨0; 0⟩.

Hume was fully aware of the problems inherent in trust game structures without iteration, i.e. one-shot-games:[9]

> Your corn is ripe to-day; mine will be so to-morrow. 'Tis profitable for us both, that I shou'd labour with you to-day, and that you shou'd aid me to-morrow. I have no kindness for you, and know you have as little for me. I will not, therefore, take any pains upon your account; and should I labour with you upon my own account, in expectation of a return, I know I shou'd be disappointed, and that I shou'd in vain depend upon your gratitude. Here then I leave you to labour alone: You treat me in the same manner. The seasons change; and both of us lose our harvests for want of mutual confidence and security. (Hume 2007, 334)

For the beginning we base $HUME_{1.0}$ on a trust game variant in which the *P*-agent is player 1 and delivers first by doing a prepayment. What about the amount? Since the prepayment is supposed to be the one and only payment to the *S*-agent during a single exchange, it has, firstly, to cover the *S*-agent's costs to produce the solution of the *P*-agent's problem k. Referring to the *S*-agent by an index 'S' the *P*-agent, therefore, has to pay $COSTS_{Sk}$. A payment of *only* that amount is not a positive incentive for the *S*-agent to start working—as it just covers the costs. An incentive is set, if the *S*-agents gets on top of his costs a certain share β (with $0 < \beta \le 1$) of the added value. There are at least two natural ways to do determine the total prepayment that the *S*-agent receives:

---

[9] For a detailed and careful analysis of the trust game and its importance to understand Hume's *Treatise* and *Enquiry* cf. Lahno (1995).

$$\text{COSTS}_{Sk} + \beta \cdot VALUE\$\_\$ADDED_{Sk}, \qquad (7)$$

or

$$\text{COSTS}_{Sk} + \beta \cdot \left(VALUE\$\_\$ADDED_{Sk} - VALUE\$\_\$ADDED_{Pk}\right). \qquad (8)$$

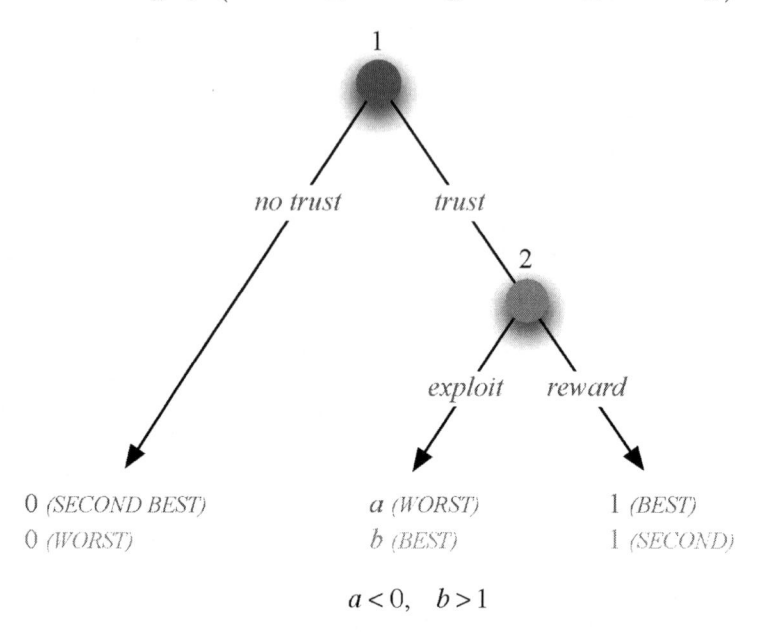

```
                       1
                  no trust / \ trust
                           /   \
                          /     2
                         /    exploit / \ reward
                        /            /   \
                       ↓            ↓     ↓
              0 (SECOND BEST)   a (WORST)   1 (BEST)
              0 (WORST)         b (BEST)    1 (SECOND)
```

$a < 0, \quad b > 1$

Figure 4: The trust game (*TG*)

In the first case the *S*-agent gets on top of his costs a fraction of the added value that he generates. In the second case it is the fraction of the difference between the added value that the *S*-agent generates and the added value the *P*-agent could generate at its own. In the first case, for the prepayment only the solution competence of the *S*-agent matters. In the second case, the competence of the *P*-agent matters as well—somehow implicitly reflecting bargaining power. However, it seems that for major—though not for all—areas of the parameter space it does not matter very much which assumption we apply. For the beginning we use the first clause.

For an exchange *P*- and *S*-agents have to be matched. Matching will be discussed later in chapter 5. In anticipation of the results, we make already here use of a very natural matching principle: a match is possible only if the *Do-it-yourself*-solution[10] is for the *P*-agent strictly worse than what the *P*-agent receives if the *S*-agent delivers the solution. As a consequence, under our assumptions about costs and values, it is a necessary condition for matching a *P*- and a *S*-agent that it holds:

---

10   Here and in the following a *solution* is a solution of a problem. Thus, a solution is *not* a strategy or vector of strategies that solves a game in a game theoretical sense.

212

$$(1-\beta)\cdot VALUE\_ADDED_{Sk} > VALUE\_ADDED_{Pk}. \qquad (9)$$

That condition can only be fulfilled if the *S*-agent's competence to solve problem *k* is strictly better than the *P*-agent's own competence. On the whole we get the trust game as given by Figure 5. Box (1) states what is guaranteed by a pre-play matching procedure (explained later). At (2) the trust game starts: player 1, i.e. the *P*-agent has to decide whether to trust or to distrust the *S*-agent. In the latter case, the *P*-agent solves his actual problem *k* on his own. In (4) the upper entry is the payoff that the *P*-agent then gets: the value of his *Do-it-yourself*-solution minus the costs he has to bear, i.e. $VALUE_{Pk}$ − $COSTS_{Pk}$ what equals $VALUE\_ADDED_{Pk}$. If the *P*-agent trusts, he has to prepay the *S*-agent at step (5). Then—in step (6)—the *S*-agent decides whether to exploit or to reward. If the *S*-agent exploits, then the *P*-agent's whole prepayment is lost. In (8), the upper entry is the *P*-agent's payoff, i.e. the *loss* of the prepayment. The lower entry is the *S*-agent's payoff, that is the prepayment of his costs plus his share of the added value of the solution *that he did not work out*. If the *S*-agent decides in (6) to reward, then the *P*-agent's payoff is given by the upper entry in (10): the *P*-agent gets a solution of his problem *k* that is worth $VALUE_{Sk}$. Minus the prepayment, the balanced account of the *P*-agent is just his share of the added value, i.e. $(1-\beta)\cdot VALUE_{Sk}$. The lower entry in (10) is the *S*-agent's final payoff: he got the prepayment and worked out the solution of k at certain costs. He, therefore, ends up with his share of the added value, i.e. $\beta \cdot VALUE_{Sk}$. It is easy to verify that under our assumptions about costs, values and possible matches the constitutive ranking of trust-game-outcomes is always fulfilled (see Figure 4).

For the beginning we assume in $HUME_{1.0}$ an exchange structure as described above and given by Figure 5. Other versions in which the *S*-agent delivers first or both exchange simultaneously (see Figure 3) can be defined analogously.

In our version of the trust game, or better, in our context of the trust game, besides the usual trustworthiness at least two additional moral dimensions are involved. Firstly, there might be an incentive to be deceptive about one's competence—simply to get 'the job'. For the *P*-agent there might be an incentive to be deceptive about his problem—simply to catch a qualified *S*-agent who would be better off working on another agent's problem. Secondly, since normally quality is costly for the producer, under-performance may be tempting for the *S*-agent.[11] Thus, in our trust game a total of three moral dimensions are involved, two of which concern only the *S*-player:

1. *Trustworthiness*: Does the *S*-agent reward?
2. *Honesty*: Does the *S*-agent really have the announced technical competence in solving problem *k*? Does the *P*-agent really have the announced problem?
3. *Reliability*: Does the *S*-agent really do his best to deliver with exactly the quality his competence allows for?

---

11 Formally, we could introduce a performance level *l* with $0 \le l \le 1$ that represents to which degree the *S*-agent is doing his best. The performance level would affect the payoffs: The *S*-agent's payoffs decrease with a higher level; the *P*-agent's payoffs increase with a higher level.

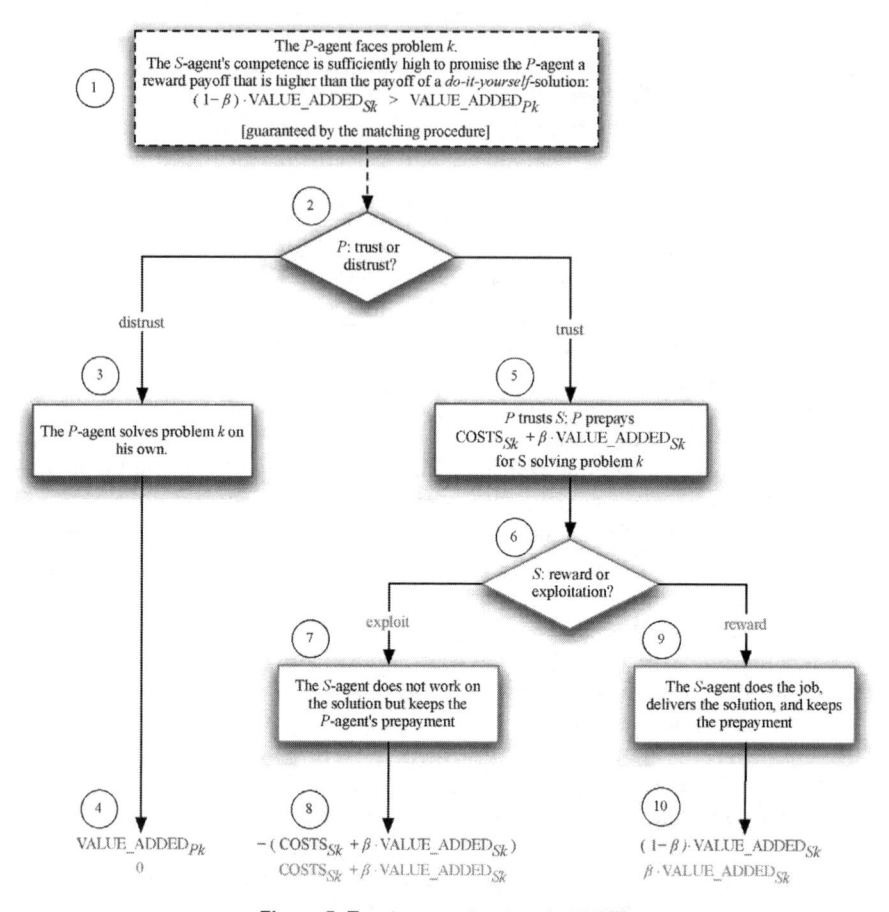

```
┌─────────────────────────────────────────────────────────┐
│                 The P-agent faces problem k.            │
│  The S-agent's competence is sufficiently high to promise the P-agent a │
│(1) reward payoff that is higher than the payoff of a do-it-yourself-solution: │
│         $(1-\beta) \cdot \text{VALUE\_ADDED}_{Sk} > \text{VALUE\_ADDED}_{Pk}$ │
│              [guaranteed by the matching procedure]     │
└─────────────────────────────────────────────────────────┘
                              │
                           (2) P: trust or distrust?
                   distrust ╱       ╲ trust
                           ╱         ╲
              (3)                          (5)
    The P-agent solves problem k       P trusts S: P prepays
          on his own.              $\text{COSTS}_{Sk} + \beta \cdot \text{VALUE\_ADDED}_{Sk}$
                                       for S solving problem k
                                                │
                                          (6) S: reward or exploitation?
                                     exploit ╱     ╲ reward
                                    (7)              (9)
                         The S-agent does not work   The S-agent does the job,
                         on the solution but keeps   delivers the solution, and
                         the P-agent's prepayment    keeps the prepayment
    (4)                       (8)                        (10)
$\text{VALUE\_ADDED}_{Pk}$  $-(\text{COSTS}_{Sk} + \beta \cdot \text{VALUE\_ADDED}_{Sk})$  $(1-\beta) \cdot \text{VALUE\_ADDED}_{Sk}$
         0                  $\text{COSTS}_{Sk} + \beta \cdot \text{VALUE\_ADDED}_{Sk}$     $\beta \cdot \text{VALUE\_ADDED}_{Sk}$
```

Figure 5: Trust game structure in HUME$_{1.0}$

However, we will *simplify* the situation in HUME$_{1.0}$ by two assumptions: Firstly, we assume direct observability of competencies and problems. Thus, deception—including self-deception—is excluded, or, to put it in another way, there is only true advertising of one's competencies or problems. Secondly, we assume that always the best quality is delivered that an agent's competence allows. This avoids that we deal with problems of effort detection. As a consequence, HUME$_{1.0}$ focuses on the dynamics of trustworthiness in an environment in which agents face special problems and special solution-competencies could evolve, which then matter in terms of payoffs. As a consequence a matching and partner selection problem arises in which at the same time trustworthiness and competence are to be considered.[12]

---

12 Trust games play an important role in the growing number of projects that study how trust can be established and maintained in electronic commerce and communities. A central problem is

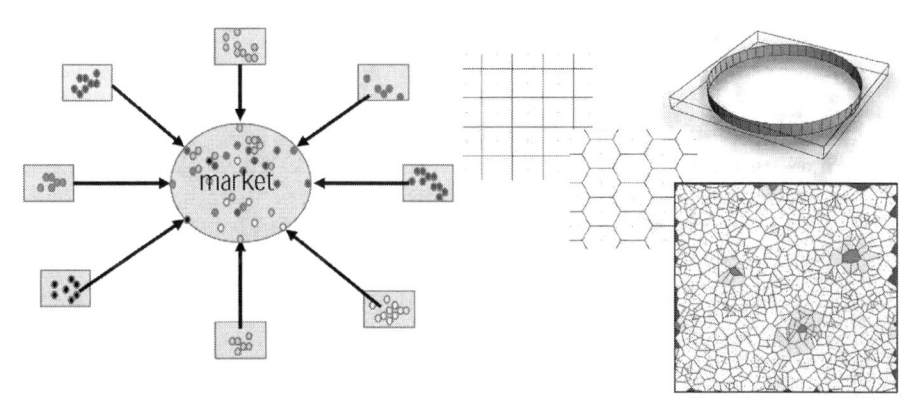

Figure 6: Two social structures: partition and market based (left) and grid distance based (right)

4. Component₃: Social Structures

HUME$_{1.0}$ analyses the evolution of trustworthiness and specialization for two different social structures. In the first scenario grid based network structures are assumed.[13] Neighbourhoods overlap and network distance matters for the choice of exchange strategies, the spread and reliability of information etc. In the second scenario the population is partitioned into non-overlapping subgroups. The agents exchange either within their subgroup or on a central market. The exchange location matters for strategies and information. To keep it simple, it is assumed for both scenarios that period-by-period nature randomly assigns a problem $k \in K$ to half of the population. Consequently, in each period 50% of the population are *P*-agents, the other 50% are *S*-agents.[14]

We refer to the first setting as the **g**rid **d**istance based scenario (GD-scenario): The agents live on a low-dimensional grid (1-dimensional, 2-dimensional, rectangular, hexagonal, irregular in the sense of Voronoi-diagrams). Neighbourhoods—defined by network distance—overlap. The agents that live on this network topology are characterised by *two* attributes that determine their decisions:

1. Within an agent-specific and dynamic radius, defined in terms of network distance, *P*-agents look for trustworthy *S*-agents, which are—given the *P*-agent's

---

how to design and implement mechanisms that allow to identify cheaters. For an overview see Ramchurn; Huynh/Jennings (2004) and Sabater/Sierra (2005).
13 For a description and discussion of grid based modelling approaches cf. Hegselmann/Flache (1998) and Flache/Hegselmann (2001).
14 In principle our framework allows that being a *P*- or *S*-agent is a role only. If so, then agents may have both roles in the same period. An agent might look for an expert to solve his actual problem while at the same time offering his special expertise to others that need it. This, however, complicates the matching procedure, therefore we do not allow it in this stage.

actual problem—as competent as possible. We refer to that radius as the P-agent's *search radius*, denoted by $r_i^{P\_search}(t)$. (The details of the matching process and the dynamics of the search radius—the latter driven by various kinds of learning—will be explained later.)

2. S-agents reward only in interactions with P-agents that live within an agent specific and dynamic *reward radius*, denoted by $r_i^{S\_reward}(t)$. They exploit if an exchange partner lives beyond that radius. (Again, details of the learning driven dynamics of the reward radius will be given later.)

Using a more compact notation, we characterise the agents in the GD-scenario by the *decision vector*

$$D_i^{GD}(t) = \langle r_i^{P\_search}(t), r_i^{S\_reward}(t) \rangle. \qquad (10)$$

Equation (10) condenses—broadly conceived—agent's *i* moral attributes at time *t* (while specific *technical* capabilities are given by the competence vector $C_i(t)$). The second component of (10) reflects Hume's virtue of justice, or better, the limits within which an agent is prepared be a just agent.

The second structure is called the **p**artition and **m**arket based scenario (PM-scenario). The agents are initially distributed among an exogenously given number of partitions, i.e. small groups (families, tribes, villages) to which they belong. To some degree—controlled by a parameter—exchange of members between groups may be possible.[15]

As in the first scenario, period by period the P- and the S-agent-role is randomly assigned to half of the population. P- and the S-agents decide where to search for partners, within their small group or on an open market. Decision behaviour is modelled by probabilities:

1. Each agent has an agent-specific and dynamic probability to enter the market if acting as a P-agent. That probability is $p_i^{P\_market}(t)$. Correspondingly, with probability $p_i^{P\_local}(t) = 1 - p_i^{P\_market}(t)$ a P-agent searches locally, i.e. within his partition, for S-agents that are trustworthy and as competent as possible. An agent's decision behaviour if acting as a S-agent is modelled analogously: $p_i^{S\_market}(t)$ is the probability to offer solutions capacities on the market. $p_i^{S\_local}(t) = 1 - p_i^{S\_market}(t)$ is the probability to stay local and offer one's competencies there.

2. S-agents reward with agent-relative and dynamic probabilities. With probability $p_i^{S\_reward\_market}(t)$ agent *i* rewards in a *market* interaction; with probability $p_i^{S\_reward\_local}(t)$ the agent rewards if he is involved in an *local* exchange. (The details about matching and learning are given later.)

---

15 Exchange of members seems to be a widely accepted fact about prehistoric societies, as anthropologists have indicated.

Again, we characterise the agents a bit more compactly by a decision vector. Due to specifics of the scenario the vector has four probabilities as its components:[16]

$$D_i^{PM}(t) = \left\langle p_i^{P\_market}(t), p_i^{S\_market}(t), p_i^{S\_reward\_local}(t), p_i^{S\_reward\_market}(t) \right\rangle. \quad (11)$$

It is the third and fourth component of $D_i^{PM}(t)$ that reflects Hume's virtue of justice and the degree to which an agent has internalised that virtue.

Obviously, there are further structural settings to be analysed in HUME$_{1X}$. Good candidates would be network structures that are *not* grid based: instead of being a constant, the number of links of network nodes may have a certain distribution (e.g. the scale free power law distribution, a Poisson distribution etc.); the network structure itself may evolve. The use of grids is a very convenient modelling approach if one has to analyse or wants to model especially local interactions with overlapping neighbourhoods. *If* such a social topology—even as a stylised one—is untypical for the target system and possibly misleading because there are reasons to believe that the difference in the topological structure matters, *then* using grids is somewhat inappropriate. For instance, the very regular and overlapping neighbourhood structure has as a consequence an extremely large diameter of grid-based networks. However, most real world networks surprise by their small diameter. Therefore, it is a very natural idea to analyse a setting, in which network distance matters, but the network itself is *not* grid-based. Another structural setting could consist of a kind of PM-scenario in which the local group has—different from the PM-scenario above—a relevant network structure that, for instance, affects learning, spread of information and reputation etc.

5. Component$_4$: Matching

Before they can play trust games—a two(!)-person game—agents have to be matched. Matching involves two problems. Firstly, *P*-agents are interested to exchange with trustworthy *S*-agents only—otherwise their pre-payment is lost. Secondly, *P*-agents and *S*-agents have an interest to be paired such that the *P*-agents actual problem *k* and the *S*-agent's competence go well together: the *S*-agent generally obtains his highest reward payoff if he solves a problem for which he is best qualified. The *P*-agent's reward payoff is the higher, the better the competence of the *S*-agent. Therefore, both types of agents are interested in finding good exchange partners. However, there might be a competition for the same *P*-agent if his problem is attractive for many *S*-agents; many *P*-agents may compete to be matched with the

---

[16] The PM-scenario has structural similarities with a model developed by Michael W. Macy and Yoshimichi Sato in Macy/Sato (2002). However, there is—among others—one important difference: we differentiate the probability for rewarding on the market from the probability for rewarding locally. That allows the analysis of conjectures and hypotheses of Macy and Sato in a similar—though more reasonable—structural setting. It is interesting to do that since the central original claims of Macy and Sato are *not replicable*; see Will/Hegselmann (2008b), Macy/Sato (2008) and Will/Hegselmann (2008a).

same *S*-agent if he has the right competence. But basically the interests of *P*-agents and *S*-agents that intend to reward, do not conflict.[17]

The first problem is a *detection problem* with regard to trustworthiness. It constitutes the moral component of matching. The second problem is different. We assumed direct observability of competencies and problems (see section 3 above) and thus there is no detection problem. The real problem for both types of agents is to establish an *efficient* pairing in terms of problems and solution competence. Consequently, the general matching problem has both, a moral and an efficiency component.

Matching is a complicated matter. As to the moral component, *P*-agents have to decide upon *S*-agents' trustworthiness. Doing that they might draw on reputation, signalling, or their own and others' past experience. Reputation is a kind of belief about the others' beliefs about somebody, a more or less inter-subjectively consistent, and more or less accurate social information that spreads with a higher or lower speed. Reputation can be build, lost, and even be managed or manipulated—distorting others' reputation may increase a *S*-agent's chance to get the job. Signalling regards all the subtle, unintentionally given signals and clues that tell something about an agent's actual intentions or character traits. Past experience, personal or communicated by more or less reliable others, can be used to form conjectures, which may be outdated since an *S*-agent's character may have changed in the meantime. As to the efficiency component of the matching problem the situation is less complicated, though complex enough. We take true advertising as given (see section 3). Nevertheless, the agents have to compare all the problems and competencies that are on offer. While some still gather information to obtain a more or less perfect overview, others may already make agreements, thereby changing what is on offer.

In HUME$_{1.0}$ we will not even try to explicitly model the social and cognitive processes and capacities involved in that kind of matching process. Instead, we use a modelling short cut. We introduce a procedure that directly generates a set of matches with certain desired properties.

For an understanding of the procedure it is important to notice the following: (a) Given the network distance between any *P*-agent *i* and *S*-agent *j*, it is in the GD-scenario already fixed by the decision vector $D_i^{GD}(t)$ (see equation (10)) whether the *S*-agent will exploit or reward in the pairing $\langle i, j \rangle$ in the actual period *t*. On the *P*-agent's side it is by *i*'s search radius, whether such a pairing is actually 'out of range' or not—and that in a very literal sense. (b) In the PM-scenario it is different. The decision vector $D_i^{PM}(t)$ consists of four probabilities (see equation (11)). That does *not* fix an agent's actual behaviour. We get a behavioural fixing by the assumption that the matching procedure starts only after, firstly, nature has assigned *P*- or *S*-agent roles and, secondly, for all *S*-agents their specific behaviour is fixed sing the probabilities given in their actual decision vectors. Let's refer to that assumption as the

---

17 With *S*-agents that intend to exploit it may be different—depending upon the values of β, σ, and ϕ. An exploiter may obtain his highest payoff by accepting a problem that does not correspond to his highest competence.

decisions-made-assumption (later follow some hints how to give up that assumption). Consequently, in both scenarios, matching starts with *S*-agents that have already made their strategy decision; within the given period their intentions are somehow fixed.

Now we can describe the ideas and assumptions for the short cut that avoids an explicit modelling of a complicated matching process.

1. In the GD-scenario, a match $\langle i, j \rangle$ is possible only if the *S*-agent *j* lives within the actual search radius of *P*-agent *i*. In the PM-scenario a match is possible only, if both agents exchange in that period at the same location, i.e. either in the open market or the same local group. All matches that do not meet the conditions are excluded.

2. A match $\langle i, j \rangle$ is possible only, if the reward payoff for the *P*-agent *i* in an exchange with *S*-agent *j* is higher than his *Do-it-yourself*-payoff. All matches that do not meet that condition are excluded. Depending upon the competencies involved, in Figure 7 only matches for which the vertical value is greater than 0, that condition is fulfilled. (It depends heavily on the *S*-agent's share β, whether that is the case or not.)

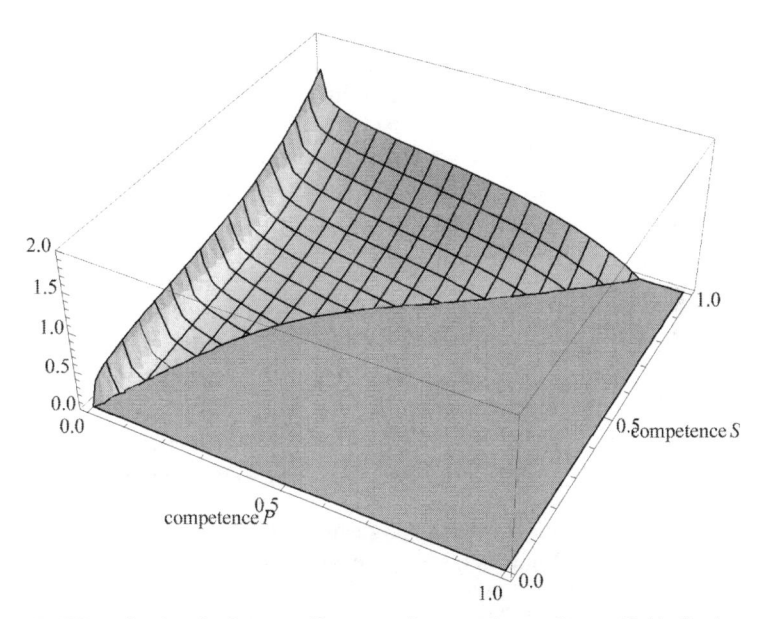

Figure 7: When is the *Do-it-yourself* worse than paying a *S*-agent? Vertical axes: The *P*-agent's surplus compared to a *Do-it-yourself* solution. ($\beta = 0.2; \phi = 4.0; \sigma = 0.25$)

3. By assumption we equip each agent with a trustworthiness detection 'technology' that works—though only to a certain degree. The technology correctly detects with a certain probability *p* the strategy decision that the *S*-agent has already made. With probability $(1 - p)$ rewarders are mistaken for exploiters

219

and vice versa. The technology is more reliable close by and becomes *less reliable* as social distance increases (as it is the case on the market or in interactions with far distant agents on a grid). The detection technology may be based on reputation, signal reading, or past experience—whatsoever and in whatever combination. *P*-agents use their detection technology and classify *S*-agents as either trustworthy or untrustworthy. If in a period *t* *S*-agent *j* was classified as untrustworthy by agent *i* then a match $\langle i, j \rangle$ is not possible. All such matches are excluded.

4. Depending upon problems, competencies, and intended strategies, the payoffs in different possible matches differ. Knowing all possible partners and the payoffs involved, both types of agents would have rank ordered preferences over the possible partners of the opposite type. We might therefore regard our matching problem as an instance of the so called *stable marriage problem* for which (type!)-optimal solutions exist.[18] Optimality is defined in terms of stability:

> A particular matching is *unstable* if there are two parties who are not matched with each other, each of whom strictly prefers the other to his/her partner in the matching [...]. A *stable* matching is [...] a matching that is not unstable (Gusfield/Irving 1989, 2).[19]

At first the idea might therefore be to resort in HUME$_{1.0}$ to the Gale-Shapley-algorithm[20] that computes such an optimal solution—as one can prove. However, doing that comes down to assuming an all-knowing central authority, an all-knowing social planner who does the matching.[21] Even extremely intelligent and very fast agents could never find the solution if their communication and knowledge is only local. The matching generated by the Gale-Shapely-algorithm can't be interpreted as the result of any 'feasible' decentralised social process with only local and limited knowledge about others.

On the other hand, matching in HUME$_{1.0}$ should *not* be random. Our decentralised matching should be less than optimal, but at the same time *better* than random. In other words, to a certain degree our agents should manage their decentralised matching in such a way that on average *more attractive matches are more likely*—and that should indiscriminately hold for *P*- and *S*-agents. For that, we transform comparatively higher payoffs into comparatively higher probabilities.

5. All *P*-agents that were not matched resort to a *do-it-yourself* solution. Possibly *S*-agents that could not be matched remain. They receive a zero payoff in the actual period.

---

18 In our case the condition of equal sized numbers of agents in both sets, strict and complete preferences, is not generally fulfilled. However, stability concepts can be extended to work under weaker assumptions (allowing indifferences, non equal sized sets etc.).
19 See also Roth/Sotomayor (1990).
20 For a description of the algorithm see Gusfield/Irving (1989), footnote 9.
21 As in case of the National Resident Matching Program (NRMP) that matches graduating medical students with hospitals in the US.

A more technical and more detailed description of the matching procedure is given in an appendix.

So far we assumed that the *S*-agents' strategic decision whether to reward or to exploit is already made when the matching process starts. The detection technology tries to detect the decisions that were made. However, in the PM-scenario the components of the decision vector are *probabilities*. An alternative approach therefore is to assume a detection technology that tries to detect these probabilities. The accuracy of the perceived trustworthiness probability should be worse on the market. For the technical details of such a matching procedure see Will (2009).

At this point the essential dialectics that drives $HUME_{1.0}$ becomes very clear: Obtaining high quality solutions at all times requires exchange with agents that are both specialised and trustworthy. Exchange with highly specialised agents normally implies exchange with more distant ones. But exchange with more distant agents is precarious since detection technologies are less reliable, and fraud is tempting for the one side and has expensive consequences for the other.

6. Excursion: *Representing Processes* versus *Generating Effects*

For both detection processes and the matching procedure in general, a short cut is used. The approach described in section 5 and in the appendix does not go into the typical or stylised details of what agents do if they have to solve a sort of matching problem as assumed here. What the matching module of $HUME_{1.0}$ does is to directly generate some effects which we, i.e. the *modellers*, believe that agents—with all the limitations we want them to have—would, or could, bring about by their capacities and activities. However, these activities and these capacities are not explicitly modelled. Of course, they could be modelled. In our case one could think of a certain range of vision agents have and that allows them to see some of the characteristics of others. In case of mutual vision, agents could address each other, make proposals and finally make a deal and so on, and so forth.

Not being explicit about the underlying processes is, trivially, a disadvantage if explicitness is the only goal. On the other hand, not being explicit and directly generating the intended effects makes it easier to control other parts the model, given one is sure about the intended effects. If in such a case, the explicit processes would not produce the directly generated effects, then, that would be a lack of adequacy. However, it may be a non-trivial task to make sure and demonstrate that an effect-generating module really produces all (and only) the effects it should produce.

Obviously, one can distinguish two different types of modules: *effect-generating* modules and *processes-representing* modules. Models usually consist of a mix of both types. In the process of modelling, corresponding types of modules can possibly be checked against each other. For instance, if one trusts more in the effect-generating module, then that module could be used to check the adequacy of a corresponding process-representing module one tries to develop.

Black box is the term that is sometimes used to refer to modules we propose and would prefer to call *effect-generating module*. For instance, the matching procedure above is not a process-representing module. Nevertheless, one can't say that the pairing mechanism is a black box since everything going on in the module is transparent, clear, and even 'explicit' in a certain sense.

It might be a good idea that even on the level of flow charts and pseudo code, effect-generating modules are marked as such and, at the same time, get assigned an accompanying plausible narrative (again marked as such) that tells a plausible and well informed informal short story about the processes that probably are or might be involved. Of course, somehow almost all modules need some informal interpretation and explanation. However, the point is, that for an effect-generating module it is part of the accompanying plausible narrative that the effect-generating module is not the true story, i.e. does not represent the real processes at work—not even in a stylized form and under a fairly liberal understanding of 'representation'.

7. Component$_5$: Learning Morals

Agents are characterised by their technical competencies and their moral character traits. The former is given by the competence vectors $C_i(t)$ as defined in (1); the latter is given by the decision vectors $D_i^{GD}(t)$ and $D_i^{PM}(t)$ (cf. definitions (10) and (11) in section 5). By working on problems, special technical competencies evolve in a learning process as described in section 2.

Moral character traits change as well. They develop, evolve, or erode over time: In the GD-scenario, the *P*-agents' search radius or the *S*-agents' reward radius may increase or decrease. In the PM-scenario, all four probabilities in the decision vector can change. It may become more or less likely that agents enter the market or stay local, and that they reward or exploit. Thus, agents somehow learn or unlearn morals.

There are many types of learning. But whatever the learning mechanism may be, we assume along with Hume that learning is always success driven—with success measured in terms of payoffs. Morals spreads, if it pays off to be moral. Morals erodes, if it is a 'looser strategy'.

Two important types of learning are *imitation* and *trial and error*. In our context imitation could mean to imitate the decision vectors of more successful others. It therefore implies a kind of *social comparison*. Trial and error works *individually*: in our context, the agents could experiment with different values of the components in their decision vectors; the better the outcomes of decisions based on the values the more likely it becomes that they are used again (*reinforcement learning*). Obviously, lots of variants exist for both types of learning mechanisms.

For the beginning we implement in HUME$_{1.0}$ a variant of imitation. The essence is to adopt components of the decision vector of a 'role model', namely a *most successful* agent close by. The details are:

1. Success is measured in terms of payoffs. But it is the *aggregated* payoff, not only the actual payoff. Let $\pi_j(t)$ be an agent's *j* payoff in the actual period *t*. The aggregated payoff then is

    $$\Pi_j(t) = \pi_j(t) + \gamma \cdot \Pi_j(t-1). \tag{12}$$

    In equation (12) the factor γ with $0 \le \gamma \le 1$ discounts past payoffs. In the model γ is an exogenously given parameter. For $\gamma = 1$ success is the total sum of all payoffs over all periods; for $\gamma = 0$ only the present period counts.

2. The pool of agents from which agent *i* selects his role model is differently defined in both scenarios. In the PM-scenario, that pool is a randomly selected subgroup of agent *i*'s partition. The size is an exogenous parameter. In the GDscenario the learning pool is a neighbourhood, defined as a radius in terms of grid distance. The radius is given as an exogenous parameter. Thus learning may be more or less local. The learning radius is constant over time. A comparatively small radius seems to be the natural starting point for the evolution of morals.

3. Given there is a most successful agent *j* in *i*'s learning pool with $i \ne j$ and $\Pi_j(t) > \Pi_i(t)$, then agent *i* imitates agent *j* in the following sense: component by component each value of agent *j*'s decision vector is copied with probability ζ into the corresponding component of agent *i*'s decision vector. ζ is exogenously given. If there isn't any more successful other in *i*'s learning pool, then *i* is his own role model—and nobody is imitated.

4. This type of learning generates new combinations of values in decision vectors. But it does not generate new values to be newly combined. To eliminate this lack of innovation, we introduce *mutation* as an additional component. In each period, with a small probability θ each component of the agents' decision vector is subject of mutation. Another parameter ζ sets the absolute size of the mutation, while the direction of change is random. Both, θ and ζ, are exogenously given parameters.

8. First Results and Research Perspectives

In sections (2) to (7) we described the main components of HUME$_{1.0}$. Period by period, the model runs through a loop in which all components are involved. Figure 8 shows how the components work together in the main loop.

The loop implements a dialectical structure and process: high quality solutions require exchange with trustworthy specialists. Exchange with highly specialised agents almost always implies exchange with more distant ones. Exchange with distant others is precarious since detection technologies are less reliable at such distances. Fraud therefore becomes increasingly tempting for the one side and increasingly expensive for the other. At the same time a lot of wealth can be generated and accumulated if trust into strangers and globalised trustworthiness would evolve.

```
┌─────────────┐
│    Start    │
└──────┬──────┘
       ▼
```

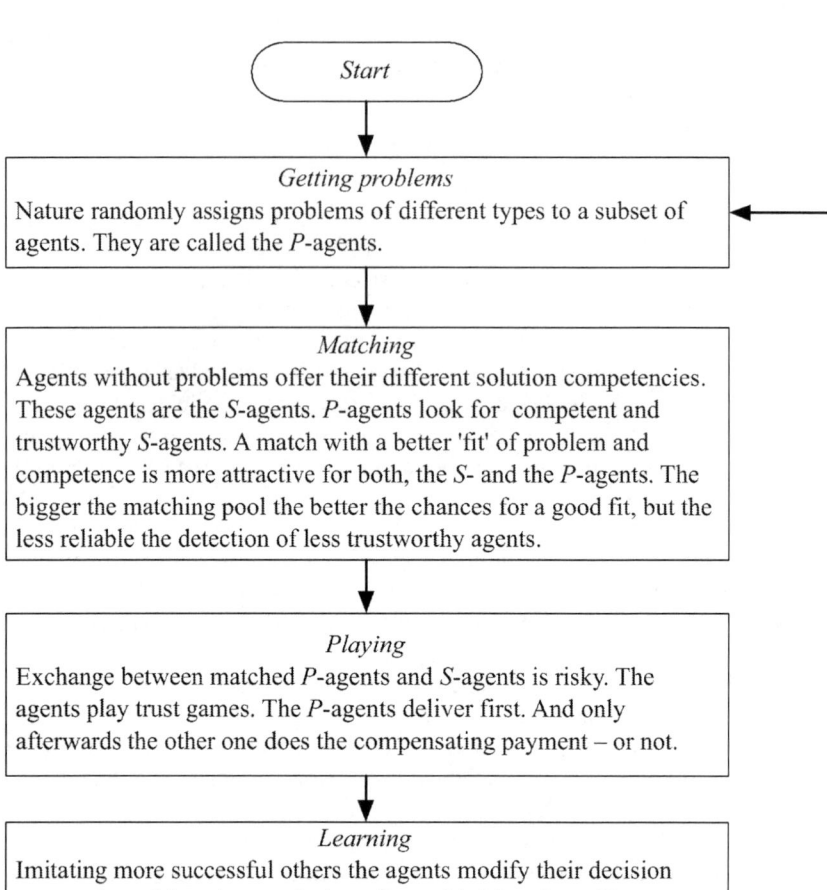

Getting problems
Nature randomly assigns problems of different types to a subset of agents. They are called the *P*-agents.

Matching
Agents without problems offer their different solution competencies. These agents are the *S*-agents. *P*-agents look for competent and trustworthy *S*-agents. A match with a better 'fit' of problem and competence is more attractive for both, the *S*- and the *P*-agents. The bigger the matching pool the better the chances for a good fit, but the less reliable the detection of less trustworthy agents.

Playing
Exchange between matched *P*-agents and *S*-agents is risky. The agents play trust games. The *P*-agents deliver first. And only afterwards the other one does the compensating payment – or not.

Learning
Imitating more successful others the agents modify their decision vectors (moral learning: evolution of morals). Mutation adds additional behavioral innovation. By solving a certain type of problem an agent becomes better in solving that type of problem (technical learning: specialization, division of labor).

Figure 8: The main loop in HUME$_{1.0}$

HUME$_{1.0}$ runs. In one version it implements the PM-scenario. Another version implements a GD-scenario in a 1-dimensional world: 500 agents live in a ring and can exchange with their neighbours to the right and left (see Figure 6 right). HUME$_{1.0}$ allows experiments with artificial societies in an artificial world. A convenient control panel is used to set the parameters for the societal dynamics under study.

HUME$_{1.0}$ allows a statistical analysis of the ongoing dynamics. The results can be easily monitored. One such monitoring window is given in Figures 10 and 11. For the GD-scenario they show the frequency dynamics of the decision vectors $\langle r_i^{search}(t), r_i^{reward}(t) \rangle$. The *x*-axis gives the search radius. The *y*-axis gives the reward radius. Therefore each $\langle x, y \rangle$ combination is one of the possible decision vectors.

Different shades of grey indicate the frequency of such a vector. Consequently, if over time the distribution of vectors moves to the north-east, then the artificial world is on an evolutionary path towards globalized exchange.

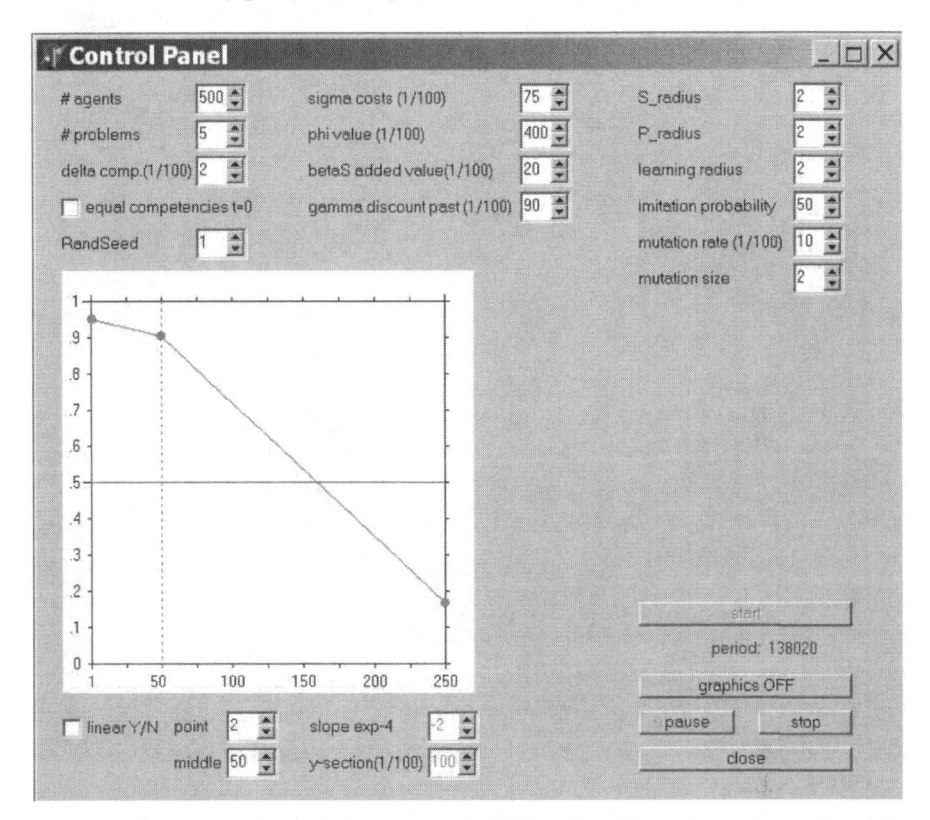

Figure 9: Control panel for the GD-scenario of HUME$_{1.0}$. The white window is used to define linear or non-linear detection functions by mouse clicks: As the network distance (x-axis) increases, the probability for a correct classification decreases (y-axis).

HUME$_{1.0}$ has not been seriously analysed so far. Systematic experimentation and exploration is only now beginning. However, there is one main impression from 'playing around' with the various parameters (i.e. more or less intelligently designed worlds): the evolution of globalized exchange based on division of labour, trust, and trustworthiness, is not an easy-going process. Sometimes it does work, but often it fails.

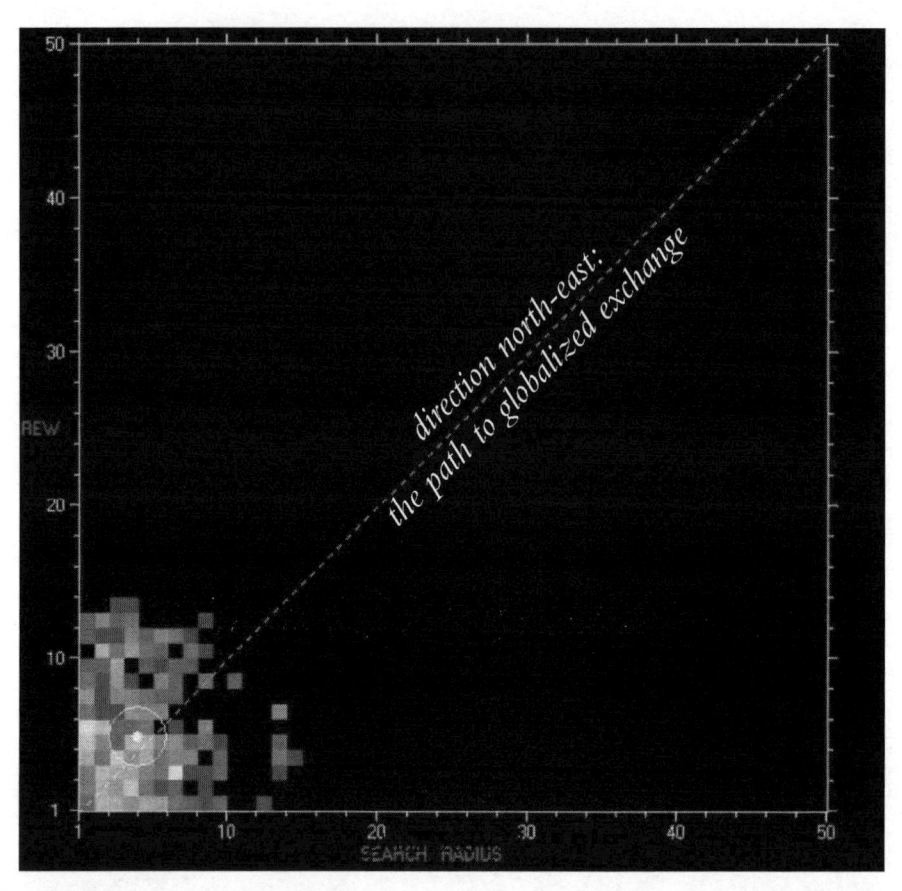

Figure 10: Frequency dynamics of decision vectors in the GD-scenario. *x*-axis: search radius. *y*-axis: reward radius. Shades of grey indicate the frequency of a certain combination. Black: No such combination exists. Along with Hume, a world is typically started with a frequency distribution that concentrates bottom left. White circle: Mean value for the actual period *t*.

There are many problems to be analysed. Below are a few.

1. Efficiency of exchange.

    (a) Are there typical conditions and constellations under which decentralized moral control suffices to let a wealthy society of *P*- and *S*-agents evolve, in which high specialization almost always allows high quality solutions?

    (b) Are there typical conditions and constellations under which decentralized moral control typically does not work and a central monitoring, enforcing and punishing agency seems to be necessary?

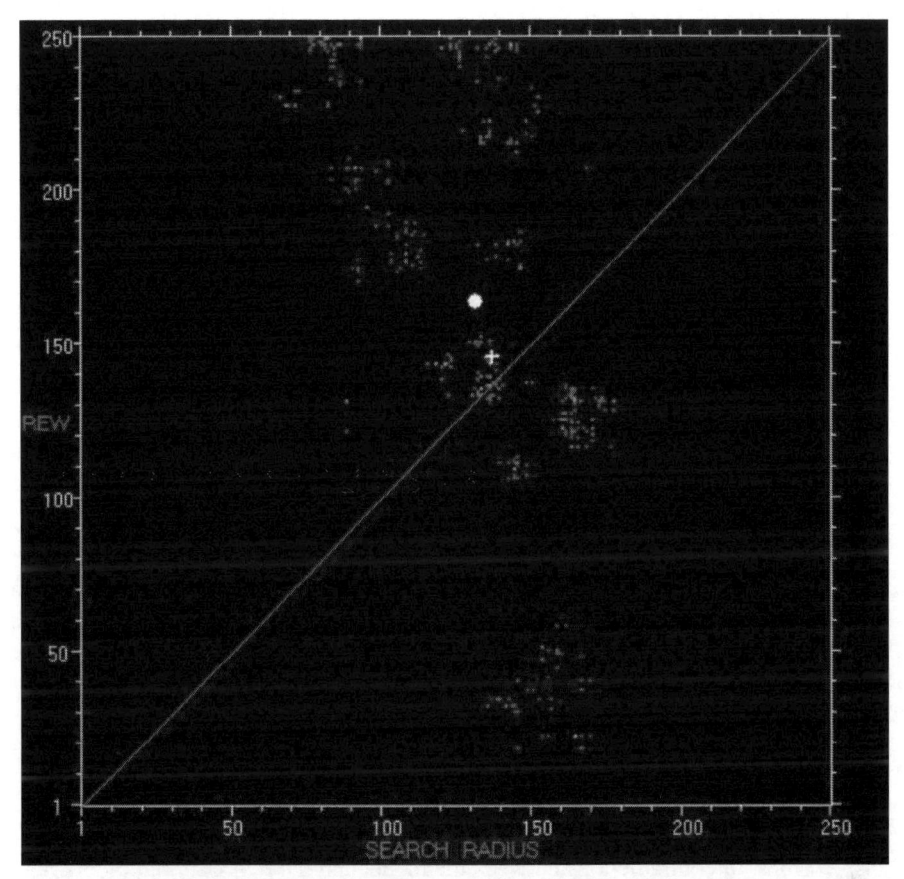

Figure 11: The dynamics that started in Figure 10 thousands of periods later and now on a larger scale for the radii. White circle: actual mean value. White cross: actual median value. Obviously this world is on an evolutionary path towards a more globalized exchange.

2. The path to globalized exchange.

   (a) Are there 'typical' trajectories of the values in the decision vectors $D_i^{GD}(t)$ and $D_i^{PM}(t)$? Is it a linear or more stepwise process?

   (b) If morals and division of labour evolved, what are the possibilities, likelihoods, conditions and circumstances of—more or less severe—setbacks or death spirals?

3. Learning morals:

   (a) Does the type or speed of moral learning—as controlled by the parameter ζ—matter? Is it important that there is a certain inertia as to the agents' moral character traits? Is it important that bad examples, i.e. wealthy cheaters, are not too visible? Does the size of the learning pool matter?

(b) How much does discounting past success—as controlled by the parameter γ—matter for the evolution of morals? Is it important that long term success matters for the imitation of others? Or has γ to be in the right interval—not too high and not too low?

4. Detection capabilities.
   (a) How strong does the reliability of the detection technology affect the evolution of a more globalized or more local exchange?
   (b) How bad can the detection capabilities be but still result in 'reasonable' quality solutions?

5. Technical learning and division of labour.
   (a) How important is the—so far—exogenously given and constant number of different problems?
   (b) What happens if the number of problems is endogenized and increases as specialization increases? Does that favour more globalized exchange and more universalised trust?

By answering these questions we have two hopes. The first is to understand better the mechanisms of one of the most obvious and puzzling developments in human societal life, the evolution of large societies based on division of labour and a high proportion of trust and trustworthiness among people without any personal ties. The second is to present modelling and simulation as a fruitful approach to interpret and to reconstruct rich informal theories. $HUME_{1.0}$ allows a kind of experimental interpretation; by experimentation one can try to find out with increasing precision the effect of specific assumptions. It allows us to check the validity of intuition based conjectures.

Of course, the assumptions on which $HUME_{1.0}$ is build, are not sacrosanct. Conflicts, tensions, or contradictions between the model and the rich informal theory may suggest changes in the model. But then, again, the modified model is a useful tool to clarify and check the rich informal theory.

9. Appendix

The basic ideas for the matching process in the GD-scenario are informally described in section 5. Here follows a more *technical* description. It should be detailed enough to allow a *replication* of the matching module.

The core of the matching module are certain matrices and iterated operations on them.

1. Let m be the number of P-agents and S-agents. We generate a $(m+1)\times(m+1)$ matrix. The first column is used to enlist the indices of the P-agents, the first row to enlist the S-agents' indices. (Position $\langle 1,1 \rangle$ is *not* used.) Based on the

decision vectors and the detection technology we determine for each possible pairing if:

(a) the S-agent lives within or beyond the P-agents search radius;
(b) the S-agent intents to reward or to exploit;
(c) the P-agent detects the S-agent's intention correctly or not.

That information is coded and stored in the matrix. We refer to the matrix as the *status matrix* M^{status}

2. The status matrix is then used to calculate two payoff matrices, one for the P-agents, $M_P^{payoffs}$, and one for the S-agents $M_S^{payoffs}$. Later the payoff entries will be transformed into probabilities that then are used for a kind of *matching lottery*. The payoff entries in both matrices are generated as follows:

(a) Positive payoff entries get only pairs of P- and S-agents for which it holds, that the S-agent lives within the search radius of the P-agent and, additionally, was classified as a rewarder—correctly or mistakenly. All other entries in both matrices are zero.

(b) In the P-agent payoff matrix the entries are the P-agents' reward payoffs, given their specific problems and the S-agents' specific competencies.

(c) In the S-agent payoff matrix the entries are—depending upon the intended strategy—either the S-agents' reward or their exploit payoff.

3. For a P-agent, a match with a S-agent that he classified as trustworthy is interesting only if his reward payoff is higher than his *do-it-yourself* payoff. Row by row, column by column, for each pair with a positive payoff in $M_P^{payoffs}$ and $M_S^{payoffs}$, respectively, it is checked whether, given the problems and competencies, the P-agents' reward payoffs are higher than their *do-it-yourself* payoffs. If not, then in each case that information is added to the entries in M^{status}. The corresponding entries in $M_P^{payoffs}$ and $M_S^{payoffs}$ are set to zero.

4. Now payoffs are transformed into probabilities, which are used later in a matching lottery. The probabilities are generated as follows:

(a) P-agent by P-agent the rows of $M_P^{payoffs}$ are checked. If in a row non-zero payoff entries exist, then for all such row entries their normalised value is calculated. Normalisation means a linear transformation such that the row sum of all normalised payoff entries equals 1. The normalised values become the entries in a third type of equally structured[22] $(m+1)\times(m+1)$ matrix, the probability matrix M_P^{prob}. If in a row all payoff entries are zero, then the corresponding entries in M_P^{prob} are set to zero as well.

---

22 *Equally structured* means that again the first row is used to enlist the indices of S-agents while the first column enlists the indices of P-agents. Position $\langle 1,1 \rangle$ is not used.

229

(b) Analogously, *S*-agent by *S*-agent the columns of $M_S^{payoffs}$ are checked. If in a column non-zero payoff entries exist, then for all entries in that column their normalised value is calculated. The values become the corresponding entries in the second probability matrix, M_S^{prob}. If in a column all payoff entries are zero, then the corresponding entries in M_S^{prob} are set to zero as well.

5. The matching lottery starts. Several probabilities are involved:

    (a) We count in M_P^{prob} the number of *P*-agents that—after all exclusion principles have been applied—can be matched with at least one *S*-agent. That number is the number of *rows* in M_P^{prob} that contain non-zero probabilities. Let n_P be that number. The number of *S*-agents that can be matched is the number of *columns* of M_S^{prob} that contain non-zero probabilities. Let n_S be that number. To avoid type or role privileges we base a matching with probability $\frac{n_P}{n_P+n_S}$ on M_P^{prob}; with probability $1 - \frac{n_P}{n_P+n_S}$ the matching is based on M_S^{prob}.

    (b) If M_P^{prob} is the basis, we randomly select one of the n_P *P*-agents. Let *i* be the selected agent. In 'his' row of M_P^{prob} exist non-zero probabilities for interactions with *S*-agents, identified by their index in the first row of the column of each probability. With the probability that is give in 'their' column one of the *S*-agents is selected for a match with *P*-agent *i*. Since higher payoffs imply higher probabilities, matches with more attractive *S*-agents are more likely. If M_S^{prob} is the basis, we randomly select one of the n_S *S*-agents. Let *j* be the selected agent. In 'his' column of M_S^{prob} exist non-zero probabilities for interactions with *P*-agents, identified by their index in the first column of the row of each probability. With the probability that is give in 'their' row one of the *P*-agents is selected for a match with *S*-agent *j*. Since higher payoffs imply higher probabilities, matches with more attractive *P*-agents are more likely.

6. Once a match $\langle i, j \rangle$ is established, both agents are *excluded* as possible interaction partners for others: in $M_P^{payoffs}$ and $M_S^{payoffs}$ all payoffs from interactions with *i* or *j* are set to zero.

7. Steps 4 to 6 are repeated until there is no *P*-agent or no *S*-agent left to be matched with an agent of the other type. All *P*-agents that were not matched resort to a *do-it-yourself* solution. It is possible that unmatched *S*-agents remain. They receive a zero payoff in the actual period.

For *P*-agents and *S*-agents, there are *no one-sided type privileges* (as they exist—as gender privileges—in some versions of the *optimal* algorithms mentioned above). Both types have the same chance to find matching partners. There is no guarantee that everybody is matched—even if logically that would have been possible. Finally, there is no guarantee that matches are stable in the sense as defined above for the stable marriage problem. However, this effect is on purpose and an intended consequence: basically we want to generate a matching as it plausibly *could have been brought about by decentralised interactions of agents that have only limited knowledge of the search pool and the agents therein.* Under such conditions, stability should be a rare event.

A warning: so far we do not know enough about the matching procedure described above. Firstly, we do not know how much better, compared to random matching, our matching algorithm behaves. Secondly, we do not know how much unstable matches our procedure generates. Both should be known. In the near future we will find out.

Bibliography

Baurmann, M. (1996), *Der Markt der Tugend*, Tübingen

Binmore, K. (1994), *Game Theory and the Social Contract – Vol. 1: Playing Fair*, Cambridge

Clark, G. (2007), *Farewell to Alms: A Brief Economic History of theWorld*, Princeton

Flache, A./R. Hegselmann (2001), Do Irregular Grids Make a Difference? Relaxing the Spatial Regularity Assumption in Cellular Models of Social Dynamics, in: *Journal of Artificial Societies and Social Simulation 4(4)*, http://jasss.soc.surrey.ac.uk/4/4/6.html

Gibbard, A. (1990), *Wise Choices, Apt Feelings: A Theory of Normative Judgment*, Cambridge

Gusfield, D./R. W. Irving (1989), *The Stable Marriage Problem – Structure and Algorithms*, Cambridge/MA

Hardin, R. (1982), Exchange-theory on Strategic Bases, in: *Rationality and Society 21(2)*, 251–272

— (2007), *David Hume: Moral and Political Theorist*, Oxford

Hegselmann, R./A. Flache (1998), Understanding Complex Social Dynamics – A Plea For Cellular Automata Based Modelling, in: *Journal of Artificial Societies and Social Simulation 1(3)*, http://Jasss.soc.surrey.ac.uk/1/3/1.html

Hume, D. (1998), *An Enquiry Concerning the Principles of Morals*, Oxford

— (2007), *A Treatise of Human Nature*, London

Kliemt, H. (1985), *Moralische Institutionen – Empiristische Theorien ihrer Evolution*, Freiburg

— (1986), *Antagonistische Kooperation*, Freiburg

Lahno, B. (1995), *Versprechen – Überlegungen zu einer künstlichen Tugend*, München

Lucretius (1922), *De rerum natura*, Oxford

Mackie, J. L. (1980), *Hume's Moral Theory*, London

Macy, M./Y. Sato (2002), Trust, Cooperation, and Market Formation in the US and Japan, in: *Proceedings of the National Academy of Sciences 99*, 7214–7220

— (2008), Reply toWill and Hegselmann, in: *Journal of Artificial Societies and Social Simulation 11(4)*, http://jasss.soc.surrey.ac.uk/11/4/11.html

Plato (1997), *Complete Works*, Hackett

Ramchurn, S. D./D. Huynh/N. R. Jennings (2004), Trust in Multi-Agent Systems, in: *Knowledge Engineering Review 19(1)*, 1–25

Roth, A. E./M. A. O. Sotomayor (1990), *Two-sided Matching – A Study in Game Theoretic Modeling and Analysis*, Cambridge

Sabater, J./C. Sierra (2005), Review on Computational Trust and Reputation Models, in: *Artifical Intelligence Review 24(1)*, 33–60

Skyrms, B. (1996), *The Evolution of the Social Contract*, Cambridge

Smith, A. (1979), *An Inquiry into the Nature and Causes of the Wealth of Nations*, Oxford

Sugden, R. (2004), *The Economics of Rights, Co-operation and Welfare*, 2nd ed., New York

Ullmann-Margalit, E. (1977), *The Emergence of Norms*, Oxford

Will, O. (2009), An Agent-Based Model on the Evolution of Trust in Strangers and Division of Labour, in: *MABS 2009 forthcoming*

Will, O./R. Hegselmann (2008a), Remark on a Reply, in: *Journal of Artificial Societies and Social Simulation 11(4)*, http://jasss.soc.surrey.ac.uk/11/4/13.html

— (2008b), A Replication That Failed: On the Computational Model in "Michael W. Macy and Yoshimichi Sato: Trust, Cooperation and Market Formation in the U.S. and Japan. Proceedings of the National Academy of Sciences, May 2002", in: *Journal of Artificial Societies and Social Simulation 11(3)*, http://jasss.soc.surrey.ac.uk/11/3/3.html

Giulia Andrighetto

The Micro-Macro Link as a Recursive Loop
A Comment on Rainer Hegselmann and Oliver Will

1. Introduction

In their contribution to the workshop *Norms and Values. The Role of Social Norms as Instruments of Value Realization*, Hegselmann and Will present a computational model (Hume$_{1.0}$) of Hume's moral and political theory (Hume 1739f.[1998]; 1751[2007]). In particular, they are interested in modelling and checking by simulation the theory on the origin of artificial virtues—i.e. justice and government—the British philosopher handed down to posterity. Hume$_{1.0}$ is an insightful and rigorous reconstruction of Hume's informal theory through which the authors explicitly operationalize the *interplay of mechanisms* in force of which virtues, specialization and wealth prosper, thus testing how robust these parameters are. This work contributes to the workshop with an important perspective: it provides a framework in which the moral character and its dynamics can be investigated by means of social simulation.

Social simulation can be defined as the study of social phenomena through computer simulation: agents' behaviour, their interactions and the environment are explicitly modelled in order to investigate the micro-based premises that explain the macro regularity of interest. It helps modelling and understanding the *generative* process between premises on a micro-level and the consequences that agents' interactions originate over time at the macro level of analysis.

Joshua Epstein, probably the best known advocate of the generative approach in social science, argues that generating a social phenomenon by means of agent-based simulation means "situate an initial population of autonomous heterogeneous agents (see also Arthur) in a relevant special environment; allow them to interact according to *simple* local rules, and thereby generate—or 'grow'—the macroscopic regularity from the *bottom up*" (Epstein 1999, 41; italics added).

HUME$_{1.0}$ adopts such a generative perspective: it explores the micro mechanisms—the bottom-up processes—allowing the evolution of large societies based on division of labour and the emergence of trust and trustworthiness among strangers. Although the authors point out a bunch of problems needing further exploration and experimentation, the results obtained with Hume$_{1.0}$ are enlightening and contribute to a more fine-grained understanding of the evolution of globalized exchange based on division of labour, trust and trustworthiness.

Nevertheless, I consider the notion of *emergence* the authors refer to, intended as a one-way process from micro to macro, to be formulated in a somewhat unsatisfactory way, namely as just a bottom-up process (as defined by the vast majority of the simulation and computational models of social and economic processes). The *downward* process from social properties to local rules is not taken into account. As argued by Conte (2009), one of the effects of ignoring the downward causation dynamics is that of limiting the explanatory and generative power of simulation.

In this commentary, I will endeavour to show what are the advantages of integrating the generative perspective with a theory of downward causation, providing a view of the micro-macro link as a recursive loop, in which emergent effects at the macro-level retroact on the lower levels, modifying them.

2. Emergence as a Complex Loop

This brief commentary is not the forum for a survey on the epistemological and philosophical debate on the notion of emergence, a very intricate and contradictory phenomenon (Alexander 1920; Broad 1925; Coleman 1990). Thus, I will focus on the way back of this dynamics, from the macro to the micro level, i.e. the process of *downward* causation (Campbell 1974).

In a recent paper (Conte et al. 2007), two main ways in which downward causation occurs in human and multi-agent societies have been distinguished:

- *Simple loop*, in which the emergent effect retroacts on the generating systems, determining new properties that might interfere negatively or positively with the micro systems' further activity. This is the case with a number of properties, such as rights, social status and social power, as well as the evaluations that agents form about one another (for example, reputation).[1]
- *Complex loop*, in which the emergent effect determines new properties at the micro-level by means of which the effect is reproduced. A *recursive interaction* between both levels is established in a complex feedback loop. This includes two sub-processes:
    → 2nd order emergence: i.e. the process by means of which, once produced, an emergent effect is *recognised* by the producing systems and by this means the effect is likelier to be reproduced (Dennett 1995; Gilbert 2002).
    → Immergence, i.e. the gradual and complex process by which the macro-social effect emerges while immerging in the minds of the agents producing it, thus generating a number of *intermediate loops*. Before any global effect emerges,

---

1   One example of simple downward causation are dependence networks. In a common environment, actions done by one agent take effects on the goals of other agents. These are limitedly self-sufficient in the sense that they not always possess all the resources required to achieve their goals. Under these conditions, social dependence networks (Sichman et al. 1994; Sichman/Conte 2002) emerge as interconnections among agents endowed with a finite number of goals and resources for achieving them. In turn, this non-uniform distribution of exchange power determines a new effect at the lower level: agents derive an equal power of choice, or, as we called it, negotiation power. Here the emergent macrostructure—the dependence network—affects the lower level, creating a distribution of negotiation power among individual agents at the generating micro-level, that will interfere positively or negatively with their successive achievements.

specific local events affect the generating systems, their beliefs and goals,[2] in such a way that agents force one another into converging on one global macroscopic effect (Castelfranchi 1998; Conte et al. 2007).

Unlike self-reinforcement, where the replication of a given behaviour increases with its past occurrence, in downward causation macro-social forces (e.g., institutions, norms) retroact on local systems by getting them to act. To understand this process we must assume that macro-social properties *generate* new properties at the local level.

A good example of downward causation, and in particular of immergence, is social norms. There is not a consensus on a common definition of social norms: in this commentary I will refer to the one provided by Ullman-Margalit: "Social norms are a prescribed guide for conduct which is generally complied with by the members of society." (1977, italic added) It is important to point out that the prescription through which a norm is transmitted is a special one: a prescription that is *requested* to be adopted because it is a norm and it is *fully applied* only when it is complied with for its own sake (Hart 1961; Durkheim 1951). In other words, in order for the norm to be satisfied, it is not sufficient that the prescribed action is performed, but a *normative belief* has to be generated into the minds of the norm addressees, and the corresponding *normative goal* has to be formed and pursued.

In accordance with this view of norms as two-sided, external (social) and internal (mental) objects (Conte/Castelfranchi 1995; 2006), a norm emerges as a norm only when it immerges into the minds of the agents involved; in other words, when agents recognize it as such. Thus, immergence is a necessary correlate of emergence of at least a subset of macro-social phenomena, such as social norms.

In order to test this view of norm emergence as a complex loop, some agent based simulations have been carried out (Andrighetto et al. forthcoming; Campennì et al. 2009; Troitzsch 2008; Lotzmann et al. 2008). These simulations models are based upon a complex architecture of the agent: they make use of agents capable of influencing each other by direct communication, recognizing norms, generating new normative beliefs and acting on the basis of these beliefs. This kind of agent modelling adds a further level of complexity at the micro level by introducing cognitive properties inside the agents' behaviour, thus making possible for the macro-social effect to immerge into the minds of the agents.

One interesting result of these simulation studies is that they have made visible something unexpected: that the emergence of social norms is preceded by the insurgence of proto-norms (candidate normative beliefs) into the agents' mind. In other words, simulations' results seem to suggest that norms have a *latency time*: the time interval between the normative belief appearance into the agents' minds and the agents convergence on the corresponding action. The recognition of this mental process has an important impact on the theory of norms and on the understanding of

---

2   Throughout the commentary, I will refer to goals from the point of view of computer science and autonomous agent theory. In particular, a goal is a wanted world-state that triggers and guides action (see Conte, forthcoming).

their emergence. It can be seen as a preliminary evidence of the fact that the immergence process occurs before the emergence one, but it takes time for the emergent effect to become visible.

A view of the micro-macro link as a recursive loop, in which emergent effects at the macro-level retroact on the lower levels, modifying them, thereby provides a more dynamic, generative view of the micro-level entities. Furthermore, such a theory might contribute to preserve the generality and plausibility of local rules: there is no need for ad hoc local rules if macro-social properties are allowed to emerge from them in non-trivial ways (which include feedback loops).

Therefore, in order to provide a valid model of the evolution and emergence of social norms and of other social phenomena—such as artificial virtues—the individual mechanisms and mental processes allowing these processes to take place should not be neglected. Experimenters ought first to model how this dynamics takes place and what its requirements are, and not be content with a set of simple, at most plausible local rules.

Hegselmann and Will explicitly say: "In HUME$_{1.0}$ we will not even try to explicitly model the social and cognitive processes and capacities involved in that kind of matching process. Instead, we use a modelling short cut. We introduce a procedure that directly generates a set of matches with certain desired properties." They provide a very detailed and sound replication of Hume's informal theory, of which the British philosopher would have been very grateful. But I wonder whether Hegselmann and Will could have been able to surprise Hume with some unexpected results, if only they had been more demanding as to the agent model.

Bibliography

Alexander, S. (1920), *Space, Time, and Deity*. 2 vols., London

Andrighetto, G./M. Campenni/F. Cecconi/R. Conte (forthcoming), The Complex Loop of Norm Emergence: A Simulation Model, in: *Lecture Notes in Artificial Intelligence*

Broad, C. D. (1925), *The Mind and Its Place in Nature*, London

Campbell, D. T. (1974), Downward Causation in Hierarchically Organized Biological Systems, in: F. J. Ayala/T. Dobzhansky (eds.), *Studies in the Philosophy of Biology*, London, 179–186

Campenni, M./G. Andrighetto/F. Cecconi/R. Conte (2009), Normal = Normative? The Role of Intelligent Agents in Norm Innovation, in: *Mind and Society 2009, 10.1007/S11299-009-0063-4*

Castelfranchi, C. (1998), Simulating with Cognitive Agents: The Importance of Cognitive Emergence Multi-Agent Systems and Agent-Based Simulation, in: *Lecture Notes in Computer Science (LNCS) 1534*, 26–44

Coleman, J. (1990), *Foundations of Social Theory*, Cambridge/MA

Conte, R. (2009), From Simulation to Theory and Backward, in: *Lecture Notes in Computer Science (LNCS) 5466*, 29–47

— (forthcoming), Rational, Goal Governed Agents, in: *Encyclopedia of Complexity and System Science*

— /G. Andrighetto/M. Campenni/M. Paolucci (2007), Emergent and Immergent Effects in Complex Social Systems, in: *Proceedings of AAAI Symposium, Social and Organizational Aspects of Intelligence*

— /C. Castelfranchi (1995), *Cognitive and Social Action*, London

— / — (1999), From Conventions to Prescriptions. Towards a Unified Theory of Norms, in: *AI and Law 7*, 323–340

— / — (2006), The Mental Path of Norms, in: *Ratio Juris 19(4)*, 501–517

Dennett, D. (1995), *Darwin's Dangerous Idea: Evolution and the Meanings of Life*, New York

Durkheim, E. (1951), *Suicide*, New York

Epstein, J. M. (1999), Agent-Based Computational Models and Generative Social Science, *Complexity 4(5)*, 41–60

Gilbert N. (2002), Varieties of Emergence, in: D. Sallach (ed.), *Proceedings of the Agent 2002 Conference on Social Agents: Ecology, Exchange, and Evolution*, University of Chicago, Oct. 11–12 2002, 41–56

Hart, H. L. A. (1961), *The Concept of Law*, Oxford

Hume, D. (1998), *An Enquiry Concerning the Principles of Morals*, Oxford

— (2007), *A Treatise of Human Nature*, London

Kelsen, H. (1979), *General Theory of Norms*, Oxford

Lotzmann, U./M. Möhring/K. Troitzsch (2008), Simulating Norm Formation in a Traffic Scenario. Paper presented at the fifth annual conference of the European Social Simulation Association, (ESSA), University of Brescia, Sept. 1–5 2008

Sichman, J. S./R. Conte (2002), Multi-agent Dependence by Dependence Graphs, in: *Proceedings of Autonomous Agent & MAS, AAMAS*, 483–91

— / — /C. Castelfranchi/Y. Demazeau (1994), A Social Reasoning Mechanism Based on Dependence Networks, in: A. G. Cohn (ed.), *Proceedings of the 11th European Conference on Artificial Iintelligence* (ECAI), Baffin Lane, 188–192

Troitzsch, K. G. (2008), Simulating Collaborative Writing: Software Agents Produce a Wikipedia. Paper presented at the fifth annual conference of the European Social Simulation Association (ESSA), University of Brescia, Sept. 1–5 2008

Ullman-Margalit, E. (1977), *The Emergence of Norms*, Oxford

von Wright, G. H. (1963), *Norm and Action. A Logical Inquiry*, London

Gerhard Schurz

Global Value Distribution and Value Clashes

1. Clash of Civilizations?

With his article "Clash of Civilizations" (*Foreign Affairs 1993*) and his book (1996) Samuel P. Huntington created world-wide attention, which was amplified through the tragic event of September 11th, and whose consequences culminated into a still lasting world-wide debate. Huntington's position can be summarized in the following three theses.

Huntington's thesis no. 1: After the era of colonialism and the consecutive era of cold war, which ended with the breakdown of communism, the world has entered a *new* era, in which the artificial political division of the world is replaced by the more natural division of the world in historically old world-wide 'civilizations' which through the process of global networking come more and more in mutual conflict:

1st World War	Collapse of Communism	Since 1990s:
Era of colonialism Western hegemony	*Era of cold war* Artificial division of world into two blocks	*Era of clash of civilizations* Natural division of world into worldwide cultures

Huntington's thesis no. 2: Our world is naturally divided into *civilizations* or *world-cultures*. These are *historically enduring* constitutions of human societies, primarily characterized by religion, and secondarily by common history and by geographical region.

Huntington distinguishes the following eight world-cultures. Four of them are historically very old and more-or-less independent, while the other four are partly derived (the last one is a 'family'):

Four large and historically old cultural blocks:

1) The *Sinic* or *Chinese* world-culture, which begins 1500 B.C. and is mainly *Confucian*.
2) The *Hindu* world-culture on the Indian subcontinent, which begins around 1500 B.C.
3) The *Islamic* world-culture, which begins around 700 A.D. and has spread from the Arabic peninsula to central Asia and parts of the Indian subcontinent and of Indonesia.

4) The *western* world-culture, which, according to Huntington, begins around 700 A.D., is mainly determined by *Christian* religion, and has spread from Western Europe to North America and Latin America.

In part historically derived are:

5) The *orthodox-Christian* world-culture in the *ex-communistic* countries of Eastern Europe and North Asia.
6) The *Latin-American* world-culture, which is closely related to the western world-culture.
7) The *Japanese world-culture*, which has developed from the Chinese world-culture and begins between 100 and 400 A.D.
8) The *African family* of cultures—because of the diversity of tribal identities it is questionable, says Huntington, whether one can speak here of *one* world-culture.

Huntington's critics have soon noticed several *general* problems which are involved in Huntington's classification of world-cultures, such as the following:

- Can the major characteristic of contemporary world-cultures be really defined by religious attributes?
- Are these world-cultures really historically enduring characteristics—haven't these world-cultures drastically changed through historical time?
- Does an Orthodox-Christian world-culture really exist—aren't these countries similar because of their ex-communistic history? (Greece, for example, is orthodox but doesn't belong to this group.)
- Is the Western world-culture really homogeneous?

Apart from these general problems, which will be analyzed in the next sections, several *special problems* have popped up during the Huntington-debate. For example: Why is Buddhism missing (the fifth 'world-religion'; cf. Huntington 1996, 61)? Why is the starting point of western culture located at 700 A.C. (and not, for example, at 600 B.C. with the ancient Greek empire)? If Japan is included, why not Korea? What stands behind the 'family' of African cultures? However that may be, it does not tackle Huntington's third, major and most provocative thesis, which is the following:

Huntington's thesis no. 3: The western ideal of *universal modernization*—western democracy & free-market economy as the direction in which all countries will develop if one gives them independence and imports western know-how (the 'world-wide Marshall plan')—*is false*.

Rather, our world divides itself naturally along the above world-cultures. They are more-or-less in *mutual conflict* with each other, and in part even *incommensurable*. They should better not be mixed.

Western societies, and in particular the USA, should retreat as a *leading model* from the international level. At the same time they should *protect* their culture against too many immigrants from incommensurable cultures (Huntington 1996, 524).

Huntington supports his theses citing the following evidence:

⇨ Non-western countries have taken over western technology, science and economy. But at the same time, they have kept or even strengthened their own cultural traditions. This is especially true for the east-Asian countries which had an enormous economic boom—Hong Kong, Taiwan, Southern Korea, Singapore, China, Malaysia, Thailand, and Indonesia (Huntington 1996, 129, 156–9, 167).

⇨ Scientists who research religion speak about a world-wide *come-back* of religious orientations with increasing fundamentalist tendencies—especially in the Islamic countries, in India, in South America, in the ex-communist countries, and even in the USA (cf. Huntington 1996, 135, 144, 149; Kienzler 1996, 28ff; Riesebrodt 2000, 122). According to Huntington, the reason for this come-back is an *intrinsic crisis of modernity*: as a reaction to post-modern orientation-less and moral de-stabilization people turn back to religion-based absolute value systems (Huntington 1996, 146).

2. Huntington's 'World-Cultures' from an Evolutionary Viewpoint

I think that Huntington's view of world-cultures as historically enduring characteristics is wrong. The following simple observation makes this plain:

Anti-thesis to Huntington: the western-Christian world-cultures in Europe's pre-modern time, from 800 to 1800 A.D., are much more similar to the contemporary non-Western societies (e.g. the Islamic countries) than to the modern Western societies.

My anti-thesis can be supported by many facts, and I mention only a few of them:

⇨ Contemporary Confucian values fit quite well with the conservative values of the European citizens in 19th century (cf. Müller 1998).

⇨ There are many parallels between contemporary Islamic countries and European countries in the times when they were ruled by Christian religion: Jihad had its parallel in Christian crusades, the submission of females under males was also once central to Christian morality, and post-modern liberties, e.g. concerning permissive clothing fashions, would have shocked my grandmother in a similarly drastic way as they currently do Islamic fundamentalists. In general, Jewish, Christian and Islamic religions are very similar to each other and share historical roots.

Therefore I arrive at the following evolutionary diagnosis:

> *Evolutionary diagnosis:* Huntington's so-called world-cultures seem to be momentary developmental stages of certain cultural evolutionary processes. The reason for the contemporary clashes between world-cultures lies not so much in their intrinsic differences, but is the effect of the huge *temporal displacement* ('time shift') between their development stages—concerning economic and industrial development, and concerning secularization and democratization.

In fact, the secularization of Christianity was a slow and difficult historical process, and given that Mohammed came six centuries later than Christ, one may expect that the secularization of Islam will simply need some more centuries of time.

But even if my evolutionary diagnosis is true, there is an important *successor question* to the controversy about the clash of world-cultures:

> Does the long-term development of societies go into more-or-less the same direction, into the direction of modernization?
> Or do different cultures develop into different directions in which case Huntington's third thesis maintains its validity?

These are the central questions of Inglehart's empirical investigation, to which I turn to in the next section.

3. Ronald Inglehart's World Value Survey: Empirical Investigation of World-Cultures

Most of the recent discussions about Huntington's theses are very critical and strongly value-laden, lacking *systematic empirical evidence* (cf. Metzinger 2000 as a typical example). One notable exception are the empirical studies of the *Word Value Survey (WVS) project* which has been founded by Ronald Inglehart at the University of Michigan and which can be accessed via the WVS homepage *http://www.worldvaluessurvey.org*. In this project, social scientists have developed and successively improved detailed questionnaires, by which people in more than 65 countries are asked questions concerning:

- their attitudes towards religion, authority, labor, family, political organization, personal self realization, gender roles, homosexuality, liberty, etc.
- their lifestyle: married or single, how much time they spend for work, family, clubs, etc.

Each answer to a question corresponds to one *empirical variable* (which is standardized on an interval scale: mean = 0, standard deviation = 1). In order to interpret the more than 250 variables (answers), Inglehart has performed a factor analysis. In several independent WVS-studies or 'waves' (1990; 1995; 2000; 2005), two stable (statistically independent) factors have been obtained which explain more than 50%

of the total variance of the empirical variables. The factor analysis has been performed with nations as empirical units, i.e., with the mean values for each country. The two obtained factors or 'theoretical parameters' correspond to latent causes of highly intercorrelated empirical variables; and they are best understood by recognizing the types of answers with which they have high correlations (or 'loadings'):

Factor 1: tradition-religious versus secular-rational orientation:
Correlates with: religious vs. rational-secular value-orientation, importance of family bonds vs. individual freedom, national pride high vs. low, respect vis-à-vis state authority high vs. low, birth rate high vs. low, estimation of labor high vs. low.

The transition on the 1st factor axis from traditional-religious to rational-secular values corresponds to the social transition from *agrarian* to *industrial* civilizations—the so-called *process of modernization*.

Factor 2: survival values versus self-expression values:
Correlates with: low vs. high economic standards of life, importance of existential security & work vs. pleasure & life-quality, low vs. high appreciation of gender equality, rejection vs. acceptance of homosexuality, intolerance vs. tolerance towards foreign immigrants, low vs. high interpersonal trust, acceptance vs. non-acceptance of authoritarian regimes, devaluation vs. appreciation of democracy.

The transition from survival to self-expression values corresponds socially to the transition from industrial to post-industrial societies with a high prosperity level and a dense social service infrastructure—the so-called *process of post-modernization*.

In his earlier books (cf. 1998), Inglehart defended a version of modernization theory in which more-or-less all nations follow in their development the same major modernization trends:

agrarian ─────────────▶ industrial ─────────────▶ post-industrial societies

    modernization (factor 1)   post-modernization (factor 2)

Because of the WVS-data, Inglehart later weakens his view and recognizes a large amount of *culture-specific path-dependence* in this development (cf. Inglehart 2004, 141). In fact, it seems to me that Inglehart's modernization theory is even less supported by the WVS-data as Inglehart seems to think. In part, the WVS-data support a modified Huntington-type thesis about *divergent developments* of world-cultures, although Huntington's own classification of world-cultures is falsified by the data in many respects.

4. Global Distribution of Cultural Values

Fig. 1 shows the most recent cultural world map of nations based on the WVS-data of 2000 and 2005 (they include more nations than 1995). Some typical attitudes which correspond to different positions on this cultural world-map are shown in fig. 2. A closer inspection of figure 1 leads to the following remarkable observations:

Figure 1
The cultural world-map. Most recent data from 2000 and 2005. (Source: http://www.worldvaluessurvey.org.)

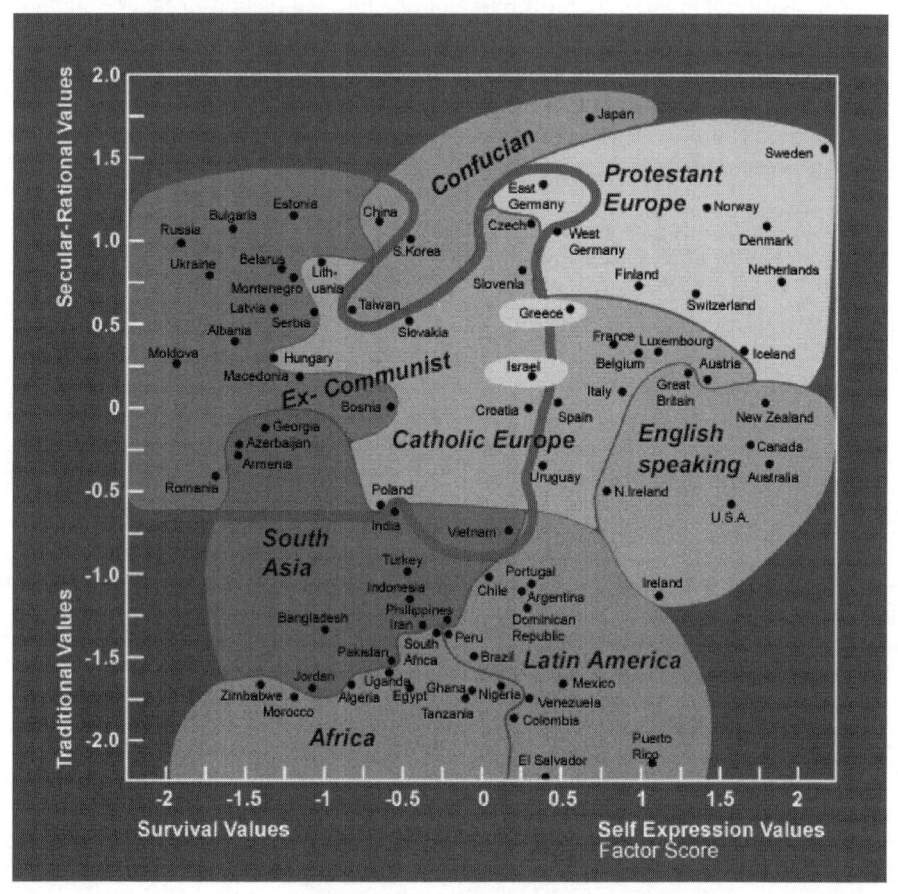

⇨ The nations are not correlated along one path—for example along the path 'first upwards, then to the right' which is predicted by the simple modernization theory. Rather, they are statistically independent along the two factors. Already this fact proves that there is a large amount of cultural divergence which cannot only be explained by temporal displacement in development.

Figure 2
Typical attitudes which correspond to different positions on the cultural world-map. (Source: http://www.worldvaluessurvey.org)

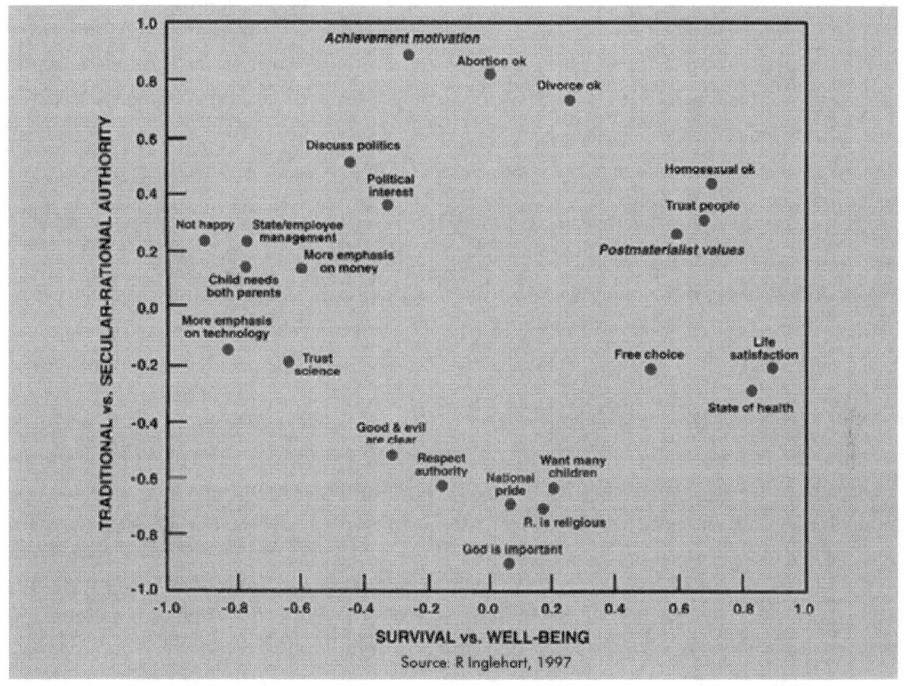

⇨ The map exhibits cultural world-regions and to that extent is in support of Huntington. But only some of Inglehart's cultural world-regions are in conformity with Huntington.
⇨ The Islamic countries are, as to be expected, in the lower-left corner, representing high traditional religious and survival values. Only the African countries are even more traditional.
⇨ The ex-communist countries have a striking position, highly rational-secularized though not post-modernized. This supports the view that their ex-communist history rather than orthodox Christianity is the major cause of their similarity. But also the east-Asian countries fit in this area: they also have an ex-communist history; but in addition their Confucian tradition was secular from early historical times. In this respect the east-Asian countries differ strongly from other world-cultures.
⇨ The so-called western Christian world-culture is very *divergent*—so divergent that it is doubtful whether its members should be subsumed under *one* world-culture. At least, the religious characterization 'Christian' seems to have little content. The *cultural distance* between extremely post-modernized countries in protestant Europe (say Sweden) to rather medium-positioned countries in catholic Europe (say Italy) is bigger than the distance between the latter countries and, e.g., the Islamic countries.

⇨ Western and eastern European countries taken together make up two thirds of the entire cultural map—which means that the task to establish a cultural *European identity* is *almost as difficult* as to establish a cultural *world identity*.
⇨ The English speaking countries have a characteristically different position than the continental-European countries: the former combine highly traditional-religious orientations with high level of post-modernization—which is, by the way, roughly the opposite combination than that of the ex-communist countries.

5. Some Methodological Problems of the WVS-Approach

An empirical-statistical analysis of cultural values, as it is attempted by the WVS project, has to face several methodological problems. In this section I discuss six of them:[1]

⇨ *Problem No. 1—to what extent are the data reliable and representative?* The four independent WVS studies have yielded similar general factor-analytic patterns. This fact speaks in favor of the reliability of the general result. To what extent the particular positions of the nations on the cultural world-map are robust should be investigated by repetition studies.

⇨ *Problem No. 2—are the empirical questions (variables) representative indicators for the latent causes which make up cultures and cultural values?* Concerning this question, the following points of defense can be made: (a) The more than 250 questions of the WVS cover a broad range of indicators, not only concerning verbally asserted values by also concerning lifestyles, etc. (b) The questionnaire is anonymous, and is introduced by the interviewers in an appropriate manner. (c) It can be expected that the answers are by and large trust-worthy. Even if people's verbally asserted values deviate from their actual behavior, they reflect accepted norms of their society.

⇨ *Problem No. 3—are the two factors causally representative?* Only in part, because they explain just slightly more than 50% of the variance. This calls for much more detailed re-evaluations of the huge data corpus with a focus on particular subsets of data (some authors began to do this in Inglehart 2003).

⇨ *Problem No. 4—are the two factors independent?* According to Inglehart's own theory, the large majority of nations should go first upwards along factor 1 (modernization) and then horizontally to the right along factor 2 (postmodernization). If this were true, then both factors would not come out as statistically independent. The assumption that the two factors are statistically independent may well be an artifact of the chosen factor-analytic method (principal component analysis).

---

[1] A philosophical analysis of factor analysis as common cause abduction is found in Schurz (2008a, §7.3; 2008b). On philosophical aspects of statistical methodology see Schurz (2006b, ch. 4).

Therefore, a re-evaluation with the help of factor-analytic methods which do not assume independence would be important.

⇨ *Problem No. 5—information about statistical dispersions is missing.* The spread of cultural diversity may partly be an artifact, because the *mean values* are based on *nations* which have very different population sizes. For example, China is just one point on the map, but it has more inhabitants that Europe and USA taken together. If China would be divided in different parts of the country (including urban as well as rural parts), how strongly would it disperse? I regard this problem as significant. A re-evaluation of the WSV data w.r.t. statistical dispersions would be important.

⇨ *Problem No. 6—how important is nationality as an indicator for cultural values in comparison to other indicators such as income or education?* For example, if one would perform a WVS-factor analysis of all academic people worldwide, or of all farmers worldwide, separating again into nation-wise units, how close together would these nation-wise units lie on the cultural world-map? Would the dispersions of the nations of academics be smaller than the dispersion of different worldwide social groups, e.g. farmers vs. academics? Also in this respect, a re-evaluation of the WSV data w.r.t. statistical dispersions would be important.

It seems to me that none of these problems constitutes an obstacle in principle. But significantly more effort is required to evaluate the huge bodies of data collected by the WVS project in a careful and reliable way. Generally speaking, the value of the global and coarse-grained picture which is produced by the factor-analysis of the WVS-data lies in its heuristic function for finding the relevant problems and asking the right questions for more fine-grained explorations.

6. Correlations of Cultural Value Distributions with Other Variables

As a defender of modernization theory, Inglehart believes that (post-)modernization goes hand in hand with economic progress, progress in freedom and democracy, and increase of happiness and self-satisfaction. But not all of these claims are supported by the WVS-data.

For example, that the development in both factor-dimensions is correlated with economic progress is shown in fig. 3. However, the correlation of modernization, i.e. of factor 1, with economic progress in fig. 3 is rather weak. For example, in the category 5.000 to 15.000 $ we have a variation factor 1 of 100%. Postmodernization, or factor 2, correlates better with economic progress, which is reasonable since a high level of postmodern values requires a high level of economic welfare. One should also be aware that if China's economy should go on in its progression to western standards without a significant change of its present cultural values, then fig. 3 would have to be re-drawn completely.

Figure 3
Correlation of the two factors with economic progress. GNP/capita = gross national product per head). Findings from 1995. The fig. is based on all nations; only some are drawn into it. (Source: http://www.worldvaluessurvey.org)

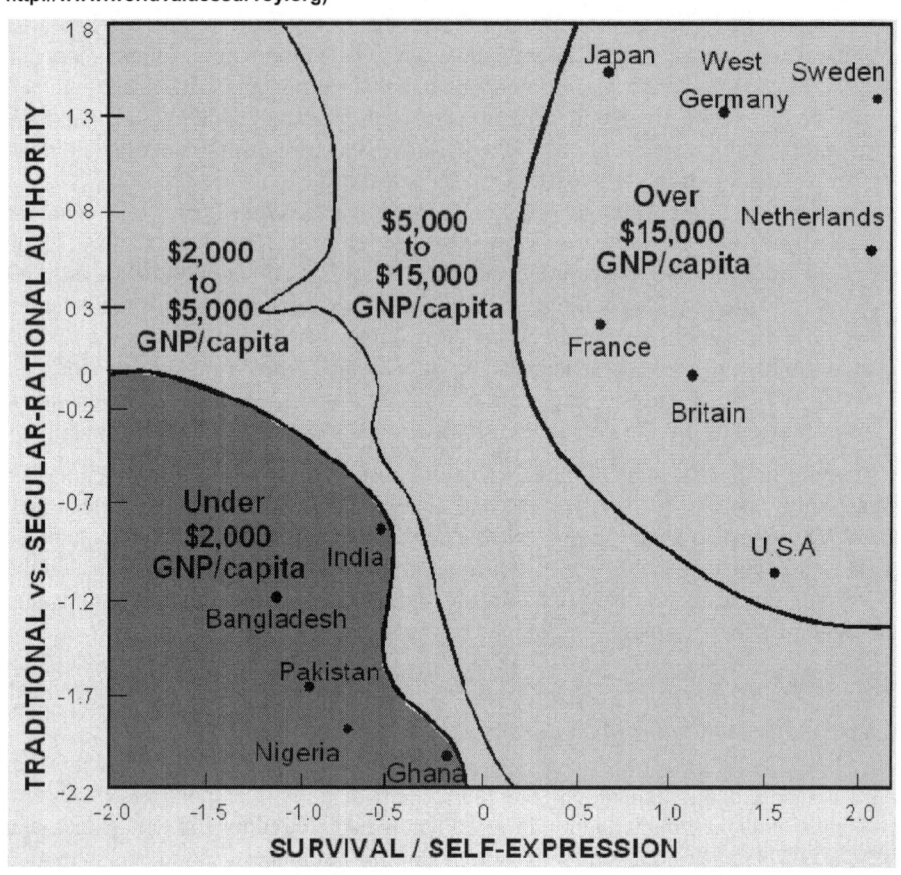

In other studies Inglehart (cf. 2006, 161) has shown that the degree of postmodernization correlates with the degree of democratic development as measured by the so-called *Freedom House index*. That this correlation holds is quite plausible.

On the other hand, what remains doubtful is the correlation between self-satisfaction and economic modernization. This can be seen from figure 4 (findings from 1995), in which self-satisfaction is measured by the mean of the percentages of people who say that they are happy and who say that they are satisfied with life as a whole. On peculiar historical reasons, the ex-communist countries have a special position which gives the false impression that there would be a high correlation between the two axes of fig. 4. If they are omitted from fig. 4, the correlation is low: people in Ghana, China, or Mexico are not less happy than those in Austria, France or West Germany, although their economic position is almost on the opposite end. On the other hand, differences between rich countries, such as France or Netherlands, are rather high.

Figure 4
Correlation of happiness/self-satisfaction with GNP per capita. (Source: http://www.world-valuessurvey.org)

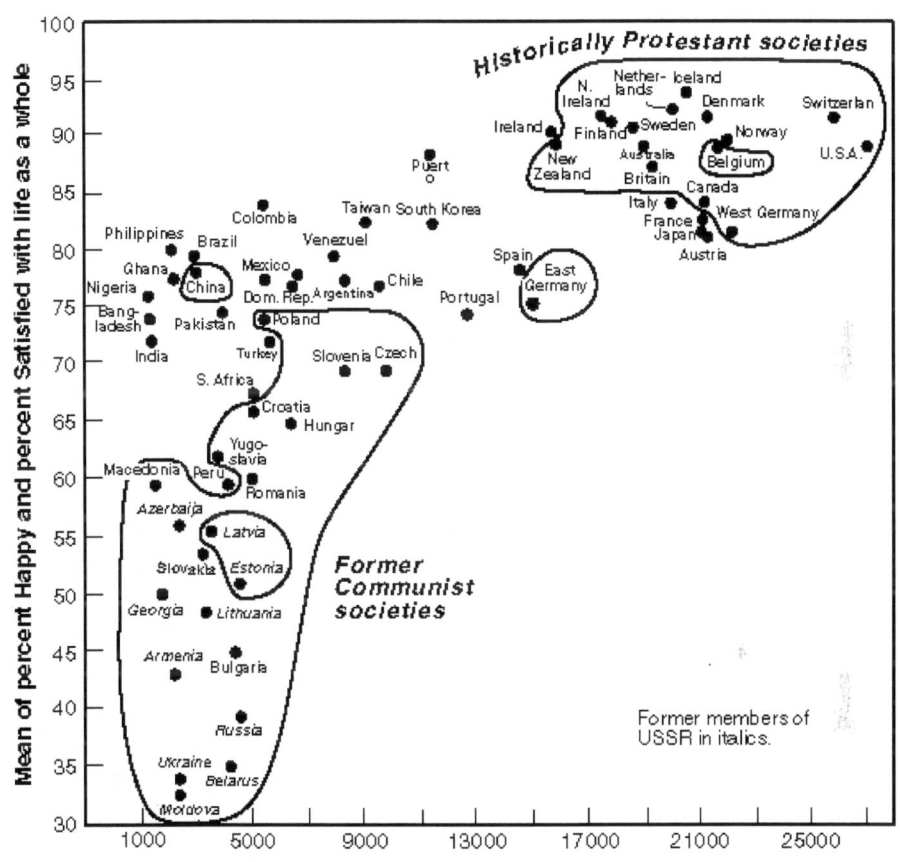

The dissatisfaction of the people in the ex-communistic countries is caused by the fact that these people had very high expectations towards the new 'free' society which was promised to them after the breakdown of communism, and their expectations had been strongly disappointed. This is shown in figure 5 which contains data from Russia representing three historical periods that span a total of 15 years: the percentage of people who say that they are satisfied with their life has fallen down from 70% in the year 1981 to only 48% in 1990 and 38% in 1996.

Figure 5
Dissatisfaction in ex-communist countries—diachronic data for Russia. (Source: http://www.worldvaluessurvey.org)

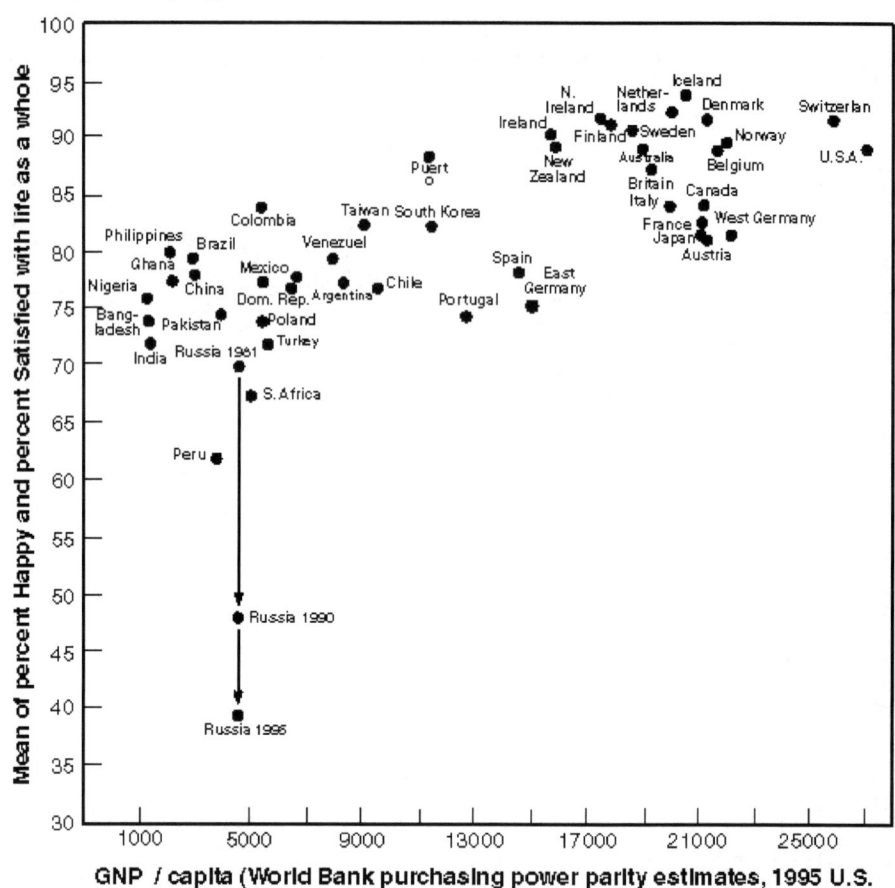

7. Empirical Data on Evolutionary Trends

Developmental data are available only concerning the last few decades. Figure 6 shows the change of the cultural positions of 39 countries in the years from 1981 or 1990 to 1997 (the time intervals are different because not all countries have been investigated in earlier questionnaires).

Figure 6
Change of cultural positions of 39 countries in recent decades. (Source: Inglehart/Baker 2004, 161. See also http://www.worldvaluessurvey.org)

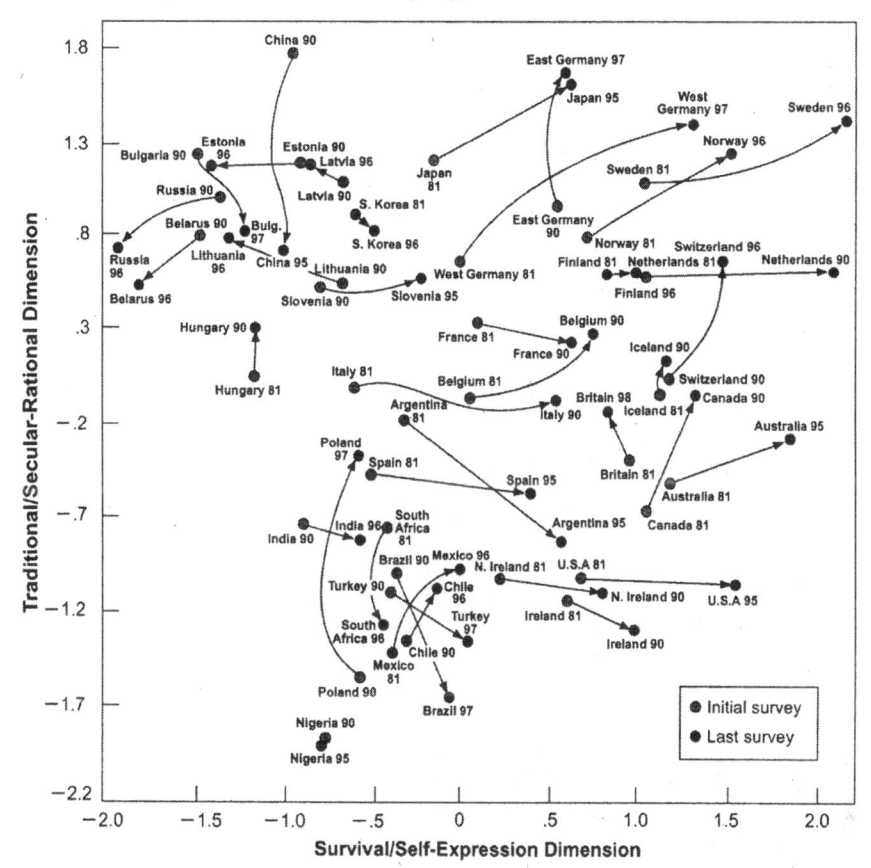

It can be seen from fig. 6 that the rate of cultural changes as well as their directions are rather diverse:

⇨ From 39 countries only 18 have followed the direction of modernization, i.e. have developed forward along both axes—where 'forward' and 'backward' have to be read in quotation marks.

⇨ 6 countries (Russia, Belarus, Estonia, South Africa, Nigeria and China) have developed backwards along both axes.

⇨ 12 countries have developed backwards to the traditional side, along the axes traditional vs. rational (Bulgaria, Brazil, Argentine, Turkey, India, Ireland, North Ireland, Spain, Italy, France, USA, South Korea).

⇨ 3 countries (Latvia, Lithuania, Britain) have developed backwards to the survival side, along the axis survival versus self-expression.

⇨ The most rapid cultural change has taken place in Poland, East-Germany and other ex-communist countries. Also Western Germany, Netherlands and Sweden experienced a fast cultural change.

In conclusion: modernization theory is hardly supported on the short term scale. One may object that modernization is a *long term development* and cannot be judged at the level of decades—short time reversals are compatible with a long term modernization trend.

So let us finally ask: are modernization and post-modernization really stable universal long-term trends?

⇨ *Concerning post-modernization:* So far, the question of its long term stability cannot be answered. The shift towards post-modern values is a *very young phenomenon* which has taken place in the Western generations after the Second World War. This is shown by figure 7, and is supported by similar diagrams (cf. Norris/Inglehart 2004). Insofar as post-modernization is characterized by a retreat of traditional family values, by low birth rates, and by an increase of single lifestyle, it is doubtful that it can lead to an enduringly stable cultural equilibrium because post-modernization depends on high economic prosperity, and it is doubtful that the high prosperity on which post-modern values depend can be realized for the majority of humans living on earth.

Figure 7
The transition towards dominantly post-modern attitudes is a very young phenomenon. (Source: http://www.worldvaluessurvey.org)

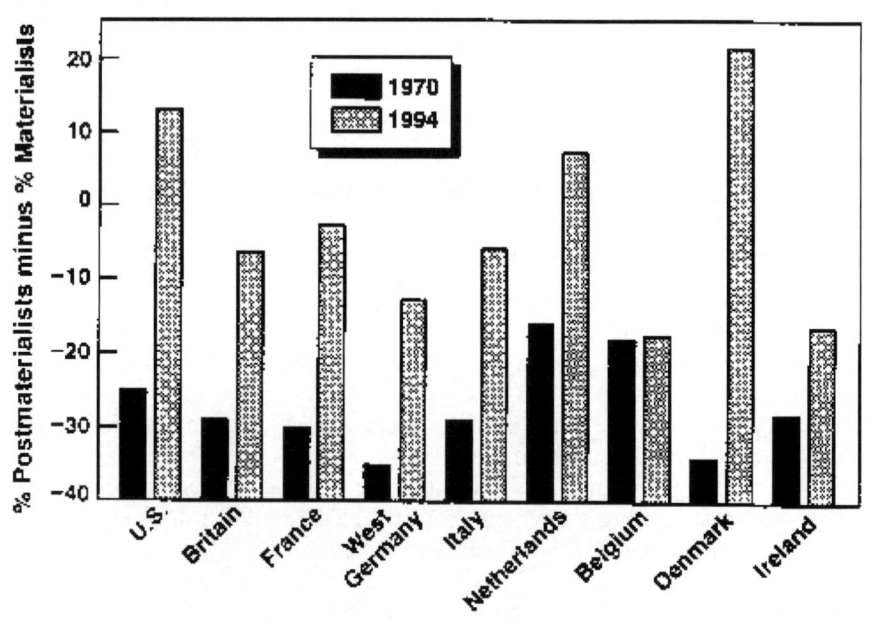

⇨ *Concerning modernization:* Rationalization, increase of education, secularization, democratization and the realization of equal human rights have been *long term* modernization developments in the Western countries for several centuries. But even here things are not so simple: while religious activities have declined during this development, religiosity as such has dropped down a little, and has recovered during post-modernization. Figure 8 shows that while the attendance of religious activities has declined in post-industrial societies, identification as religious and belief in life after death have increased a little bit. So it seems that, at least to some degree, humans have a desire towards religious orientations independent of the degree of modernization (see also Wenegrat 1990 and Wilson 2002, who support this conclusion by independent evolution-theoretic considerations).

Figure 8
Importance of religion in agrarian, industrial and postindustrial societies. (After Inglehart/Norris 2003b, 55; table 3.2)

	Agrarian	Industrial	Postindustrial	Total
% Believe in God	91	80	79	83
% Believe in life after death	83	62	68	69
% Religion 'very important'	87	60	55	64
% Identify as religious	73	58	59	61
% Comfort from religion	74	51	46	54
% Attend religious service regularly	47	45	21	28
Mean religiosity 100-point scale	73	54	53	58

In *conclusion*, the data show that religion is compatible with modernized democratic societies—but of course, only in its *secularized form*, in which the religious authorities are separated from the state authority. In this respect, Islamic countries are clearly in a pre-modern stage.

Although religion and many specific history-dependent cultural values and habits *may survive* in modernization, one may still ask: *Are at least secularization, progress towards democracy and towards equal human rights three major trends which must go hand in hand with economic & technological progress?*

Interesting in this respect is a recent investigation of Inglehart and Pippa Norris: their data show that the true cultural clash between Western and Islamic cultures does not lie (so much) in their attitude towards democracy vs. state authority, but in their values concerning family life and gender roles (in combination with religious attitudes). Inglehart and Norris (2003a; 2003b) have compared 11 Islamic countries (Albania, Algeria, Azerbaijan, Bangladesh, Egypt, Indonesia, Iran, Jordan, Morocco, Pakistan, and Turkey) with 22 Western Countries (9 West-European, USA, Australia, New Zealand, and 10 ex-communist countries). Fig. 9 presents the data.

Figure 9
Difference in attitudes between 11 Islamic vs. 22 Western countries (9 ex-communist). Based on WVS-questionnaires 1995–6 and 2002–2. After Inglehart/Norris (2003a, 69f.)

(%-Agreement)	Western countries	Islamic countries
Democracy performs well	68%	68%
In favor of democracy	86%	87%
Rejection of authoritarian political leaders	61%	61%
Rejection of religious political leaders	62%	39%
Gender equality is good	82%	55%
Divorce should be admitted	60%	35%
Abortion should be admitted	48%	25%
Homosexuality should be admitted	53%	12%

According to the data in fig. 9, the people in the Islamic countries *want democracy*. But one could ask—do they really mean the same with this word as Western societies? Or are their values concerning religious authority and in particular concerning the individual freedom in one's choice of life-style *in conflict* with a democratic constitution? Are these people really *mature* for democracy? These questions bring us to the last section, the question about which descriptive and normative conclusions can be drawn from the analysis of the WVS data.

8. Some Moderate Conclusions

As a general *descriptive conclusion* of this paper I suggest the following one: cultural evolution does not follow a uniform trend, but stands under *opposite evolutionary forces*, whose strength are mainly dependent on the level of economy and education. The *location of cultural equilibria* in the cultural world-map—the regions in which societies stay stable for a long time—are largely dependent on the constellation of these forces. A sketch of this view is illustrated in fig. 10 (for more details cf. Schurz 2006a; 2007).

Figure 10
Cultural Evolution under the Pressure of Opposite Evolutionary Forces

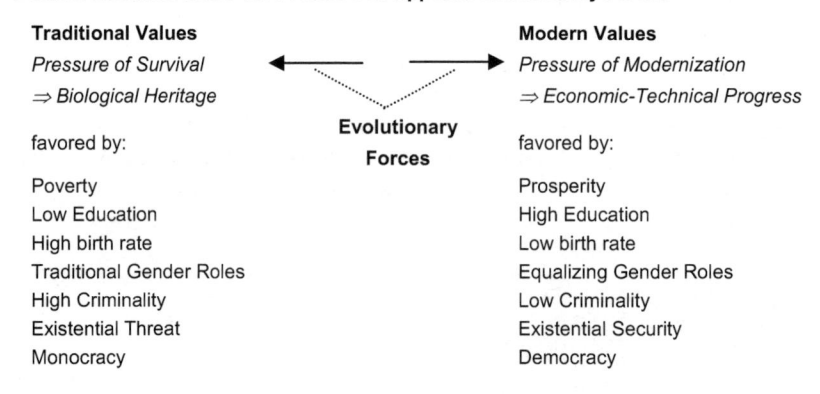

Traditional Values		Modern Values
Pressure of Survival	←——————→	Pressure of Modernization
⇒ Biological Heritage		⇒ Economic-Technical Progress
favored by:	**Evolutionary Forces**	favored by:
Poverty		Prosperity
Low Education		High Education
High birth rate		Low birth rate
Traditional Gender Roles		Equalizing Gender Roles
High Criminality		Low Criminality
Existential Threat		Existential Security
Monocracy		Democracy

But what are the *normative conclusions* one should draw from these findings and their descriptive interpretations? This is a slippery slope, on which one is inclined to draw those conclusions which agree with one's general political values. For example, can one draw the normative conclusion from the data in fig. 9 that one should strive for the establishment of democracy in these countries by external (military or economic) powers? Or should one rather draw the conclusion—towards which I personally would be more inclined—that instead of attempting a *forceful* establishment of democracy onto countries whose people have pre-modern values, the western countries should *wait* until people in these countries are mature for democracy and are able develop it on their own feet. In the meantime, the most important task would be the sustainment of a *peaceful co-existence* of the different world-cultures—which does not exclude fostering democratic developments in these countries by peaceful means such as economic or educational support.

Let me take a systematic stance on these questions: how can one arrive at such normative recommendations at all in a justified way? The important point to realize here is Hume's famous *is-ought-gap*: there is no way to infer normative conclusions from descriptive premises without so-called *Is-Ought bridge principles*. In Schurz (1997) various versions of this thesis are proved by rich logical means. Note that the descriptive premises may, of course, include assumptions about the *de-facto* normative or evaluative orientations of people—this does not change their nature as being descriptive assertions.

If we apply this insight systematically to the question under consideration, we arrive at the following possible positions. First of all, the exercise of influence on the development of other nations can only be appropriate if something like the descriptive assumption (D1) and the bridge-principle (B1) is accepted:

(Descriptive assumption D1): Certain types of societies (S) (e.g. democracy, etc.) increase certain desirable qualities of human life (Q) (e.g. absence of suffering, freedom, happiness, self-realization, etc.), which cannot be achieved otherwise. We allow that (S) includes several types of societies.

(Bridge principle B1:) If assumption (D1) is true, then it is morally appropriate to exert influence on a given nation in order to increase its development towards a socitey of some type in (S), under the constraint (C) that negative side-effects (in terms of Q) are small.

The application of assumption (D1) requires, of course, a specification of the societies in (S) and the qualities in (Q). Note that assumption (D1) does not presuppose a full modernization theory—it only assumes that certain types of societies outside of (S) (e.g. dictatorship, anarchy. etc.) *prevent* the achievement of qualities (Q). This is compatible with a pluralism of types of societies in (S) which perform equally well with respect to the achievement of qualities (Q).

Assumptions (D1) + (B1) together with agreement about the concretization of (S) and (Q) justify the exercise of *soft* pressure, such as political or economic pressure, assuming that in this case negative side-effects are small, i.e. constraint (C) is not violated. In contrast, since the exercise of influence by military power has unavoidable and strongly negative side-effects which violate constraint (C), military power cannot be justified merely by assumptions (D1) and (B1). It requires specifically strong justifiers (e.g., endangerment of international peaceful coexistence of nations, according to the UNO-declaration, or extreme violation of human rights such as genocide, etc.). This concludes my logical snapshot of the problem of drawing normative conclusions from the descriptive findings of the WVS studies via bridge principles—a detailed normative-political analysis would have to be the topic of another paper.

Bibliography

Huntington, S. P. (1996), *Kampf der Kulturen*, München; engl. 1996, *The Clash of Civilizations*; quotations refer to the German edition

Inglehart, R. (1998), *Modernisierung und Postmodernisierung*, Frankfurt/M.; engl. 1997

— (2003) (ed.), *Human Values and Social Change: Findings from the Values Surveys*, Leiden

— (2004), Kultur und Demokratie, in: S. P. Huntington/L. E. Harrison (eds.), *Streit um Werte*, München, 141–166

— /W. Baker (2000), Modernization, Cultural Change, and the Persistence of Traditional Values, in: *American Sociological Review 65*, 19–51

— /P. Norris (2003a), The True Clash of Civilizations, in: *Foreign Policy March/April 2003*, 67–74

— / — (2003b), *Rising Tide: Gender Equality and Cultural Change around the World*, Cambridge/MA

Kienzler, K. (1996), *Der religiöse Fundamentalismus*, München

Metzinger, U. (2000), *Die Huntington-Debatte*, Köln

Müller, H. (1998), *Das Zusammenleben der Kulturen. Ein Gegenentwurf zu Huntington*, Frankfurt

Norris, P./R. Inglehart (2004), *Sacred and Secular. Religion and Politics Worldwide*, New York

Riesebrodt, M. (2000), *Die Rückkehr der Religionen*, München

Schurz, G. (1997), *The Is-Ought Problem. An Investigation in Philosophical Logic*, Dordrecht

— (2006a), Clash of Civilizations, in: C. Kanzian/E. Runggaldier (2007) (eds.), *Cultures*, Frankfurt, 277–294

— (2006b), *Einführung in die Wissenschaftstheorie*, Darmstadt

— (2007), Kampf der Kulturen? Eine empirische und evolutionäre Kritik der Huntington-These, in: K. Gabriel (ed.), *Technik, Globalisierung und Religion*, Freiburg, 123–172

— (2008a), Patterns of Abduction, *Synthese 164*, 201-234; online version: http://dx.doi.org/10.1007/s11229-007-9223-4

— (2008b), Common Cause Abduction and the Formation of Theoretical Concepts, appears in: C. Dégremont et al. (eds.), *Essays in Honour of Shahid Rahman*, London

Wenegrat, B. (1990), *The Divine Archetype: The Sociobiology and Psychology of Religion*, Massachusetts

Wilson, D. S. (2002), *Darwin's Cathedral*, Chicago

Annette Schmitt

Why Still Criticize Huntington?
A Comment on Gerhard Schurz

Without subscribing to the view that 'de mortuis nil nisi bene', I wonder: Why still criticize Huntington? Regarding the severe conceptual and methodological problems in Samuel Huntington's *The Clash of Civilizations*, it seems that everything has already been said in the legion of comments published since 1996. And as far as the explanatory value of his work is concerned: Huntington himself never claimed to produce a theory, in the sense of a deductive system featuring causal laws. His contribution to the understanding of international relations consists, so he claims, in an interpretative heuristic, a "simplified map of reality" (1996, 29) which may be good today but "[not] good forever" (1996, 37), for understanding the antecedent conditions of conflicts in the 21st century and for predicting future developments.

What is the attraction, then, of still criticizing this book? Is there a need continuously to point to its deficiencies because so many contemporaries—scholars, journalists, terrorists etc.—talk about the 'clash of civilizations' as if it were a fact of 21st century life? Is it because 'clash of civilizations' has become a catch phrase like 'end of history' or 'survival of the fittest' (cf. Steinfeld 2008), a handy arrangement of words, but devoid of any scientifically exploitable meaning? Or is it because the monstrous assaults of 9/11 and subsequent terrorist attacks have been interpreted as dramatic evidence of the predictive value of Huntington's book? It has been claimed that Osama bin Laden declared the terrorist attacks of 09/11 as the "first climax of the 'clash of civilizations'" and that Huntington was appalled by this: "Osama bin Laden's goal is […] to turn this war by a terror organisation on civilised society into a clash of civilisations between Islam and the West. It would be a disaster were he to succeed." (Huntington, cited in Geyer 2008) Has talk about the clash of civilizations become a self-fulfilling prophecy? And how does all this connect to the topic of the present collection of papers on norms and values?

The link may be forged like this: If we interpret the terrorist attacks by Muslim fundamentalists as a violent challenge to 'Western Civilization'—which, I think, is quite in accordance with Huntington's prediction of rising religious fundamentalism (1996, 37) and of future conflicts predominantly occurring between "the West and the rest" (1996, 183)—and if, again with Huntington in mind, we characterize 'Western Civilization' in terms of its Christian roots, its conception of the individual as a bearer of rights and its conception of the state as legitimate only if ruled by laws protecting these rights, then we may well conclude that since 2001 'Western' norms and values have been under fire. And how does 'the West' fare in this confrontation? Not very well, to say the least.

By this, I do not refer to the problems of fighting terrorism by means of the military and the police which have been debated extensively under the heading of 'asymmetric warfare'. Rather, I refer to the fact that with respect to terrorism 'the West' has adopted, as Cass Sunstein puts it, a strong version of the precautionary principle. According to this maxim, applied to our topic, actions which may threaten national security are to be prohibited *if it cannot be proven that they do not pose a threat*, and all measures necessary to prevent such actions are to be taken—"even if the supporting evidence remains speculative and even if the [...] costs of regulation are high" (Sunstein 2005, 24). Consequently, governments have been debating, devising and employing instruments which, some claim, must not even be discussed, and much less made use of, if the 'West' does not wish to undermine and weaken the very values and norms it set out to protect (as, e. g., the dignity of human beings protected by the German Basic Law, the *Grundgesetz* [GG]). This idea is not new, either. But it involves pressing and important issues which warrant continued attention much more than the academic inadequacies of Huntington's book. How does 'the West' contribute to destroying its value basis? Three observations will be presented:[1]

1. Privacy Invaded

It is only reasonable not to wait until the bomb is ticking, but to seek actively to forestall disaster at the earliest possible stage. Furthermore, there is no earthly incentive to discourage suicidal terrorists from detonating the bomb; thus the only way to avoid catastrophe is to thwart its planning. Prevention presupposes information which must be gathered, processed and communicated efficiently to the respective authorities: the law enforcement agencies and, possibly, the military. But the pursuit of this prudent goal, as is well known, has various repercussions which, from a liberal point of view, are problematic. By way of example, I will mention only two:

- The prevention of 'deindividualized' 21st century network terrorism seems to require that everybody be treated as a potential threat, as a possible 'sleeper' disguised as a law-abiding citizen (Huster/Rudolph 2008, 14f.). In order to stand a chance of discovering these persons, it is necessary, or so it seems, to monitor the population closely: the steps people take in the public space—it is said that there are some 500.000 CCTV cameras installed in London—but also the moves they make at home. Among the measures proposed and implemented (at least temporarily, until prohibited by the Constitutional Court) in Germany during the past decade were the so-called 'Big Bugging Operation', the storage of data gathered at toll stations or forcedly provided by telecommunication companies, and secret computer surveillance aimed at spying out private data. Obviously, the individu-

---

1 'The West' is here reduced to the USA and Germany, and the three observations my claim is based upon are presented in a slightly biased fashion, owed primarily to spatial restrictions.

al's right to privacy in general and to data privacy in particular has been substantially restricted by these measures in order to meet alleged security needs (cf. Huster/Rudolph 2008, 18).

- To improve communication, and, in the words of former U. S. Attorney General John Ashcroft, "to build strong teams" (2006, 21), the strict separation between law enforcement and secret service has been given up. Now, police officers can access data gathered by intelligence agencies, and data are jointly analyzed. At Germany's Joint Terror Defence Centre (*Gemeinsames Terrorabwehrzentrum*), for instance, analysts from the Federal Office of Criminal Investigation (*BKA*) and the Federal Office for the Protection of the Constitution (*Bundesamt für Verfassungsschutz*), the intelligence agency for domestic affairs, exchange and process information in order to discover potential dangers at the earliest possible stage and to coordinate respective operations. If it is true that 9/11 could have been prevented if the FBI and the secret services had been better at exchanging data, that seems to be a good idea. But we must not forget that it is for a reason that law enforcement and the intelligence apparatus are to be strictly separated. By joining the information gathering possibilities of the secret services with the executive competences of the police a power centre is created that every liberal democrat should be wary of.

2. Dignity Violated

In the face of a terrorist threat, the state's responsibilities are frequently reduced to its Hobbesian duty to guarantee physical security. Governments are asked to do everything necessary to preserve their citizens's lives (cf. Ashcroft 2006, 27; Depenheuer 2007, 7; Brugger 2006, 13). Even when the 'everything' is conditioned by the formula 'within the law' (as in the case of Ashcroft), it is fairly obvious that this is a matter of paying lip service to a formal conception of the rule of law and that the lawmaker is expected to authorize all measures deemed necessary.

The situation is characterized as one of 'supreme emergency' in which, as Daniel Statman points out, the following conditions prevail: there is "(a) a grave threat of an evil [...], (b) conventional means [...] are unable to counter the threat, and (c) unconventional means [...] can prevent the otherwise inevitable catastrophe" (2006, 58f.).

This is the ground on which the discussion about the legitimacy of torture flourishes. In Germany, as probably in 'Western' democracies in general, for many decades the legitimacy of torture was not an object of debate. Torture was considered to be absolutely prohibited as a logical consequence of the (uncontested) premises that (1) torture is incompatible with human dignity and that (2) human dignity must not be violated (Art. 1 GG). Then, two things happened:

- In September 2002, a boy was kidnapped. When the kidnapper was arrested, he refused to reveal the boy's whereabouts, and the local chief of police ordered to threaten him with the infliction of severe pain; the threat was effective: the kidnapper gave the desired information; the threatened action was not carried out. The chief of police and another police officer were subsequently tried and convicted for threatening to torture a suspect, and a public debate about whether or not torture might be justified under the exceptional circumstances of a 'supreme emergency' was opened.

- In February 2003, a new commentary on Art. 1 GG[2] was published. Written by the German constitutionalist Matthias Herdegen, it challenged the interpretation of his colleague Günther Dürig which had been the basis of the prevailing opinion in German constitutional law since 1958 (Maunz/Dürig 1958). According to Dürig, Art. 1 GG constitutes the basis of the German Constitution, the "unconditional and, with respect to its implementation, non-negotiable highest principle of the constitutional order" (Hesse 1999, marginal n. 116) from which all basic rights are derived (cf. Maunz/Dürig 1958, marginal n. 4). Herdegen rejects this categorical interpretation (cf. 2003, marginal n. 11); in his view, Art. 1 GG does not absolutely dominate other basic rights. Especially with respect to the right to life and physical integrity (Art. 2.2.1 GG), he states that "the protection against physical destruction [...] is *a priori* no less valuable than the respect for human dignity" (2003, marginal n. 22).[3] Life, in fact, constitutes the "vital basis of the guarantee of human dignity" (2003, marginal n. 23). Therefore, there is no potential collision between Art. 1 GG and Art. 2.2.1 GG. For the state to respect human dignity implies, as a necessary condition, to protect life and limb (cf. 2003, marginal n. 45). With respect to the legitimacy of torture, Herdegen concludes: A perpetrator threatening the life and physical integrity of a person does not respect the victim's dignity. It is the state's duty by Art. 1 GG to protect the victim's rights according to Art. 2.2.1. At the same time, the dignity of the perpetrator as a human being must be respected too, but "just how much 'respect' [...] is owed [to him] depends on his or her own past behavior and the associated threat he presents to the life and dignity of other human beings" (2003, marginal number 45). Hence, under certain circumstances, Herdegen thinks, torture—an attempt to break a person's will—does not violate the right to dignity of this person because the amount of respect owed to her is diminished by her disrespect of other persons's dignity (cf. 2003, marginal n. 45).

Ever since, the permissibility of torture has been the object of both public and academic debate in Germany. It is currently discussed primarily with respect to the

---

2 Art. 1 GG [on human dignity] reads:
   "(1) Human dignity is inviolable. To respect and protect it is the duty of all state authority. (2) The German people therefore acknowledge inviolable and inalienable human rights as the basis of every community, of peace and of justice in the world. (3) The following basic rights shall bind the legislature, the executive, and the judiciary as directly applicable law [...]."
   http://www.iuscomp.org/gla/statutes/GG.htm#1 (Jan. 29, 2009)
3 All quotes from Herdegen have been translated by the author of this contribution with the kind support of 'our man in Essex', Kai Arzheimer.

question of whether or not it is legitimate to use torture as a means to prevent terrorist attacks. This threat is visualized as a 'ticking bomb' that will kill thousands of innocent persons if we do not summon the 'courage' to do 'what is necessary' to the person in possession of the relevant knowledge, i.e., the terrorist (cf. Beestermöller/Brunkhorst 2006, 7; Brugger[4] 2000, 165). While some argue, like Herdegen, that torture is compatible with our most basic values, others replace the "rights-based outlook with a consequentialist one" (Statman 2007, 59): what is the dignity of one person—the evil terrorist—compared to the lives of thousands of innocent citizens?

I will not try to reproduce the arguments advanced on both sides of the debate, as this is not the place for such a discussion.[5] What I wish to stress, though, is the fact that the content of our value basis has come under debate, and it does not stop here. There is also a tendency—and that is the real danger I wish to point to—to ban our most basic values and the norms protecting them from consideration in the debate about the best way to fight terrorism.

3. The Rule of Law Sacrificed

As was pointed out above, some interpret the current state of 'Western' liberal democracies as one of latent supreme emergency where unconventional means are warranted in order to ward off the grave danger posed by international terrorism. If this is a correct characterization of our current situation, what are the implications for the rule of law under such conditions?

While liberals such as Stephen Breyer, Associate Justice of the U. S. Supreme Court, insist that "[t]he Constitution applies even in times of dire emergency" (2006, 13), conservative lawyers, politicians and officials increasingly seem to subscribe to Cicero's maxim that "inter armas enim silent leges".

Otto Depenheuer,[6] for instance, claims that the German Constitution "is not armed" to prepare the legal ground for authorizing the measures necessary to face the threat of international terrorism successfully (cf. 2008, 20; 22) and that it, thus, needs to be tacitly amended. This is so, according to Depenheuer, for two reasons: The fathers and mothers of the *Grundgesetz* did not foresee the kind of challenge posed by international terrorism, and the Basic Law does not allow to distinguish between citizen and enemy.

---

4   The Heidelberg law professor Winfried Brugger already in 1995 argued against the absolute prohibition of torture.
5   I tend to hold with Kant that there are things human beings must not do to other human beings, regardless of the circumstances, but this is, of course, a contested view.
6   Otto Depenheuer, a German constitutionalist at the University of Cologne, is not without influence in German political circles and the public at large. The book which is the basis of the discussion presented here, *Selbstbehauptung des Rechtsstaates* [*Self-assertion of the State under the Rule of Law*], e. g., has been publicly recommended by the current Minister of the Interior, Wolfgang Schäuble.

- The *Grundgesetz* informs us how to deal with criminals and hostile foreign powers, but not with the very special kind of threat posed by terrorists (cf. Depenheuer 2008, ch. II). Criminals burden the state during 'normal times'. They break the law but do not threaten the integrity of the state as such. They are the responsibility of the law-enforcement agencies whose task it is to prevent crime and arrest criminals on the basis of the law designed to rule in times of peace. 'Normal times' end when the state is threatened as a cultural, political and legal entity, for instance by a hostile foreign power. In such an 'exceptional case', the military takes over and the law of peace is replaced by emergency law (cf. Depenheuer 2008, 51). Terrorists, however, are not criminals, and although they threaten to inflict grave and massive evil they do not catapult the state into a state of war, either. The special feature of 21st century terrorism, according to Depenheuer, consists in the confrontation of liberal democracies in 'normal times' with the kind of existential threat characteristic of 'exceptional times' (ibid., 50). These are circumstances, he claims, for which the *Grundgesetz* has not been designed.

- In order to meet the challenge of terrorism, Depenheuer recommends, the laws devised to rule in times of peace and the laws made to meet the challenges of supreme emergency must be effective simultaneously (cf. ibid., 51), the laws of peace being applicable to regular criminals, the laws of emergency to terrorists. As terrorists operate both from the outside and from within (e. g., the above-mentioned 'sleepers'), the state, furthermore, must be able to distinguish between regular criminals and terrorists—which the *Grundgesetz* does not foresee. Thus, politicians must remember what politics is all about, at least according to Carl Schmitt, namely, that it is about the ability to distinguish between "friend and foe" (Schmitt 1997, 38)—and that means also between ordinary crook and enemy of the state (cf. Depenheuer 2008, 54). Terrorists must be considered enemies of the state and as such, Depenheuer concludes, cannot claim to be protected by the law which they seek to destroy (cf. ibid., 62). Terrorists, in general, must be treated as outlaws (cf. ibid., 64) to whom, due to the special circumstances, one single right must be conceded: the right to a full hearing at court, so that a judge may determine whether someone is to be treated as an enemy terrorist or merely as a criminal citizen (cf. ibid., 65).

Depenheuer is not the only legal scholar advocating the treatment of terrorists according to enemy law. In 2004, Günther Jacobs published a widely noted paper on "citizen criminal law and enemy criminal law", raising the question whether "the obligation to respect a perpetrator as a person does not impose restrictions on the state which are inappropriate in dealing with a terrorist who does not justify the expectation of acting like a person" (2004, 92).

In the United States, the idea of denying basic rights to persons considered enemies of the state has played an important role in legislation in general. There is, for instance, the widely practiced disenfranchisement of felons: As the 'Sentencing Project' points out, in all but two states offenders are not allowed to vote while in prison. That is not a very unusual measure; but in some states, ex-offenders are denied the right to vote "even after having completed their sentence", and, in general, the "process of restoring voting rights [... is] so cumbersome that few ex-offenders are able to take advantage of them" (The Sentencing Project 2008). Other examples are 'Broken Windows' and 'Three Strikes' laws. In both cases, perpetrators are treated not as persons who violated the law and are to be punished in proportion to the severity of the offense but as enemies of public order against whom the public must be protected (cf. Kötter 2004, 391). But the most disturbing cases of persons considered 'enemies' and, therefore, denied as basic a human right as *habeas corpus* are those of the so-called 'unlawful enemy combatants' who have been incarcerated at Guantánamo for many years. In this rights-free space, they have been treated in a manner fundamentally incompatible with any conceivable conception of the human being as a bearer of unalienable rights (cf. Koch 2008). Guantánamo drastically illustrates that the enactment of enemy law signifies the end not only of a substantially constrained rule of law, but even of the formal rule of law, as it represents a zone where the law no longer rules: The presumption of innocence is sacrificed. *Habeas corpus* is denied: the majority of prisoners had a hearing before a military tribunal, if at all, but not before an independent judge. The principle of proportionality has been suspended. Questions about the status of suspects and the legality of interrogation methods were decided by the executive on the basis of arcane criteria.

And where does it stop? Heiner Bielefeld is right: "The law-free-zone, at first reserved to the 'enemy', does not stop at the borders of the state, but necessarily spreads out across the state as a whole, thus altering its normative basis." (2006, 6)

This is not what Huntington had in mind when he recommended, as preconditions for avoiding international conflicts, "to support in other civilizations groups sympathetic to Western values and interests; to strengthen international institutions that reflect and legitimate Western interests and values and to promote the involvement of non-Western states in those institutions" (1996b, 25). But all is not lost yet. 'Yes, we can' face the damage done to a rights-based rule of law and begin repair works. Shutting down Guantánamo is the most important first step, and shame forbid that the German government will go on stubbornly refusing to receive any of the detainees who without due process have been deprived of many years of liberty. Furthermore, proving that the 'West' takes its values and norms seriously, and not only in times of peace and quiet, is a matter not only of restoring international credibility and working off shame, but a moral imperative.[7]

Bibliography

Ashcroft, J. (2006), Preserving Life and Liberty, in: T. E. Baker/J. F. Stack (eds.), *At War with Civil Rights and Civil Liberties*, Lanham, 17–23

---

7   I would like to thank Ruth Zimmerling for her, as always, very helpful comments.

Beestermöller, G./H. Brunkhorst (2006), Folter: Sicherheit zum Preis der Freiheit?, in: G. Beestermöller/H. Brunkhorst (eds.), *Rückkehr der Folter—Der Rechtsstaat im Zwielicht*, München, 7–10

Bielefeld, H. (2006), Zur Unvereinbarkeit von Folter und Rechtsstaatlichkeit, in: *Aus Politik und Zeitgeschichte 36*, 3–8

Breyer, S. (2006), Liberty and Security, in: T. E. Baker/J. F. Stack (eds.), *At War with Civil Rights and Civil Liberties*, Lanham, 11–17

Brugger, W. (2006), Einschränkung des absoluten Folterverbots bei Rettungsfolter?, in: *Aus Politik und Zeitgeschichte 36*, 9–15

— (2000), Vom unbedingten Verbot der Folter zum bedingten Recht auf Folter?, in: *Juristenzeitung 55*, 165–216

Depenheuer, O. (2008), *Selbstbehauptung des Rechtsstaates*. 2nd ed., Paderborn

Geyer, C. (2008), On the Death of Samuel Huntington: A Portentous Buzzword, retrieved 1-30-2009 from the WWW: http://www.qantara.de/webcom/show_article.php/_c-478/_nr-849/i.html

Herdegen, M. (2003), Art. 1 GG, in: T. Maunz/G. Dürig (eds), *Grundgesetz Sonderdruck. Kommentierung der Art. 1 und 2 Grundgesetz*, Munich, margin nos. 1–114

Hesse, K. (1999), *Grundzüge des Verfassungsrechts der Bundesrepublik Deutschland*. 20th ed., Heidelberg

Huntington, S. P. (1996), *The Clash of Civilizations*, Sydney

— (1996b), The Clash of Civilizations?, in: *Foreign Affairs. The Clash of Civlizations? The Debate*, New York, 1–25

Huster, S./K. Rudolph (2008), Vom Rechtsstaat zum Präventionsstaat?, in: S. Huster/K. Rudolph (eds.), *Vom Rechtsstaat zum Präventionsstaat*, Frankfurt/M., 9–22

Jacobs, G. (2004), Bürgerstrafrecht und Feindstrafrecht, in: *Online-Zeitschrift für Höchstrichterliche Rechtsprechung im Strafrecht 3/2004*, 88–95. Retrieved 1-29-2009 from the WWW: http://www.hrr-strafrecht.de/hrr/archiv/04-03/index.php3?seite=6

Klingst, M. et al. (2007), Das Klima ist nervöser. Interview with Wolfgang Schäuble, in: *DIE ZEIT 30/2007*, 4. Retrieved 1-28-2009 from the WWW: http://www.zeit.de/2007/30/Das_Klima_ist_nervoeser?page=1

Koch, E. (2008), *Die CIA-Lüge. Foltern im Namen der Demokratie*, Berlin

Kötter, M. (2004), Subjektive Sicherheit, Autonomie und Kontrolle, in: *Der Staat 43(1)*, 371–397

Maunz, T./G. Dürig (eds.) ([1958]2009), *Grundgesetz. Loose-leaf commentary*. 53rd ed., Munich

Nowak, M. (2006), Das System Guantánamo, in: *Aus Politik und Zeitgeschichte 36*, 23–30

Schmitt, C. (1997), Der Begriff des Politischen, in: H. Münkler (ed.), *Politisches Denken im 20. Jahrhundert*. 2nd ed., Munich, 37–46

Statman, D. (2006), Supreme Emergencies Revisited, in: *Ethics 117(1)*, 58–79

Steinfeld, T. (2008), Zum Tod von Samuel P. Huntington: Der Parteiliche, in: *Süddeutsche Zeitung 29.12.2008*, retrieved 1-30-2009 from the WWW: http://www.sueddeutsche.de/kultur/66/452764/text/

The Sentencing Project. Felony Disenfranchisement Laws in the United States. September 2008. Retrieved 1-29-2009 from the WWW: http://www.sentencingproject.org/Admin/Documents/publications/fd_bs_fd_lawsinus.pdf

Sunstein, C. (2005), *Laws of Fear*, Cambridge

III. Social Values and Collective Choice

Werner Güth and Hartmut Kliemt

The Impossibility of Social Choice and the Possibilities of Individual Values: Political and Philosophical Liberalism Reconsidered

1. Introduction and Overview

As human beings we tend to ascribe mental states to collectivities. We also routinely conceive of our community as a whole as making 'social choices'. Therefore what is going on in research on 'we-intentions', 'team-reasoning', 'social ontology' etc. is important and interesting.[1] Nevertheless, there seem to be good reasons for assuming that the largest entity to which we cannot only ascribe actions and mental states but for which we also have a clear conception of how the 'causa finalis' is operating seems to be the 'individual' (in the common sense use of the term). This is not meant to deny that beyond its primary use there are secondary uses of the term 'choice' that may be legitimately applied in some contexts.[2] Yet we emphasize that, in the paradigmatic sense of the term in which individual choice as made by a person is possible, social choice is impossible. In truly interactive choice making social results are not 'chosen' by a single individual (at least not in the original sense of the term 'choice') but necessarily *emerge from the separate choices of individuals* (whether they occur within organizations like firms, across markets, or in politics).[3]

As opposed to the impossibility of social choice, evaluations of social states by individuals are, however, possible. The evaluations of individuals can rank order the emergent social results in the narrow sense of the term 'evaluation' (as made by a specific person placing value). Such personal evaluations can be partial or impartial. They can lead to non-moral or to moral as well as to so-called ethical preference orders of an actor (see Harsanyi 1977) which in turn can be represented by personal utility or personal welfare functions. For the following the specifics concerning an evaluative concept are not important. It must, however, be kept in mind that evaluations are distinct from institutionalized norms.

We start our discussion of the particular—or should we say 'peculiar'—relationship between (liberal) institutionalized political norms and (philosophical) evaluations of such institutionalized norms with a few conceptual clarifications (2.). Then follows an endorsement of what may be called a 'public' and a rejection of a

---

1 See for very recent examples some of the papers in Peter and Schmid (2007).
2 And this might go to sub- as well as supra-individual entities; see Ainslee (1992) for the former and Coleman (1990), Vanberg (1982) for examples of the latter.
3 As a direct consequence of the preceding an ethics in terms of consequences of 'social choice making' cannot employ the same meaning of terms as an ethics addressed directly to individuals and their choices.

'social' choice perspective on institutionalized norms and rules that define the game of politics (3.). Turning to personal evaluations of the game of politics and its results we focus on two problems of forming a 'welfarist' personal social welfare function that represents the ethics of a person as depending on the 'ethical values' of the persons concerned (4.). The first is the 'circularity problem' (4.1) the other the 'liberal paradox' (4.2). In the final section we conclude that in view of the impossibility of social choice, liberals should focus on institutions (and possibly appropriate values or opinions supporting them) while neglecting theoretical problems of welfare economics like that of circularity or the liberal paradox (5.).

2. Conceptual Preliminaries

By the term 'norm' we will understand basically *institutionalized* regularities that are embodied in and exhibited by overt behavior. 'Value' we will very broadly understand as referring to individual reasons for rankings of social states or institutionalized regularities (norm systems). We will sometimes commit the rather harmless blunder of calling the rankings (orders) that emerge from reasons for the ranking of alternatives 'values', too.

We will use the term 'public choice' for the *institutional* process in which 'social outcomes are generated through social institutions or systems of social norms'. The term 'Public Choice' in capital letters we will reserve for the explanatory *theory* of the norm-based institutional process of public choice.[4] As opposed to this we will use 'Social Choice' exclusively for the *theory* addressing issues of the judgmental ranking of social states or outcomes of the social process.

Because literally speaking there is no *choice* of social results the proper purpose of the rankings developed in Social Choice[5] perhaps needs to be somewhat further clarified.[6] The following table may be helpful for that purpose.

---

4 Normative Constitutional Political would be the corresponding normative theory ranking institutional orders.
5 Social Choice in the preceding sense can be found in ethical and in welfare economic normative *theory*. It is applied by individuals in forming their personal welfare functions for the collectivity.
6 To be completely clear about this. Social choice was a very misleading bit of terminology from the outset. However, since there is the established tradition of using the term we keep using it, too, but suggest to reign in its confusing use to a core meaning which is related to evaluation rather than to institutionalized norms.

Table 1

social process or social choice	institutional perspective	judgmental perspective
Public Choice as a theory of how social states are brought about	X	?
Social Choice as a theory of forming value judgments on social states	?	X

Much confusion arose because the off diagonal entries were seen as meaningful. But, to put it bluntly, they are not. Public Choice as we understand it here deals with games played within institutionalized norms. Social Choice again as we will use the term subsequently concerns evaluations and rankings of social states (and possibly, on the level of 'constitutional choice', institutionalized normative orders).

3. Public Choice as a Theory of the Game of Politics

At a closer look the very term 'public choice' must seem as strange as the term social choice. 'The public' is not—at least not in the primary use of the term—a choice making entity (like a personal actor). Therefore, to imply by our phrasing that 'it' is 'making choices' in the sense a person does, contains a metaphorical element.[7] Using the term public choice there is no presumption that there is a specific choice making 'social' entity whose involvement would separate public from other kinds of choices. Quite to the contrary like on markets, in the realm of politics, results *emerge* from choices of persons (or, perhaps, agents) but social results are not chosen *by* any person.

On markets and in politics—in fact within any organizational unit and its norms and regularities of conduct—individuals interact with each other according to certain 'rules of the game' defining the organization (the game). And, results emerge within these rules; where the theoretical concept of a 'rule of the game' is taken as comprising causal laws (natural) as well as man-made (artificial) rules (norms and laws).[8]

---

[7] At least it may lead our intuitions astray the same way Rawls believes that it is leading us astray if we would, like the utilitarians, neglect the separateness of persons and conceive of society as if it were a unitary actor when we intend to rank order social states ethically.

[8] As opposed to the Hayekian usage of terms which treats spontaneously emergent rules as 'natural' (see Hayek 1973; 1993) rules need not be deliberately enacted to qualify as 'artificial' if we use terms as proposed here. The crucial point is that the artificial would be otherwise if men acted or desired otherwise (see related to this Heinimann 1987; 1945, and Buchanan 1979).

Game theoretically speaking, the so-called 'rules of the game' comprise everything that is beyond choices or the causal influence of the decision making entities *in* a play of the game.[9]

Since the implications of the homo oeconomicus model of forward looking opportunity taking behavior began to be spelled out in the early sixties in more detail in non-co-operative game theory (with Schelling and Selten leading the 'pack') almost exactly when Public Choice (with Buchanan and Tullock leading the 'other pack') started its rise, the two seemed natural allies.[10] Ultimately there is one game of life with one type of rational individuals populating that world. Specific results derive from the specific rules of partial or lower order specific games (or from 'structure' as political scientists might want to say).[11] Any sound explanation of behavior should be based on a *universal* explanatory model for which the 'rules of the game' are antecedent clauses while the model of individual behavior as such must be governed by the same set of behavioral laws across games.[12]

It is assumed by non-co-operative game theory[13] that players have full control over their individual moves but, exactly for that reason, except for special cases of deterministic trivial 'games against nature', no player has full control over results.[14] For an illustration of this simple but much too often neglected point consider a 2 x 2 matrix game like the one in table 2 below. As in particular James M. Buchanan in his use of the metaphor of the 2 x 2 matrix game for 'social choice' has always insisted, we cannot properly speaking say that the two players 'choose' a result. They can either choose a column—as column player—or a row—as row player. Each can choose one of the two moves open to each of them but none can (unilaterally) choose one of the cells.[15] This is impossible unless the other player were just a puppet on the strings of the choosing actor. Then the choosing actor merely would play against 'nature' rather than a strategic game against a co-player who herself is an independent center of choice making.[16]

---

9   Including preferences, values and artificial rules/norms as well as natural features of the situation that are beyond the strategic influence of the players in *plays of the game considered*.
10 It seems fitting that the Pubic Choice Society meetings until rather recently were combined with those of the Economic Science Association and their focus on game experiments.
11 Specific games like markets or voting in politics etc. are merely abstracted from the broader context to make them analytically tractable.
12 This, of course, does not rule out that some rules of a lower order game are to be explained as emergent or artificially created in a higher order game as most obviously but not most typically in rules of self-amendment; see on this Suber (1990).
13 Which is distinguished from co-operative game theory by the assumption that the description of the game model contains all rules explicitly, including any that may guide choices.
14 The functions—actions—mapping states of the world into results would each have to assign a constant result under all circumstances.
15 See on this, in particular Buchanan (1975; 1996) and his earlier criticisms of the Social Choice paradigm as reprinted in Buchanan (1999, vol. 1).
16 Of course from an external point of view the other player may as well be seen as part of nature and subject to natural laws. There is no theory of free will implied that would be incompatible with soft determinism. We only stress the fact that an actor from her first person perspective

The insight that even in the most simple case of a 2 x 2 matrix game the results of a play of the game are not chosen but are necessarily emergent obviously extends to games with any number of players, moves, and strategies. It holds true if we do not commit the—regrettably rather common—blunder to assume that a strategy can be chosen as an act and not merely as a plan.[17] Therefore *any conceptualization of a social interaction in terms of non-co-operative game theory will imply that results cannot be chosen.*

Since the framework of non-co-operative game theory explicitly models all moves and thereby all causal influences of individuals[18] on each other and their environment, it forms the most detailed and basic conceptual scheme for representing any form of social interaction.[19] In this sense we may conclude that according to our fundamental models of the world *results of public choice cannot be chosen.*[20] They emerge within the norms structuring social interaction (while these norms themselves emerge within a higher order interaction etc. according to the same principles without social choice in the narrow sense ever taking place[21]).

When we conceptualize interactive choice making in the political realm as a game there is only public choice. The thesis of the impossibility of social choice is merely a corollary of the game conceptualization rather than a substantive insight in the structure of the world. Conceivably there might be other conceptualizations but we believe that none of them could have the credentials that non-co-operative game modeling commands as a basic conceptual scheme. Moreover, there seem to be good reasons for claiming that within any adequate conceptual scheme there is a categorical distinction between choice making in the narrow sense of bodily movements of

---

phenomenologically must distinguish between making a choice and predicting it (including in particular her own choices).
17 If some illustration is desired, consider a pd. Transform the pd in a perfect information game in which the second mover knows the actions of the first mover. Write down the corresponding strategic game table. It is a two by four (not a two by two table). Assume now that the strategies are not merely plans but can be chosen as acts. Write down the graph and get a tree with imperfect information and eight end nodes. This will drive home the message if you need to receive it at all. Speaking of strategies as if they could be chosen in one act smuggles in commitment power without noticing it.
18 See on the more game theoretically minded modelling side Güth and Kliemt (2007).
19 But in an adequate account of what is going on that knowledge is merely expressed by game theoretic language tools (and it is expressed as part of the rules of the game). Game theory does itself not provide the empirical information expressed in the rules of the games analyzed. It does not contain any empirical 'natural' behavioral laws but *represents* them along with 'artificial' rules of games as for instance norms (as complex practices and regularities).
20 See in particular Buchanan (2001). One should, however, bear in mind that classical or, to use Ken Binmore's, see Binmore (1987/88) apt term, "eductive" (non-co-operative) game theory is not a behavioural theory at all but rather a 'theory of reasoning about knowledge' (in the sense of Fagin et al. 1995).
21 Of course, we say that we choose to enact norms by, say, processes of voting. But strictly speaking nobody makes the choice of enactment. The enactment emerges, chosen are acts like *saying* yes or no.

phenotypes and choice making in the metaphorical sense of the 'movements' of an 'extended phenotype'.

4. Two Problems with Social Choice

If there is no social choice then, as a theory, Social Choice does not seem to have an object. Nevertheless, like non-co-operative game theory, which provides the tools to represent and to analyze games characterized by systems of institutionalized norms, Social Choice provides conceptual tools to evaluation processes. The 'social welfare function' which can be used to analyze the evaluative or judgmental side of ranking games and their outcomes as a whole is one such conceptual tool. Since no collectivity 'makes'—properly speaking—'social choices' we assume that a social welfare function always represents an *individual's* preferences over collective outcomes (or whole sets of rules or norms governing the process leading to such outcomes).

A personal social welfare function yields a complete ordering of the results of public choice according to the values of the individual whose values are represented by the function. If the evaluating individual happens to endorse 'welfarist' values, then he or she ranks games and outcomes of games according to how the concerned players themselves rank the outcomes of the game they play.

To be more specific, suppose that there are $n > 0$ individuals who have the preference orders R_i, $i = 1, 2, ..., n$ forming the profile $(R_1, R_2, ..., R_n)$. An individual j's welfare function w_j is welfarist if it expresses j's ethical values as a function $w_j(R_1, R_2, ..., R_n)$ of how the concerned individuals $i = 1, 2, ..., n$ themselves rank the states of the world. Depending on whether the individual j is internal or external to the relevant community different problems emerge. If the ranking is regarded as the (ethical) preference order of an external individual $j \notin \{1, 2, ..., n\}$ who forms it on the basis of the game playing individuals' evaluations of outcomes there is no principal problem to formulate such a function. In this external observer case problems arise only if we impose additional requirements on that function. We will deal with that case and the problems of a 'liberal' welfare function in the next section (see the section 4.2). In the case of a participant $j \in \{1, 2, ..., n\}$ internal to the interaction the very formation of a welfarist function w_j may become problematic because it tends to make the evaluation of everybody dependent on that of each. Forming individual (second order) preferences on the basis of individual preferences concerning outcomes of the game seems to run the risk of circularity (or the risk of a progression to infinity).

4.1 The Circularity Problem

It is conventionally assumed that the preferences operative in the play of the game include already everything relevant to the ranking of end-results. With such satiated preferences there seems no room for an additional individual ranking on the basis of the profile of individual rankings.[22]—We first explore the possibility that the preferences which form the arguments of w_j are non-satiated, then look at the case of satiated preferences and end this section with an example that exemplifies both.

Referring to the preferences in the game—guiding within rule choices—as 'tastes' and preferences that concern the game as a whole—guiding rule choices—as 'values' the problem of circularity may indeed be avoided.[23] If we do not want to impose specific trade offs between tastes we can assume that there are as many taste based social welfare functions as there are individuals. Each function is expressing the taste based ethical preferences of an individual who evaluates a game not only on the basis of her or his 'within game'-tastes but also in the light of the 'within game'-tastes of all other individuals concerned. Since the evaluation of the game as a whole is not based on evaluations of the game but merely on individual 'within game'-tastes circularity is avoided.[24]

Relying on non-satiated preferences the economist is taking the preferences not as given after all things have been considered by the individual holders of these preferences themselves. He still starts from given tastes but preference formation is taken into account. However, taking preferences into account but avoiding the introduction of tastes as distinct from preferences when considering preference formation makes preferences dependent on preferences. We have to form a preference order as a function of a profile (list) of individual preferences of which the preference order is itself a part. If each individual intends to make her or his own preferences a function of the preferences of the other individuals we get an interdependence that would require that we have $(R_1, R_2, ..., R_n) = f(R_1, R_2, ..., R_n)$, 'a fixed point' of the function $f(\cdot)$ in other words. To put it slightly otherwise, if we assume that welfare functions w_i, $i = 1, 2, ..., n$, that express the individuals' ethical values, exist, then these n personal welfare functions could each be functions of the satiated preferences of all individuals only if $R_i = w_i(R_1, R_2, ..., R_n)$, $i = 1, 2, ..., n$. There might be several such fixed points, yet only a fixed point can fulfill the requirement of making the preferences of each a function of the preferences of all individuals.

Lengthy abstract considerations are fortunately unnecessary to illustrate the essential aspects of the preceding considerations. A very simple ultimatum game example suffices to exemplify them: The proposer X can propose a division (x,y) with $p \geq x \geq p/2$ and $x + y = p$ of the monetary pie $p(>0)$. The responder Y can

---

22 See on this criticism of Arrow's approach to welfare economics, of course, already Little (1952).
23 Pattanaik (2005) discusses the criticisms of Arrow offered early on in Little (1952), Bergson (1954), and takes them as seriously as they deserve. To Pattanaik's excellent analysis we want to add merely that we distinguish not only tastes and values but also an institutional and an evaluative approach. This indicates that the present discussion is not only complimentary to Pattanaik's great paper but also intends to be complementary.
24 We do not go into the details of forming a preference order on an enlarged space of 'procedures cum results' as in Pattanaik/Suzumura (1996).

accept $(\delta(x,y)=1)$ or reject $(\delta(x,y)=0)$ the proposal (x,y). The monetary payoffs, depending on the choices, are $\delta(x,y)x$ for X and $\delta(x,y)(p-x)$ for Y.

Now, modeling preferences as dependent on preferences or tastes is a special case of introducing other regarding concerns explicitly into the model. More generally speaking other regarding concerns could be based

(i) on the material payoffs $\delta(x,y)x$ and $\delta(x,y)(p-x)$ and
(ii) on the individual evaluations $u_X(\delta(x,y)x)$ and $u_Y(\delta(x,y)(p-x))$ of such outcomes.

In case (i), each individual X and Y is free to evaluate results by not just considering only her own monetary payoff but that of the other as well. This can express itself as altruism, e.g. in the additive form

$$U_X(\delta(x,y)x,\delta(x,y)(p-x)) = \delta(x,y)x + \alpha_x \delta(x,y)(p-x)$$
$$U_Y(\delta(x,y)x,\delta(x,y)(p-x)) = \delta(x,y)(p-x) + \alpha_y \delta(x,y)x$$

with $\alpha_x, \alpha_y > 0$. It can also adopt the form of inequ(al)ity aversion (Loewenstein et al. 1989; Bolton 1991; Bolton and Ockenfels 2000; Fehr and Schmidt 1999) as expressed by functions

$$U_X(\delta(x,y)x,\delta(x,y)(2x-p)) \text{ and } U_Y(\delta(x,y)(p-x),\delta(x,y)(2x-p))$$

which depend positively (negatively) on their first (second) argument.

The material payoffs, and their individual evaluations $U_X(\cdot,\cdot)$ and $U_Y(\cdot,\cdot)$ are distinguished and circularity can be avoided.

In case (ii), we can read $u_X(\cdot)$ and $u_Y(\cdot)$ as representing 'tastes'. Then the latter could become arguments of individual welfare functions

$w_X(u_X, u_Y)$ and $w_y(u_Y, u_X)$.

This also would avoid the circularity problem. The problem, however, emerges when assuming satiated preferences.

Let us distinguish the latter as case (iii) from the two preceding. Consider functions

(iii) $w_X = w_X\left[\delta(x,y)x, w_Y\right]$ and $w_Y = w_Y\left[\delta(x,y)(p-x), w_X\right]$

that due to 'altruism' are increasing in both their arguments. According to such an interdependent altruism (in the spirit of Becker 1981) or such a characterization of interdependent welfare, one can derive a fixed point provided that appropriate existence conditions are met by $w_X(\cdot,\cdot)$ and $w_Y(\cdot,\cdot)$:

$$(w_X, w_Y) = \begin{pmatrix} w_X\left[\delta(x,y)x, w_Y\langle\delta(x,y)(p-x), w_X\rangle\right], \\ w_Y\left[\delta(x,y)(p-x), w_X(\delta(x,y)x, w_Y)\right] \end{pmatrix}.$$

We do not believe that such considerations are particularly important within the ordinary business of life. Yet they may play a role for ethical theory formation if the assumption that there is an external point of view from which an ethical theorist or welfare economist can form her personal welfare judgments for the collectivity is deemed unacceptable. An evaluator who conceives of herself as a participant rather than an external observer in the process of ethical deliberation may be confronted with circularity problems if she intends to take the ethical preferences of all into account and knows that the others adopt the same participant's point of view.[25] If we assume that the moral point of view is external to the collectivity whose welfare is evaluated the circularity problem vanishes. However, those who adopt such an external point of view with the intention to respect the given preferences of others and simply to ratify them might run into problems, too.

4.2 The Liberal Problem[26]

Consider an evaluator j, $j \notin \{1,2,....,n\}$, external to the collectivity of n individuals. Such an individual j may rank the institutionalized norms defining the game of politics according to some criterion of better or worse without restricting himself to the results of the game. There is no reason why in particular preferences of a procedural type could not be formed. Problems arise only if a specific 'welfarist' economic perspective on *evaluation* is mixed up with *institutional* issues of bringing about results.[27]

We can make a simple yet fundamental distinction between two forms of liberalism, political and evaluative. *Political liberalism* is institutional (or constitutional). It is embodied in the structure of the game or the norms and other rules of the game defining 'the game form' (basically the moves open to players disregarding the payoffs).[28] *Philosophical liberalism* is 'judgmental'. It concerns itself with how to *evaluate* game results on the basis of individual values (or perhaps tastes if the preceding distinction is made).

In political liberalism the liberal element is embodied in the rules (norms, institutions). In philosophical liberalism the liberal element is entailed in how we form ethical opinions. Though we personally prefer to conceive of liberalism in terms of institutionalized norms[29] and believe that such political liberalism is the core of what

---

25 Not necessarily the point of view Strawson had in mind but something akin to it, Strawson (1962).
26 Regarding political or institutional liberalism, Robert Sugden got it basically right on 'rights'. Others went into similar directions. Some of the discussion is summed up usefully in Gaertner (2006, chap. 4) though strangely enough without mentioning Sugden, e.g. Sugden (1985; 1994).
27 This is not about tastes vs. values. The relevant distinction is one between institutions or mechanisms and the evaluations thereof. It clearly has something to do with alternative conceptualizations of rights, as characterized for instance in Gaertner et al. (1992), yet the distinction we intend to make is even more elementary and plain.
28 The values supporting it may typically be procedural.
29 In this political 'norm focused' reading the fact that pd incentive structures may emerge and lead to Pareto dominated results is entirely trivial and no paradox (of liberalism or other). Payoff dominated results can, of course, emerge from rational play.

liberalism stands for, we do not deny that there seems to be another use of the term 'liberalism'. The latter characterizes a position that is judgmental or evaluative. For simplicity we refer to this evaluative view as 'philosophical' though it is endorsed not merely by philosophers but by economists as well.

Armatya K. Sen identified, we think, quite correctly a philosophical problem for the not uncommon type of a liberal economist who endorses welfarist welfare functions along with a Robbins type meta-ethics to express his self-restraint or his respect for 'given preferences' in passing value judgments. According to Sen an *evaluation* is 'liberal' in a minimal sense, if it fulfils

L: individual rankings of 'other' are owned in judgment of self sometimes
P: respect for unanimity (Pareto) are respected by judgment of self
U: unrestricted acceptance of other's values or neutrality in judgment of self.

Somebody who intends to pay due respect to individuals' desires may be naturally inclined towards these requirements on forming his own value judgments. James M. Buchanan's approach seems to be a paradigm case in point. He is of the opinion—endorses the value—that respecting the values of others is essential when forming our own value judgments for society. Leaving aside the fact that for Buchanan—due to norms of inter-personal respect—on the ultimate level of justification *only* Pareto improvements may count as ethical improvements,[30] the three conditions named above seem indeed to express what it means to refrain from 'playing God' in Buchanan's sense. The answer why, emerges from a series of questions deemed rhetorical by 'philosophically liberal economists':

> Who are you, to say that some of the preference orders endorsed by the individuals should not be taken into account? → You accept universal domain, U.
>
> Who are you, to say that a Pareto improvement should not be realized? → You accept that being a Pareto improvement is sufficient for ranking a social result higher in your ethical value order than another one, P.
>
> Who are you, not to go along in your own ethical evaluations with the individuals' evaluations at least *sometimes* (and regardless of the value judgments of others in the collectivity whose social states you order) → You accept condition, L.[31]

If we intend to render our own welfare judgments subservient to the value judgments of those who are themselves concerned (i.e., respect the 'given preferences') we should accept the preceding line of argument. In forming our own values we want to *ratify* values of those concerned rather than impose our own. We do not only intend to 'live and let live', we evaluate states of the world according to the personal

---

30 Being a Pareto improvement becomes necessary rather than merely sufficient for legitimacy. Only if a proposed measure is a Pareto improvement the autonomy of others in forming their value judgments receives full Kantian respect.
31 Or, for that matter, Sen's condition L' of minimal liberalism.

'liberal' maxim that—other things being equal—the world is a better place if people get more rather than less of what they themselves prefer to get. Rather than let them have what we prefer them to have we ratify their views.

As in case of the circularity problem a specific example may be helpful. The so called 'paradox of liberalism' can be used to illustrate what is at stake here. With some inessential modifications of Sen's original story (see Sen 1970) we can present the paradox starting from a simple two by two matrix:[32]

Table 2

Lascivious

		non-read	read
Prude	read	3,3	1,4
	non-read	4,1	2,2

As the story runs, Prude is chiefly interested to keep Lascivious 'out of the fire' of reading Lady Chatterley's Lover. Lascivious deems it most important that Prude reads the book. Yet, if Lascivious reads, then Prude prefers not to read. If Lascivious does not read, then Prude also prefers not to read. So regardless of what Lascivious does, Prude prefers not to read. Likewise, regardless of what the other does, Lascivious prefers to read. However, the evaluation of the state (read, non-read) ranks higher than (non-read, read) in the value rankings of both.[33]

Now, order the cells of the table 2 in a vector

$$v := \big((\text{read, non-read}), (\text{read, read}), (\text{non-read, non-read}), (\text{non-read, read})\big)$$

and represent the personal ethical value rankings *for* society (these might be simple tastes if we were to respect tastes) by Prude and Lascivious, respectively, by the two corresponding vectors of ordinal ranking numbers (3, 1, 4, 2), (3, 4, 1, 2). We get then $w_{\text{impartial observer}}((3, 1, 4, 2); (3, 4, 1, 2))$. This function will rank-order the entries in v.[34] If we restrict the condition L to something akin to Sen's minimum L' the function should respect the preference of Lascivious in the value ranking for the collectivity over at least two pairs of alternatives, eg. the pairs (non-read, non-read), (non-read, read). If Lascivious ranks them '(non-read, read) $P_{\text{Lascivious}}$ (non-read, non-read)' then this should be 'ratified' by the impartial observer:

'(non-read, read) $P_{\text{impartial observer}}$ (non-read, non-read)'

---

32 We are not interested in the game form conceptualization as already implicitly in Buchanan (1975; 1996), also Gaertner et al. (1992) and, of course, again Sugden (1994).
33 For each it is more important that the other co-operates with his wishes than to realize his own preferences between acts. But this is in the end an inessential interpretational aspect.
34 This is not necessarily leading to a contradiction if we think of it as ascending in a hierarchy of value orderings based on lower order value orderings.

The respective ordering of Lascivious is represented by the personal impartial function $w_{\text{impartial observer}}$ ((3, 1, 4, 2); (3, 4, 1, 2)) showing the impartial observers ranking of the entries in v as a function of the preferences of Prude and Lascivious; i.e.:

$w_{\text{impartial observer}}$ ((3, 1, 4, 2); (3, 4, 1, 2)) ((non-read, read)) >

$w_{\text{impartial observer}}$ ((3, 1, 4, 2); (3, 4, 1, 2)) ((non-read, non-read))

Likewise the impartial observer can ratify and in this sense respect the preference, say, '(non-read, non-read) P_{Prude} (read, non-read)' of the prude individual only if

$w_{\text{impartial observer}}$ ((3, 1, 4, 2); (3, 4, 1, 2)) ((non-read, non-read)) >

$w_{\text{impartial observer}}$ ((3, 1, 4, 2); (3, 4, 1, 2)) ((read, non-read))

If the value ranking emergent for the impartial observer is to comply with the preceding we have

(non-read, read) $P_{\text{impartial observer}}$ (non-read, non-read)

and

(non-read, non-read) $P_{\text{impartial observer}}$ (read, non-read)

With transitivity we get

(non-read, read) $P_{\text{impartial observer}}$ (read, non-read)

which contradicts the requirement that value judgments of the impartial observer should respect Pareto improvements. This amounts to stating that one cannot let individuals dictate one's own value orders—make them 'dictators' as far as one's own ordering is concerned—and at the same time restrict their dictatorship by the Pareto principle. Neutral ratification to which the philosophical liberal aspires according to his central value of not imposing his own values on others is impossible. He must take a stance and cannot simply ratify in the ways intended.

Stated that flatly the whole thing seems entirely trivial. But let us emphasize that we are concerned with the sphere of *evaluations*. The discussion is about forming values not about norms, it is about opinion not about institutions. We are concerned with rankings rather than with bringing about results. Therefore the argument that results of interaction necessarily emerge and cannot properly be chosen does not apply. Of course, individuals can meaningfully form their individual rankings over social results even if they cannot in the proper sense of that term 'choose' them.

Philosophical liberalism can meaningfully be formulated by characterizing the structure of the *evaluation function* (welfare function). However, this will not result in confusion only if liberalism is strictly seen as a matter of liberal *evaluations* and *not* of liberal political *institutions*. To put it slightly otherwise, the impossibility of a liberal evaluation does not at all amount to an impossibility of liberal political institutions. It points out a problem of a welfarist framework in Social Choice and not at all of liberal institutionalized normative orders or political liberalism. Seen in this light it is entirely clear that the 'paradox of liberalism' has nothing to do with political rights and the norms that define those rights. It is irrelevant for liberal policies.

However, as far as formulations of philosophical or judgmental liberalism are concerned Sen has a point.[35] The requirements L, P, U, on the opinion formation process of a *judgmental* 'Paretian Liberal' are *an* explication of what a 'value skeptical' economist intends to accomplish when he rejects 'playing God' in the formulation of his social welfare function for the collectivity. As the theorem shows that explication is inconsistent.[36] The economist cannot keep sitting on the fence altogether when it comes to formulating his personal welfare function for the collectivity. If he intends to let each separate individual dictate his own ethical *judgment* concerning at least the ordering of one pair of social states, he cannot meaningfully let the individuals concerned dictate his ordering of social states. He cannot merely ratify.[37]

To put it bluntly, those who prefer liberal political institutions will have to defend that value judgment on substantial grounds. They cannot derive it from any meta-ethical assumptions about how value judgments should be formed. The ideals guiding the formation of value judgments do not imply norms guiding behavior.

5. Conclusion

Like in Popper's plea for intolerance towards the intolerant somebody may be willing to impose the constitution of a free liberal order on others. Yet in a literal sense this imposition by an individual is impossible. There is no individual who can choose an institutionalized norm order. Somebody can, however, develop the desire that the order be of a certain form. What he believes to have good reason to desire is shaped by the contingent facts of his institutional experience. He may be induced to develop dispositions to choose in a certain way after such experience, and, liberal institutions may in fact instill values that support these dispositions which in turn support the liberal institutions.

Contrary to that a process of (ethical) preference formation based on given preferences, as in welfarist welfare economics, in all likelihood does not help at all to support liberal institutions. It is not generally true either that we need liberal values in the sense of philosophical liberalism (as explained here) to support a politically liberal normative order.[38] We need people who adopt an internal point of view (see

---

35 Making the argument appear more relevant by blurring the distinction between the institutional and the judgmental perspective was, of course, an illegitimate strategy.
36 There may be other ones but they will lead to analogues of the variant of the Gibbard's paradox within the sphere of evaluation.
37 Again it should be no surprise that such dictatorship even over the value rankings of an individual as exerted by the value rankings of another individual will be infectious and lead to a clash if there are two dictators of the kind.
38 It is presumably generally untrue.

Hart 1961) to the norms of the *politically* liberal order and who support it by their norm abiding and norm enforcing behavior (for what reasons ever).

To make a long story short, in a literal sense and for trivial reasons only individuals make choices and are guided by values. We must acknowledge that, if we take the causal mechanisms under which we operate seriously. Once we do that the liberal paradox, though a real problem for some forms of *philosophical* attitudes towards forming welfare judgments, becomes irrelevant for choice making within established sets of institutional norms (which may or may not be liberal in the political sense). Philosophical liberalism is politically irrelevant. However, philosophically it is a potential source of confusion. If we start to confuse norms and values as in the mistaken evaluation-based rather than norm-based conceptualization of rights in the discussion of the liberal paradox we should not be astonished that collective confusion emerges though it has not been collectively chosen. In a way, this paper sorts out the confusion of one of its authors. Friedrich Breyer was right in pointing to this confusion (see Breyer 1996) but the explanation why the confusion arose may be of some interest, too: the Paradox of Liberalism has nothing to do with classical political liberalism at all but Sen made an effort to let it seem so.

Bibliography

Ainslee, G. (1992), *Picoeconomics*, Cambridge

Becker, G. S. (1981), Altruism in the Family and Selfishness in the Market Place, in: *Economica 48*, 1–15

Bergson, A. (1954), On the Concept of Social Welfare, in: *The Quarterly Journal of Economics 68*, 233–252

Binmore, K. (1987/88), Modeling Rational Players I&II, in: *Economics and Philosophy 3 & 4*, 179–214 & 179–155

Bolton, G. (1991), A Comparative Model of Bargaining: Theory and Evidence, in: *American Economic Review 81*, 1096–1136

— /A. Ockenfels (2000), ERC: A Theory of Equity, Reciprocity and Competition, in: *American Economic Review 90*, 166–193

Breyer, F. (1996), Comment on the Papers by Buchanan and by de Jasay and Kliemt, in: *Analyse & Kritik 18*, 148–152

Buchanan, J. M. (1975; 1996), An Ambiguity in Sen's Alleged Proof of the Impossibility of a Pareto Liberal, in: *Analyse & Kritik 18*, 118–125

— (1979), *Natural and Artifactual Man*, Indianapolis

— (1999), *The Logical Foundations of Constitutional Liberty. Vol. 1*, Indianapolis

— (2001), Game Theory, Mathematics, and Economics, in: *Journal of Economic Methodology 8*, 27–32

Coleman, J. S. (1990), *Foundations of Social Theory*, Cambridge/MA and London

Fagin, R./J. Y. Halpern/Y. Moses/M. Y. Vardi (1995), *Reasoning about Knowledge*, Cambridge/MA-London

Fehr, E./K. Schmidt (1999), A Theory of Fairness, Competition, and Cooperation, in: *Quarterly Journal of Economics 114*, 817–868

Gaertner, W. (2006), *A Primer in Social Choice Theory*, Oxford

— /K. Suzumura/P. K. Pattanaik (1992), Individual Rights Revisited, in: *Economica 59*, 161–177

Güth, W./H. Kliemt (2007), The Rationality of Rational Fools, in: F. Peter/H. B. Schmid (eds.), *Rationality and Commitment*, Oxford, 124-149

Harsanyi, J. C. (1977), *Rational Behavior and Bargaining Equilibrium in Games and Social Situations*, Cambridge

Hart, H. L. A. (1961), *The Concept of Law*, Oxford

Hayek, F. A. v. (1973; 1993), Law, Legislation and Liberty: A New Statement of the Liberal Principles of Justice and Political Economy, in: *Rules and Order. Vol. Bd. 1*, London

Heinimann, F. (1987; 1945), *Nomos und Physis*, Darmstadt

Little, I. M. D. (1952), Social Choice and Individual Values, in: *Journal of Political Economy 60*, 422–433

Loewenstein, G./L. Thompson/M. Bazerman (1989), Social Utility and Decision Making in Interpersonal Contexts, in: *Journal of Personality and Social Psychology 57*, 426–441

Pattanaik, P. K. (2005), Little and Bergson on Arrow's Concept of Social Welfare, in: *Social Choice and Welfare 25*, 369-379

— /K. Suzumura (1996), Individual Rights and Social Evaluation: A Conceptual Framework, in: *Oxford Economic Papers 48*, 194–212

Peter, F./H. B. Schmid (eds.) (2007), *Rationality and Commitment*, Oxford

Sen, A. K. (1970), The Impossibility of a Paretian Liberal, in: *Journal of Political Economy 78*, 152–157

Strawson, P. F. (1962), Freedom and Resentment, in: *Proceedings of the British Academy*, 187–211

Suber, P. (1990), *The Paradox of Self-Amendment*, New York

Sugden, R. (1985), Liberty, Preference, and Choice, in: *Economics and Philosophy 1*, 213–229

— (1994), The Theory of Rights, in: H. Siebert (ed.), *The Ethical Foundations of the Market Economy*, Tübingen, 31–53

Vanberg, V. (1982), *Markt und Organisation. Individualistische Sozialtheorie und das Problem Korporativen Handelns*, Tübingen

A. Michael Kirmes

Political and Philosophical Liberalism Re-Reconsidered
A Comment on Werner Güth and Hartmut Kliemt[*]

1. Social Choice: More Than Just an Evaluation of Outcomes?

The paradigm case of choice making is the choice action of an individual. Güth and Kliemt (henceforth GK) argue that *social choice* in this sense is (trivially) impossible. In the narrow sense of that term results of a social interaction cannot actually be 'chosen' in the way a single individual can choose. Instead, results emerge from the separate choices of individuals, who act according to certain 'rules of the game' (i.e. the aspects of the game that are unalterable by any actual play of the game). The institutionally guided process of generating social results in interaction is called *public choice* by GK, and the explanatory theory of such processes is referred to by the term *Public Choice* (with capital letters). Since GK's definitions of terms render the preceding statements practically tautological, not much can be objected.

In contrast, then, GK define *Social Choice* as an evaluative theory "addressing issues of the judgmental ranking of social states or outcomes of the social process". The main point of GK's paper is to establish this dichotomy of an 'institutional perspective' (as used in Public Choice and *political* liberalism) on the one side and a 'judgmental perspective' (as used in Social Choice and *philosophical* liberalism) on the other. From this, they eventually conclude that the *Liberal Paradox* (Sen 1970) is an entirely philosophical (evaluative) problem, which is "irrelevant for liberal policies". However, while GK hope to resolve a long-lasting confusion (namely, between said institutional and judgmental perspectives), I will argue that they have stopped one step short of achieving this goal, thereby adding to the confusion.

A judgmental and an institutional perspective are clearly not disjoint opposites. Public Choice can be an opposite of Social Choice if it is, as GK suggested, a merely explanatory theory, in contrast to Social Choice's being judgmental. Philosophical liberalism can be juxtaposed with political liberalism, if it is concerned merely with (individuals' evaluations of) outcomes instead of institutional (or procedural) issues (how the outcome is 'brought about'). However, the two dimensions of outcomes and of procedures should be kept apart better than by GK. Social Choice can in two ways take an 'institutional perspective' on 'collective decision-making': it may suggest that institutions be set up for a specific result to emerge, and it may base an evaluation of a social state on 'how the state is brought about'.

---

[*] I want to thank Ruhiye Keskin for initial inspiring discussions, and Hartmut Kliemt and Bernd Lahno for helpful hints, suggestions and corrections.

2. You Should Do What's Best for You

Pattanaik (2005), whose paper GK intend to complement, at length discusses Bergson's interpretation of Arrow (Bergson 1954) that Social Choice's task is to counsel "the public official whose sole aim in life is 'to implement the values of other citizens as given by some rule of collective decision-making'", which Arrow (1963) "emphatically endorses" (Pattanaik 2005). Pattanaik in turn suggests that Welfare Economics, or Social Choice, can (and should) have both functions: in a first phase, it can be a means for individuals' to form welfare judgments about all social states (an evaluative approach), and in a second phase, it can counsel a (fictitious?) public official to implement the 'social result', which is evaluated as best according to an aggregate of individuals' values, by setting up the required institutions that in turn lead to the desired result (a normative approach). Similarly, Sen (1983) introduces a "normative choice" interpretation: "x is socially preferred to y" can be interpreted as "decision making in the society should be so organized that y must not be chosen when x is available".

In this light and contrary to GK's definition, Social Choice seems to be not only evaluative and in this sense 'philosophical', but also normative. The 'social preference' does not only indicate the 'best' social state, but it also implies that this social state then ought to be realized. Therefore, contrary to what GK state, problems such as Sen's paradox should concern policy more than philosophy. The problems show the inconsistency of the combination of certain values, which is, from a philosophical standpoint, an important merit. But the problems may be even more important for the following process of implementation and institutionalization.

Of course, Social Choice can only indicate the 'socially preferred' result to the public official; it does not tell him how to effectively get there. This would be a job for social engineering informed by Public Choice.[1] However, institutions, such as norms, are inherently procedural (they can only tell individuals what to do, but not a collective to chose a result) and should be set up independent of individuals' specific preferences, to allow for the emergence of the 'best' result in every case. In order to do so, it seems sensible to translate the values which are used as conditions for the social welfare function into norms. This may in some cases be easier than in others, as I will argue in the fourth part. But first, I will establish what I call *procedural values*.

3. The Journey is the Reward

In their (philosophical) interpretation of Sen's Liberal Paradox, GK base the ranking of social states merely on individuals' evaluations of the social state's outcomes. Indeed, for a long time, and pretty much up until today, Social Choice has predomi-

---

[1] Which is, in this respect, also normative.

nantly been understood as dealing with the evaluation of outcomes. However, when ranking social states, we may very well also want to take the processes leading to these social states into account. Indeed, in the section 'The Decision Process as a Value' of *Social Choice and Individual Values*, Arrow (1951) is concerned with such procedural values:

> For example, the belief in democracy may be so strong that any decision on the distribution of goods arrived at democratically may be preferred to such a decision arrived at in other ways, even though all individuals might have preferred the second distribution of goods to the first if it had been arrived at democratically. (Arrow 1951, 90)

In line with this, Sen (1995, 11) stresses the importance of judging both "the 'rightness' of procedures, and the 'goodness' of outcomes". Indeed, it was Sen himself, who—if inadvertently—stimulated incorporating such procedural values into Social Choice theory through the condition of 'Minimal Liberalism' in his Liberal Paradox (Sen 1970). Sen defined liberalism by referring solely to individuals' evaluations of social states (thereby relying much on terms and formulations used by Arrow (1951) in his impossibility theorem). But Nozick (1974) convincingly argued against Sen's formulation that liberty should rather be defined as giving people *control* over some decisions. Sugden (1981) joined in on this by arguing that Mill's view on liberty, which Sen allegedly had picked up, was one about procedures. In a later article, Sugden (1985) described the liberal thought in the following way:

> Value is being attached to the *act* of choice rather than to the things that are chosen. It is not that liberty is good because people tend to choose good plans for themselves; rather, these plans are good because they are the ones people have chosen for themselves. (Sugden 1985, 216)

Sugden proposes the use of game forms to represent such procedural requirements.[2] The game form approach lends itself to any kind of procedural formulations. In his argument on the procedural dimension of liberty, Sugden is discussing value judgments concerning game forms. Someone's belief in the liberal value that people should choose certain things on their own and unrestricted by others is concerned with a procedural value. He endorses a value judgement discriminating between alternative game forms and the decision sets assigned by them to individuals.

Even though there may be cases where an outcome- or desire-based approach to liberty is perfectly adequate, it at least does make sense as well to formulate the liberal thought as a procedural value, as even Sen himself recognized (Sen 1992). However, whether procedures or outcomes are evaluated has nothing to do with GK's separation of (real) institutional issues and (theoretical) evaluations. In their effort to do justice to Sen's original argument, GK explicitly take evaluations of outcomes into account only. But this only adds confusion to the debate: why should philosophical (evaluative) liberalism only be allowed to consider outcomes of a process, but not the process itself, while political liberalism—according to GK—demands or sets up certain (inherently procedural) institutions?

---

2 Since rights are usually *institutionalized* norms, this is where the confusion between institutional and evaluative issues argued against by GK came from.

4. Paradoxical Policies?

It is important to note, that with procedural values, one is much closer to the institutionalization of norms. If I believe that it is best to let people choose freely (a procedural value), it also makes sense for me to strive for institutionalized norms that allow people to actually choose freely. In contrast, if I believe that in some realm people should get whatever they prefer (a preference- or outcome-oriented value), the translation into a corresponding norm is more complicated (it has to take an indirect form such as 'people should only be allowed to choose in such a way that the outcome is the one that people prefer'). Since each outcome is linked to a procedure that leads to it, restrictions on outcomes limit procedures as well, and vice versa. Even if one claims not to put restrictions on procedures (allowing 'individual free choice'), putting restrictions on outcomes of course limits the range of possible procedures as well.

Thus, the impossibility of a 'Paretian liberal' boils down to the impossibility of having a 'liberal dictator'. On the one hand, one wants to give individuals unlimited free choice (at least, for minimal liberalism, concerning two states, or one aspect, of the world). On the other hand, demanding (and not only 'respecting', as it is usually called) Pareto-optimality, one effectively limits the outcomes that can possibly be accepted (or 'preferred by society'), and with them, the range of possible procedures. Obviously, this makes the liberal 'paradox' seem rather trivial and not very paradoxical at all. However, I disagree with GK's contention that the "paradox of liberalism has nothing to do with political rights and the norms that define those rights". The impossibility of a combination of liberal and Paretian values does not disappear entirely when one starts looking at actual (or conceivable) institutions (or procedures) instead of outcomes.

Nevertheless, I agree that neither Sen's nor Gibbard's paradox (Gibbard 1974) pose a problem for genuine liberals—but for a different reason: genuine political liberals are entirely procedurally liberal or, at least, give priority to procedural liberty. Thus, as a rule, they subordinate Pareto-optimality or other outcome-related conditions.[3] (Procedural) liberals do demand free choice, and they often claim that this will lead to Pareto-optimality, but most of them are also aware that Pareto-optimality is not always reached through this choice (because of externalities, free rider problems etc.). Indeed, it would appear somewhat strange if a liberal would first demand that people should decide freely and on their own, and afterwards force

---

[3] Of course, in Gibbard's paradox (Gibbard 1974), the Pareto condition cannot be the problem. In this case, it is the implicit demand that the outcome should be such that no individual that had an influence on this outcome may have the wish (or preference) that he or she had chosen differently before. Both the conformist and the non-conformist face a decision under uncertainty with no dominant strategies, and will thus have a hard time deciding what to do. Evidently, once they each have independently made their individual choice, one of them is bound to not have his preference fulfilled. But from a (procedurally) liberal standpoint, this outcome cannot to be criticized, because both of them chose freely and therefore brought the outcome upon themselves.

a Pareto-improvement upon them if they have not reached a Pareto-optimal social state by their deliberate choices. Even though a Pareto-improvement actually makes everyone better off, forcing a Pareto-improvement upon people seems rather illiberal.[4] There is a huge difference between 'respecting' Pareto-improvements that actually are achieved through individuals' free choices (which would, however, already be part of the Liberal condition) and saying that every Pareto-improvement *should* indeed be realized.[5]

5. Conclusion

Although GK are right in claiming that—in contrast to Public Choice—Social Choice should not be perceived as 'institutional', it is, still, not only concerned with the evaluation of outcomes but also—and in some cases essentially—with procedures. Moreover, Social Choice also provides normative judgment by helping to answer questions about which social state ought to be realized. This realization can only happen through 'right' institutions, which enable the procedures required for the desired result to emerge. Herein lies a problem for policy, if the ranking of social states relies on inconsistent values. However, purely procedural ('true') liberalism is not inconsistent, but only becomes inconsistent when paired with other ('welfarist') values that are not inherently liberal.

Bibliography

Arrow, K. (1951), *Social Choice and Individual Values*, 1st edition, New York
— (1963), *Social Choice and Individual Values*, 2nd edition, New York
Bergson, A. (1954), On the Concept of Social Welfare, in: *The Quarterly Journal of Economics 68*, 233–252
Gibbard, A. (1974), A Pareto-Consistent Libertarian Claim, in: *Journal of Economic Theory 7*, 388–410
Nozick, R. (1974), *Anarchy, State, and Utopia*, New York
Pattanaik, P. (2005), Little and Bergson on Arrow's Concept of Social Welfare, in: *Social Choice and Welfare 25*, 369–379
Sen, A. (1970), The Impossibility of a Paretian Liberal, in: *Journal of Political Economy 78*, 152–157

4 If Robinson and Friday trade fish against pineapples, which makes both of them better off, would a true liberal condemn them because they have not instead traded oranges against steaks, which would have been even better for both of them? They might be blamed for not being rational, and the outcome might be regretted from an efficiency point of view, but the choices cannot be disapproved from a liberal standpoint, as both of them chose perfectly freely.
5 Interestingly, Buchanan indeed does see a possible remaining task of politics to realize Pareto-improvements that have not been realized by individuals themselves. In this respect, he seems to be more a contractarian than a true liberal.

— (1983), Liberty and Social Choice, in: *The Journal of Philosophy 53*, 5–28
— (1992), Minimal Liberty, in: *Economica 59*, 139–159
— (1995), Rationality and Social Choice, in: *The American Economic Review 85*, 1–24
Sugden, R. (1981), *The Political Economy of Public Choice*, Oxford
— (1985), Liberty, Preference, and Choice, in: *Economics and Philosophy 1*, 213–229

Robert E. Goodin

Norms Honoured in the Breach[*]

Max Weber offers one clear instance of how people might orient their behaviour around social norms even when they are not strictly being guided by them. We would be hard-pressed to explain why the thief operates under cloak of darkness, except by reference to the norm that he is violating and the sanctions that attach to its violation (Weber 1947, 125). Here I shall point to another such example—one that derives from a fundamental feature of norms that has heretofore been too little noticed.

Norms are paradigmatic 'orders without authority'.[1] They share this feature with customary law in traditional societies. Both are sets of rules that bootstrap their own authority. It is purely the practice of the community subject to them that makes those rules rules. There is no one who is duly authorized to 'issue' the orders, or interpret them, or apply them. It is purely a case of those who are subject to the rules 'doing it by and for themselves'. The rules being treated as rules is all that makes them rules.

In terms famous from H. L. A. Hart's *Concept of Law*, norms thus constitute a set of 'primary rules' without any 'secondary rules' (Hart 1961, ch. 5).[2] Primary rules are simply injunctions to 'do this!' or 'don't do that!' There are plenty of rules like that among both social norms and customary law. But what both sets of rules lack are any secondary rules—rules to authorize anyone to issue those orders, or to dictate how anyone can change or apply or authoritatively interpret those primary rules. That absence is what Hart sees as the characteristic feature of customary law. That is what I shall be focusing upon as the neglected feature of social norms.

The aims of this article are firstly to point out that fact about social norms and secondly to trace out the implications of living under a set of primary-without-secondary rules. How can people 'doing it by and for themselves' manage to perform the various functions that are performed by way of secondary rules in more developed legal systems? And what peculiar practices must people adopt when op-

---

[*] An earlier version of this chapter was presented at the ECPR Joint Sessions in Lisboa in April 2009. I am grateful for comments, then and later, from Joel Anderson, Michael Baurmann, Lina Eriksson, Nic Southwood and Kai Spiekermann.
[1] As Weber (1947, 126) says, writing of uncodified systems of social order, "For sociological purposes there does not exist, as there does for the law, a rigid alternative between the validity and the lack of a validity of a given order."
[2] Hart systematically refers to 'sets' of primary-without-secondary rules, supposing it is the existence of secondary rules that transforms a 'set' into a 'system' of rules; but here I shall use the two terms interchangeably.

289

erating in such unstructured normative environments, to avoid costly errors and misunderstandings?[3]

1.

Some aspects of the problem of how to operate in a world of primary-without-secondary rules are fairly straightforward. At least they are in theory, however hard they may be solve in practice.

How do you get a new rule adopted in the absence of any secondary rule of recognition that specifies when some new rule has been formally adopted? Well, you simply get enough other people around to you to say it is a rule.

In a developed legal system, there would be a rule of recognition that is itself backed by serious social pressure from some sufficiently substantial portion of the community. It is by reference to that rule of recognition that we would decide what the primary rules of that system are (Hart 1961, 84–5). In the absence of any rule of recognition, the same thing that would have made the rule of recognition the secondary rule—serious social pressure from some sufficiently substantial portion of the community—is required to underwrite each and every primary rule of the system.

A cognate question is how to get some particular interpretation of the rule established, in the absence of any secondary rule appointing authorized interpreters. Again, you simply get enough other people to say that that is the right interpretation. Roughly speaking, that is how the common law emerges—and the common law is of course merely the customary law of the courts (Simpson 1973). One judge issues a ruling, and other judges go on to rule in like manner.

Or again, how do you change the rules, in the absence of any secondary rule specifying how to amend the first-order primary rules? Again, you must simply get enough other people around you to say that that is the new rule.

The dynamics of all this are intensely interesting, and there are various particular forms that they might take. Sometimes the process involves a fairly formal two-stage process, whereby in the first stage you go around collecting 'I will if you will' promises from all and sundry, and in the second stage you go around collecting on all those 'conditional promises' (Frohlick/Oppenheimer/Young 1971). International negotiations often look something like that. Think for example of the sequence of treaties governing emission of ozone-depleting CFCs: first there was the 1985 Vienna Convention for the Protection of the Ozone Layer promising to do something, then there was the 1987 Montreal Protocol on Substances that Deplete the Ozone Layer that actually committed signatories to (moderately) binding targets.[4]

---

3 In a companion paper, I address similar issues as they arise with customary international law. See Goodin (2005).
4 I discuss the differences between these two agreements more fully in Goodin (1990).

More often, the dynamics depend on bandwagon-style mechanisms driven by differential sensitivities.[5] Some people suppose that something is a norm only if 80 percent of the relevant community say it is. Those people are going to be among the last to be won over. But there are some people who suppose that something is a norm if only 40 percent of the community say it is. And there are others who suppose that something is a norm if only 10 percent of community say it is (not unreasonably, provided everyone else is indifferent either way). So you start the bandwagon rolling by getting people with low thresholds to agree; and as more of them come on board you cross progressively higher thresholds triggering yet more people to agree, until you eventually have everyone agreeing. It is a classic case of a 'normative cascade'.[6]

As stories told about how norms get established, these are familiar ones. That is much the most discussed part of the problem of how to manage a in a world of primary-without-secondary rules. But as I have said, the same sorts of stories can probably be pretty readily adapted to provide answers to the allied questions of how norms get interpreted and how they get changed.

2.

For the remainder of this article, let us focus on the *changing* of primary-without-secondary rules, and the peculiar problems that that poses.

In a system with proper secondary rules, there are mechanisms for changing the primary rules of the system. The processes that those secondary rules prescribe may be slow and cumbersome, or they may be quick and efficient. Contrast, for example, the arduous amending of a constitution with the instantaneous rescinding of an Executive Order.

In a system that does not have any secondary rules, changing the primary rules will *necessarily* be a slow and tedious process. There, the only way rule-change can ultimately happen is by some people beginning to follow different primary rules of conduct and enough other people then following suit. Of course, you can do all sorts of things to encourage them to follow suit, talking up the proposed new norm and such like. But talk up the proposed new norm as you will, it does not actually become the new norm unless and until enough people actually start complying with it. As with making rules, so too with re-making rules, in a system of primary-without-secondary rules: "we must [simply] wait and see whether a rule gets accepted as a rule or not." (Hart 1961, 229) And that invariably takes a fair bit of time.

The 'stickiness' of social norms—their slowness to change—is of course a familiar feature that has already attracted much comment. Here I offer yet one more explanation. Systems of primary-without-secondary rules are always slow and cumber-

---

5   On bandwagons more generally, see Brams (1978).
6   And they are more stable in this form than the ones Timur Kuran writes about in, for example, Kuran (1998).

some to change, giving them something of a 'static character'.[7] Norms are conspicuous examples of such systems. That is one reason (doubtless among many others) that for the familiar 'stickiness' we observe in social norms.

A further fact emerges from the absence of secondary rules for changing social norms. Anyone who attempts to introduce changes in such rules inevitably finds herself in the precarious plight of having her actions easily misinterpreted.

In the absence of secondary rules, how do you go about proposing changes to the system of rules? There is no formal procedure for 'moving an amendment'. Without secondary rules, ultimately the only way to 'formally' move an amendment to change to a rule is to break that rule.[8] Of course you hope your new pattern of behaviour will eventually catch on and becomes the new rule. But in the meanwhile—and certainly in first instance—you will inevitably be breaking the rule.

Assuming some serious social pressure stands behind rules as they currently stand, that sets a potentially serious penalty on proposing changes in this, the only way one can, to systems of primary-without-secondary rules. That further exacerbates the static character of such systems (Akerlof 1984).

Not only is there a serious disincentive of that sort facing anyone who proposes changes in systems of primary-without-secondary rules. There is also a serious difficulty facing others trying to interpret their behaviour and to frame their own reactions in response.

Such observers need to know whether the rule-breaker is just a common-garden rule-breaker or whether she is hoping to become a rule-(re)maker. In the former case, her behaviour should be sanctioned and her model shunned. In the latter case, observers should at least consider whether the rule-breaker's proposed rule-revision has merit, and whether hers is a model that should be emulated. But in systems of primary-without-secondary rules, it can be hard to distinguish between breaches of primary rules that are intended as proposals for alterations to those rules and breaches that are just plain breaches with no such implication.

---

7   As Hart remarks, bemoaning the 'static character' of systems of primary-without-secondary rules, "The only mode of change in the rules [...] will be the slow process of growth, whereby courses of conduct once thought optional become first habitual or usual, and then obligatory, and the converse process of decay, when deviations, once severely dealt with, are first tolerated and then pass unnoticed. There will be no means [...] of deliberately adapting the rules to changing circumstances, either by eliminating old rules or introducing new ones: for, again, the possibility of doing this presupposes the existence of rules of a different type from the primary rules of obligation by which alone the society lives." (1961, 90)
8   Of course you can 'talk it up' as discussed above. That's just what I'll be exploring below. But actually to *move* the amendment requires a breach, and that motion is subsequently ratified if and only if others follow suit.

3.

Where people have to breach a rule to propose changing that rule, yet another complication arises. Sometimes a person breaches a rule without in any way wanting the rule to be changed. But precisely because breaching is the way changes are proposed, the breach might easily be misunderstood as advocating alteration. Elaborate rituals are required to forestall that misinterpretation.

Consider the contrasting case of breaching primary rules of a legal system with a fully panoply of secondary rules for making, interpreting and altering the primary rules. There, there is considerably less scope for misunderstanding what a breach is supposed to imply.

To be sure, breach of laws *is* sometimes meant to signal that the laws should be changed. Sometimes there is indeed an orchestrated refusal to obey some particular enactment, with a view to proving it unworkable. Classic cases of civil disobedience are like that (more of which later).

Much more ordinarily, however, breach is just plain breach, and nothing further for the larger legal system is supposed to follow from that. For the most dramatic illustration of that what I will call 'callous breach', consider the theory of 'efficient breach' proposed by Richard Posner and the Chicago School of Law and Economics more generally (Posner 1972, 57–61).

The Chicago thought is just this. If you can afford to pay the legally-prescribed penalty for breaking a law, and still be better off than you would have been complying with the law, then the efficient thing for you to do is to breach the law. That is not merely the efficient thing from your personal point of view. Assuming the legally-prescribed penalties have been set properly—by which economically-minded lawyers mean, in such a way as to reflect the full social costs of your breach—then it would be most efficient from the point of view of society as a whole for its members to break the law.[9]

'Efficient breach' doctrine was developed with reference to, and makes most sense as applied to, the law of contracts. There, it is quite uncommon for courts to compel 'specific performance', and require that the contracting parties do exactly what they contracted to do. More typically, courts merely require payment of monetary damages for breach of contract, in sums sufficient to compensate the wronged party for the loss of what was contractually owed. That really does make it look very much as if you are being invited (or anyway permitted) to breach your contract whenever it would be cheaper for you to pay the damages than it would be for you to perform as promised.

But taking the Chicago Law and Economics programme to its logical conclusion, there is no reason that 'efficient breach' ought be applied to contracts alone. Other

---

9 You could pay the penalties and still come out ahead—that is all that is required to say that it is socially efficient for you to breach. That is not necessarily to say that you actually should pay the penalties—that, economists would say, is a separate distributional question which is outside the realm of efficiency.

branches of the law—torts and especially criminal law—assess punitive damages as well as or instead of compensatory ones. Nonetheless, the same principle should still apply. If the penalties have been set properly, and reflect the full social 'cost' of your breaching the law, then it would be efficient (socially, and not just personally) for you to breach the law whenever complying would cost you more.

Of course, there are plenty of people—legal scholars and ordinary folk alike—who would be aghast at this theory of efficient breach. 'Contracts are promises', they would say, 'and as such they should be kept even when inconvenient' (Fried 1981). All the more, they might insist: 'The criminal law is not just a price schedule; it is a set of prescriptions for behaviour.' And while everyone may agree that a violator who has 'paid her debt to society' should be reintegrated into society rather than shunned forever, the breach of law was wrong in ways that can never be put fully to right by payment of the penalties.

I introduce the theory of efficient breach of law not to take sides in that controversy. My aim is merely to point out that that would be a much more plausible (even if perhaps ultimately wrong) way to think about breaching laws that have a full panoply of secondary rules behind them than it would be of thinking about the breach of norms lacking any secondary rules.

Such a callous breach of primary rules is more viable where there are secondary rules standing behind them, precisely because there is no danger there that one's breaking the rule will be misconstrued as a proposal for changing the rule. A separate set of procedures is in place for making and considering proposals of that sort.

In systems of primary-without-secondary rules, there are no such procedures in place. There, the way you change a rule is to break it. In consequence, anyone who breaks a rule might well be (mis)understood as proposing a change to the rule. If the rule-breaker wants to avoid that implication, she has to go to extraordinary lengths to 'honour the rule in the breach', explaining why that is the right rule to follow even if due to some extraordinary circumstances she now finds herself breaking it.

'Conscientious' as contrasted with 'callous' rule-breaking is thus required in systems of primary-without-secondary rules. In such systems, people cannot merely let their actions speak for themselves. Instead they must conjoin their actions with explanations of what is meant by them. There may be some default assumption—perhaps, for example, that breaking a rule will be taken as a suggestion for changing the rule, unless any further explanation is offered (or maybe the opposite). But if you want your rule-breaking not to be understood that way, you must actually say so. And insofar as there is a real risk of different observers operating according to different default assumptions, you all the more emphatically had better actually say what you mean to convey by your breach.

That, I suggest, is one of the principal things (doubtless again among many others) that gives rise to the sort of elaborate account-giving that so often surround breaches of social norms and mores (Mills 1940; Tilly 2006). Of course, people try to wiggle off the hook when caught in violation of a legal obligation as well. But the touch and tone is characteristically quite different. When offering excuses or entering pleas in mitigation in cases of legal breaches, people focus primarily on their own special circumstances. Again, of course people do some of that when explaining why they have breached social norms as well (more of which below). But people violating a norm often go to great lengths to emphasize their endorsement of the value and importance of the norm they have violated, in a way that is much less common in cases of broken laws.

The closest we find to that in the formal legal system is the discourse of civil disobedience. There is an important difference, of course: what the civil disobedient is emphatically reaffirming is her allegiance to the larger legal system, not the very law (banning blacks from riding in the front of the bus, or whatever) that she is insistently disobeying. With social norms, there is no 'larger system'.[10] Still, the attitude of 'conscientiousness' attending the breach is similar.

In the discourse of civil disobedience, 'conscientious' means two things. The first is that the breach of law was motivated by a 'claim of conscience' (morality rather than material self-interest, for example). The second is that the law was breached 'conscientiously', publicly and in a way that pays due respect to the larger legal system.[11] A canonical statement of that appears in the *Letter from Birmingham City Jail* by Martin Luther King, Jr.:

> One who breaks an unjust law must do it openly, lovingly [...], and with a willingness to accept the penalty. I submit that an individual who breaks a law that conscience tells him is unjust, and willingly accepts the penalty by staying in jail to arouse the conscience of the community over its injustice, is in reality expressing the very highest respect for law. (Reprinted in Bedau 1969, 78–79)

Note that there is definitely something a little odd in saying that you respect the larger legal system at the same time as finding this particular enactment utterly unconscionable. How could it *fail* to reflect badly on the larger system of lawmaking that it resulted in this enactment that my conscience finds so intolerable?

That issue does not arise with social norms, of course. There, there is no system of secondary rules for you respect. There is only a bunch of unconnected primary rules. In such circumstances, what might violators of a norm be professing respect for, as they set about 'conscientiously' violating the norm in question? Maybe they could be swearing full allegiance to all the *other* primary rules, whilst refusing to comply with this particular one. But if those really are just a whole pile of other unrelated norms, you would not be professing allegiance to any larger system of norms. You would just be professing allegiance to a long list of unconnected commandments.

'Honouring a norm in the breach' is thus importantly different from 'honouring a law in the breach'. Once again, that is precisely because social norms, unlike laws, are not embedded within a system of primary plus secondary rules. There is in con-

---

10 Defined in terms of second-order rules anyway.
11 Hugo A. Bedau (1961) writes: "Civil disobedience is necessarily *public*" (656); and "Conscientiousness [...] requires that the dissenter acknowledge that the law, no matter what it is, makes some claim on his obedience, no matter how readily this claim may be overriden by other claims." (660) See similarly Cohen (1971, 16–22).

sequence no 'larger system' to honour, while breaching some subordinate part of it. In the unsystematized world of primary-without-secondary rules, there are no subordinate or superordinate parts of the normative environment. It is all on one plane.

When honouring social norms in the breach, therefore, you must engage in the more florid and rhetorical displays associated with civil disobedience. You acknowledge the rule that you are breaking, and (*modulo* what I shall go on to say below) you openly acknowledge that you are indeed breaking it. You engage in lots of hand-wringing, you go on and on about how hard the decision was, how very atypical were the circumstances in which you found yourself. You promise faithfully comply with the norm under other circumstances in the future, and you entreat others to do likewise. You emphasize that your action should not be taken as a precedent by others.

Such displays would of course be transparently disingenuous if you engaged in them too often. So to be taken as sincere, your breaches and accompanying protestations must be relatively rare. But if sufficiently rare, you might in this way be able to convince (enough) others that you really did not mean to propose a change to the norm or undermine others' adherence to it, through your own violation of it.

Of course, breaching a norm can be contagious, even when the breaching party does not intend for her model to be emulated. In any Prisoner's Dilemma or Public Goods game, when other people defect from cooperative patterns of play, you do likewise—not so much to punish them as to protect yourself. In iterated N-person games of that sort, the more people who defected in the previous round, the more others who will defect in the next, and so on until a new 'norm' of non-cooperation is established—much to the chagrin of everyone (not least the initial defector's).

So 'misunderstanding' of the signal that the norm-violator meant to send by her violation of the norm is not the only risk to worry about, here. That sort of 'unraveling' of a norm can easily occur, even if there was no misunderstanding.

My point here is merely that misunderstanding is easy, in the realm of social norms—and that can easily lead to the undermining of norms, even when the strategic structure of the situation would not itself lead to this sort of unraveling.

4.

'Honouring a rule in the breach' is thus a device whereby you hope to persuade others to persist in their adherence to a rule that you yourself violate. What sort of story can you tell to make it plausible that they should abide by it at the same time as you should (or should be allowed to) violate it?

One of the things that you insistently say, in such situations is, that this is not exactly the sort of case covered by the rule. The civil disobedient often says, along these lines, that the law she is breaking is 'not really law'. In his letter to fellow clergymen, Dr. King claimed that the law that he violated was not really law because it contravened God's law (*ibid.*, 77). Other civil disobedients claim that the laws they violate are not laws because they violates are contrary to the Constitution or federal statutes that override state law. Or, if they had been reading too much early Dworkin, civil disobedients might say that the laws they violate are not laws because they are contrary to the 'principles' underlying the legal 'rules' (Dworkin 1967). And as with laws, so too with norms.

The more interesting case comes when someone concedes that she is genuinely violating a rule, but insists that the rule is the right rule regardless—not 'for others but not herself' but for herself as well. How can one plausibly assert both that it is the right rule and that it is all right to violate the rule?

One way that argument might work is through some appeal to 'weakness of will'. You concede that it is the right rule, but you simply cannot bring yourself to act upon it. Or, as a variation on that theme, you might say that some very special features of your present circumstances make the rule 'overly demanding' for you in those circumstances.

Here is a second and more interesting way that argument might work. Both laws and social norms are necessarily rules that are general in form. They are designed to cover lots of cases of a standard sort. There will inevitably be very particular circumstances where the 'spirit of the rule' would indeed require a different resolution. But rules work best if stated simply and easy to access intuitively. So there is a very good reason for not building absolutely all exceptions—however infrequently they might arise—into the rule.

Hence it is perfectly plausible for me to say that both (a) my case is an exception to the rule and also (b) I think it would be wrong for all such exceptions literally to be written into the rule. That is the sort of situation in which you honour the rule in the breach. You agree you are breaching the rule as it stands; you agree that that is precisely what the rule should be, rather than appealing for any amendment to incorporate your exceptional circumstances. Yet you also argue that your breach is to be condoned, somehow.

5.

It is a characteristic feature of norms is that they are 'orders without authority'. Like customary law, norms are systems of primary rules without secondary rules governing how to make them, interpret them or change them.

Given that there is no authority—no *grundnorm*, no secondary rule—standing behind them, norms must be established and re-established by being reiterated on each occasion. Honouring in the breach is a way of reaffirming the a norm, even whilst breaching it.

Bibliography

Akerlof, G. (1984), A Theory of Social Custom, of which Unemployment May Be One Consequence, in: *An Economic Theorist's Book of Tales*, Cambridge, 69–100

Bedau, H. A. (1961), On Civil Disobedience, in: *Journal of Philosophy 58*, 653–665

— (1969) (ed.), *Civil Disobedience*, New York

Brams, S. J. (1978), *The Presidential Election Game*, New Haven

Cohen, C. (1971), *Civil Disobedience: Conscience, Tactics and the Law*, New York

Dworkin, R. M. (1967), The Model of Rules, in: *University of Chicago Law Review 35*, 14–46

Fried, Ch. (1981), *Contract as Promise*, Cambridge/MA

Frohlick, N./J. A. Oppenheimer/O. R. Young (1971), *Political Leadership and Collective Goods*, Princeton

Goodin, R. E. (1990), International Ethics and the Environmental Crisis, in: *Ethics & International Affairs 4*, 91–105

— (2005), Toward an International Rule of Law: Distinguishing International Law-breakers from Would-be Law-makers, in: *The Journal of Ethics 9*, 225–46

Hart, H. L. A. (1961), *The Concept of Law*, Oxford

Kuran, T. (1998), Ethnic Norms and Their Transformation through Reputational Cascades, in: *Journal of Legal Studies 27(2)*, 623–59

Mills, C. W. (1940), Situated Actions and Vocabularies of Motive, in: *American Sociological Review 5*, 904–13

Posner, R. A. (1972), *Economic Analysis of Law*, Boston

Simpson, A. W. B. (1973), The Common Law and Legal Theory, in: A. W. B Simpson (ed.), *Oxford Essays in Jurisprudence*, 2nd series, Oxford, 77–99

Tilly, Ch. (2006), *Why?*, Princeton

Weber, M. (1947), *Theory of Social & Economic Organization*. Trans. A. M. Henderson and T. Parsons, New York

Holly Lawford-Smith

The Importance of Being Earnest, and the Difficulty of Faking It
A Comment on Robert Goodin

1. Introduction

Goodin's *Norms Honoured in the Breach* is the companion to his earlier paper *Toward an International Rule of Law: Distinguishing International Law-Breakers from Would-Be Law Makers* (2005). In the domestic context there are set procedures for legal reform, so the straightforward way to distinguish law breakers from would-be law-makers (i.e. those seeking legal reform) would be to look at whether they break the existing laws, or instead take the appropriate steps to change the existing laws. But international law is an interesting case, because there is little by way of set procedure for reform—and in fact little by way of genuine law, if you think that enforceability is necessary to render law 'genuine'. One way to push for legal reform in a system with no set procedures for doing so is to *break* the law. But that poses an interesting question: how can we tell when a state is simply breaking international law, and how can we tell when it is pushing for international law reform? In his (2005) paper Goodin considers several answers to that question, arguing in general that would-be lawmakers will break the law publicly, accept the accompanying sanctions, and accept the legitimacy of other states acting in the same way for the same reasons. Presumably, would-be law-making is normatively acceptable, under the same conditions that conscientious objection in the domestic case is normatively acceptable.

In his article in this volume, Goodin exploits his earlier work, extending the conditions that distinguish a would-be lawmaker to cover domestic norm breakers. The paper might be read uncharitably as a handy 'how to' guide for the would-be social cheater. Goodin offers his readers some useful tips: don't break norms too often, or your excuses will start to seem disingenuous; make sure to sincerely protest your special reasons for breaking the norm, and your otherwise firm commitment to it; and it wouldn't hurt to throw in a little hand-wringing for effect. In short, the lesson is that the very behaviour that makes both international and domestic law-breaking normatively acceptable can be emulated to allow successful social defection. Very well. Goodin has adopted the perspective of the social agent concerned to cheat and get away with it; here I shall take the perspective of the society concerned to identify the threat of such ingenious defectors. The discussion shall proceed covering two central questions. Firstly, I'll ask whether there's actually anything wrong with the odd well-disguised defection. If there's not, maybe there's nothing that society needs to protect itself from. Secondly, I'll discuss the likelihood of society actually being confronted by Goodin-style cheaters. I will draw upon arguments of the evolutionary biologists to suggest firstly that sincerity of the kind Goodin proposes is hard to fake, and secondly that norm-breaking, whether accompanied by justification or not, might still signal unreliability as a cooperative partner.

2. What's Wrong with a Little Defection Every Now and Then?

Whenever there is large-scale cooperation without the presence of a central authority, norms are usually wheeled in to explain it. But what is a norm? To some extent any definition depends on a theorist's purposes. Sociologists might prefer to define norms in terms of expectations, or values, while philosophers might prefer a behavioural definition. Robert Axelrod, in one of the early studies using game theory to analyze cooperation, preferred a behavioural definition on the grounds that it allowed us to infer the presence of a norm from behaviour, and it permitted our being able to say that norms were present to greater or lesser degrees (Axelrod 1984; 1986). Philip Pettit more recently defines a norm in similarly behavioural terms as "a regularity that actually prevails among members of a group" (Pettit 2008). He qualifies that by adding that the behavioural regularity must attract a high approval rating, where the high approval rating should help to explain why the norm is generally instantiated. That a regularity satisfies those three conditions should in general be a matter of common awareness.

Consider two quite different cases involving norms. In the first case, a homosexual couple choose to challenge a firmly-held social norm against public displays of homosexual affection by walking through their town centre holding hands. In the second case, a student chooses to fly from Berlin to London rather than taking the train, despite a strong social norm in favour of environmentally friendly travel. What should be immediately obvious is the different normative status of each of these acts. The homosexual couple breaks the norm against public display of homosexual affection in the hope of changing it. Most people would agree that such a norm is oppressive and lacks reasonable justification, and would therefore welcome both the challenge to it and the possibility that the challenge trigger a 'normative cascade' whereupon more and more people defect from the norm in question. In general, we think that the breaking of discriminatory or otherwise pernicious social norms is a good thing. The second case is quite different. The norm is in place for a reason, namely that countries *must* lower their carbon emissions. Moreover, the student doesn't break the norm because she particularly wants to change it. We can suppose that she doesn't care much either way, or that she prefers other people to conform to the norm so long as she can be the exception. Whatever it is, we think there's something wrong with the fact that she breaks the norm, not least because of the risk, which Goodin discusses extensively, of her defection triggering similar behaviour in others. In general, we think the breaking of fair or otherwise desirable social norms is a bad thing.

Goodin's focus is squarely upon cases of this second kind. He wants to investigate the possibility of a person breaking a norm while avoiding the risks of triggering defection in others. In game-theoretic terms, he takes the perspective of an economically self-interested player in a cooperation game. The dominant strategy in many such games (or at least the dominant strategy for someone unlikely to have future interactions with his fellow players and lacking preferences for anything other than the accumulation of economic goods) is to cheat. That strategy obtains the maximum possible payoff. But in real world terms, the defection can't be admitted to be such, because that would be to invite retaliation, or at least imitation. That would likely put a fragile arrangement such as conditional cooperation to produce some public good (or worse, and more topically, to not lose some fundamental public good which is under threat) at risk of systemic collapse. Hence the title of this section, 'what's wrong with a little defection now and then?' Obviously it's at least sometimes, if not always, permissible to break pernicious social norms; but it's not obvious that it's permissible to break the good ones. 'Defection' is a term usually reserved for the latter, i.e. social transgressions generally contrary to public or collective welfare.

Whether you think there's anything wrong with a little defection every now and then will depend largely on background views about norms, duties, and obligations. A preliminary question to ask involves the connection between social norms and moral duties. It can't be that it is morally obligatory to obey all social norms, because we've already considered cases of pernicious social norms where we think the right thing to do is to break them, in the hope of changing them. But it might be that certain social norms are grounded in the right reasons, like recently developing norms toward more environmentally-friendly behaviour. Assuming that it is morally obligatory to obey some subset of social norms, e.g. the good ones, it still doesn't follow that *everyone* has to obey them. This is where things will depend on the controversial nature of rules and obligations. If you think obligations are categorical and exceptionless then you'll think the person who breaks a positive social norm has morally transgressed. If you think rules and obligations are hypothetical and conditional, then you might not think there is moral transgression at stake in a defection. And regardless of whether you think there's a moral debt being incurred, there's a practical question of harm done.

That is to say, if we're strict consequentialists, then the important questions are about outcomes. Obviously if a person defects on a positive social norm and triggers a normative cascade such that the norm collapses, they've done potentially irreparable damage. But Goodin's point is that the would-be defector can emulate the strategies of the conscientious objector and the international law re-maker in order to avoid precisely that outcome. And if he does that, then the only damage done is the moral damage of his own transgression, which might look fairly minor compared with the alternative just considered.

The problem is that there will be cases where non-compliance with a norm creates a remainder, and cases where it does not. In cases where, say, there is a norm of praying at morning meals, the fact that one person alone stops doing this has no effect on anyone else. That kind of case is a perfect candidate for the kind of response that says a little defection every now and again doesn't matter. The only harm accrued is to the person who broke the norm. But more often we will be dealing with cases where defection means that a person fails to do their fair share, which will entail that the rest of a community of cooperators have to absorb the cost of defection. If one person always buys the tea and coffee for the tea room, and another person never puts the agreed donation in the money jar, the person doing the buying is forced to absorb the defector's costs. If everyone in a flat agrees to go without heaters to drive the cost of the electricity bill down, and one person surreptitiously defects, the others will have to pay costs for which they receive no benefit. And so on. Where duties are divisible among persons and there is defection, the defector's duties will accrue to others. That means others must do more than their fair share, which affects their welfare compared to those who have to do a normal share, and especially compared to the defector who took no share at all. We can get around at least a subset of these cases by doing theory that assumes imperfect compliance (which anyone designing policy in the real world does, although some would argue that perfect compliance is just a matter of arranging the costs and incentives in the right way). Then the important thing is to figure out how much defection a policy can withstand, and to find ways to keep cooperation above that level. The only risk of that kind of set-up is that if people know that not everyone has to cooperate, there'll be a kind of 'race to the bottom' in order to be the one to get the fruits of cooperation without paying the price.

One final thought on this point is that rather than taking Goodin's discussion to be a 'how to' guide for the would-be defector, a more charitable interpretation might be that he hopes to persuade the would-be defector to minimize damage to collective endeavors. He tells the would-be cheater that there's more at stake than her own selfish preferences; he asks her to consider the *effects* which her cheating might have, the greatest of which is the potential normative cascade. Or indeed he tells the person who genuinely *is* an exception to a norm and is excused in violating it how to avoid being misinterpreted (this reading is consistent with his talk of 'conscientious' contrasted with 'callous' rule-breaking). This cascade was a good thing in the case of norms in need of reform, but stands to be potentially disastrous in the case of norms allowing for social cooperation. Instead of reading him as saying 'cheat if you like, and here's a good way to get away with it!' then, we might read him as saying 'if you must cheat, or already have done, you ought at least to minimize the damage ... and here's how'. The risk is that too many people cheat-and-minimize-the-damage, which places the norm at risk. In the next section, we will look in more detail at that risk.

3. Goodin-style Cheaters in the Real World

To what extent should we expect to find Goodin-style cheaters in the real world? Let's take another look at what is required of his defector:

> When honouring social norms in the breach, therefore, you must engage in the more florid and rhetorical displays associated with civil disobedience. You acknowledge the rule that

you are breaking, and (*modulo* what I shall go on to say below) you openly acknowledge that you are indeed breaking it. You engage in lots of hand-wringing, you go on and on about how hard the decision was, how very atypical were the circumstances in which you found yourself. You promise to faithfully comply with the norm under other circumstances in the future, and you entreat others to do likewise. You emphasize that your action should not be taken as a precedent by others. (296)

Goodin's would-be norm-breaker must publicly acknowledge that he's breaking the norm (presumably because protestations are not so convincing if caught trying to get away with something), must appear visibly distressed, must make convincing promises about the future, must persuade others not to follow his defection. He must have the charm to pull all of this off without arousing suspicion. In terms of acknowledging the rule that is being broken, Goodin suggests five ways of escaping the obligation. a) Say that the norm people follow is not the 'true' norm, while the one you followed is, perhaps appealing to God as the Author of the true norms. The problem with this escape is that if others believe you, they're likely to want to follow the true norm too, thus triggering the normative cascade, and if they don't believe you, they'll take you as defecting, which opens up the possibility of their like defection (but doesn't necessitate it; they might think you made an honest mistake). Either way, there's a risk of norm collapse. b) Say you're adhering to the principles that underly norms, perhaps principles about social cohesion. But the response to this will be just the same as the response just given. c) Claim weakness of will, saying that the norm is a good one but you couldn't bring yourself to obey it. The problem with this excuse is that there's no reason why others shouldn't use it, and it won't fly in cases where the duty wasn't very difficult. d) Claim overdemandingness, saying that the norm is a good one but it only applies to people who can fulfill it, and you can't. This is similar to e) claim that you're an exception to the rule, but that you don't advocate rule change to allow for exceptions because you believe that rules should be general in form.

Both (d) and (e) raise the question of whether obligations are conditional or unconditional in form. If they are unconditional, then neither excuse will work. 'Impossible' isn't the same as 'really hard', and the response will just be that you're required to do your duty (e.g. obey the norm) whether you find it difficult or not; overdemandingness should be reserved for cases where a duty is strictly impossible for an agent to fulfill. And claiming to be an exception won't work either, because if the rule was meant to allow for exceptions you might expect people to generally act in a way consistent with there being exceptions, and not be angered by defections that obviously occur in special circumstances (although perhaps the real difficulty here is the opacity of people's reasons for action). But it can't be that *all* of our obligations are conditional instead. If that's true, then it means that only if conditions x and y are satisfied, do I have an obligation to do z. If a person is robbed and I am the only person around, then I have an obligation to help them. But that creates two problems.

Firstly, it would commit us to thinking that there are no unconditional obligations, for instance to help people in need. Secondly, it would seriously violate Occam's Razor and clutter up our moral ontology. Rather than a limited set of unconditional principles covering infinite actual cases, we'd find ourselves with an infinite set of complicated conditional requirements, designed to cover all possible eventualities and say what is required of people under each of them. Surely even if most of our obligations are conditional, there are some unconditional requirements, or there is a way of expressing the conditional requirements in a way that makes them general (perhaps we can do without a conditional operator and express them as primitives). If our obligations do work in this way, then (d) and (e) stand a chance of succeeding. Then the argument would be that the norm in question applies to cases meeting criteria p and q, which are met for most people most of the time, but not for cases meeting criteria n—which may well be that fulfilling the norm would be too difficult—which you yourself happen to meet. The obvious limit on this kind of defection is that there just won't be that many plausible excuses, exceptions which other people don't also fall into. People who find themselves in a similar situation can either take themselves to be excused from obeying the norm, or take you to not be. This is a good thing so far as society is concerned, because it is likely that it can absorb the rare impact of norm-breaking in exceptional circumstances. It is less good news for the social cheater concerned to exploit Goodin's conditions to his own advantage, because it means opportunities will be extremely infrequent.

In *Passions within Reason*, Robert Frank argues that certain signs of reliability, such as those Goodin's cheater would have to perform, are hard to fake. He introduces three principles of signaling. Firstly, for something to function as a reliable signal, it must be difficult (or costly) to fake. The example he uses is the reliable correlation in toads between their size and the depth of their croak, and how physical limitations simply prevent a very small toad from emitting a very deep croak. Secondly, having some characteristic must have benefitted the first individual who had it, and this will usually mean that signals evolved for reasons unrelated to the signaling benefit they came to have. Thirdly, the fact that someone signals positive information forces others into full disclosure about their own quality, because if they remain silent they will be assumed to be worse that they actually are.

> The general message of this full-disclosure principle is that a lack of evidence that something resides in a favoured category will often suggest that it belongs in a less favoured one. (Frank 1988, ch. 5; see also Akerlof 1970)

Frank distinguishes passive from deliberate signals, arguing that all three conditions must hold in the case of the former, and only the first and last in the case of the latter. Because Goodin's cheater will be attempting a deliberate signal of trustworthiness and sincerity (breaking the norm but attempting to justify the breach) we should look more closely at how hard to fake that might be.

Frank runs through a whole host of physical events that occur to people under stress, and that happen under occurrence of genuine emotion but can be deliberately manipulated only by very few people. The underlying idea is that certain types of physical responses are instinctual (he uses the example of a dog preparing to fight, with its hair standing on end, teeth bared, back arched, and muscles tense), and that imitating them will be slow and difficult. There are what psychologists call 'reliable' facial muscles, which only a small portion of the population can control. For instance the downward pull of the mouth without movement of muscles in the chin can be achieved deliberately by only about 10% of the population, but we all make that movement automatically when experiencing grief (Frank 1988, ch. 6). Also difficult is the eyebrows raised and furrowed associated with sadness, grief and distress (which about 15% of people can control), the eyebrows raised and pulled together associated with fear and terror (which less than 10% can control), eliminating the fleeting micro-expressions which will cross the face before the deliberate expressions can replace them, holding a steady gaze, non-dilation of pupils, blinking at regular speed, normal levels of mouth moisture (the mouth dries under stress, which can show up in pronunciation), avoiding blushing, and managing regular modulation of voice, because experiments show that about 70% of subjects' voices go up in pitch when emotionally upset (Frank 1988, ch. 6; see also Ekman 1985).

Frank suggests that perhaps the best way for a cheater to cheat successfully, i.e. to avoid giving the game away with any of these manifold physical slips, is to deceive himself into thinking he really *is* innocent of cheating, or really *did* have a good reason that made him an exception to the social norm or rule. But the problem Frank points out is that self-deception must sacrifice guilt (if you believe you were right in cheating, then you can't simultaneously feel guilty for cheating). And if a person cannot express guilt, then they will be assumed not to feel it at all (by the full-disclosure principle).

A further complication Frank suggests for the cheater is that experimental evidence shows people to have a tendency toward discounting negative possibilities if they are in the distant future as opposed to the near future. This means that when confronted with an opportunity to cheat (even one with a high likelihood of getting caught) many people will be tempted to take the risk, knowing that they will receive *now* the short term benefit of whatever goods their cheating gains them. Frank suggests that a good reputation can nonetheless function as a reliable indicator of trustworthiness because the reliable person will have internalized a preference against cheating, in which case the potential guilt from doing so will sufficiently offset the short-term gains that cheating promises. Someone who is fine with cheating will have no such off-setting mechanism, and therefore be more likely to cheat, and so more likely to get caught, thus risking their reputation. Returning momentarily to the charitable and uncharitable readings of Goodin, the consequences of sincerity being hard to fake will be different for each. The cheater really is faking, so he is subject to the difficulties just discussed in a way the genuine exception (or the person who takes themselves to be a genuine exception) is not. And the harder sincerity is to fake, the more we can be sure that the only norm-breakers getting away with norm-breaking will be those who genuinely 'honour the norm in the breach'.

It has been fairly well-established that one way to stabilize human cooperation is to punish those who defect on a cooperative scheme. But punishment itself creates a public goods problem: punishing is costly to the individual punisher, but the benefit of punishing accrues to the whole group (although this does depend on the kind of sanctions involved. Alienating someone or restricting their liberty will be much more costly than merely expressing disesteem toward them, which might be cost less). Costly signaling theory, the main rival of both strong and conditional reciprocity theories, suggests that the sanctioning of individuals who defect on their collective obligations, or free-ride upon others' contributions, can act as a costly signal of the signaler's quality. Fairness norms act as a test of people's willingness or ability to pay their fair share, thus identifying defectors as unreliable or undesirable partners in cooperative ventures. Smith and Bliege Bird (2005; see also 2000) argue that defection from a prosocial norm might signal one of three things, depending on the context: inability to pay one's share, which is a signal of low quality, leading to reduced social status; withdrawal, if the cooperation is a competition for status; or flaunting the norm to signal superior social status or power, a reliable interpretation so long as violating the norm is more costly than paying one's share (Smith/Bliege Bird 2005, 136). They suggest that the enforcement of fairness norms may be as much about ensuring the reliability of signals, and the solution of status-competition games, as it is about the importance of ensuring equality itself (137). Along similar lines, Joseph Bulbulia has argued that following religious norms is a costly signal of altruistic intentions, making the signaler a more attractive cooperation partner (Bulbulia 2004), and Samuel Bowles and Herbert Gintis have argued that certain kinds of prosocial cooperation, including the unconditional sharing of resources, participating in group defense, and punishing norm violation, is a costly signal of being a worthy mate, coalition partner, or competitor (Bowles/Gintis 2001). Neither of these latter two explicitly defends the idea that accepting the costs of punishing normbreakers is an honest signal of quality, but to the extent that provision of punishment is just another public good which an elite few may provide to the whole group, the same arguments can be expected to apply.

One interesting issue to flag here is the distinction between merely obeying social norms that everyone else (or almost everyone) obeys, and obeying social norms that only an elite group can obey, e.g. where a few people provide a public good for the whole group. The idea is that costly signaling theory can explain how what looks like a puzzlingly altruistic set of actions, e.g. engaging in dangerous and physically demanding hunting to supply a communal feast (Smith/Bliege Bird 2000), or as suggested above, being the person willing to absorb the costs of punishing the noncooperators, can be explained by virtue of being a costly signal of quality, which will have benefits for the signaler. The person who defects on the first order norms runs a double risk. The first, as Smith and Bliege Bird suggested, is signaling unreliability as a cooperative partner, by virtue of defection meaning in inability or an unwillingness to pay the cost associated with obeying the norm. The second is the risk of being sanctioned by the second-order norm follower looking to signal quality by punishing first-order defection. And it's not necessarily the case that a convincing justification of the norm breach will avoid those risks, because it might be the case that the association between norm-breaking and cooperative unreliability has become automatic or instinctual as a cognitive heuristic to calculating the likelihood of being cheated.

4. Conclusion

Goodin suggests that precisely the kinds of behaviours that allow conscientious objectors and international law reformers to break norms without gaining a reputation as a norm-breaker in the pejorative sense could be emulated in the domestic case to allow successful defection from social norms. In this paper I have asked whether the kind of well-contained norm breaking he suggests is actually worth worrying about. I argued that it is, because of the burden it places on others in a context where defection creates a remainder. I have also asked whether Goodin-style defectors are likely to be common in the real world, and I argued, for various reasons stemming from the difficulty of faking sincerity of the kind required, and the risk that defection poses to the individual defector, that we can expect such cheating to be fairly rare.

Bibliography

Akerlof, G. (1970), The Market for Lemons, in: *Quarterly Journal of Economics 84*, 488–500

Axelrod, R. (1984), *The Evolution of Cooperation*, New York

— (1986), An Evolutionary Approach to Norms, in: *American Political Science Review 80*, 1095–1111

Bulbulia, J. (2004), Religious Costs as Adaptations that Signal Altruistic Intentions, in: *Evolution and Cognition 10(1)*, 19–42

Ekman, P. (1985), *Telling Lies*, New York

Frank, R. (1988), *Passions within Reason*, New York

Gintis, H./E. A. Smith/S. Bowles (2001), Costly Signalling and Cooperation, in: *Journal of Theoretical Biology 213(1)*, 103–119

Goodin, R. (2005), Toward an International Rule of Law: Distinguishing International Law-Breakers from Would-Be Law Makers, in: *The Journal of Ethics 9*, 225–246

Pettit, P. (2008), Norms, Commitment and Censure, paper presented at colloquium *Hart/Fuller 50 Years On*, Australian National University, Canberra, December 2008

Smith, E. A./R. Bliege Bird (2005), Costly Signalling and Co-operative Behaviour, in: H. Gintis/S. Bowles/R. Boyd/E. Fehr (eds.), *Moral Sentiments and Material Interests*, Massachusetts, 115–150

— / — (2000), Turtle Hunting and Tombstone Opening: Public Generosity as Costly Signalling, in: *Evolution and Human Behaviour 21*, 245–261

Russell Hardin

The Story of Qiu Ju[*]

1. Introduction

In *The Story of Qiu Ju*, Zhang Yimou presents the tale of a partially literate woman who is offended by her village Chief's abusive treatment of her husband, Wan Qinglai. Qinglai insults the Chief with the taunt that he only has hens, a grievous taunt in their culture, in which boys are highly valued and girls are not. They fight and Chief Shantang beats Qinglai and viciously kicks him in the groin. The beating itself might have been justified by the norms of the community, because Qinglai and Qiu Ju have illegally built a shed in which to store chili peppers, their main source of income. They have violated rules that keep land in productive agricultural use and that bar building structures without permission. But the vicious, injuring kick was clearly beyond the pale for Qiu Ju. It was unduly hurtful, offensive, and indecent, and she demands an apology for the action, which might damage her marriage and, if Qinglai's 'plumbing' is damaged, might even wreck the chance of her having a second child after the birth of the child she now visibly carries (*Story*, 00:05:16).[1] Her distended belly is often at the center of the screen and, to maintain her balance, she leans backwards as she walks. Qiu Ju and her sister-in-law Meizi take Qinglai in a two-wheel cart to the village to see a doctor. It is at this point that the movie begins, with the background told later.

In a decent society, the Chief would be expected to apologize for his action and would show proper humility to restore his relationship with Qiu Ju and Qinglai. In an abstract urban society, the focus is commonly on the regularity of decent behavior and therefore on enforcement of rules and norms. The Chief has an official hierarchical role in the village and is therefore not entirely bound by the informal, spontaneous order of the village. Indeed, he seems unable to subject himself to communal norms. His hierarchical position can upset the harmony of the village's spontaneous order—as in his dealings with Qiu Ju and Qinglai. For example, he rudely rebuffs Qiu Ju's request for an apology.

Qiu Ju attempts to invoke higher authorities against the Chief to compel his apology. She goes first to Officer Li, who says he cannot force an apology but who negotiates an agreement for the Chief's payment of Qinglai's medical costs and lost work time. This might have settled the issue except that, when Qiu Ju comes to

---

[*] I wish to thank Andrea Belag and Nora Ng for discussions of this paper.
[1] References to *The Story of Qiu Ju* are noted at their time in the film: (hour:minute:second). Quotes from the film are from the English subtitles with apparent typos silently corrected.

collect the money, Chief Shantang insults her and she walks away without the money. She then appeals to the county town Public Service Bureau (PSB), a mediating body, which proposes an identical settlement. She appeals this decision to the higher level municipal PSB, also a mediating body. Again she fails and is told she can go to court if she wishes to overturn their judgment affirming the decision of the county town PSB.

To go to court is utterly to transcend the communal order of her world and such an action is foreign to Qiu Ju, who does not like her role in the official proceeding. Moreover, going to court means suing Director Yan of the municipal PSB, the one official who has been kindest to her in all of these proceedings. Only when Yan encourages her suit does she let it go forward. Again, the outcome is to reaffirm that the Chief owes nothing more than compensation for any injury he has done to Qinglai, although the Court marginally increases his payment. He owes no apology or humility, which he apparently believes would disgrace him in his hierarchical role in the Village. But that is to say that he owes no communal tie, no rich communal relationship. He owes only a formal recognition of harm that can be made good through mere payment of a small sum, which Qiu Ju does not want and finally refuses to take. She apparently thinks the Chief should be bound by fealty to the community and its norms of decency even if that means lowering his hierarchical status.

I wish to lay out the changing, often conflicting systems of norms that govern and drive the interactions in *The Story of Qiu Ju*. The norms and, indeed, the whole system of these norms are in transition to fit the transitions in the larger society, especially in its demography and economy. The norms change because the structure of the society changes, and therefore the problems and the structures of interaction that must be regulated change. The transitions that are sweeping such communities as that of Qiu Ju carry the villagers *from norms that are local, informal, and personal, to norms that are abstract, formal, and impersonal*, with variation in degrees on all these dimensions.

The communal norms of Qiu Ju's village are not likely to work very well in organizing a much larger social order in which each person interacts with very many others more or less daily, including many others with whom there is no ongoing relationship. For people in the village, a change of scale may therefore come as a sad loss. For many aspects of daily relations, however, the older norms might partially survive the transition to a larger social order. They will govern a much smaller part of life, especially if mobility takes the village apart and breaks many of its relationships, as it has done in another of Zhang's movies, *The Road Home*. The mobile, modern society requires a more abstract and more uniform order. Expectations could be quite stable in the spontaneous order of Qiu Ju's village. They are apt to be very stable in the larger society only if they are in essence codified and managed. They may still work with spontaneity case by case, but their design and content must be less spontaneous than they were in an earlier era.

Qiu Ju's life is already partially in the world of abstract relationships. For example, she and Qinglai grow chili peppers to sell on the market. The peppers are so numerous that they frame their home in vast red hangings. Qiu Ju and Qinglai specialize for market production just as Adam Smith, David Hume, or Bernard Mandeville would advise and as modern economic relations demand. But otherwise almost all her relationships are in the village, where presumably they are regulated almost entirely by local norms. It is only a part of her and her husband's life to enter the somewhat abstract and impersonal market order.

My purpose here is not to evaluate the rightness or goodness of various social norms, although one might be able to do that from the perspective of a particular moral theory. My purpose is the naturalistic explanation of certain norms. The norms at issue are those that contribute to and regulate social order and, in particular, help organize social cooperation. The content of such norms is inherently contingent on social structures and relationships through which they must govern behavior and attitudes. I will be concerned here with attitudes only to the extent that they affect behavior. The relevant attitudes in this context are, of course, commitment to particular norms, commitment that might or might not drive behavior. For example, in some meaningful sense you might be strongly committed to a norm of honesty and truth-telling. But you might sometimes or even often violate that norm in your own behavior because other considerations, including your own interests, trump your commitment to honesty. As David Hume ([1739–40] 2000, book 3; see Hardin 2007, 33–6) argues more generally for morality, even a passionate belief need not motivate behavior.

Here is the outline of her efforts to obtain redress through a restoration of good relations with the Chief. Her Chief beats up Qinglai; the chief refuses to apologize; she goes to Officer Li to get him to compel an apology from the Chief. Li negotiates a payment of 200 yuan (about US$ 26 at current rates of exchange) to cover Qinglai's medical expenses and lost work time but without an apology. Qiu Ju is apparently willing to settle until the Chief insults her, and she refuses the payment. She appeals to the county town Public Service Bureau, a mediating body that handles such conflicts. The PSB denies Qiu Ju's appeal of Li's proposed settlement; she appeals to the higher level municipal PSB, which also denies her complaint. She is therefore at the end of the process of mediation through these boards, and as her next step she must sue the municipal PSB.

After setting the context and character of her communal norm system, let us then expand on these bare outlines of Qiu Ju's tale to explicate the range of norms at issue and to interpret the behaviors of the principals. In many senses, they are faced with new experiences and they have to invent ways to cope with these from their old norms, which have not evolved to fit the current issues and which are likely to be put under pressure, as are the principals. Spontaneous creativity while struggling to hew to their norms is the hallmark of their tale.

2. Two Systems of Humiliation

Although his focus is on relatively highly developed, modern societies, the nature of what Avishai Margalit calls a decent society emerges from his analysis of the corrosive functioning of humiliation in its many forms. He is concerned in particular with institutional humiliation, which is built into many of the institutions and arrangements of a government or a state, perhaps especially of its legal system. Margalit (1996, 4) notes that the state has an especially great potential, both normatively and factually, for institutional humiliation. Such humiliations are available in societies of many types, including the small village society of Qiu Ju and Wan Qinglai.

Consider a gross attempt at humiliating Qiu Ju. When Chief Shantang offers his 200 yuan payment to Qiu Ju, he throws the money on the ground before her, saying, "There are twenty 10 yuan notes there. Bow your head and pick them up." (00:19:43) "For each one you pick up, you bow your head to me. When you've done that 20 times, we can call it quits."

But Qiu Ju stands above the groveling that Shantang seems to have expected and walks away, because her concern remains with decency, which must include apologies for wrongs, now compounded by the Chief's indecent arrogance with the money and his rude remarks to her. Although Qiu Ju's concern with decency is probably common in her community, the strength of her commitment to the communal norms is extraordinary. "The thing could have been done with", she says. "But he flung the money on the ground. Said those terrible things. I can't believe there's no justice." (00:20:39) She would apparently much prefer to receive the decency of an apology than to receive 200 yuan, despite its value. Her husband, Qinglai, who has directly borne both the harm and the insult of Chief Shantang's action of kicking him, wants to drop the issue. Qiu Ju, however, pushes further with her quest.

Qiu Ju's concern with decency is commonly, after all, at its core a concern with humiliation (Margalit 1996), and the Chief's action in his handling of the 200 yuan seems clearly intended to humiliate Qiu Ju further by making her grovel before him—she would get a little acknowledgement with the 200 yuan, but she would pay for it in face-to-face humiliation. The Chief is also foremost concerned with humiliation, but in his case presumably the worry is that being humiliated will undercut his authority. Humiliation drives both of them, but in very different ways. For Shantang, the issue is relatively impersonal. He is partly the embodiment of a form of social organization that is managed by hierarchical role holders.

There are two systems of humiliation here that drive distinctively different norms, loosely characterized as an official norm of authority and its dignity, and the personal norm of decency. Chief Shantang has crossed over these two by kicking Qinglai in the groin in a way that humiliates and is therefore personally indecent. The entire interaction begins with humiliation and retaliatory humiliation, both personal. The retaliatory humiliation, however, crosses from personal to official. Chief Shantang's action in response to personal insult and humiliation brings his authority into question because it goes beyond what his authority would justify. As Qiu Ju says to the Chief, "You're the head of the village. You can't kick a man where he lives." (00:07:20) Evidently, she grasps the difference between the norms that govern him as an official and those that govern all of the villagers as individuals.

Chief Shantang snarls, "So I kicked him—what did you want now?" (00:07:24)

Qiu Ju goes with Meizi, Qinglai's sister, to the village to Officer Li to seek redress. Meizi tells Li much of the story, and Officer Li supposes that a fight must have involved two people, both in the wrong in some way. "What did your brother [Qinglai] say?" he asks (00:14:09).

"He cursed the Chief; said he'd have no heirs. Said he could only raise hens."

"Your brother was wrong then."

"Everyone knows that the Chief only has daughters."

"Your brother's words cut him where it hurts. The family planning policy means he'll have no heirs. It's cruel to remind him of it."

In response to an official reprimand for his illegal shed, Qinglai retorted with a personalized insult. Although this is surely not an uncommon move in such contexts, it is a violation of the separate norm systems, crossing over from one to the other. More often than not, such crossovers may go in this direction, from official to personal, as though the latter were more basic, as though it were even a last resort. Or perhaps it merely eliminates the official gulf by reducing the official to a mere person. Although the move partially licenses the person who is attacked in this manner to go personal as well, doing so leaves the official norm system torn and, in this case, it undercuts the authority of Chief Shantang. He has demeaned himself in his role.

3. Bodo Ethics

Consider the normative structure of a very simple, highly but spontaneously organized society in which the norms are virtually all local, personal, and informal, even though they may be very specific and determinate. Dyadic and small-number relationships are central to such spontaneous regulation of a small communal social order. Large-number coordination may stand behind broader social norms, such as decency in everyday relationships. These might carry over to many local communities or villages, so that we might find similar norms across some large region. But the norms are likely to be *enforced within the local community* without any extra impetus from outside, so that the force of such a norm is almost entirely from its local backing. It is likely to work through the threat of exclusion, either with mild shunning or with draconian total exclusion from the community. That is to say that it is likely to be a norm of exclusion (Hardin 1995, chapter 4).

Unfortunately, a norm of exclusion cannot work very well for the village Chief, whose role is already partially outside the community and who is backed by still higher outside authorities, with whom he seems to identify more than he identifies with his fellow villagers. The higher officialdom might be expected to line up in defense of his prerogatives and actions against claims from the villagers. In essence, his role is extra-communal; it is part of the organization of the larger society and its governance. The role is somewhat analogous to that of a foreman in a factory. The foreman is at the intersection of management and the workers and is neither of the one nor of the other.

Axel Leijonhufvud (1995) characterizes the village society of tenth century France in which the villager Bodo lived. We have detailed knowledge of that society from the parish records of the abbey of St.-Germaine-des-Pres. Today one would say that that abbey is in the center of Paris, but in Bodo's time it was a rural parish distant enough from Paris that many of its inhabitants may never have seen Paris. Virtually everything Bodo consumed was produced by about eighty people over his entire lifetime, all of whom he knew well. Indeed, most of what he consumed was most likely produced by his own family. If anyone other than these eighty people touched anything he consumed, perhaps it was salt, which would have come from the ocean and would have passed through many hands on the way to St.-Germaine.

In life as organized in Bodo's village, everyone could assess everyone else and their contributions to their own families' lives as well as to the lives of all the other villagers. They had the epistemology to do for their villagers what modern states can still do only relatively poorly today.[2] All in that village were known intimately to all. The situation of Bodo's village, although not of France in general, was very nearly that of Gerrard Winstanley's ([1652]1973) vision for the organization of economic life, each family producing primarily for itself.

Ethics in Bodo's society must have been a compound of religious values and social reciprocity. We must rely on each other to some extent and our failures of reliability will be known to everyone. Any of us who are utterly unreliable are likely to become pariahs to everyone else. Much of the simplistic morality of common sense fits such a society fairly well. That morality is a set of minatory constraints: do not lie, do not cheat or steal, do not fail to fulfill your obligations, and so forth. Bodo ethics is essentially a set of rules, norms, or expectations for regulating daily life in small communities with generally close knit relations. Bodo ethics may still be much of the quotidian ethics of people today. But it cannot ground a full system of social order or a legal system in a large and complex society. And it cannot even be very good for regulating broader relations with those—virtually everyone—outside a very close-knit community.

A striking feature of Bodo ethics is, again, that it is relatively enforceable by the community. An individual need not rely on self-regulation to be moral. The knowledge that the whole community has of each individual's adherence to the local moral code allows community members to sanction miscreants. An enormous part of the debate about morality in the modern secular world is about how individuals can be motivated to act morally.[3] That question is answered easily for Bodo's world. The

---

2 Differences in the epistemologies of states and individuals are important in many contexts, especially in the law (Hardin 1994).
3 A major reason for the modern interest in classical Greek moral philosophy is that the Greeks were de facto also secular and could not invoke a vengeful god to intervene in an afterlife to compel morality in this life. Between the Greeks and the era of Hume, Kant, and other moderns, the hierarchical Church regulated morality in the European world.

community spontaneously enforced its morality as a set of compulsory norms. This did not guarantee compliance, but it must often have exacted a toll for non-compliance

4. From Informal to Formal Norms

The sets of norms that govern the interactions between Qiu Ju, the Chief, and various others can be arranged hierarchically from the most informal to the most formal, which is to say from the most personal to the most institutionalized. As they rise to the more institutionalized level, the norms become increasingly impersonal and independent of what anyone specifically wants in a particular case. Instead, the formal institutions define what the stakes are and take over the regulation of the interactions. Qiu Ju's interactions over Qinglai's injury follow this hierarchy as though she were passing through a historical development in telescoped order at almost instantaneous speed over very few months.

She moves from a world nearly like Bodo's to one that is urban and densely crowded with people whose behavior is governed by diverse normative visions and expectations, people whom Qiu Ju does not know and will never know. Even in the historical development of these norm systems in various times and places in the world, however, there have perhaps usually been overlapping systems. The use of heavy institutional devices is too cumbersome for many low stakes issues at the two-person face-to-face level. Norms of decency are local, and often they are strictly dyadic. A decent society depends on decent relationships within each pair or small number group. It also depends on decent institutional arrangements, with institutions that do not abuse or offend those who have to use them or rely on them.

The claims for decency, or any other normative ordering, are not inherently claims about social scale. A large society can be graced with decency or a small one can be utterly indecent. For an example of the latter, Edward Banfield (1958) shows how norms for social cooperation can go badly awry in an impoverished southern Italian community, which he calls Montegrano. That community, as it showed itself to Banfield, may long since have disappeared in the face of economic advancement in Italy. Those who still live there two generations later must live better lives than their forebears, although there might be few of the descendants still living there. If so, it has presumably not been changing norms so much as changing structural circumstances that have made the difference. In this limited respect, that village compares to Qiu Ju's fictional village in recent China.

The way practical morality commonly works is through norms, which gain their force from group and social sanctions rather than from their moral content. But that means a host of other norms, some of them quite ugly and even brutal, that could hardly be called moral on any standard moral theory are on roughly equal footing with norms that have the content of standard moral theories. For example, in many societies, norms of racism may be far more powerfully motivating than norms of honesty or decency. In general, the force of norms is essentially unrelated to their moral content but only to what one could call their strategic content or structure. In particular, because norms with genuinely moral content are usually universalistic, such norms will be less well enforced than norms that are exclusionary, even exclusionary to the point of violence.[4] The transition from such communities as that of Bodo or Qiu Ju to larger, more diverse societies entails *a transition in the very basis of practical morality away from communally enforceable norms to ingrained principles and to legally enforced constraints.*

After failing to get redress—a mere apology from the Chief—at three levels of mediation and appeal, Qiu Ju must quit or sue for her cause. Her suit would have to be against Yan, the director of the municipal PSB, because he is the official ultimately responsible for the decision that Qiu Ju rejects. In remarkable exchanges with her lawyer, Wu, and then with Director Yan, Qiu Ju reveals both her naiveté and her normative stance to the world, the stance of decency. Qiu Ju has no fight with the Director, who has been very kind to her, even giving her a lift in his official car. But it was his PSB that denied her satisfaction by rejecting her claims against the Chief at the final available level of mediation. Qiu Ju thinks one could only sue a bad person, not so sweet a man as Director Yan. To lawyer Wu she says, "I won't do it, I'm suing the Chief. How can I drag Director Yan into this?" (01:13:27–9)

Director Yan appears and greets Qiu Ju, saying it's time to go into the court hearing. She says she will not go, "I'm not going to sue you".

Yan explains again the structure of the legal process for matters such as hers. The emphasis is on mediation to settle them amicably, without lingering animus, and to restore good relations. One might suppose that this is a central device for a decent society, one in which Qiu Ju would want to live. In suing the Municipal PSB, of which Yan is the Director and therefore the responsible party, she is nominally suing him, but in essence she is suing his role and not his own person. He is in the realm of the impersonal and the justice system will treat him impersonally.

Director Yan says, "Qiu Ju, in civil and administrative lawsuits, the defendants are not necessarily bad people".

She seems a bit taken aback. "You mean good people can sue each other?"

"Of course!" Director Yan says.

Qiu Ju is still bothered, possibly because she has an ominous view of the impersonal, bureaucratic courts and their power. As though to get a glimpse into the black box of that bureaucracy, she asks, "Director Yan, if you lost, what would happen to you?" (01:15:21) She does not wish to be indecent toward this warmly decent person who has no personal responsibility for the harms done to her husband.

---

4 See further, Hardin (1995, chapters 4 and 5) on exclusionary and universalistic norms, respectively.

5. The Chief's Restoration

Eventually, the Chief's membership in the community is restored in Qiu Ju's eyes when he uses his authority to marshal help to take her to a hospital when her child's birth goes badly wrong. That happens on the eve of the new year when everyone in the village wants to enjoy a classical Chinese opera performance and no one wants to spend the late, wintry evening carrying Qiu Ju on a stretcher to the distant hospital. Only the Chief can get them to do so, and he takes action in Qiu Ju's favor despite their hostile relationship.

For the community's traditional celebration of the child's first full month of life, Qiu Ju insists that the Chief must be included and must come. He has ostensibly helped her because it is his role as chief to tend to such needs of the villagers and not because he strives to restore communal or friendly relations with her. In all likelihood no one else could have mobilized several strong men to help carry her on a stretcher to get competent medical care before it would have been too late. Shantang does not want anyone mistakenly to suppose he helps Qiu Ju in order to placate her. It is his role that requires such action, as has been true in the past for other cases as well. Her suit against him can go forward, he insists, but she sees otherwise. She now has grounds from decency to forget the past and to thank the Chief for his wonderful kindness in helping to save her life. It is of course a single event, but for him the story is of a formal duty, while for her it is of a personal action. Behind his action, he sees himself always as an official; she sees him as a decent person. For him it is also face-saving to insist on his duty because that means he has not in some sense capitulated to her demands for what she thinks is justice in the case of her husband's being kicked. The Chief's kicking and his helping are unrelated actions, not morally connected actions.

6. The Normative Stages of Qiu Ju's Quest for Justice

Qiu Ju goes through many levels of norm systems in her quest for what she expects will be just redress for the wrong she and her husband have suffered from Chief Shantang, as discussed already. A beauty of her various moves is that they include many of the possible stylized moves in the world of normative regulation of social order, including several of the most important of these. Many other things might be going on as well, as in such specific familial relationships, but the focus here is only on social order more generally and therefore on relationships that characterize the larger or more pervasive forms of social organization. A more detailed discussion of the norms along the way will give an instructive accounting of how these work, how they interact with each other, and, of special interest in this context, how they are altered or superseded in response to ongoing transitions in the larger society that are reaching down to the small village level, even eliminating villages that have poor resources.

(1) The first and most natural step for Qiu Ju is to recur to the very informal, spontaneous norms of her Chinese equivalent of Bodo's ethics, norms that are not in any sense legislated or otherwise officially promulgated or backed. The villagers are likely to take these normative principles as matters of truth, as though they were natural and even universal. In her village, a principal background norm is decency, somehow defined in varied contexts. Hence, Qiu Ju appeals personally for an apology from Shantang. This is to invoke a highly personal and informal norm in the order of their society. This might be the only normative system she actually understands or that actually governs her own interactions with others.

(2) When she is rebuffed by the Chief, Qiu Ju must either give up on reliance on decency or she must find a way somehow to enforce it, which sounds almost like a contradiction of the norm. Often, we can restore damaged relationships through recourse to mediators or mutual associates who can bridge our conflict or insult of the moment. She moves into the more nearly formal world of asking Officer Li to intervene with the Chief, to get him to apologize. She still has only the informal concern with decency, not a larger concern with legality or formal resolution of her complaint. The resolution she seeks would presumably be very informal in the sense that it would not be part of an official protocol or record of judgment. Indeed, it would be an attempt to avoid any such official or bureaucratic regulation despite the role of an official in the proceedings. In keeping with this informal quality of his intervention, Li has no authority to compel the Chief to apologize or to admit wrong; he can only mediate. Li's main argument to the Chief is from communal norms of amicability and of basic human equality, both of which are part of the system of decency. Shantang must live with Qiu Ju and Qinglai, so they all must want an amicable outcome. Decency in that relationship requires equal treatment and recognition of equality; and they are not really very far apart on their community hierarchy of social roles.

In this instance, after failing to get an apology from Shantang, Qiu Ju has gone outside the local community to a larger, more encompassing official community. She crosses one context with another, official with personal. Oddly, in attempting to gain a decent outcome, she goes outside the informal normative system of decency into the somewhat formal, official system of coercion or at least of official pressure, even though in that system, decency is not a major concern. She leaves her own normative world to appeal to the more nearly official world of Chinese government and institutions. From actions such as hers, arguably motivated by necessity, her own normative world is crumbling.

Li reaches an agreement that the Chief will pay for Qinglai's medical expenses, thus implicitly admitting a wrong. He will not apologize, apparently because he fears that that would reduce his dignity as Chief. Losing face is a major concern for him; maintaining face is an essential, core norm of his hierarchical position. Li implores Qiu Ju not to force Shantang to lose face, not to humiliate him, to accept the 200 yuan that he will pay, and to call it quits (00:18:15).

The next morning Qiu Ju goes to Shantang with medical receipts. As she is about to take the money and to end the conflict, Shantang retorts to her assertion that she only wants justice. "Justice?" he says. "You think I've given in? It's only that Officer Li came so far. I can't let him lose face." (00:19:35)

The Chief evidently supposes that he will not himself lose face from giving her the money if his action is taken to preserve the dignity of Officer Li. It is humiliation and the threat of humiliation all around. Li brings gifts that he says Chief Shantang offers in apology. Qiu Ju immediately suspects that Li has bought the gifts to try to settle the conflict, and she soon returns them. She wants only an apology from the Chief. The gifts, intended as a proxy for an apology, might be adequate if they are really from Chief Shantang and are voluntarily offered by him, but not if they are a ruse from Officer Li, with whom Qiu Ju has no brief and who owes her nothing beyond his official duties toward her in certain contexts.

When in the end his efforts at persuasion fail, Officer Li attempts to fool Qiu Ju by covering for Shantang with his lie about the gifts supposedly offered by the Chief. This ploy presumably could never have succeeded in the long run, because Shantang would eventually have revealed his lack of any intention to apologize or to admit wrong. He genuinely seems to believe he has done no wrong as though he thinks his kick merely went awry and did more harm than he intended. Hence, Chief Shantang's resolution of the conflict, with payment of Qinglai's medical bills plus a small gift of seeming contrition, has the character of a tort liability without fault, as in a system of strict liability. As in such a system, the Chief owes payment but he is guilty of no wrong.

If Li's efforts were to succeed, with payment of medical costs for the injury to Qinglai and a falsely implicit admission of wrong, and his subterfuge were later to become open, the whole outcome would likely have seemed indecent to Qiu Ju. She seems to have read both of these parties well enough to see through Li's subterfuge. Oddly, Li should have been grateful for her discovery and rejection of his ploy, because eventual knowledge of it might have undercut his credibility and his authority in their community. The crossover of personal and impersonal, of official and informal norms is most evident in his complex role. Li is not sufficiently strategic in his analysis of the situation to act well in his own interest—or in the larger communal interest. He is too short sighted in his focus on the particular conflict of the moment.

(3) The next step for Qiu Ju is to go to mediation, which is a blend of formal and informal devices. The goal of mediation is to obtain de facto agreement by all concerned on a resolution that puts the issue in the past. In Qiu Ju's case, the third-party mediator, the county town PSB, is a formal, official body. It proposes a settlement that might actually work, but eventually it is undermined by Shantang's continued arrogance. In many such mediation systems, the parties are brought together to work out their conflict. In the system that Shantang and Qiu Ju face, they are not brought together with the mediator; instead, the mediator takes their inputs and comes up with a proposal that the mediator, the PSB, thinks is fair and likely acceptable. No doubt, the weight of the PSB is an added consideration for the parties in accepting the PSB's proposals, but the absence of face-to-face mediation may undercut their acceptability.

Still, the system is relatively personal because it works with what the parties want rather than with rules that determine outcomes. Two seemingly identical cases could get substantially different outcomes to fit the idiosyncrasies of the involved parties. That the outcome of our case might differ from that of another very similar case would not be a ground for protesting the resolution or for saying it is unfair. Fairness is not an abstract notion here. It is defined and measured by those reaching a resolution. It can be heavily affected by social mores and practices, by the history of a relationship, by expectations and hopes of various kinds, and by vagaries of the moment. It would be wrong to suppose that we could, as in John Rawls's ([1971] 1999) theory of justice, go behind a veil with all of our own history and character somehow left out of consideration as we try to determine what would be fair. What would be fair is what we as the actual people we are will accept as fair in our case.

(4) When, in Qiu Ju's eyes, mediation by the county town PSB fails by simply agreeing with the proposed resolution of Officer Li, she appeals to a higher level, the municipal PSB. This is apparently not in principle different from the lower level PSB, except that it has more the character of an appeal of a prior decision than of an initial direct mediation. Therefore it drifts closer to the nature of an appeals court, but still without all of the formality of an ordinary appeals court and without the supposed precision in fact finding of usual courts of first instance. Moreover, the mediation is at a higher, more encompassing level and is plausibly therefore more abstract and less personal.

(5) When Qiu Ju appeals the resolution of the municipal PSB, which essentially goes against her claims by commending the rightness of the lower level PSB's proposal, avenues of mediation have run out and she must now go to court to sue that PSB. Here she enters the realm of the heavily formal world of distant judges and institutions. As Lawyer Wu says, "The PSB only mediated, but now it's a lawsuit" (01:09:21). Now formality, indeed, formalism takes over. The role of the courts and judges is more to establish the facts and the abstract character of the case at hand than to find what would be a resolution that would be acceptable to the parties in conflict. Its decision is binding independently of its acceptability, although its decision can be appealed further. When acceptability of any particular resolution ceases to be a central concern, the abstract qualities of the case at hand are likely to become the focus of decision. That a decision might make both parties to the resolution of a particular conflict very unhappy is not a major issue or concern of a court.

Yet again, Qiu Ju loses.

(6) We may count as a sixth stage in the resolution of Qiu Ju's case the events of new year's eve, when Chief Shantang helps to get Qiu Ju to a hospital and probably saves her life. It is, of course, his authority in the community that enables him to impress several men away from the annual opera in Wang Village and into the arduous task of carrying Qiu Ju on a stretcher the considerable distance to the hospital. Qinglai knows that he cannot mobilize the necessary help for his wife ("Who's gonna pay me any mind?" he asks the Chief in imploring him to take charge [1:21:36]). The Chief might rightly say that his effort on her behalf is completely unrelated to their case in conflict, that it is entirely from his duties as Chief that he acts. "This

has nothing to do with the law suit", he insists (01:25:17). But this might also merely be another face saving claim to protect himself against a charge of acting only to stop Qiu Ju from continuing her suit, as though he were buying her off.

Qiu Ju is virtually incapable of thinking that way, and she instinctively supposes that the Chief has personally done her a great service. For her, therefore, the issue is how to weigh his decency overall. She must primarily weigh two things: the Chief's perhaps errant kick and his generous rescue of her from the trauma of a birth gone wrong. Clearly the latter of these is more important and trumps the former. She is not likely to think that the Chief is duplicitous and merely self interested in acting on her behalf. Rather, his action is evidence that he is a decent, well meaning person. Hence, at this stage, she takes the issue back into the realm of the local, informal, and personal, away from the realm of the abstract, formal, and official. For her, all is forgiven.

(7) There is a final stage in the conflict between the Chief and Qiu Ju, a stage in which their conflict is transformed for everyone into a legal matter, so that it is in fact no longer their conflict. This transformation leaves all of the personal and informal character of the conflict aside to focus on legal responsibility, wrong, and punishment. This transformation takes us into the world of humiliation and estrangement. The stakes are escalated from mere insult and minor injury when it is discovered from x-ray that Qinglai has suffered a broken rib from the Chief's assault. At that point the institutional system takes over regulation of the interaction, which is now defined as criminal (01:33:14).

The evidence of Qinglai's x-ray is unfortunate for communal norms. Assault is a serious infraction in the rule of the larger society, and the Chief must be brought to justice according to the larger society's devices, which rule that he must go into detention for fifteen days. This is justice as punishment or vengeance, not as restoration. Qiu Ju has only demanded decency through the restoration of a damaged relationship, not vengeance or punishment, neither of which she could possibly want. But the formal law of assault trumps her local norm of decency and Shantang must serve his time.

Without the serious injury, the Chief would not have been brought under the institutionalized system of criminal law. The interaction between Qiu Ju and Shantang virtually ceases to be an interaction between the two of them. It is now almost absolutely impersonal; it is an interaction between one individual—the Chief—and the state. It no longer even involves Qiu Ju. In seriously injuring Qinglai, the Chief has acted against the law and the state. That it was also action against Qinglai is merely a formal fact, no longer a personal matter. The spontaneous, personal norm system of the villagers no longer matters. Similarly spontaneous norms might be in the background to support the workings of the legal system, but in a legal proceeding institutions take over and displace the villagers' norms.

Officer Li interrupts the one-month celebration to tell Qiu Ju and Qinglai that the Chief is being taken away for his detention. At any point earlier on, Qiu Ju could have released the Chief from responsibility for harm to Qinglai, but now she can do nothing on his behalf. "I never asked them to take him away", she says forlornly

321

(01:33:30), but what she has asked is irrelevant in the world of the law in this criminal case. Qiu Ju has wanted to find justice in her world. She has found it but it is not in the form of what she wanted. It is cold, abstract, and unrelenting. Qiu Ju runs off to try to stop the Chief from being arrested or at least to see him, but she is too late. Zhang ends his film with the face of Qiu Ju—Gong Li, ravishing despite being dressed down for her peasant's role—in distress as she stares down the road toward the city, the city whose institutions she has now helped to override her communal norms and morals. She stands forlorn between her communal and her broader citizen self.

The Chief's rescue of her that awful evening of the new year's opera also counts for nothing in determining his guilt and his punishment for seriously injuring Qinglai. All that matters here is not testimony about the man Shantang, but testimony about the rib and the x-ray that reveals that it has been broken. One might agree fully with the view of the issue as essentially that of a tort under strict liability, without fault. But Shantang is charged with a crime, for which there is no strict liability to defuse the sense of guilt for wrongdoing. As someone liable for his actions and harms, he is now to be humiliated. His sentence of fifteen days of detention, while seemingly minor, has potentially major consequences in his official role and in his personal relationships in the village. Recovering face will be a daunting task, especially for him with his arrogant personality.

The transformation of the Chief's offense into assault may also rescue officialdom and its system from accusations that might otherwise seem plausible, namely that the officials stick together in defending each other against charges from mere citizens. This is a worry that bothers Qiu Ju. When she takes her appeal against Officer Li's recommended resolution to the county town PSB, an official there says, "Officer Li has dealt with this already" (00:28:59). "Why come to us?" She answers, "Officer Li might have favored the Chief. I want the county government to handle it." The Chief has earlier asserted to Qinglai that as an official he will be supported by "the higher ups" (00:59:23). And Qiu Ju has asked Director Yan how she can be sure that government officials, including Yan himself, do not all band together (01:07:38). Yan grants that her suspicion is not unreasonable. But when the charge is against a person as an individual rather than as an official, it is not officials and officialdom who are on trial.

7. Concluding Remarks

Many of the films of Zhang and some other leading directors in China are primarily social psychological in their portrayal of how the transitions in China affect a vast range of relatively ordinary people. This may not be a specifically deliberate choice of topics because the issues must be varied and far reaching in today's China with its many ongoing transitions. They show people being swept up or even swept aside in changes that to them might seem to be micro-level alterations of their relationships with others, including old and new others. But many of the changes are, of course, systemic and pervasive, and they are inescapable for most people. They transform economic relations so massively that they transform virtually all relations, including intra-familial and village-level relations. In part they do this by giving opportunities and incentives for mobility that breaks up families and village communities, as in Zhang's *The Road Home*. Such mobility could, of course, take many people from a single village into a single new locale within a large city or even within a city in a foreign country. First immigrants might recruit others from their own village or area, thus sustaining the community to some extent despite migration. But much of the mobility shatters erstwhile communities forever and must, even in the best of circumstances, complicate the normative structures of cooperation and social order.

Zhang's films often present this conflict between these two worlds, both of which are in transition, although the communal world is buffeted and largely swallowed by the world organized under law and bureaucracy, which cannot be long deflected by communal norms and concerns. Zhang's characters stand at the cusp of this sometimes brutal transition and they are commonly forlorn and dismayed, often as shown in stunning visions of an individual's face, as in the case of Qiu Ju as she stares at the end of the film into the unfamiliar world that has engulfed her and distorted her intentions and that now makes her seem as cruel to Chief Shantang as he was to Qinglai. In this arena, Zhang is implicitly a keen observer of the social mores of our time, and especially of China's time, which has come in full force. It is perhaps unintended irony that Qiu Ju stares toward the city, which, of course, cannot be seen at this distance, so that she stares at nothing, at the emptiness and virtual invisibility of the impersonal institutions that have taken Chief Shantang away and that are now changing the normative order of her village.

There is a deep and some might say sad irony of the title of Zhang's *The Road Home*. For these people 'home' is on the verge of ceasing to have any of the standard meanings of the word. Their former home still sparks attachments from children and students of the revered, now deceased teacher, Changyu Luo, of the village. But the village and its life spark little attachment, which perversely comes only through a death. That death is likely to be the final attachment for some of the next generation. Many of his former students return to help carry their revered teacher on foot the long trip from the provincial hospital's morgue to his burial in his home village on a hill overlooking the crumbling school where he taught for forty years. The next generation of villagers do honor to him, not to their former community, which has essentially died long before he has, because all of the young have left the village to go the city. As Luo's widow, Di, says to her son, our children must leave home. There are so few, mostly elderly people, remaining that they recruit people from another village to help carry the casket.

In the end more than a hundred people, mostly returning students, join the effort. In what would have been a half-day journey by tractor, they walk into the night through a snow storm to carry Teacher Luo back to what was genuinely his home, although it is no longer theirs. Most of them probably have him to thank for easing their way into the larger, new society of today's dynamic China. In all likelihood, most or all of them are fulfilling the demands of this traditional communal norm for the last time. That norm is passing and will cease to govern behavior hereafter. Even in this instance, they do honor to their teacher, not to their former normative system. The teacher's widow may be the last person still committed to the norm of carrying the dead back home for burial out of a traditional belief that they might otherwise forget their way home.

Their teacher educated them well, enabling them to move with the best opportunities. These are, of course, the best personal, not societal, opportunities. It is not the village but its former members who make the move to modern China. Many of them might now have no place to call home. They share the fate of Thomas Wolfe (1934) from more than seventy years ago: they cannot go home again, and for two reasons. Home is no longer there and they are no longer the people who were there when it was home. Unlike Wolfe, however, they do not individually meet this fate because of years away in university; they collectively meet it because the entire society is being transformed from under them and they are being transformed together. They are in transition—except that for some of them, transition may seem to be a permanent condition of their lives, not merely an intermediate stage on the way to a quasi permanent condition. If there is to be a permanent condition, it will come in the distant future.[5]

As of now, however, Qiu Ju has felt the abstract, impersonal and tenacious grip of the modern state. *That state has intervened harshly to show her just how little her communal norms count once the law has regularized relationships, thus undercutting the communal norms even while that law is ostensibly designed to protect the people in the community.* She shares with the teacher's widow the fate of living by norms that are trumped by her own society. Her new born son may never honor many of those norms, which may die as his generation is born.

Bibliography

Banfield, E. C. (1958), *The Moral Basis of a Backward Society*, New York

Hardin, R. (1994), My University's Yacht: Morality and the Rule of Law, in: I. Shapiro (ed.), *The Rule of Law*, New York, 205–227

— (1995), *One for All: The Logic of Group Conflict*, Princeton

— (1999), From Bodo Ethics to Distributive Justice, in: *Ethical Theory and Moral Practice 2*, 337–363

— (2007), *David Hume: Moral and Political Theorist*, Oxford

Hume, D. ([1739–40] 2000), *A Treatise of Human Nature*, Oxford, ed. D. F. Norton/M. J. Norton

---

5   Some of those moving into a new status will have Wolfe's experience of the transformation. His character says, "I have violated the standards of decency again and again, but in my heart I've always wanted to be decent. I don't tell the truth, but there's a kind of bitter honesty in me for all that. I'm able to look myself in the face at times, and tell the truth about myself and see just what I am." (Wolfe 1934, 290)

Leijonhufvud, A. (1995), The Individual, the Market and the Industrial Division of Labor, in: C. Mongardini (ed.), *L'Individuo e il mercato*, Rome, 61–78

Margalit, A. (1996), *The Decent Society*, Cambridge/MA

Rawls, J. ([1971] 1999), *A Theory of Justice*, Cambridge/MA

Winstanley, G. ([1652] 1973), *The Law of Freedom in a Platform or, True Magistracy Restored*, New York, ed. R. W. Kenny

Wolfe, T. (1934), *You Can't Go Home Again*, New York

Zhang, Y. ([1991] 1993), *The Story of Qiu Ju*, a film. Quotes from the film are from the English subtitles, noted at their time in the film by (hour:minute:second), and with apparent typos silently corrected.

Kieran Healy

Social Structure, Gifts and Norms in *The Story of Qiu Ju*
A Comment on Russell Hardin

1. Introduction

Hardin's paper is a reading of the film *The Story of Qiu Ju*, focusing on how different systems of norms work, how people are caught up in them in various ways, and how they try—with mixed success—to get what they want from them. In the film, Qiu Ju's husband, Qinglai, gets in an argument with the village Chief. He insults the Chief, they fight, and the Chief beats Qinglai and—adding the crucial insult to the initial injury—the Chief kicks Qinglai viciously in the groin. This kick is a blow too far, and Qiu Ju demands that the Chief apologize to her husband for it. He refuses, and the film follows her efforts to obtain an apology by various means.

The paper argues that the film presents "changing, often conflicting systems of norms that govern and drive" people's interactions. These range from the very local, small-scale, informal but very concrete system of village norms (what the paper calls "Bodo Ethics"), up to the more abstract, more formal and legal rules of a large-scale social order co-ordinated by the market and the bureaucratic state. As Qiu Ju moves up this hierarchy of regulation—from the village to the local council to a regional legal authority—the norms become "increasingly impersonal and independent of what anyone specifically wants in a particular case". That is, these more general normative systems are powerful, and so have the capacity to force an outcome or resolution to the conflict, but by the same token escape the efforts of Qiu Ju to control what that outcome will be. The pathos of the film is found in the unexpected consequences for all concerned of Qiu Ju's quest for a just apology.

There are seven or eight key events in the sequence of the plot, which happen in five or six different settings. But we can boil these down to three main layers: things that happen in the local village; things that happen at the meso-level district; and things that happen in the big city.

You can look at these events in a number of ways. One option is to see them as representing, as Hardin says, "many of the possible stylized moves in the world of normative regulation of social order". That is, the film shows a kind of menu of options for the normative and legal regulation of a social order. A stronger reading, and one of the main themes of Hardin's discussion, is to see these moves as ordered both hierarchically and temporally. Most of Qiu Ju's decisions propel her up the ladder of Chinese society, away from informal norms and toward formal legal regulations. Hardin suggests this can also be seen as representing a temporal transition: Chinese society as a whole is moving away from the small-scale world of face-to-face relationships to the more abstract and impersonal world of city life. So Qiu Ju's journey recapitulates in miniature the development of the society as a whole, "as though she were passing through a historical development in telescoped order at almost instantaneous speed over very few months". The ontogeny of the film recapitulates the phylogeny of Chinese society.

Hardin does qualify this, saying that such development has usually resulted in "overlapping systems" with the local persisting in the midst of the more general. Nevertheless, he thinks that "norms change because the structure of the society changes, and therefore the problems and the structures of interactions that must be regulated change". The transition from the small scale and homogeneous to the large scale and differentiated "entails a transition in the very basis of practical morality away from communally enforceable norms to ingrained principles and to legally enforced constraints"—and, by implication, to norms with real moral content: a move from how the word 'normative' is used in sociology (meaning whatever system of norms prevails) to its more philosophical sense (meaning principles of action grounded in a defensible moral theory).

A second theme of the paper is what I shall call the problem of restitution or rebalancing of the moral order, in the wake of a breach of some kind. To be fair to Hardin, I may be reading my own interests into the paper on this point. But it does seem to me that it illustrates some interesting aspects of the role of money, on the one hand, and the workings of generalized reciprocity or gift exchange, on the other. The participants in the drama try to impose obligations on each other, find ways to deny the force of these obligations, and look for ways to reset the system of exchange when it is out of balance.

A third theme, and one that is discussed in the paper a little more extensively, is the role of decency and humiliation in the enforcement of norms. Hardin argues that Shantang, the Chief, and Qiu Ju are both driven by humiliation, but in different ways: he is concerned primarily with the dignity of his official role, which has been compromised by the original argument and his violent response to it. Qiu Ju, Hardin suggests, is more concerned with decent behavior on the level of persons.

2. Social Structure and Norms

Let us begin with the main theme. "The norms change because the structure of society changes", the paper argues. This is a familiar story, recalling Durkheim's argument in *On the Division of Labor*, amongst other such accounts (Kumar 1978). As the social structure grows larger and more differentiated, and the material density of a society increases, its moral order moves from an intense, determinate and concrete system of norms to a less intense, less determinate and more abstract system. All societies need a moral order and a basis for social solidarity, but the large, differentiated societies cannot be bound together in the same way as smaller ones. There are other parallels, too: the move from the concrete to the abstract, from dyadic interaction within a village to anonymous interactions governed by laws. We find these ideas very much to the fore in classical sociological theories of social change. But there is a key difference between the world of the film and Durkheim's image of things. Durkheim thought that the institution of punishment in structurally simple societies was basically retributive, whereas in a more complex division of labor justice is served through restitutive means. In the film, however, things are more complex. The village norms emphasize the restitution of the prior balance through the medium of an apology or other appropriate exchange. The lower layers of the state bureaucracy provide informal and formal means for mediation. It is the state's criminal code that is activated at the end, and the state that exercises retribution against the Chief for his assault.

In sociology there have been two main critical responses to the classical vision of social change. The first is to accept the broad story, but to emphasize the persistence in large and complex social systems of what might seem like earlier forms of normative enforcement. So instead of a wholesale transformation, the new society gets layered on top of the old one, with pockets of the simpler local order persisting, just as local communities and cultures reconstitute themselves in cities. This is consistent with Hardin's remarks that normative systems may overlap, even as the modern, legal-rational system is ultimately more powerful than more local alternatives.

A second response questions an implicit premise of the story. It is tempting to think that the structural changes that come with role differentiation in modern society amount to an escape from moral order as an encompassing cultural system. Although we may leave behind the communally enforced—and as Hardin notes, often quite vicious—norms of a small-scale society, the more general moral principles and legal constraints of a complicated, differentiated society do not mean actors are disembedded from culture. Modern society may be increasingly rationalized, but it remains intensely ritualized (Meyer/Boli/Thomas 1997). Durkheim recognized this, arguing that what the members of a modern society shared was a strong conception of their distinctive individuality, and so moral solidarity in a differentiated social order was achieved by making the individual the subject of a kind of sacred cult. At least in this respect, the concern with personal decency in the practical morality of Bodo Ethics, and the emphasis on the personal dignity of individuals in contemporary societies are not so far apart.

3. Restitution, Rebalancing, and Self-Interest

Throughout the film, as Qiu Ju tries to get various people to help her sort things out, the third parties at the local level (and to some extent the Chief himself) insist that the best way to resolve things is for both parties to just admit they were wrong and then put the incident behind them. Over and over, the villagers say things designed to restore the status quo by sharing the blame around and promoting a kind of forgetfulness. Things like this:

- It takes two to fight, says the Officer.
- Let's call it quits, says Shantang.

- She is as pig-headed as the Chief, says Qui Ju's father in law.
- Let's forget the past.

Qiu Ju and the Chief resist this pressure, at least to begin with. We might be tempted to say that this kind of moral accounting is typical of and confined to the world of Bodo ethics. But this kind of approach to solving grievances is not just a survival in modern societies, it thrives in highly rationalized and discursively elaborated legal settings, such as Truth and Reconciliation commissions, or in informal political bargains to forget the past. In these cases, too, the goal is to acknowledge that it takes two to fight, to decide it's best to call it quits, and to resolve that it is time to forget the past. I do not say that justice in some general sense is served by doing this kind of thing. But this approach to repairing or resolving breaches is not by any means a historical curiosity of simple societies.

Before the film's final, ironic moments, Qiu Ju and the Chief are in fact reconciled. Hardin characterizes the moment as follows.

> Shantang does not want anyone mistakenly to suppose that he helps Qiu Ju in order to placate her. It is his role that requires such action, as has been true in the past for other cases as well. Her suit against him can go forward, he insists, but she sees otherwise. She now has grounds from decency to forget the past and to thank the Chief for his wonderful kindness in helping to save her life. It is of course a single event, but for him the story is of a formal duty, while for her it is of a personal action. Behind his action, he sees himself always as an official; she sees him as a decent person. For him it is also face-saving to insist on his duty because that means he has not in some sense capitulated to her demands for what she thinks is justice [...]. The Chief's kicking and his helping are unrelated actions, not morally connected actions. [...] 'This has nothing to do with the lawsuit,' he insists. But this might also be merely another face saving claim to protect himself against a charge of acting only to stop Qiu Ju from continuing her suit, as though he were buying her off. Qiu Ju is virtually incapable of thinking that way, and she instinctively supposes that the Chief has personally done her a great service. [...] Hence, at this stage, she takes the issue back into the realm of the local, informal, and personal, away from the realm of the abstract, formal, and official. For her, all is forgiven. (317/20f.)

This sequence of events very strongly recalls theory on the character of gift exchange. The life of the village happens through a system of ongoing, reciprocal exchanges. Gifts and gift exchange are everywhere in the film. Almost every time someone visits someone else we see rituals of hospitality and the gift of food—have some tea, have a drink, eat some noodles; you've come so far, you must stop and have something to eat. Even when she goes to the city to find a civil official, Qiu Ju brings him some fruit and a painting she buys at the side of the road.

Now, from the point of view of explicitly calculated exchange in a market or rationalized decision-making within a bureaucracy, gift exchange systems have some features that can look quite perverse (Healy 2006). In particular, it is extremely important that any semblance of self-interest or calculation be repressed in exchanges, even when a return gift is clearly redressing a debt and creating a new obligation to be returned in the future (Bourdieu 1998). In the moral economy of the village, the Chief's kicking and his helping are understood very much related actions, but for the implied exchange to work it is important that this link be actively denied. For that reason, I disagree with Hardin's remark that Qiu Ju is "incapable" of thinking of the actions as unrelated and that her supposition is "instinctive" or somehow mistaken. I think she knows that the Chief has done her a great service, and she also knows that this service—saving her life—far outweighs and erases the previous wrong. But in public this cannot be acknowledged. Similarly, the Chief is confident that his actions mean he cannot now lose face whatever the outcome of the lawsuit, even to the point where he is comfortable having reference to the original insult surface again at the moment of reconciliation.

4. Humiliation and Overlapping Systems

Finally, what about the relationship between the local and the general systems? The wider world enters into the local in two main ways. The first is through the medium of money. The second is through the apparatus of the state and its legal system. The way that Qiu Ju treats the offer of money from the Chief is consistent with what we know about the importance of marking and classifying exchanges over and above their strictly economic value (Zelizer 1995). The Chief throws the 200 yuan on the ground in front of Qiu Ju, so if she picks it up she will have to bow her head to him. So of course she rejects the offer with contempt, even though it is a lot of money. Again, the only way Qiu Ju would have accepted the money would have been in the form of a gift accompanied by an apology. It is not that the purchasing power of the cash is irrelevant to her or that she is somehow too pure a soul to take it. Rather, the money cannot really compensate the underlying wrong directly, and it is easy to turn a payment into an insult if you mark the exchange the right way. The two false or failed gift exchanges—first when Officer Li brings presents to Qiu Ju pretending that they come from the chief, and second when the Chief insults her with the money—should be contrasted with the real gift exchange that goes with his assistance during her Labor, when he gives his help freely.

The second way the wider world comes in is through the apparatus of the state, and its legal system, which provides the final, terrible moment of the film when the Chief is taken away to be imprisoned for assault. For Hardin, the hard lesson of the film is that the "state has intervened harshly to show [Qiu Ju] just how little her communal norms count once the law has regularized relationships, thus undercutting the communal norms even while that law is ostensibly designed to protect the people in the community" and thus her fate is to be "living by norms that are trumped by her own society". And that is what happens, in this case. But the film reminded me of *The Majesty of the Law*, a short story by the Irish writer Frank O'Connor (1982). That story, also set in a rural part of the world, is ostensibly about a visit one evening between a poor farmer and a police officer. They go through a ritual of polite discussion as the farmer, whose name is Dan, insists that the Sergeant stay to have some tea and then take a drink of potín, or illegally distilled liquor. At the end of this conversation, the Sergeant leaves, apparently with nothing having transpired. But then he returns momentarily and asks—diffidently, while out of sight around the doorway—"I suppose you're not thinking of paying that little fine, Dan?" This of course is the true purpose of the Sergeant's visit. We learn that Dan,

> a respectable old man, had had the grave misfortune to open the head of another old man in such a way as to require his removal to hospital, and why it was that he couldn't give the old man in question the satisfaction of paying in cash for an injury brought about through the victim's unmannerly method of argument.

Dan says he isn't going to pay, and they make a quick arrangement about when it would suit Dan to come town to the town. The word 'prison' is not mentioned in their conversation, and only appears as the very last word of the story. In his longest speech in the story, Dan explains why he would rather go to jail.

> 'You see, sergeant', Dan said, looking at another little cottage up the hill, 'the way it is, he's there now, and he's looking at us as sure as there's a glimmer of sight in his weak, wandering, watery eyes, and nothing would give him more gratification than for me to pay. But I'll punish him. I'll lie on bare boards for him. I'll suffer for him, sergeant, so that neither he nor any of his children after him will be able to raise their heads for the shame of it.'

So here we have a case slightly different from Qiu Ju's, where there is a fight between two more or less equal characters in a village. As in the film, the authority of the state is ultimately exercised in its strongest form, as one of the characters goes to prison for a crime. But the state's authority is also co-opted by a much more local game of honor and decency. Dan's punishment at the hands of the state is also his moment of glory in his own eyes, because he uses it to shame his neighbor. Although things do not work out that way for Qiu Ju, it is not inevitable that the majesty of the law should trump or obliterate the communal norms of the village. It is also possible for the legal system to become tangled up in local concerns in spite of itself, or in a way that goes over the heads of the officials entirely. A slightly different sequence of events in Qi Ju's story would us you a very different impression of the relationship between a local moral order and a rationalized system of justice administered by a bureaucratic state.

Bibliography

Bourdieu, P. (1998), *Practical Reason: On the Theory of Action*, Stanford

Healy, K. (2006), *Last Best Gifts: Altruism and the Market for Human Blood and Organs*, Chicago

Kumar, K. (1978), *Prophecy and Progress: The Sociology of Industrial and Post-Industrial Society*, Harmondsworth

Meyer, J. W./J. Boli/G. M. Thomas (1997), World Society and the Nation State, in: *American Journal of Sociology 103*, 144–181

O'Connor, F. (1982), The Majesty of the Law, in: *Collected Stories*, New York, 320–327

Zelizer, V. (1995), *The Social Meaning of Money*, New York

IV. Epilogue

Ernesto Garzón Valdés

Radical Evil, Absolute Evil, and Norms. Responding to Extraordinary Violence[*]

In the 20th century we have witnessed enormous calamities brought on by human hatred and fanaticism. In fact, they have reached such overwhelming dimensions that some observers believe that they have gone beyond what is comprehensible for the human mind, and that it is therefore impossible to think of adequate ways and means to eliminate them in the future or to punish them whenever they occur.

I will argue in what follows that these beliefs are false, that human evil is always capable of provoking still greater horrors than those we have known in the past (section 1), that forgetfulness and impunity are morally unacceptable, and that the only sensible means available to us for dealing with the calamities of the past are a strong, persistent memory and the relentless and non-selective application of the criminal law, nationally and internationally, in each and every known case (section 2). I shall illustrate my position with examples from the Argentine judicial system and its reaction to crimes committed during the times of state terrorism in that country (section 3).

1. Radical Evil and Absolute Evil

1. In the past century, the difficulty of comprehending the extremes of human evil was most clearly spelled out by Hannah Arendt with her conception of "radical evil", used to designate the almost unspeakable horrors of the Holocaust. As the source of the term "radical evil", Arendt of course refers to Kant. However, for the sake of conceptual precision, it must be noted that Kant's radical evil has nothing to do with the enormity of an inflicted harm, nor with the impossibility of comprehending it.[1]

---

[*] This is a revised and extended version of a paper given in the context of the international conference on *Norms and Values. The Role of Social Normas as Instruments of Value Realisation* at the ZIF in Bielefeld, on May 8, 2008. I wish to express my gratefulness to Michael Baurmann and Geoffrey Brennan for offering me the opportunity to present some theses about a topic of undisputable moral and legal relevance which also affects me personally, as an Argentine forced into exile by the criminal aberrations of state terrorism. Special thanks also to Ruth Zimmerling for, as always, helpful comments and for the translation of this paper.

[1] In this sense, the connection made by Hannah Arendt between Kantian radical evil and the Holocaust is mistaken. Richard Bernstein (2002, 20) is right when he observes: "Despite the striking connotations of the term 'radical', Kant is not speaking about a special *type* of evil or evil maxim. He would not agree with Arendt when she declares that radical evil is a phenome-

The expression "radical evil" appears in Kant's *Religion within the Limits of Reason Alone*.² Unlike Leibniz, Kant did not believe that we live in the best of all possible worlds and that one must accept the crimes of a Borgia or the rape of Lucretia as if they were merely the darker shades in the picture of an evolving history which on the whole is morally irreproachable. But he also did not believe that humanity, so far from Paradise, was inevitably marching towards its ruin. He could not even deny the historical evidence of evil having been committed by agents who were not ignorant of the existence of the moral law. This is precisely why he took recourse to the conception of *radical evil*:

> [T]he proposition, Man is evil, can mean only, He is conscious of the moral law but has nevertheless adopted into his maxim the (occasional) deviation therefrom. [...] [W]e can call this a natural propensity to evil, and as we must, after all, ever hold man himself responsible for it, we can further call it a *radical*, innate *evil* in human nature [...]. (§ 21)

> This evil is *radical*, because it corrupts the ground of all maxims; it is, moreover, as a natural propensity, *inextirpable* by human powers. (§ 27)

It is fitting to recall these passages of Kant, to avoid misunderstandings and to bring out more clearly what his radical evil amounts to.³

---

non that 'confronts us with its overpowering reality and breaks down all standards we know' (Arendt 1976, 459). And he certainly does not mean anything like what Arendt means when she claims that 'radical evil has emerged in connection with a system (totalitarianism) in which all men have become equally superfluous'."

2 [*Translator's note*: The quotations from this work follow the translation by Theodore M. Greene and Hoyt H. Hudson, *Religion within the Limits of Reason Alone* (New York 1960) as given in the e-text version first prepared by Stephen Palmquist of Hong Kong Baptist University and now available in a modified edition at the Chinese University of Hong Kong website: www.arts.cuhk.edu.hk/Philosophy/Kant/rel (May 13, 2003).]

3 According to Joan Copjec (1996), Kant's "radical evil" has two possible interpretations: "in admitting the innateness or radicality of evil, Kant could seem either to have discarded his belief in the powers of reason and the perfectibility of man and reverted instead to a belief in original sin, or to have found in the Enlightenment notions a new source of evil. It was easier for his contemporaries to take the former position, to think that Kant had in his old age returned to one of the traditional religious views against which they were battling. To us the latter position comes more easily; we almost spontaneously assume that Kant must have begun to renounce his former optimism and to fear that the Enlightenment principles he had so long preached might themselves become the doctrine of a modern-day religion, more dangerous than the kind it superseded." Copjec favors the second interpretation, arguing that "between Kant's contemporaries and us there have intervened numerous colonialist battles and two all-out world wars which have been borne by a kind of implacable fury and devastation that could not possibly have existed during the centuries before Kant wrote and of which even he could only have had abstract glimmerings". This is also the view often shared by those who nowadays speak of "radical evil" in Hannah Arendt's sense. Personally, I don't find this very convincing, for the very reasons Copjec mentions: given that Kant obviously could not have had the experience of the failure of reason that we have, it seems rather adventurous to attribute to him the fear that the consequences of Enlightenment might be for the worse. For his conception of radical evil, Kant needed to take into account only undisputable facts: "That such a corrupt propensity must indeed be rooted in man need not be formally proved in view of the multitude of crying examples which experience *of the actions* of men put before our eyes." (§ 22) On the interpretation

Of course, someone might argue that the crimes my generation has witnessed not only perversely affected the human will to some extent, but consumed it altogether, without leaving a trace of any good. Hence, we would be dealing not merely with an occasional deviation from the moral law, but with its total destruction. We would thus have reached what I would like to call *absolute, diabolic evil*—an evil that is in a sense worse than what Kant was willing to accept, an inexhaustible evil, with a potentially infinite number of victims.[4]

The practitioners of such *absolute evil* see in their victim not only an enemy that must be subdued, but a member of a class of people who must be eliminated for some equally *absolute* reason. While in the case of Kantian *radical evil* there is room for a bad conscience, the perpetrator of *absolute evil* feels redeemed by his very acts and knows no regret, as he believes to have not merely excuses, but justifications for them.

2. Kant thought that the workings of radical evil at all times and everywhere are historically verifiable facts, and Peter Singer has illustrated with examples from the Bible and Greek history that human cruelty and genocides are not exclusive to our recent past. His examples come indeed close to what I mean by *absolute evil*:

> [T]he [*Book of Numbers*, EGV] shows that the Holocaust that engulfed my grandparents was new only in that modern technology and communications enabled the Nazis to murder far more people in a relatively brief period of time than had ever happened before. (Singer 2003, 95f.)

Examples abound, and we should be careful with the alleged impossibility of a repetition of certain calamitous atrocities which, as Peter Singer pointed out, are rather made easier by the steady improvement of an ever more efficacious technology of genocide.

3. For *radical evil*, understood in the Kantian way, the number of victims is irrelevant. The murder of just a single person is already an expression of this human propensity to violate the moral law. For *absolute evil*, by contrast, numbers do matter, as does the kind of crime. Genocide is an example for the relevance of numbers, torture an example for the relevance of the kind of crime.

4. We are living with the memory of *absolute evil* that has been committed as well as with that of the persistent practice of *radical evil*. This would not have surprised Kant who repeatedly observed that human nature is made of "crooked timber". In the next section, I will consider the position a society that takes human dignity seriously should adopt when confronted with extraordinary violence.

---

of radical evil in the sense of Copjec, cf. Staten (2005). For an excellent presentation of the question of radical evil from Augustinus to Arendt, cf. Pranteda (2002).

4 Note that Hannah Arendt too speaks of "absolute evil", but in contrast to the distinction I propose, she links it to "radical evil": "And if it is true that in the final stages of totalitarianism an absolute evil appears (absolute because it can no longer be deduced from humanly comprehensible motives), it is also true that without it we might never have known the truly radical nature of Evil." (Arendt 1976, viii–ix)

2. Responding to Extraordinary Violence

1. There are two possible mental attitudes for dealing with the past which are mutually exclusive and jointly exhaustive: forgetting and remembering. My considerations about these two options will refer particularly to the question what individual and/or institutional reactions can be adopted in postdictatorial situations for dealing with criminal acts or extraordinary violence perpetrated by the former rulers and their agents. I will be particularly concerned with the moral relevance of these reactions. The crimes I am talking about—torture, rape, sexual slavery, enforced disappearance of persons, imprisonment or other severe deprivation of physical liberty, among others—are expressly considered "crimes against humanity" in art. 7 of the *Rome Statute* of the *International Criminal Court*; they are seen as crimes which "deeply shock the conscience of humanity" (Preamble). Though I will concentrate particularly on systems that promote state terrorism[5] since that is where extraordinary violence is perhaps most notoriously committed, the following observations also apply to some other, analogous cases.

Obviously, the relevance of forgetting or remembering depends on the relevance of the things forgotten or remembered. This applies just as much to private or intimate events concerning only individuals as to events of a public nature. In private as in public, forgetting or remembering certain events which mark an individual's or a collectivity's trajectory can be stimulated: one can try to erase facts of the past from one's mind as if they never happened,[6] or one can keep them alive every day, for instance by mentioning the names of their protagonists or erecting monuments to them. There is, however, an essential difference between the effects of forgetting and remembering: memory reasserts and reinforces the past, whereas forgetfulness attempts to ignore it. Ignorance of facts, however, does not affect their reality.[7]

---

5 On the distinction between dictatorship and state terrorism, cf. Garzón Valdés (1991). Below, I will briefly refer to non-institutionalized terrorism and to Günther Jakobs's peculiar proposal of a theory of enemy criminal law.

6 Friedrich Nietzsche (1997, 62) emphasized with eloquent vehemence the positive effect of forgetfulness on the mental and physical health of persons and peoples: "Forgetting is essential to action of any kind, just as not only light but darkness too is essential for the life of everything organic. A man who wanted to feel historically through and through, would be like one forcibly deprived of sleep, or an animal that had to live only by rumination and ever repeated rumination. Thus: it is possible to live almost without memory, and to live happily moreover, as the animal demonstrates; but it is altogether impossible to *live* at all without forgetting, or, to express my theme even more simply: *there is a degree of sleeplessness, of rumination, of the historical sense, which is harmful and ultimately fatal to the living thing, whether this living thing be a man or a people or a culture.*"

7 A notorious example of an attempt to deny the reality of facts is Henri IV's Edict of Nantes which stipulates in Art. 1 that "the recollection of everything done by one party or the other, between March, 1585 and our accession to the crown, and during all the preceding period of troubles, shall remain obliterated and forgotten, as if no such things had ever happened." Art. 2 reiterates: "We prohibit all our subjects, of whatever state and quality, to stir the memory, to attack, to resent, to insult or to provoke each other by reproach of what has happened, for whatever reason or excuse ..." Antonio Elorza (2001) has collected numerous cases of enforced for-

Thus, to forget the past can amount to self-deception—and how that is to be morally assessed depends, of course, on the moral quality of what one attempts to forget. If what is stimulated is the dis-memory of a shameful crime, the disvalue of that crime carries over to the self-deception implied by the desire to forget it.

2. Institutional forgetfulness has a very long tradition. In European history, from the peace treaty between Lothar, Louis the German, and Charles of France in 851 to the Treaty of Lausanne in 1923 which was expressly called an "act of oblivion", appeals to the need to forget as a prerequisite for international peace have been frequent. But the apologetic strategy of forgetting also exists on the national level. One of the oldest testimonies to this effect is the edict of Thrasybulus at the conclusion of the Tyranny of the Thirty in Athens (403 BCE) which stipulated that the crimes of the deposed oligarchs should not be prosecuted. Philippe Raynaud (2004, 270) has plausibly observed that "this decision by Thrasybulus which for centuries was considered an eminent example of prudence and even of political wisdom, today amounts to a dubious concession to the enemies of democracy which, besides, implies renouncing to a reparation of the damages suffered by the victims, and thus to an injustice". Shortly after Caesar's assassination, Cicero proposed that the murderers should be forgotten: *oblivione sempiterna delendam*; the *Act of Indemnity and Oblivion* put an end to the English civil wars; the French Constitutions of 1814 and 1830 underscored the importance of forgetting; Jorge Semprún has called the Spanish transition an "intentional collective amnesia";[8] and in Poland, in his first speech

---

getfulness at the national level. Let me mention just a few: In the 3rd century BCE, the first emperor of a unified China, Qin Shi Huang, decided to destroy not only the symbols of the deposed sovereigns but also "the obstacle that the prestige of the tradition supported by scholars and their Confucian mentality could represent". His solution for this problem was a general burning of books, the prohibition to invoke the past, and the execution of the Confucian scholars. That is what his chancellor Li Si proposed to him: "Whoever by referring to the past criticizes the present will be executed together with all members of his family. Officials who fail to comply with their duties will likewise be punished. Those who 30 days after the promulgation of this ruling have not destroyed their books will be branded with redhot irons and send to build the Great Wall." (Elorza 2001, 88) In 1562, Diego de Landa, bishop of Yucatán (Mexico), ordered the public burning of the religious books of the indigenous population for similar reasons. "The forging of nation-states in the 19th and 20th century follows the pattern of the French Revolution, and to the extent that each one of them attempts to base itself on a national history the main elements of which can be disseminated to a large part of the population through the schools, it becomes necessary to suppress all cultural, linguistic or historical elements that might be dysfunctional for that purpose." (Elorza 2001, 89)

8 On December 26, 2007, the so-called 'Law of historical recollection' came into force in Spain which ever since has been the object of an interesting political, legal and moral debate, as it is understood as a revocation of the amnesty or 'collective amnesia' that had accompanied the return to democracy. Let me quote only art. 2 sect. 1 of this law: "As an expression of the right of all citizens to moral reparation and to the recuperation of their personal memory and the memory of their family history, the radically unjust nature of all judicial sentences, sanctions and forms of personal violence produced for political, ideological or religious reasons during the Civil War, as well as of those suffered for the same reasons during the Dictatorship, is acknowledged and declared." Those who oppose the law do so with the same arguments that

before the democratic parliament, Tadeusz Mazowiecki said that Poles should "draw a thick line between the past and ourselves". This list of examples could easily be extended.[9]

It is also a well-known fact that one of the arguments often heard in attempts to ensure social peace in democratic transition processes is that of the alleged need to forget the past.[10] That is the only way, it is alleged, to gain the indispensable cooperation of those who held power in the dictatorial regime. As Avishai Margalit (1997, 193) remarked:

> This means that a new beginning is necessarily always accompanied by an appeal to forget the past. Memory is an obstacle on the way to reconciliation and forgiveness.

In a similar vein, Tzvetan Todorov (2004, 26) observed that

> one of the great justifications given by the Serbs for their aggression against the other peoples of former Yugoslavia is historical: the sufferings they inflict today are only a revenge for those the Serbs suffered in the recent (World War II) or remote past (the fights

---

have been heard in other countries against the so-called truth commissions or against reports such as the one published in Argentina in 1984 by the National Commission on the Disappeareance of Persons under the title of "Nunca más" *(Never again)*: that history should be written by historians in the future, not by investigative commissions today; that stirring up the past will reawaken old hatreds and tensions; that what society needs is to forget and let the wounds of the past heal. I cannot pursue this issue here; but cf. García (2008) (the author was a member of the UN Commission for Historical Clarification in Guatemala). In the Federal Republic of Germany, four phases of dealing with the Nazi past are distinguished: the first, from 1945–49, is marked by activities of the powers who won the war; in the second, rather long period there was an amnesty for Nazi criminals; the third phase begins in 1963 with the Auschwitz trial and is seen as ending in 1985 with the famous speech by the Federal President Richard von Weizsäcker on occasion of the 40th anniversary of the end of the war; and the fourth is the present one, marked, some say, by a memorial culture rather than a struggle for memory (cf. Prantl 2007).

9 The interested reader can find more examples, as well as arguments in favor of forgetfulness, in Garton Ash (1998).

10 Stephen Holmes (1988, 27) has insisted on the importance of "gag rules" for such processes: "Consider the decision of several [...] restabilized democracies to offer immunity from criminal prosecution to military leaders who wielded power in the old regime. Although guilty of atrocities, some of these officers have been willing to relinquish power peacefully to a civilian government. But they did so only in exchange for a legislative and judicial vow of silence about their past wrongdoings. Amnesties, in fact, are classic examples of democracy-stabilizing gag rules. [...] By closing the books on the past, keeping retribution for former crimes off the political agenda, the organizers of a new democracy can secure the compliance of strategically located elites—cooperation which may be indispensable for a successful transition from dictatorship to self-government." I have my doubts about the moral status of silence and gag rules. On Nov. 28, 2004, the so-called 'Valech Report' was published in Chile; it contained information on 28,000 cases of torture during the rule of Augusto Pinochet. Ricardo Lagos, then President of Chile, gave a speech with the title "Never to live it again, never to deny it again" in which he asked: "How could we live in silence for 30 years? Surely, out of fear. [...] this understandable silence increased the injury inflicted by the sufferings that were not shared, by what we preferred to hide, to cover up, to erradicate from the archives of our history" (cf. Verdugo 2004, 13). The case of Chile is a good example of a silence imposed to hide ignominious acts, which burdened the transition to democracy with an unacceptable moral cost.

against the Turkish Muslims). Perhaps the Israelis and Palestinians assembled around a table in Brussels in March 1988 were right when they expressed their conviction that 'in order merely to begin to talk, we must put the past between brackets?'

For the case of Latin America, the Chilean writer Jorge Edwards has illustrated this point:

> Now, because of an intricate web of circumstances, we are forced to look back, to poke around in our recent past, like it or not. [...] we have been condemned to being statues of salt, as in the biblical story. We must firmly look back and are not allowed to let our eyes wander around, to more agreeable sights [...] always looking at a dark, violent past, without the right to turn the page [...]. (Edwards 1999, 11; for a vigorous reply to Edwards, cf. Sepúlveda 1999, 17)

Another well-known Chilean said some years ago:

> We should not look backwards. The only alternative is to forget. That is impossible if we reopen the judicial cases and throw people in jail.

The author of that advice was Augusto Pinochet himself who on the occasion of the 22nd anniversary of the coup that brought him to power recommended to forget the past:

> It's best to remain silent and to forget. It's the only thing to do. We must forget. And forgetting does not set in by opening cases, putting people on trial. Forget. That is the word, and for this to occur, both sides must forget ... (quoted from Kattan 2002, 102)

The strongest argument of this defence of forgetfulness is the one alleging that reconciliation, to which every transition process must aspire if it is to be successful, will be impossible until the page is turned on the past and resentment subsides.

The problem with forgetfulness, however, is the simple psychological fact that forgetting is not a voluntary act. We cannot wish to forget and make it become true. Forgetting is not something we do, but something that happens to us, whether we want it or not.[11] Certainly, forgetting can be helped by eliminating things that keep a memory alive—by "turning the page", as Edwards would say. But a single person who does not wish to turn the page, who does remember, is enough to bring back a past that has not been overcome. Ironically, attempts to foster forgetfulness often have a directly opposite effect from the one pursued by the advocates of amnesia. In Germany, for instance, the Adenauer administration tried to have Germans forget about the Nazi past, only to have its memory explode in 1968, followed by a long sequence of violent acts. Unfortunately, impunity has also protected criminal prota-

---

11 I think Jon Elster (1984, 50) is right: "You can *make* someone forget something, but not by telling him to forget it, which quite probably will have the opposite result if he takes the injunction seriously. *A fortiori* you cannot simply decide to forget something either; unless, once again, you bind yourself in some manner by setting up some roundabout machinery to induce forgetfulness." "Trying to forget" is a "contradictory project" (Elster 1984, 151). That is not the opinion of Brendan Depue, a psychologist at the University of Colorado. He claims that experiments conducted at his department show that human beings have the ability to repress traumatic memories by "locking" certain areas of the brain. However, colleagues of Depue have qualified that as a "clinical myth" (cf. *Science*, July 13, 2007).

gonists of the darkest period of German history: In 1987, Ulrich Klug, an eminent German lawyer and philosopher of law, published a significant essay about the impunity enjoyed by the judges of the Nazi *Volksgerichtshof* (Peoples Tribunal) which had arbitrarily condemned more than 5,000 innocent persons to death. All these judges received their retirement pensions and enjoyed the advantages of a *Rechtsstaat* until the end of their lives.[12]

Coming back to our central subject, it is also interesting to take into account that every command to forget implies necessarily a command to remember what is to be forgotten: if A commands B to forget X, B must necessarily remember X in order to obey the command of A.

3. If we reject the option of forgetfulness, we must accept memory. Those in favor of memory usually rely on two kinds of arguments. One could be called the 'argument from identity',[13] the other one the 'argument of the pedagogical value of history' or the 'public use of history argument', to use a phrase of Jürgen Habermas (1987, 252).

In philosophy, communitarians have underscored most forcefully the importance of memory as the backbone of individual and collective identity. Alasdair MacIntyre's considerations on the relevance of the memory of slavery for the identity of the United States is one example. This is not the occasion to take a closer look at this issue, or at Habermas's position in the so-called 'Historikerstreit'.[14]

Note that what I have said above about forgetfulness also applies to memory. To remember is not a voluntary action; it is merely the internal negation of forgetting. The impossibility of their voluntary realization is the same for both of these mental states of affairs. Baruch Spinoza was perfectly clear about this:

---

12 Cf. Klug (1994). Elster (2004, 55) likewise observed: "The failure of denazification is perhaps best seen in the total absence of a purge of the West German judiciary system inherited en bloc from the Nazi period." Considering the impunity of the Nazi judges, one can hardly avoid the to think, with bitterness, that perhaps Jörg Friedrich is right, after all, when he says: "It was possible for a lawyer born in 1900 to look back on an extraordinary career on reaching retirement age in 1965. Had he not consistently been a man without qualities, he would not have made it through. In the founding years of the Republic that was a calming disvcovery. No anti-constitutionalism, no sabotage, only concern about economic security. The opportunism of the old Nazis stabilized the state. Perhaps it has indeed been proven that *the rule of law can be erected on a judicial mass grave.*" (Friedrich 1983, 16; emphasis added)

13 One of the first thinkers who underscored the importance of memory for the identity of individuals was Augustine: "There [in memory, EGV] also I meet myself and recall myself—what, when, or where I did a thing, and how I felt when I did it. There are all the things that I remember, either having experienced them myself or been told about them by others. Out of the same storehouse, with these past impressions, I can construct now this, now that, image of things that I either have experienced or have believed on the basis of experience—and from these I can further construct future actions, events, and hopes; and I can meditate on all these things as if they were present." (*Confessions*, book X, ch. 8, no. 14) On the relationship between historical memory and national identity, cf. Kattan (2002, 105ff.).

14 On this dispute, cf. e.g. Wehler (1988).

> [I]t is not within the free power of the mind to remember or forget a thing at will.[15]

If that is correct, then neither memory not forgetfulness can be the object of legal or moral norms; it makes no sense to impose a duty to remember or a prohibition to forget if one cannot do it intentionally. We might thus conclude that there cannot be such a thing as an ethics of memory.

However, against this somewhat discouraging conclusion Avishai Margalit has argued, using the example of a promise, that it is in fact possible to prohibit forgetfulness: When someone who has broken a promise claims not to have complied with it because he forgot, this means that the claim of having forgotten serves as an excuse for the violation of an obligation.[16] Hence, remembering or forgetting is something that may be required. For this to be possible, there must be some way of control over them. To remember or to forget is not like having a nervous tic that is beyond our control.

Margalit's reasoning is certainly suggestive, but I think it is wrong. The obligation he is referring to is that of keeping a promise. The excuse for not complying with it works precisely because it claims that forgetting is beyond our control. That is just the normal way of excuses: If A doesn't keep her promise of meeting with B at 5 p.m. on Tuesday because at 4 p.m. a bridge she would have had to cross in order to make it on time collapsed, that is not imputable to A but serves as an excuse. In other words, an excuse works only if it refers to a state of affairs that was not intentionally produced by the actor.[17]

Should we then conclude that forgetting or remembering morally relevant events is not moral significant? In my view, this conclusion would be premature. Even if we agree that memory and forgetfulness are states of affairs that are not under our voluntary control, this does not cancel our responsibility for the voluntary production of situations or events that may foster memory or forgetfulness.[18] We can and

---

15 Spinoza, *Ethics,* Part III, Prop. II. In Greco-Roman antiquity, the question whether memory is inborn or acquired was one of the favorite topics of rhetoric, which promised techniques to improve it.
16 Cf. Margalit (2003, 57).
17 Against this argument, cf. Blustein (2008, 31): "we certainly do sometimes praise people for remembering and blame them for forgetting. [...] a moral imperative to remember makes sense if for no other reason than that our moral responsibilities endure over time and have implications for future conduct, and in order to fulfill them we have to remember them. If control is a precondition of legitimately holding someone morally responsible, there are ways of having control over one's memory that are well within the capacities of most people."
18 One way to stimulate the memory of instances of what I have called "absolute evil" is the foundation of memorial museums. Such museums are often erected at the very places where the atrocities were committed, as in the cases of the Terezin Memorial in the Czech Republic for the victims of the Holocaust on the soil of the former Nazi extermination camp; the National Civil Rights Museum in the United States in the building of the Lorraine Motel where Martin Luther King, Jr. was assassinated; Constitutional Hill in the Republic of South Africa which occupies the former Old Fort Prison Complex where political leaders such as Mahatma Gandhi and Nelson Mandela had been incarcerated; Gulag Pern-36G in Russia, in memory of the approximately 36 million people that passed through the Soviet Gulags; or the Museum of Memory in Buenos Aires which is being installed in the building of the ESMA (the Navy

must choose the events we consider worthy of being remembered or that it would be better to forget.[19] Every society has its criteria for the selection of memorable events; that is in fact an important element of its cultural and social identity. Moreover, the consideration of the selection criteria for memorable events can be a good method for the evaluation of the moral quality of a political culture.

4. When considering the present normative relevance of past events, we must distinguish between remote and recent pasts. This is especially important when it involves criminal acts. Indeed, one of the basic functions of legal punishment is to eliminate or rectify a past situation in which a damage was inflicted. In civil-law cases it may even be possible to restore the previous state of affairs. In criminal-law cases, by contrast, that is very rare. Penal sanctions have a rather different meaning than civil damages.

In the case of criminal acts committed in a remote past, it is practically impossible to punish the personally guilty, and the imputation of legal responsibility to their descendents is also a tricky issue because it involves the reconstruction of past situations by chains of counterfactual arguments.

However, in the cases of South Africa, Argentina or other Latin-American countries which suffered regimes of state terrorism, the situation is quite different. Using the title of the first German movie drama after 1945, directed by Wolfgang Staudte, in these cases we can perfectly well say "The murderers are among us"; there is no "uncertainty of history" (to use an expression of Paul Ricoeur) that would give us a reason to foster forgetfulness. In any case, one cannot forget the present. The current situation in Argentina, for instance, is similar to the situation in Germany when Karl Jaspers wrote his famous essay on guilt. In Argentina, the surviving victims, the direct relatives of the disappeared/murdered and the perpetrators of those crimes are still living together in society. In such cases, we don't need to invoke communitarian arguments about the role of history for the creation of a collective identity, or the topic of the pedagogical function of memory for the construction of the future. The question here rather is how to deal with the immediate living memory.

5. If one accepts the alternative of memory, rather than forgetfulness, then regarding the treatment of the crimes committed we can distinguish three individual, personal attitudes:

(a) revenge,
(b) forgiveness,
(c) reconciliation;

and three institutional strategies:

School of Mechanics) which during the military dictatorship was one of the most horrible torture centers (cf. Zommer 2007).

19 It is obvious, I think, that our memory of the past cannot be but selective; I do not mean to argue in favor of an ideal as represented by "Funes the Memorious", that famous protagonist of Jorge Luis Borges's truly unforgettable short-story whose life was made miserable by his perfect memory of everything he ever did or saw.

(d) pardon,
(e) prescription, and
(f) punishment.[20]

(a) Revenge

Revenge, as an individual behavioral strategy, has at least two severe defects which make it morally unacceptable. First, rather than putting an end to a conflict, it may initiate a chain of reactions that are as violent, or even more so, than the original crime. Second, through revenge the victims become judges on their own behalf. On this, it is useful to recall John Locke's wise observations:

> I doubt not [...] that it is unreasonable for men to be judges in their own cases, that self-love will make men partial to themselves and their friends, and, on the other side, that ill-nature, passion, and revenge will carry them too far in punishing others, and hence nothing but confusion and disorder will follow ... (Locke 1975, 9)

The "proper remedy" Locke proposed to "restrain the partiality and violence of men" was, of course, the establishment of civil government, i.e., the institutionalization of a state monopoly on violence. I will come back to this below.

(b) Forgiveness

The opposite of revenge is forgiveness. Unlike forgetfulness, forgiveness is the result of a voluntary act, and it can only refer to actions one remembers. What you forgot you cannot forgive. When you don't know what the past was like, you also don't know what there might be to forgive. Forgiveness is also not an issue when one is indifferent and does not see any negative aspect in an action. In this sense, forgiveness is similar to toleration: in both cases, an agent consciously abstains from doing something which their (moral or legal) normative system would authorize them to do and which would have negative consequences for the addressee (of a pardon or of toleration, respectively). The difference is only that tolerating something means abstaining from a *prohibition* whereas forgiving something means

---

20 In what follows, I will refer only to situations where perpetrators and victims come from a recent past; and I will not treat the issue of collective responsibility. Everyone knows examples of verbal accusations or legal persecution for actions in the remote past in the name of nation-states. They are sometimes even acknowledged by those states, as was the case, e.g., when the Spanish King Juan Carlos asked for forgiveness in the name of Spain for the expulsion of the jews in 1492; and it is also the case of the French law of May 21, 2001, whose art. 1. stipulates: "The French Republic acknowledges that the overseas treatment of blacks in the Indian Ocean, on the one hand, and the acts of slavery committed in the Americas and the Caribbean, in the Indian Ocean and in Europe against the African, Amerindian, Malagasy and Indian population, on the other, constitute crimes against humanity." Regarding the legal condemnation of the past, cf. Truche (2004).

abstaining from a *sanction*. And just as toleration, if it is not to be the 'idiotic' toleration Herbert Marcuse rejected, requires the existence of good reasons for lifting a prohibition, forgiveness, if it is not to be 'blind', requires at least the repentance of the offender.

Jeffrie Murphy correctly observed that

> It is not unreasonable to want repentance from a wrongdoer before forgiving that wrongdoer, since, in the absence of repentance, hasty forgiveness may harm both the forgiver and the wrongdoer. The forgiver may be harmed by a failure to show self-respect. The wrongdoer may be harmed by being deprived of an important incentive—the desire to be forgiven—that could move him toward repentance and moral rebirth. (Murphy 2003, 35)

However, while it is "not unreasonable" to make forgiveness depend on repentance, this does not mean, Murphy says, that one should coercively induce repentance as a necessary prerequisite for forgiveness:

> When a person comes to repentance as a result of his own spiritual growth, we are witness to an inspiring transformation of character. Any expressed repentance that is nothing more than a response to a coercive external incentive, however, is very likely to be fake. (Murphy 2003, 37)

Given that repentance is an individual mental state that becomes manifest only through verbal statements or other behavior of the respective person, there is obviously always the possibility of lying and cheating. Still, I think that from a conceptual point of view it is not only reasonable, but necessary that repentance precede forgiveness.[21] Repentance means that the respective person has intentionally behaved in a way in which he now wishes he had not behaved, precisely because it is blameworthy. Otherwise, what sense could it make to say that (a victim) *A* forgives (a perpetrator) *B* for a conduct *c*, if *B* does not think that *c* is blameworthy? What would there be to forgive, in that case? It could even be the case that *A* and *B* agree on the description of the physical movements involved in the acts in question, but not in their interpretation and moral relevance. Recourse to the theory of double effect is a well-known source for that kind of disagreement: *A* claims to have been tortured by *B*, whereas the latter asserts that what he did was not an act of torture, but merely an investigation of a situation that was relevant for public security. On this line of thinking, actions are defined by the actor's intention, not by external criteria alleged by those affected by the actions or by onlooking third parties. An unrepentant perpetrator will interpret a pardon as an insult because he will, plausibly, argue that the pardon implies the assessment of an action as blameworthy which he (the perpetrator) himself sees as unobjectionable, and possibly even as praiseworthy.[22] Rafael Videla, the Argentine dictator, has expressed this very clearly:

---

21 Allais (2008, 37) disagrees: "forgiveness is elective in the sense that it can be given without repentance of the wrongdoer, without the forgiver necessarily making a moral mistake."
22 Similarly, Card (2002, 174): "Offenders who do not acknowledge wrongdoing [...] may perceive offers of forgiveness as arrogant and offensive." The interpretation of forgiveness as an "unconditional or unilateral gift" (Allais 2002, 39) cannot account for such cases.

> It is not enough to pardon and release us. Argentine society is indebted to us. To begin with, it must ask for our forgiveness and restore us in our ranks and honors. (Quoted from García 2007)

Thus, the strategy of forgiving necessarily presupposes that those who are guilty of a crime must acknowledge this. And that is precisely what has been lacking, e.g., in the transitions in Argentina and Chile. Until this day the authors and actors of state terrorism in those countries are reiterating their conviction that they did absolutely nothing wrong, and that their's was a just war.[23]

On the other hand, freely granting unconditional pardons only serves to make the impunity even more notorious, causing new harm to the victims.[24] But this refers to what we may call 'institutional forgiveness'. Concerning individual victims, they cannot be thought to have a moral duty to forgive without previous repentance by the offender—that would be a supererogatory act which cannot be demanded from them.

And even if the offender has expressed repentance, it does not follow automatically that the victim has a moral obligation to forgive. Forgiveness presupposes repentance, but it is quite another question whether repentance necessarily imposes forgiveness. Claudia Card's observations on this point seem plausible to me:

> Although forgiveness cannot be compelled, one can be at fault in failing to offer it to those who deserve it or refusing to grant it when asked by those who have done all they can to atone. (Card 2002, 174)

By contrast, Hannah Arendt held that not only is it wrong to suppose that repentance always imposes forgiveness, but that some actions are so perverse that they belong to the category of the unforgivable and also the unpunishable:

> It is [...] a structural element in the realm of human affairs, that men are unable to forgive what they cannot punish and that they are unable to punish what has turned out to be unforgivable. This is the true hallmark of those offenses which, since Kant, we call 'radical evil' and about whose nature so little is known [...]. All we know is that we can neither punish nor forgive such offenses and that they therefore transcend the realm of human affairs and the potentialities of human power ... (Arendt 1959, 217)

I tend to think that the relationship she establishes between the possibility of forgiveness and the possibility of punishment leads to rather unreasonable conse-

---

23 According to Augusto Pinochet, "Some, very strangely, say we should ask for forgiveness. Whom should we ask? Those who tried to kill us, who tried to destroy the country? Whom? They are the ones that should ask forgiveness from us! [...] The Armed Forces have nothing to ask forgiveness for. [...] If someone wants to ask for forgiveness, let him do it. But I will not ask forgiveness on behalf of my institution, ever. [...] There were excesses on both sides." (Quoted from Lefranc 2005, 164–165)

24 Unconditional forgiveness tends to foster forgetfulness of crimes. An amnesty—that "shared amnesia", as it has been called—can plausibly be seen as an institutional form of unconditional forgiveness. A particularly disgusting form of unconditional institutional pardon is the auto-amnesty as imposed in Argentina and Chile by the dictatorial governments to avoid all risks of legal prosecution. In Lefranc's words (2005, 268), this is a "caricature of a pardon: the pardon of the offender by the offender".

quences. *A* may think that the harm inflicted on her by *B* is unforgivable without necessarily thinking that it cannot be punished. Certainly, it is not always possible to implement the desire to bring crime and punishment in an adequate relation; and it may well be that in cases of extreme evil any kind of punishment seems insufficient, not only from the point of view of the victims. We need only think of the so-called crimes against humanity. When such crimes are punished with prison terms of hundreds of years, such sentences serve to demonstrate the severity of the crime rather than to indicate the actual possibility that the term could be served. Besides, the alleged relationship between unforgivability and impossibility of adequate punishment has the peculiar consequence that beyond a certain degree of severity of a crime the reasonableness of punishment decreases, with the implication that at some point it would be rational for an offender to increase the severity of his crime in order to push it beyond the threshold and make it unforgivable and thereby unpunishable, thus ensuring impunity. If that reasoning were correct, then prosecutors and judges who attempt to prosecute and sentence those who commit crimes against humanity would also be unreasonable. This does not seem tenable to me.

Moreover, if must not be forgotten that forgiveness cannot erase the perversity of the conduct of a repentant criminal. The effect of forgiveness is rather of a mental kind: it makes the repentant perpetrator feel freed from the resentment and potential revenge of the victim who, in turn, can see in the criminal's repentance an expression of empathy with her suffering. Forgiveness thus changes the relationship between the forgiver and the forgiven. That is why it seems to make no sense to say that we can forgive a dead person, as Allais says (2002, 37), or that forgiven the repentant is superfluous, as Aurel Kolnai claims:

> [T]he question is often raised how we can forgive the unrepentant without condoning their offenses, tacitly approving them, and thereby tacitly encouraging their emulation. The question is also raised what remains to be forgiven when an offender does repent and regenerate? [These two questions] together suggest that forgiveness is either inappropriate or else redundant. Without repentance, it seems inappropriate. With repentance, it seems redundant. (Quoted from Card 2002, 178)

(c) Reconciliation

One means often employed for making a pardon look less supererogatory or paradoxical is to assert that the idea is not that it should be a unilateral voluntary act, but that what matters is reciprocity. This is the strategy of so-called "reconciliation". In the words of Walter Wink:

> Reconciliation [...] requires that I and the other from whom I have been separated by enmity, mutually forgive each other and together walk into a common future. Forgiveness is thus a component of reconciliation, but only a first step. We may forgive our enemies in our hearts, but reconciliation requires that we pick up the phone or meet face to face and try to work things out. (Wink 1998, 14, quoted from Little 1999, 69)

This idea of reconciliation has inspired the activities of the South African Truth and Reconciliation Commission (TRC) established on July 19, 1995, with a Committee on Human Rights Violations, a Committee on Amnesty and a Committee on Reparation and Rehabilitation. In other countries, similar commissions have been set up, such as the Bosnia and Herzegovina Truth and Reconciliation Commission, the Truth Comission of El Salvador, or the Rettig Commission in Chile, among others. Just as in the unilateral strategy of forgiveness, in all these cases strong religious overtones invoking the value of forgiveness and of understanding human weaknesses which are the cause of sins and crimes are clearly perceptible. In 1997, André Du Toit, professor at the University of Cape Town, observed:

> As religious leaders und churches became increasingly involved in the commission's work, the influence of religious style and symbolism supplanted political and human rights concerns. (Quoted from Minow 1998, 55)[25]

In South Africa, the prevalent argument was the following:

> To achieve unity and morally acceptable reconciliation, it is necessary that the truth about gross violations of human rights must be established by an official investigation unit using fair procedures; fully and unreservedly acknowledged by the perpetrators; made known to the public, together with the identity of the planners, perpetrators, and victims. (Quoted from Minow 1998, 55).

In Argentina too, the issue of reconciliation has recently returned to the attention of the public. On August 3, 2003, an editorial in the important newspaper *La Nación* (p. 24) stated:

> we must insist on the idea that we Argentines need to become aware of the value of moral and institutional gestures that could lead us definitely to overcome the historical antinomies and the resentments of the past [...] What we demand is that when it comes to decisions that affect the supreme national interest, the court must take into account the importance of promoting, among other things, the reconciliation of the Argentine people.[26]

---

25 Cf. also Lefranc (2005, 77): "The opening remarks of the president [of the Commission, EGV] were usually preceded by a prayer; a commemorative candle was lighted, and hymns and songs were sung. When Archbishop Desmond Tutu presided the session, he wore his purple habit [...]. During the last sessions, when he was not present, other religious leaders were asked to lead a prayer. Also, local community groups often sang songs and organized a ceremony."

26 In 1989, President Carlos Menem had already asserted: "The central idea of these times is national reconciliation. [...] The executive authority of the nation intends [...] to create the conditions and the necessary platform for national reconciliation, mutual forgiveness and national." But note that the idea of "mutual forgiveness" conceptually presupposes the acknowledgement of guilt on all sides. Hence, speaking of reconciliation, I think the observations of another Latin-American president, the Chilean Patricio Aylwin, on March 4, 1991, are more to the point: "This is the hour of forgiveness and reconciliation. [...] Who could not desire this? However, if we want to achieve this we must begin by establishing who were the offended who must be asked for forgiveness, and who were the offenders who should be forgiven. I cannot forgive anybody in the name of others. Forgiveness cannot be decreed. Forgiveness presupposes repentance on one side and generosity on the other." (Quoted from Lefranc 2005, 163–164)

It is rather obvious that a necessary condition for reconciliation is that the truth about the crimes that were committed is known. But this leads to an unsolvable moral problem because one of the consequences is that for *collective reconciliation* to have any rational foundation *collective guilt* must be assumed. We can in this context think of a secular version of the biblical metaphor of the stone that may be thrown by those and only by those who are innocent. Hence, it is not surprising that advocates of the strategy of reconciliation usually insist that *all* citizens who lived under a regime of state terrorism or under *apartheid* are somehow guilty, which enables them to invoke the Christian admonition just mentioned. In Argentina, even before and briefly after the military regime was ousted, the phrase 'All are guilty' was heard. In July 1982, Reynaldo Bignone, the last of the top protagonists of the Argentine 'Process of National Reconstruction', expressed the condition for possible reconciliation when he literally said that "He who is without guilt may throw the first stone"; to which from the city of Córdoba Arturo Illía, a former President who has always been honest, replied: "I have a lot of stones in my hands" (quoted from Tcach 1996, 44). On November 16, 1985, Cardinal Raúl Primatesta gave an ecclesiastic version of the idea of collective guilt:

> We have all been wrong, *we must all seek forgiveness, grant it and ask for it*, and look to the future to construct something new. (Quoted from Fernández 1987, 43)

And on June 20, 1998, Carlos Menem—at that time President of Argentina— spoke of "a past at which no-one may throw the first stone".

Unless one believes that the alchemy of reiteration makes falsity become true, I do not see how this much-repeated admonition could make sense (on the discussion about whether everyone is guilty, cf. also Ciancaglini/Granovsky 1995, 331ff.). Still, the stoning metaphor has remained in fashion:

> We must put an end to the preaching of resentment. We must extinguish the flames of discord before they become a huge fire that pushes us into disintegration and anarchy. [...] He who believes to be without any responsibility for the horrors of those past years may throw the first stone. (Letter to the editor by Alberto Rogríguez Varela, *La Nación*, August 29, 2003, 16)

Let me reiterate that reconciliation conceptually presupposes that all sides have valid complaints against all others. Only if the initial situation is understood in this sense one can also understand why reconciliation is often said to restore the state of affairs prior to the offenses. Reconciliation is about establishing a symmetrical relationship of a positive kind, in reversal of a negative symmetrical relationship which existed while the parties, neither of which is supposed to be innocent, were locked in confrontation.

If that is correct, then certainly collective reconciliation is *not* what should be suggested when a regime of state terrorism is overturned. As state terrorism is a regime in which offenses are always dealt out *asymmetrically*, such systems necessarily produce innocent victims. For a proposal of reconciliation to make sense to these victims, one would have to demand that *a posteriori* they accept part of the blame. Such a demand would ask not only for a supererogatory, but for an altogether irrationally masochistic attitude. I simply cannot imagine a victim of the stubbornly unrepentant Pinochet to 'pick up the phone' and make plans with the latter for 'a common future'—just as I cannot imagine a telephone conversation of this kind between a survivor of the holocaust and, say, a neo-nazi.

Besides, it seems strange—to say the least—that a criminal should be able to exchange truth for impunity[27] According to that logic, the perpetrator who confesses his crime must go free, whereas a person who denies being guilty should be punished. That is why the argument for reconciliation has always seemed dishonest and frustrating to me: it opens the way for the impunity of the guilty while smearing the innocent with the suspicion of guilt. Often, it is used simply as a means to cover up a lack of political will or the impossibility to apply the law, either because there never was a window of opportunity or because one has let it pass.[28] It is a 'crutch

27 This is not merely a rhetorical assertion. The introduction to the report of the South African TRC edited by Desmond Tutu (quoted, and retranslated, here from an excerpt published in Spanish in the Mexican journal *istor. Revista de historia internacional* vol. II no. 5 [2001]) literally states that "Freedom was granted in exchange of truth" (12). On the whole, that introduction contains remarks I find astonishing. A few examples: "Frequently, we uncovered the lies and deceptions that were at the very root of *apartheid* [...]. We know who bombed Khotso House. We remember how Mr. Adriaan Vlok, former Minister of Law and Order, publicly [...] lied about it; how without any shame whatsoever provoked the detention of Shirley Gunn with her infant son as responsable for that act. In his favor, it must be said that during his plea for amnesty Mr. Vlok gentlemanly [sic!] presented his excuses to Ms. Gunn." (12) "There were some who thought that we should follow the post-war example and bring those guilty of severe human rights violations to justice, as the allies did in Nuremberg. [...] [I]n South Africa that was an impossible option. Neither of the two parties in conflict (the government and the liberation movements) had defeated the other and hence neither was in the position to impose the so-called winner's justice." (9) In my view, it is inadequate to speak of "winner's justice" when a criminal political regime is ousted. The expression "winner's justice" clearly carries a morally negative connotation which is unwarranted as much with respect to the Nuremberg case as with respect to countries like Argentina where the democratic system brought the leaders of the military dictatorship of 1976–1983 to trial. In this context, it is interesting to recall some facts collected by Jon Elster (2004, 117): "Most of the twenty-odd truth commissions that have been established since 1982 have not even named the perpetrators, let alone proposed to punish them. The commission in South Africa is the major exception, but even here the knowledge of politically motivated wrongdoings does not lead to prosecution. In Brazil, the 444 torturers who were named by the Archidiocese of Sao Paulo had already been granted amnesty." Regarding the precarious moral status of the truth commissions, cf. Robertson (2006, ch. 7, V).

28 In that sense, it is interesting to note that those who argue in favor of establishing truth commissions often do so to avoid being put to trial. One obvious example of this can be found in the following declaration, made in 1994 by Mario Enríquez, Minister of Defence of Guatemala: "We are fully in support of a truth commission. Just as in Chile: truth, not trials." The best way to ensure impunity once the findings of a truth commission are known is to grant a broadly defined amnesty. Hayner (2001, 86) presents valuable information about the relationship between the reports of truth commissions and amnesty: "In El Salvador, the release of the truth commission report was answered with the immediate passage of a sweeping amnesty law. In South Africa, justice was put up for trade: the truth commission offered freedom from prosecution in exchange for the full truth about politically motivated crimes." And: "The El Salvador truth commission's strongly worded report included the names of forty high-level officials responsible for serious abuses, despite strong pressure from the Salvadoran government not to publish names. In response to the report [...] the president of El Salvador immediately intro-

strategy' intended to help a precarious *Rechtsstaat* stay on its feet. And the most diligent manufacturers of such crutches are, of course, those who are themselves responsible for the weakness of the state. They are the ones who claim that 'time is not ripe' for implementing the penal code, and that the alternatives are either punishment and the demise of democracy or 'clean slate' and democracy's persistence. To believe in this dilemma: that is what seems wrong to me.

(d) Pardon

In contrast to amnesty, a pardon does not imply forgiveness; it merely involves the omission of punishment. A legacy of absolutism and a prerogative of heads of state, it is not always easily justified. As Kant said:

> The right of pardoning (*jus aggratiandi*), viewed in relation to the criminal, is the right of mitigating or entirely remitting his punishment. On the side of the sovereign this is the most delicate of all rights, as it may be exercised so as to set forth the splendour of his dignity, and yet so as to do a great wrong by it. (Kant 1954, 165)

From the moral point of view, when a pardon is granted to individuals who have committed crimes against humanity, as was the case of Argentina (to which I will return below), it constitutes a notorious injustice that is unacceptable.

(e) Prescription

Prescription generally involves the cancellation of a right merely because a certain amount of time has passed. Specifically with regard to the penal law, prescription means that after a certain period of time fixed by law penal consequences for some offence may no longer be considered. Prescription does not aim at erasing the memory of a criminal action. It merely closes the road for the corresponding penal action, thus extinguishing it.[29] It can be interpreted as a form of legal absolution which comes about, so to speak, by itself, without any human intervention.

In order to avoid perverse effects in the case of crimes against humanity as well as to avoid its interpretation as a kind of tacit amnesty,[30] there exists nowadays a

---

duced a bill in Parliament to award a 'broad, absolute, and unconditional amnesty' to 'all those who in one way or another participated in political crimes or crimes with political ramifications.' Just five days after the truth commission report was published, Parliament passed this sweeping amnesty proposal into law, with the support of the former armed opposition." (Hayner 2001, 91).

29 As Paul Ricoeur (2000, 611) remarks, the concept of extinction "encompasses at the same time a phenomenon of passivity, inertia, negligence, and social inaction, and an arbitrary social gesture which allows us to regard the institution of prescription as a creation of positive law".

30 On this issue, cf. Just-Dahlmann/Just (1988, 275ff., esp. 295). In the Federal Republic of Germany, a slim majority (255 votes in favor, 222 against) of the federal parliament approved in

widespread consensus that such crimes do not prescribe: their authors can be legally prosecuted without temporal limitations.[31] It is thus stipulated, e.g., in the 'Convention on the Non-Applicability of Statutory Limitations to War Crimes and Crimes against Humanity' of 1974 as well as in art. 29 of the Rome Statute of the ICC which clearly says: "The crimes within the jurisdiction of the Court shall not be subject to any statute of limitations."

(f) Punishment

Under the rule of law, punishing those who have committed crimes of absolute evil by way of due process through the judicial system is, in my view, undoubtedly the most adequate way of dealing with the memory of atrocities, taking seriously the suffering of the victims, and expressing social repugnance to those crimes, while at the same time respecting the human dignity of the perpetrators, as it is usually not done in acts of naked revenge. I therefore agree with Arne Johan Vetlesen:

> Trials conducted to seek justice in the aftermath of large-scale collective evil effect something of invaluable moral significance by virtue of their sheer legal formalism: in seeking that those guilty receive the punishment due to them, and in breaking the walls of silence previously solidifying the sorry fate of those victimized, such trials proceed on the premise that both 'parties', the perpetrators as well as the victims, are bearers of rights. (Vetlesen 2005, 270)

There has been an intensive discussion about whether it is necessary to punish *all* agents of state terrorism and perpetrators of crimes against humanity, or whether one should rather go for what has been called 'selective punishment'. The main argument in favor of the latter holds that the quality of a judicial system should not be judged by a quantitative criterion, and that because of the large number of perpetrators it is advisable to 'select' a few, imposing the pertinent penalties only on them. The deterring effects of punishment would not be affected by such a selection, it is argued, and at the same time this would enable the new regime to count on the eventual cooperation of those who only obeyed orders. Hobbes (*Leviathan*, ch. XVI) already observed that it is possible and frequent for one individual to perform an action in the name of another; the latter then is the *author* of the action, the former its *actor*. This distinction makes it possible to exempt the actor from all responsibility, imputing it solely on the author. The actor, on this account, performs a kind of 'abdication of choice' in the sense that his own beliefs and preferences play no role for the performance of the action, which is why he should not personally be held responsible for decisions made in the name of the author who gave the corresponding authorization or order.

1979 the 'Law against the prescription of murder', thus rendering certain crimes committed during the Nazi regime imprescriptible.
31 Paul Ricoeur (2000, esp. 612f.) has, in my view convincingly, spelled out the moral arguments in favor of the imprescriptibility of crimes against humanity.

That is the position that was taken in Argentina with the so-called 'Law of Due Obedience' of June 1987 concerning the prosecution of the former military *juntas* and their agents. On the theoretical side, Thomas Scanlon (1994) has been among the advocates of this thesis. Against this, I agree with Martha Minow (1998, 44f.) who regarding Alfonsín's 'Law of Due Obedience' observed:

> This made the pattern of existing and halted prosecutions so evidently selective and partial as to challenge seriously the fairness of the entire process. In addition to the fairness problem, selectivity in prosecution risks creating martyrs out of the few who are subject to trial and punishment. The distinction between law and politics seems all but erased and the truth-seeking process seems subordinated to public spectacle and symbolic governmental statements—and thus the perpetrators begin to look like victims of the prosecutorial regimen.

A more radical view of the legal (non)treatment of the past was proposed by Bruce Ackerman. In his view, the application of the Criminal Code, of 'corrective justice', in democratic transition processes has the perverse effect that it "divide[s] the citizenry into two groups—evildoers and innocent victims" (Ackerman 1992, 71). Corrective justice always looks back to the past, he says, and in the effort to find evidence that will make it possible to punish the guilty according to the provisions of a democratic *Rechtsstaat*, the most important task is neglected, which is that of avoiding that a dictatorship might re-emerge in the future. The problem for Ackerman is not so much a lack of moral support from a social majority for this undertaking, but the persistence of a legal and administrative system that collaborated with the ousted regime and that therefore "organizational resources are limited":

> This distinctive combination—high moral capital, low bureaucratic capacity—should be kept firmly in mind as successful revolutionaries try to manage the tension between corrective justice and constitutional ordering. Responses to the past must be carefully framed in the lights of predictable bureaucratic weakness. (Ackerman 1992, 72)[32]

By renouncing the "mirage of corrective justice" (cf. Ackerman 1992, 74ff.) it could be avoided that the members of a bureaucracy contaminated by its collaboration with the previous regime engage in strategies of obstruction, and the active incorporation of these very agents into the democratic system could be promoted:

> Without the threat of vindictive punishment, an enormous number of minor collaborators in the old regime will be only too happy to join the liberal revolutions and proclaim themselves born-again believers in freedom, equality, and the rule of law. (Ackerman 1992, 78)

As empirical evidence for the convenience of his proposal to forget the past, Ackerman presents precisely the case of the trials of the Argentine military during the presidency of Raúl Alfonsín:

---

32 Jon Elster (2004, 213f.) also mentions the problem of bureaucratic weakness: "The scarcity of reliable judges is a very important constraint on transitional justice. In very many cases, the judiciary have been part and parcel of the regime to be judged. The German judiciary after 1945 was especially notorious for its obstructionist attitude toward crimes of Nazi criminals, including (and especially) Nazi judges."

> [I]t was the governments's effort to move beyond the top leaders and prosecute middle-level officers that revealed the fragility that is characteristic of the moral-bureaucratic balance of insurgent regimes. [...] In the meantime, the government was obliged to cope with the predictable anxiety of theses officers and with their political efforts to rewrite the rules of the game. Two years later the prosecution began, Alfonsín was already allowing military defendants to use 'due obedience to superiors' as a defense. This concession prompted a series of further retreats [...]. This failure prepared the way for the decision by Alfonsin's successor, Menem, to pardon everybody and to release the remaining few who were still caught up in the affair. [...] It was Alfonsín, not Menem, who failed to carry through the program in a systematic fashion [...]. (Ackerman 1992, 79)[33]

If would have been better, according to Ackerman, to ignore the valid Criminal Code and resist the temptation of 'mirages'.

In my view, the thesis that a judicial system should not be judged from a quantitative point of view, i.e. by looking at the percentage or numbers of convicted offenders, is acceptable only with strong reservations. First of all, from a moral point of view it seems correct to say that *all* guilty ought to be punished. This also seems to be the meaning of the provisions of the criminal law which stipulate such things as 'Homicide shall be punished with ...' (or, more clearly, in the Argentine Penal Code: 'He who kills another shall be punished with ...'). Such formulations must certainly be read as preceded by a universal quantifier, rather than in the sense of 'Some homicides ...' or 'Some who kill another ...'.

Concerning the claim of insufficient capacity at the national level to punish genocide, the case of Rwanda is particularly interesting. In May 2003, more than 22,000 prisoners, most of them ethnic hutus accused of having participated in the genocide of 1994, were set free after spending three months in a re-education camp and several years in prison awaiting trial. Prisons in Rwanda were filled to capacity with people accused of complicity in genocide who had not yet been tried. Estimates are that there were 90,000 of them, 90% of whom were allegedly involved in killings that took the lifes of one million tutsis and moderate hutus (as reported in *El País* [Madrid] of May 6, 2003, 11).

Already in 1998, it had been calculated that the Rwandan judicial system—with a mere 900 judges trained in six-months crash courses—would need several generations to bring all the accused (most of whom would by then be dead, of course) to

---

33 What Ackerman's here refers to is the fact that when Menem took office in 1989 he pardoned 172 participants of military revolts that took place during the Alfonsín administration, besides a large number of the protagonists of the 'dirty war' who allegedly had only obeyed orders, and that one year later, he repeated the exercise: by executive orders no. 2741 to 2746, he pardoned Jorge Rafael Videla who had been found guilty of 68 murders, 4 cases of torture leading to death, 93 cases of torture, 306 illegal detentions and 26 robberies, for which he had received a life sentence; Roberto Viola, convicted for 11 cases of torture, 86 cases of kidnapping and 3 robberies and sentenced to 17 years; Emilio Eduardo Massera, found guilty of 3 murders,12 cases of torture, 69 kidnappings and 7 robberies and given a life sentence; and Ramón Camps, convicted of 73 cases of multiple torture, of whom international human rights organizations believe that he is responsable for at least 5,000 disappearances, who claims ideological sympathy for Hitler, especially for "his humanist interest in mankind and in combating the permanent communist campaign", and who had received a sentence of 25 years.

trial (as reported in *Süddeutsche Zeitung* [Munich] of March 24, 1998, 3). On the negative consequences of this inability to punish for the social peace in Rwanda the UN has since published several reports.

Argentina was not Rwanda. And in the case of other Latin-American countries too it was not difficult to observe that when people think that their condition as victims is not taken seriously, two consequences may ensue, both of which are unacceptable:

a) They may feel doubly injured. Not only have they suffered the transgression of the offender, they are also made to suffer the mental harm of feeling unprotected against the offender or other, potential future aggressors.

b) They may thus feel impelled to take justice into their own hands.

Also, in the first case, when the law is applied selectively to the guilty and does not impose the same penalty on all perpetrators of similar crimes, the fairness principle is violated—something that is unacceptable under the rule of law.

And in the second case, when the legal system ceases to be regarded as producing a powerful deterrent against violence, that is a large step towards a Hobbesian prepolitical state of affairs. When a political regime is unable to guarantee security by imposing sanctions on those who undermine it, it has lost the legitimizing justification for its monopoly on the exercise of violence: *protego ergo obligo*. That is why I find it difficult to accept the thesis of selective punishment.

So the only alternative left is that of a consistent application of the Criminal Code, with all the guarantees which the rule of law and democracy grant to the accused—who may be numerous, but will surely never include everyone, as the advocates of reconciliation claim. Reconciliation, in any case, should only be expected after punishment has been imposed since, as Alejandro Garro (1992, 23) pointed out, "reconciliation without punishment fosters criminality rather than moderating it".

What I have said so far for the national context also applies at the international level. Crimes against humanity have already specifically been dealt with in international documents, and since the establishment of the International Criminal Court we possess a court that is specifically authorized to prosecute such cases.[34] In this respect, I fully agree with Peter Singer (2003, 100):

> Just as at the domestic level, the last line of defence against individual crimes of murder, rape and assault is law enforcement, so too the last line of defence against genocide and similar crimes must be law enforcement, at a global level.

I therefore find it difficult to see the point of arguments against an international jurisdiction which, in any case, only has a subsidiary function, meant to take over when national governments are unwilling to prosecute actors accused of crimes that 'shock the conscience of humanity' or unable to do so because of the bureaucratic weakness Bruce Ackerman was so concerned about.

---

34 By mid-2008, there were 108 States Parties to the Statute, and several dozen more had signed and were awaiting ratification (www2.icc-cpi.int).

The consistent application of the rule of law and the realization of trials in which those found guilty receive the legally established sanctions, however, is not all there is to it. In addition, I think it is useful to take into account the recommendations of James Booth to stimulate what he calls "memory-justice": an imperative of memory that goes beyond the always individualizing judicial action. Memory-justice can incorporate aspects of responsibility that escape the judicial system. It can take into account the fundamental political fact that the really big crimes, the absolute evil inflicted by dictatorial state terrorism or genocide become possible only if their authors can rely on the silent collaboration of large parts of the population:

> Memory-justice [...] seems to need something else, a testimony to and a recognition of a responsibility that, although it includes individual accountability, reaches beyond it to something not reducible to guilt. [...] What is wanted is a self-understanding on the part of the members of a political community as co-responsible even if not legally accountable. This we could call, in the aftermath of mass crimes, for a sense of shame that emerges not from direct authorship of actions but from membership in a community implicated in these deeds. [...] Memory as shame [...] seems to be part of the demand of memory-justice, and it ranges far beyond the issue of guilt that is at play in criminal trials. The absence of such a sense of shame, of the recognition of the responsibility of a community, is one of the things that struck Hannah Arendt during her 1950 visit to Germany. [...] Not only can a trial not attain to that wider form of responsibility, but it also (and therefore) offers another type of premature closure as well: as if by seeing the guilty leaders punished we have freed ourselves of the burden of responsibility for these crimes. (Booth 2006, 136–137)[35]

Rather than claiming that it is impossible legally to punish absolute evil, these observations point to the fact that the assessment of moral responsibility for it requires a broader perspective.

Finally, I wish to mention one last aspect concerning trials for crimes that amount to absolute evil and the sentencing of those convicted of such crimes. In my view, only the judicial proceedings as established in the law of liberal democracies are morally acceptable. Obviously, this excludes the proposal of special treatment for those suspected of crimes against humanity in the sense of an "enemy criminal law" *(Feindstrafrecht)* as recently proposed, e.g., by Günther Jakobs (2004). According to Jakobs, we should distinguish between a "citizen" as a "person within the law", or simply "person", who may break the law here and there in single instances, without

---

35 There exists an abundant scholarship on the question to what point the population of a country where state terrorism rules or genocide is committed can be expected to know about these facts. For the German case, let me just mention Longerich (2006). For Argentina, cf. Crenzel (2008), esp. 38–51, among others. Karl Jaspers (1987) spoke of "political guilt" in the case of an entire society passively watching on as the state committed crimes in its name and in its midst: "A people is responsible for its statehood" (Jaspers 1987, 40). Jaspers also thought that punishing the "guilty leaders" did not free Germans from a critical examination of their own passivity: "Every German, without exception, has a share in the political liability. [...] Not every German, rather only a small minority of Germans, must be punished for crimes, another minority must do penance for Nazi activities. [...] Every German—although in very different ways—probably has reason for a critical self-assessment from a moral point of view." (Jaspers 1987, 49)

therefore losing the status of citizen, and an "enemy" who is generally unwilling to accept the norms imposed by society and therefore is a permanent danger for the legal order. Rather than citizens and "persons within the law", enemies are qualified as "outside the law". As Geraldine Louisa Morguet observes,

> In Jakobs's view, enemy criminal law is a criminal law sui generis. It is a special criminal law in relation to the ordinary criminal law, i.e. the criminal law for citizens. In that sense, there are two opposed forms of the criminal law and its provisions (including criminal procedures): on the one hand, for treatment of the citizen to whom a sphere free of state control is conceded; and on the other hand, for treatment of the enemy who must be preemptively constrained at a very early stage and controlled because of his dangerousness. [...] The procedural guarantees of the criminal law for citizens such as, e.g., the right to a legal hearing, the principle of nemo tenetur or the presumption of innocence do not, or only restrictively, apply in enemy criminal law, because the enemy is not a legal subject; his punishment and the criminal procedures in his case must follow exclusively considerations of expediency: Permitted is whatever serves to reduce the danger. Procedural guarantees in favor of the enemy would, by contrast, reduce the efficiency of the criminal law. (Morguet 2009, 37, 58)

The typical enemy, in Jakobs's terms, is the terrorist—not only those who destroyed the Twin Towers in New York or exploded the trains at Atocha in Madrid, but all those who personify the satanic struggle against the democratic state.

I hope I don't need to clarify that when I speak of legal punishment I am not referring to such an "enemy criminal law" which leads straight to a system of detention without trial, as in the infamous camps of Guantánamo.

3. Abuse of Legal Norms: The Case of Argentine

1. Throughout this paper I have made frequent mention of individual and institutional reactions in Argentina regarding the criminal acts committed during the years of state terrorism in that country (1976–1983). To conclude, I wish to draw attention to the fact that in the case of Argentina, the strategy of selective punishment, amnesty laws and pardons does not seem to have been the best possible way to solve the problem.

2. In March 2001, a Federal judge in Buenos Aires ruled the law of due obedience unconstitutional, and in August 2003 the National Congress established the nullity of that law and of all the amnesty laws of 1989. In 2004, the Supreme Court ruled that crimes against humanity are imprescriptible and permitted the reopening of the criminal prosecutions against members of the military dictatorship suspected of having committed such crimes. Finally, in July 2007, the Supreme Court also ruled that the executive pardons signed by President Carlos Menem were unconstitutional.[36] The court's main arguments were the following:

---

36 As a consequence of that ruling, 380 members of the military were prosecuted for crimes against humanity. On June 25, 2008, the first life sentences were given to military personnel

- In the case of state terrorism as well as in the case of crimes against humanity, as they are committed every day in the form of institutionalized or non-institutionalized terror, there is no *legal* reason why they should not all be prosecuted. These crimes were legally classified as such before they were committed. In Argentina, this was expressly acknowledged in the Argentine military's 'self-amnesty' law[37] whose art. 1 grants "the benefits of this law [...] to all acts of a criminal nature committed in the context or with the motive of undertaking actions aimed at preventing, averting, or terminating the already mentioned terrorist or subversive activities, regardless of their nature or the legal value that has been harmed". Even before the 1976 military *coup*, the Argentine Criminal Code already sanctioned rebellion, defined as "taking up arms to change the Constitution, deposing one of the public powers of the national government [...or] impeding the free exercise of its constitutional powers [...]", with 3–10 years; and art. 652 of the Military Criminal Code stipulated that "while the rebellion lasts, all military personnel who participate in it are deprived of the authority and privileges inherent in their office". As the military never derogated any of these provisions, the problem of a retroactive application of criminal laws which so much troubled H. L. A. Hart in his controversy with Gustav Radbruch about the Nuremberg trials (Hart 1961, 254f.) does not arise, nor does that of a conflict between different legal systems and the application of sanctions for actions which at the time they were performed were in accord with the provisions of the system then in force, as in the case of the East German border guards who killed people trying to leave the country.
- From the constitutional point of view, it is legally impossible to pardon persons who have been involved in serious violations of human rights.
- Crimes against humanity are legally imprescriptible.

3. Those who argued against this position claimed:

- First, that the principle of firm sentence is the best guaranty for individual rights.
- Second, that the international convention on the imprescriptibility of crimes against humanity was incorporated in the Argentine Constitution only in 1995,

---

convicted of illegal detention, murder and torture. None of the convicted expressed repentance for these crimes; on the contrary, they again attempted to justify them: "We fought against marxist terrorism, without ever committing any crime" or "50 years ago, the war suddenly broke out in our country; we were trying to overcome international communism. What the marxist subversives have claimed ever since is wrong; what they call illegal repression were defense operations" (quoted from *La Nación* of August 29, 2008, 15). These criminals were sentenced 31 years after having committed their crimes; and the trials rekindled the discussion about the scope and limits of so-called transitional justice. With regard to the crimes committed by the guerrilla, by the way, the Argentine Supreme Court ruled that they were not crimes against humanity as that concept refers only to state-sponsored terrorism (cf. *La Nación* of July 14, 2007, 7).

37 Law 22.924 of the last military government, declared unconstitutional by Law 23.040.

i.e. long after the crimes were committed. And the retroactive application of the law in criminal cases is illegal.

4. The discussion about the competence of the judicial system to interpret and apply the law regarding severe crimes committed thirty years ago has divided Argentine public opinion. This is certainly not a positive contribution to social peace and collective harmony, and it shows that if we do not take seriously the importance of criminal courts judging the cases under their jurisdiction in the right moment and if instead we delay the application of the law in the name of short-term political goals (as was the case, I think, in Germany and Argentina), we run the danger not only of offending the victims but also of undermining the belief in the moral content of the criminal law.[38]

If we can learn anything at all from atrocities committed in the exercise of absolute evil and from the historical experience of countries like Germany or Argentina in dealing with a criminal past, and if we accept that in every democratic system the fundamental norms are expressions of the basic values of social peace and human dignity, then I think we must conclude that the only morally acceptable attitude is to promote memory, to reject pardon without repentance, and to apply the corresponding criminal laws without delay. The application of criminal justice has the enormous advantage that it *de-personalizes* conflict. It can thus help to avoid acts of personal revenge and social violence which tend to ensue when the punitive action citizens have entrusted to the judges under the rule of law comes to nothing. The application of the law therefore must not be left to the discretion of political authorities: it is an irrenouncable constitutional obligation.

4. Concluding Remark

The world today does not seem to be heading into a good direction. Everyday experience gives us reason to fear that the criminal phantasy of human beings will invent and carry out ever more sinister ways of perpetrating absolute evil. But this does not free us from the moral obligation to watch out and raise our voice against Manichean fanaticism and the terror caused by extraordinary violence. It should also not undermine our confidence in liberal democratic rule of law as the only instrument apt to give some force to principles which underscore the—likewise, human—striving for a life free of calamities imposed on us by the despotic arrogance of the stronger. The law is the only means we have. If we give it up, we will have lost any hope for a life that is not, in the Hobbesian sense, brutish and short.

38 According to Carlos S. Nino (quoted by Elster 2004, 228–229), "President Alfonsín decided in 1983 that the 'trials should be limited to a finite period in which public enthusiasm for such a program remained high'". The current discussion in Argentina about the moral relevance of derogating the amnesty laws of Presidents Alfonsín and Menem show that Alfonsín's assessment of the (in)convenience of the trials was wrong. Besides, making the application of the law dependent on 'public enthusiasm' does not seem a morally acceptable position.

Bibliography

Ackerman, B. (1992), *The Future of Liberal Revolution,* New Haven-London

Allais, L. (2008), Wiping the Slate Clean: The Heart of Forgiveness, in: *Philosophy & Public Affairs 36 (1),* 33–68

Arendt, H. (1959), *The Human Condition,* New York

— (1976), *The Origins of Totalitarianism,* New York

Augustine, *Confessions,* ed. and transl. by A. C. Outler (www.ccel.org/ccel/augustine/confessions.xiii.html; March 10, 2009)

Bernstein, R. (2002), *Radical Evil. A Philosophical Interrogation,* Cambridge

Blustein, J. (2008), *The Moral Demand of Memory,* Cambridge

Booth, W. J. (2006), *Communities of Memory. On Witness, Identity and Justice,* Ithaca-London

Card, C. (2002), *The Atrocity Paradigm. A Theory of Evil,* Oxford

Cassin, B/O. Cayla/P.-J. Salazar (2004) (eds.), *Vérité, réconciliation, réparation* (Revue Le Genre humain, no. 43), Paris

Ciancaglini, S./M. Granovsky (1995), *Nada más que la verdad. El juicio a las Juntas,* Buenos Aires

Copjec, J. (1996). Introduction. Evil in the Time of the Finite World, in: C. Joan (ed.), *Radical Evil,* London-New York, vii–xxviii

Crenzel, E. (2008), *La historia política del Nunca más,* Buenos Aires

Edwards, J. (1999), Las estatuas de sal, in: *El País* (Madrid), Feb. 4, 11

Elorza, A. (2001), La condena de la memoria, in: *istor. Revista de historia internacional* (Mexico City) *II (5),* 82–93

Elster, J. (1984), *Ulysses and the Sirens. Studies in Rationality and Irrationality,* Cambridge

— (2004), *Closing the Books. Transitional Justice in Historical Perspective,* Cambridge

Fernández, G. (1987), *La claudicación de Alfonsín,* Buenos Aires

Friedrich, J. (1983), *Freispruch für die Nazi-Justiz. Die Urteile gegen NS-Richter seit 1948. Eine Dokumentation,* Hamburg

García, P. (2007), Argentina derriba la última barrera, in: *El País* (Madrid), July 18, 11

— (2008), Los historiadores del futuro, in: *El País* (Madrid), Nov. 21, 27–28

Garro, A. M. (1992), Nine Years of Transition to Democracy in Argentina: Partial Failure or Qualified Success?, in: *Columbia Journal of Transnational Law 30,* 1–101

Garton Ash, T. (1998), The Truth about Dictatorship, in: *The New York Review of Books XLV: 3* (Feb. 19), 35–40

Garzón Valdés, E. (1991), Staatsterrorismus: Legitimation und Legitimität, in: H.-W. Tobler/P. Waldmann (eds.), *Staatliche und parastaatliche Gewalt in Lateinamerika,* Frankfurt, 317–354

Habermas, J. (1987), Vom öffentlichen Gebrauch der Historie, in: Various Authors, *Historikerstreit,* Munich, 243–255

Hart, H. L. A. (1961), *The Concept of Law,* Oxford

Hayner. P. B. (2001), *Unspeakable Truths. Confronting State Terror and Atrocity,* New York

Holmes, S. (1988), Gag Rules or the Politics of Omission, in: J. Elster/R. Slagstad (eds.), *Constitutionalism and Democracy,* Cambridge, 19–58

Jakobs, G. (2004), Bürgerstrafrecht und Feindstrafrecht, in: *Höchstrichterliche Rechtsprechung im Strafrecht (HRRS) 3*, 88–95 (http://www.hrr-strafrecht.de/hrr/archiv/04-03/index.php3?seite=6; March 15, 2009)

Jaspers, K. (1987[1946)], *Die Schuldfrage*, Munich

Just-Dahlmann, B./H. Just (1988), *Die Gehilfen. NS-Verbrechen und die Justiz nach 1945*, Frankfurt

Kant, I. (1954), *Metaphysik der Sitten*, Rechtslehre, II. Teil. Das öffentliche Recht. § 49, E. Vom Straf- und Begnadigungsrecht, Hamburg, partial transl. by W. Hastie (http://www.mv.helsinki.fi/home/tkannist/E-texts/Kant/Right/; March 14, 2009)

Kattan, E. (2002), *Penser le devoir de mémoire*, Paris

Klug, U. (1994[1987]), Die Rechtsprechung des Bundesgerichtshofes in NS-Prozessen, in: id., *Rechtsphilosophie—Menschenrechte—Strafrecht*, Cologne, 234–254

Lefranc, S. (2005), *Políticas del perdón*, Bogotá

Little, D. (1999), A Different Kind of Justice: Dealing with Human Rights Violations in Transitional Societies, in: *Ethics & International Affairs 13*, 43–80

Locke, J. (1975[1690]), *The Second Treatise of Government*, Indianapolis

Longerich, P. (2006), *Davon haben wir nichts gewusst!*, Munich

Margalit, A. (2003), *The Ethics of Memory*, Cambridge/MA

— (1997), Gedenken, Vergessen, Vergeben, in: G. Smith/A. Margalit (eds.), *Amnestie oder die Politik der Erinnerung in der Demokratie*, Frankfurt, 192–205

Minow, M. (1998), *Between Vengeance and Forgiveness. Facing History after Genocide and Mass Violence*, Boston

Morguet, G. L. (2009), *Feindstrafrecht—Eine kritische Analyse*, Berlin

Murphy, J. G. (2003), *Getting Even. Forgiveness and its Limits*, Oxford

Nietzsche, F. (1997[1873]), On the Uses and Disadvantages of History for Life, in: id., *Untimely Meditations*. Ed. by D. Breazeale, transl. by R. J. Hollingdale, 2nd, rev. ed., Cambridge, 57–124

Pranteda, M. A. (2002), Male radicale, in: P. P. Portinaro (ed.), *I concetti del male*, Torino, 159–183

Prantl, H. (2007), Wenn die Geschichte ruhen soll, in: *Süddeutsche Zeitung* (Munich), August 17, 2

Raynaud, P. (2004), La mémoire et le droit, in: B. Cassin/O. Cayla/P.-J. Salazar (eds.), *Vérité, réconciliation, reparation*, Paris, 269–279

Ricoeur, P. (2000), *La mémoire, l'histoire, l'oubli*, Paris

Robertson, G. (2006), *Crimes against Humanity. The Struggle for Global Justice*, Harmondsworth

Rome Statute of the International Criminal Court, 1998 (http://untreaty.un.org/cod/icc/statute/99_corr/cstatute.htm; March 15, 2009)

Scanlon, T. (1994), *Punishment and the Rule of Law*. Paper given at the Conference in memory of C. S. Nino, Yale Law School, Sept. 24

Sepúlveda, L. (1999), Chile: Un país de dos lenguajes, *El País* (Madrid), Feb. 12, 17

Singer, P. (2003), How Can We Prevent Crimes against Humanity, in: N. Owen (ed.), *Human Rights, Human Wrongs*, Oxford, 92–137

Spinoza, B. (1997[1677]), *Ethics*, transl. by R. H. M. Elwes (1883), MTSU Philosophy WebWorks Hypertext Edition (http://frank.mtsu.edu/~rbombard/RB/Spinoza/ethica3.html; March 10, 2009)

Staten, H. (2005), 'Radical Evil' Revived: Hitler, Kant, Luther, Neo-Lacanians, in: A. D. Schrift (ed.), *Modernity and the Problem of Evil*, Bloomington-Indiana, 12–27

Tcach, C. (1996), Radicalismo y dictadura, in: H. Quiroga/C. Tcach (eds.), *A veinte años del Golpe. Con memoria democrática*, Rosario, 27–57

Todorov, T. (2004), *Les abus de la mémoire,* Paris

Truche, P. (2004), Vivre ensemble avec des criminels contre l'humanité?, in: B. Cassin/ O. Cayla/P.-J. Salazar (eds.), *Vérité, réconciliation, reparation*, Paris, 173–179

Verdugo, P. (2004) (ed.), *De la tortura no se habla*, Santiago de Chile

Vetlesen, A. J. (2005), *Evil and Human Agency. Understanding Collective Evildoing*, Cambridge

Wehler, H.-U. (1988), *Entsorgung der deutschen Vergangenheit? Ein polemischer Essay zum 'Historikerstreit'*, Munich

Wink, W. (1998), *When the Powers Fall: Reconciliation in the Healing of Nations*, Minneapolis

Zommer, L. (2007), Museos de la memoria, in: *La Nación* (Buenos Aires), July 1, Sect. 7, 3

Authors

Giulia Andrighetto PhD
Laboratory on Agent Based Social Simulation
Institute of Cognitive Sciences and Technologies
Roma

Prof. Dr. Michael Baurmann
Lehrstuhl für Soziologie
Sozialwissenschaftliches Institut
Universität Düsseldorf
Düsseldorf

Prof. Cristina Bicchieri
Carol and Michael Lowenstein Endowed Term Professor
Director, Philosophy, Politics and Economics
Department of Philosophy
University of Pennsylvania
Philadelphia

Dr. Michael Biggs
Department of Sociology
St Cross College
University of Oxford
Oxford

Prof. Geoffrey Brennan
Professor of Economics
Social and Political Theory Program
Research School of Social Sciences
Australian National University
Canberra

Alex Chavez B.A.
Department of Psychology
University of Michigan
Ann Arbor

Dr. Lina Eriksson
Research School of Social Sciences
Social and Political Theory Program
Australian National University
Canberra

Prof. Dr. Ernesto Garzón Valdés
Professor für Politikwissenschaft
Bonn

Prof. Robert E. Goodin
Distinguished Professor of Philosophy
Philosophy Program
Research School of Social Sciences
Australian National University
Canberra

Prof. Dr. Werner Güth
Direktor, Max-Planck-Institut für Ökonomik
Abteilung Strategische Interaktion
Jena

Prof. Alan Hamlin
Professor of Political Theory
School of Social Sciences
University of Manchester
Manchester

Prof. Russell Hardin
Helen Gould Shepard Professor in the Social Siences
Wilf Family Department of Politics
New York University
New York

Prof. Kieran Healy
Assistant Professor of Sociology
Sociology Department
University of Arizona
Tucson

Prof. Dr. Rainer Hegselmann
Lehrstuhl für Philosophie
Institut für Philosophie
Universität Bayreuth
Bayreuth

Prof. Dr. Stefan Huster
Lehrstuhl für Öffentliches Recht
Juristische Fakultät
Universität Bochum
Bochum

A. Michael Kirmes
Frankfurt School of Finance & Management
Frankfurt am Main

Prof. Dr. Hartmut Kliemt
Professor of Philosophy and Economics
Frankfurt School of Finance & Management
Frankfurt am Main

Prof. Dr. Bernd Lahno
Professor of Philosophy
Frankfurt School of Finance & Management
Frankfurt am Main

Holly Lawford-Smith
Philosophy Program
Research School of Social Sciences
Australian National University
Canberra

Prof. Philip Pettit
Laurence S. Rockefeller University Professor of Politics and Human Values
University Center for Human Values
Princeton University
Princeton

Dr. Anette Schmitt
Institut für Politikwissenschaft
Universität Mainz
Mainz

Prof. Dr. Gerhard Schurz
Lehrstuhl für Theoretische Philosophie
Philosophisches Institut
Universität Düsseldorf
Düsseldorf

Nicholas Southwood PhD
Junior Research Fellow in Politics
Jesus College
Oxford University
Oxford

Prof. Dr. Thomas Spitzley
Lehrstuhl für Philosophie
Institut für Philosophie
Universität Duisburg-Essen
Essen

Prof. Robert Sugden
Professor of Economics
School of Economics
University of East Anglia
Norwich

Prof. Edna Ullmann-Margalit
Director, Center for the Study of Rationality
The Hebrew University
Jerusalem

Oliver Will B.A.
Institut für Philosophie
Universität Bayreuth
Bayreuth